SWEDES IN THE TWIN CITIES

SWEDES IN THE TWIN CITIES

Immigrant Life and Minnesota's Urban Frontier

EDITED BY

Philip J. Anderson

AND

Dag Blanck

MINNESOTA HISTORICAL SOCIETY PRESS

Published in cooperation with the Swedish-American Historical Society.
Published in Sweden by the Centre for Multiethnic Research, Uppsala University.

www.mnhs.org/mhspress

Manufactured in Canada

10 9 8 7 6 5 4 3 2 1

♾ The paper used in this publication meets
the minimum requirements of the American National Standard for Information Sciences—Permanence for Printed Library
materials, ANSI Z39.48-1984

International Standard Book Number
0-87351-399-1 (cloth)

This book was designed at the Minnesota
Historical Society Press by Will Powers, and
set in type by Allan Johnson at Phoenix Type,
Milan, Minnesota. The typeface is a version
of Berling, designed in 1951 by Swedish
typographer and calligrapher Karl-Erik
Forsberg. Printed by Friesens, Altona,
Manitoba.

**Library of Congress
Cataloging-in-Publication Data**

Swedes in the Twin Cities : immigrant life
and Minnesota's urban frontier / edited by
Philip J. Anderson and Dag Blanck.
     p. cm.
     Based on papers from a conference
held at the Minnesota History Center
in St. Paul, Oct. 17–20, 1996.
     Includes bibliographic references (p.)
and index.
     ISBN 0-87351-399-1 (cloth : alk. paper)
  1. Swedish Americans—Minnesota—
     Minneapolis—History—Congresses.
  2. Swedish Americans—Minnesota—
     Saint Paul—History—Congresses.
  3. Immigrants—Minnesota—
     Minneapolis—History—Congresses.
  4. Immigrants—Minnesota—Saint Paul—
     History—Congresses.
  5. City and town life—Minnesota—
     Minneapolis—Congresses.
  6. City and town life—Minnesota—
     Saint Paul—Congresses.
  7. Minneapolis (Minn.)—Ethnic
     relations—Congresses.
  8. Saint Paul (Minn.)—Ethnic relations—
     Congresses.
  9. Minneapolis (Minn.)—Social
     conditions—Congresses.
 10. Saint Paul (Minn.)—Social conditions—
     Congresses.
  I. Anderson, Philip J.
 II. Blanck, Dag.

F614.M6 S94 2001
305.83¢970776579—dc21

                                   00-52543

Swedes in the Twin Cities

Acknowledgments

Beginning in the early 1850s, Swedish immigrants began settling in the frontier river towns of St. Paul and Minneapolis, as well as other areas of the Minnesota Territory, and during the ensuing eight decades more members of this ethnic group made their homes in Minnesota than in any other state. These numerous Swedes inevitably left their mark on Twin Cities institutions, culture, religion, and politics, designating Minnesota as the "most Swedish" of the states even today.

Exploring the Swedish immigrants' various influences on and experiences in this new land, the essays in this book were originally among the papers presented at the conference "Swedish Life in the Twin Cities," held at the Minnesota History Center in October 1996. This major, well-attended event was part of a series of celebrations in the United States and Sweden marking the 150th anniversary of Swedish emigration to North America and was one of several academic conferences in both countries addressing the topic of Swedish immigration.

The conference was co-sponsored by the American Swedish Institute (Minneapolis), the Minnesota Historical Society (St. Paul), and the Swedish-American Historical Society (Chicago). The initial idea for such a fresh and substantive study of the Swedish experience in the Twin Cities, however, began much earlier. Scholars have long noted the relative paucity of research on the Swedish American experience in the Twin Cities. Therefore, such a project followed naturally from the successful conference on Swedes in Chicago, held in 1988, and the subsequent volume of essays we edited (*Swedish-American Life in Chicago: Cultural and Urban Aspects of an Immigrant People, 1850–1930* [Urbana and Chicago: University of Illinois Press, 1992]). The 1996 celebrations became an opportunity to promote new and extended work in the field.

Swedes in the Twin Cities is the result of the efforts of numerous persons and institutions. We thank all those who joined us on the conference planning committee and worked faithfully for more than two years: Roger Baumann, Wendy Egan, Marita Karlisch, Deborah Miller, Byron Nordstrom, Christopher

Olsson, Kevin Proescholdt, Mary Swanson, Mariann Tiblin, and Rudolph Vecoli. Responsibility for the detailed arrangements of the conference and surrounding activities fell heavily upon the chair of our committee, Bruce N. Karstadt, executive director of the American Swedish Institute, who deserves our deep appreciation for making thorough, time-consuming work appear so effortless. We wish to thank as well Nina M. Archabal, director of the Minnesota Historical Society, who warmly supported our conference and made available the Society's marvelous facilities and capable staff, and Craig Johnson, site manager of the James J. Hill House, who helped arrange the art exhibit and reception on the opening night of the conference. In addition, we want to recognize Harald Runblom, director of the Centre for Multiethnic Research at Uppsala University, for including the book in the publication series Studia Multiethnica Upsaliensia and for providing helpful insight along the way; Erik P. Anderson for editorial assistance; Mary Brod for preparing the index and Ronald J. Johnson for supporting its preparation; and the many contributors to this volume for their scholarly expertise on facets of Swedish life in the Twin Cities and for their conscientious responses to our numerous requests.

It has been a pleasure and a privilege to work with the Minnesota Historical Society Press under its director, Gregory Britton. We especially wish to thank Ann Regan, managing editor, who has cheerfully encouraged us from the beginning of this endeavor and has supported the book throughout its development; Shannon M. Pennefeather, editor, who has guided the manuscript into print with skill and efficiency; and other members of the Press's staff.

Several institutions have assisted this book by providing funding and material support for the conference "Swedish Life in the Twin Cities" and are hereby gratefully acknowledged: the Minnesota Humanities Commission, in cooperation with the National Endowment for the Humanities and the Minnesota State Legislature; the Charles A. Lindbergh Fund of the Minnesota Historical Society; the Swedish Information Service (New York); the Swedish Institute (Stockholm); North Park University; the American Swedish Institute; the Minnesota Historical Society; and the Swedish-American Historical Society.

PHILIP J. ANDERSON

DAG BLANCK

SWEDES IN THE TWIN CITIES

Introduction
Being Swedish American in the Twin Cities

PHILIP J. ANDERSON & DAG BLANCK

In the fall of 1850, the young city of St. Paul received a remarkable visitor from Sweden. Fredrika Bremer, Sweden's then most-celebrated novelist and champion of women's rights, arrived in the frontier town, a guest of Governor Alexander Ramsey. When Bremer returned to Sweden in 1853, she rhapsodized in her book *Hemmen i den nya verlden* (The Homes of the New World) about what she had experienced during her brief stay:

> What a glorious new Scandinavia might not Minnesota become! Here would the Swede find again his clear, romantic lakes, the plains of Scania rich in corn, and the valleys of Norrland. . . . Scandinavians who are well off in the Old Country ought not to leave it. But such as are too much contracted at home, and who desire to emigrate, should come to Minnesota. The climate, the situation, the character of the scenery agrees with our people better than that of any other of the American States, and none of them appear to me to have a greater or a more beautiful future before them than Minnesota.[1]

One of the first Swedes to visit the Minnesota Territory, Fredrika Bremer was prophetic about the attraction the future state would have during a mass migration from her homeland that not even she could envisage. In time, there would be more filiopietist interpretations of the successes of those who came. "[The Swedes] have faithfully helped in making Minneapolis the great and mighty city it is," expressed one account, "and they have not only reared beautiful and substantial homes for themselves, but have created public institutions, churches, and schools, and institutions of charity, that are among the finest in the city."[2]

Swedish immigrants and their descendants have played a major role in the history and development of the Twin Cities. During the era of Swedish mass emigration to the United States between 1850 and 1930, when more than 1.3 million Swedes arrived, Minnesota received more Swedish immigrants than any other state. The Twin Cities were a particularly common destination for these immigrants and their children, and, in 1910, at the peak of Swedish emigration to the United States, Swedish Americans were the largest ethnic group in Minneapolis and the second largest in St. Paul. Although Chicago was the largest Swedish settlement in America, with a significantly larger number of Swedish Americans, they never shaped that city's ethnic population in the same way as their counterparts in Minneapolis and St. Paul. The Twin Cities became one of the few large urban areas where Swedish immigrants and their children were among the largest ethnic groups, and it was the only one where by 1920 they had become dominant, making the history of this community both special and interesting.[3]

Swedish immigration within Minnesota was primarily a rural phenomenon prior to the greatest period of mass migration between 1879 and 1893. In 1850, there were only about 6,000 persons of European origin living in the Minnesota Territory. Jacob Falström is credited with being the first Swede to arrive in what would become the State of Minnesota. He took a claim in Washington County, near Marine-on-St. Croix, in 1837, though he had already been in the wider area for about two decades as a trader associated with the American Fur Company. Nils Nyberg (a shoemaker from Skåne) was the first Swede to arrive in St. Anthony in 1851, which was the same year that the first large group of Swedes began to settle in Minnesota. This was in the Chisago Lakes area, north of the Twin Cities. Nils Nilsson (a physician's assistant from Östergötland) and A. J. Ekman (a businessman from Göteborg) were the first Swedes to have appeared in the city of St. Paul, in 1853.[4]

Initially, St. Paul's eastern section attracted a larger number of Swedes than did the small settlement centered at St. Anthony Falls, further upstream on the Mississippi River. Only 2,676 Swedes were living in Minneapolis (across the river from St. Anthony, and platted in 1857) in 1870. That was soon to change dramatically as the mass migration of the 1880s brought directly to the Twin Cities thousands of mostly young, single immigrants looking for work and a future. The Swedish-born population of Minnesota reached its zenith in 1905 at 126,223, with the overall population numbering close to two million. Almost a third (38,000) lived in the Twin Cities, thus being the second largest concentration of Swedes in an urban area, behind only Chicago (63,000). At the time, the Swedes comprised 7.5 percent of the population of Minneapolis and St. Paul.[5]

By 1910, 70 percent of the Swedish-born population of the Twin Cities resided in Minneapolis. Geographer John G. Rice attributed this to a pair of likely reasons. First, there was a lesser degree of ethnic competition in Minneapolis when compared with the larger German and Irish representation in St. Paul. And second, as a center of trade and agricultural production (e.g., milling), Minneapolis had a more natural relation with the sizeable number of Scandinavian and other farmers who had settled in rural Minnesota and the Dakotas.[6]

By 1920, the Swedes were the largest immigrant group in both Minneapolis and St. Paul, ahead of both the Norwegians and the Germans; they made up 30 percent of the immigrant population in Minneapolis and 20 percent in St. Paul. Forty years later, in 1960, the census statistics included the immigrant generation as well as those that had been born in the United States of at least one foreign-born parent. Swedish Americans still dominated the Twin Cities at about 20 percent of the foreign stock, ahead of the Germans.[7]

The 1990 census provided data of a different nature on ethnicity. Rather than focusing on places of birth for individuals or their parents, ethnic ancestry was now a matter of self-identification. Individuals were thus asked to indicate their ethnic background(s) — regardless of when their ancestors had come to the United States. The 1990 census revealed 109,153 individuals in the Twin Cities who identified their background as Swedish. The strength of the migration to the suburbs is revealed by the 389,416 Swedish Americans living in the metropolitan area of the Twin Cities. In both instances, it places the group fourth, behind the Germans, Irish, and Norwegians. Surprisingly, not only did the Irish outnumber Swedes (and Norwegians) in St. Paul, but in Minneapolis as well. In St. Paul, however, the Swedes ranked third, narrowly ahead of the Norwegians. The census reported that nationally Swedish Americans ranked tenth in total ancestries with almost 4.7 million, 536,203 of whom lived in Minnesota. Only California had more (an additional 50,000) Swedish Americans. Regarding the Swedish-born in Minnesota, there was a decline from the 1980 census — from 6,131 to 4,550 — continuing a consistent pattern, ranking it fourth behind California, Illinois, and New York.[8]

As this book's subtitle suggests, most of the Swedish-born in the Twin Cities forged their lives in what to them was clearly an urban frontier. Not only were these two cities — distinctly different in so many ways — growing rapidly on the Minnesota frontier, the Swedes themselves were greenhorns at city living. Coming primarily from the rural, peasant backgrounds of farming, mining, logging, and so forth, the new and noisy world of neighborhoods and commercial enterprises was largely foreign to their own past. While their pre-migration experiences had done little to prepare them for big city life, they quickly adapted to it as they were absorbed into an urban Swedish American subculture, which in their youthful energy and ambition they participated in creating. Consequently, they played an important role, along with many others of American

and foreign stock, in helping to fashion two great cities, Minneapolis and
St. Paul, out of Minnesota's frontier during the last quarter of the nineteenth
century and into the twentieth.

The Swedish and Swedish American impact on the Twin Cities can be seen
on many levels. Numerous organizations of Swedish origin were formed, including a variety of clubs and lodges and social and cultural societies, as well as
churches. Many are still active. Swedish language, literature, and history have
been taught at the University of Minnesota since a professorship was established in 1883 by an act of the Minnesota legislature, and Swedish Americans
have played significant roles in both Minnesota and Twin City political life
since the late nineteenth century. Many Swedish-language newspapers were
published in the area, a number of Swedish bookstores existed, and Swedish
American educational institutions were also started in the Twin Cities. Since
1933, *Svenskarnas Dag* has attracted thousands of participants from the Twin
Cities and statewide each summer to celebrations in Minnehaha Park. The stately
American Swedish Institute is located on Park Avenue, set in what was the
heart of a turn-of-the century affluent neighborhood bordered by Swedish settlements in south Minneapolis. With more than 5,000 members, the Institute
has been at the crossroads of Swedish American cultural and fraternal life since
the 1930s.

In addition, there is an awareness of Sweden (and Scandinavia) in the area
that clearly does not exist in other American cities. One example of this is the
popularity of Garrison Keillor's nationally syndicated radio program, "A Prairie
Home Companion," broadcast from its base in St. Paul. Other popular evidence,
more noticeable perhaps to a newcomer, would be the many jokes about Swedish
and Scandinavian Americans often heard in conversation or in the media. It
can safely be argued, therefore, that the Twin Cities is the metropolitan area
that today exhibits the highest degree of Swedish American visibility or consciousness, where a sense of Swedishness still prevails.

There exists a significant body of literature on the history of Swedish immigration and the nature and characteristics of the Swedish American community. More than twenty years ago, Arnold Barton, one of the leading scholars in the field, observed that the Swedes in North America have "one of the
richest historical literatures that exists for any migrant group." Over the years,
a prolific scholarship has come from both Sweden and the United States, representing a variety of disciplines, such as history, literature, geography, ethnol-
ogy, sociology, labor, art history, and religion. Several studies have focused on
different aspects of Swedish American history in different urban communities
throughout the United States—for example, Chicago, Jamestown, Worcester,
Rockford, Moline, and Seattle.[9]

Given the size, longevity, and significance of the Swedish American group in the Twin Cities, it is surprising that the scholarly literature on the subject is comparatively sparse. What does exist is scattered, generally in articles or chapters in books. Often these studies addressed specific Twin Cities aspects of larger themes in Minnesota or Swedish American historical reflection—politics, religion, the ethnic press, organizational life, etc. There are also several contemporary or semi-contemporary accounts of Swedish emigration to the Twin Cities and of the life experiences that resulted. These publications mostly lack a critical perspective and are compilations. In comparison with the literature on Swedish American life in Chicago, for example, the body of literature on the history of the Swedish American community in the Twin Cities is meager.[10]

Swedes in the Twin Cities is an effort to address this gap in the literature and to be a catalyst for further research. It is based on papers presented at a major conference held at the Minnesota History Center in St. Paul on October 17–20, 1996, sponsored by the American Swedish Institute, the Minnesota Historical Society, and the Swedish-American Historical Society. The book includes contributions of leading scholars from both the United States and Sweden, who paint a broad picture of the Swedish American experience in the Twin Cities. The conference was a part of the 1996 celebrations when the 150th anniversary of the beginnings of Swedish mass emigration to the United States was recognized. The volume consists of twenty-two chapters, covering a variety of topics and approaches.

Some basic information about Swedes in the Twin Cities gives helpful context for understanding these essays. One fundamental lesson of immigration history is the creation of so-called migration chains. Once a migration to a particular locale has begun, it tends to continue, even though the conditions that set it off initially may have changed. A momentum has been created, and, in some ways, the movement of peoples between two places takes on a life of its own. The history of Swedish emigration to the United States, like that of many other immigrant groups, can certainly provide many examples of this process. For example, the careful and innovative work of the geographer Robert C. Ostergren has shown how such migration chains were established between sending areas in Dalarna, in central Sweden, and Isanti County, north of the Twin Cities. The history of Swedish emigration to the Twin Cities also illustrates this process. Even after the cessation of Swedish mass migration to the United States at the end of the 1920s, Swedes continued to move to the Twin Cities, albeit on a smaller scale than before. This immigration from Sweden has, in fact, continued up until the present time.[11]

This means that a sizeable and multifaceted Swedish American community has existed in the Twin Cities for well over a century. In terms of generational composition, the community has always included individuals born in Sweden and those born in America with parents, grandparents, or great-grandparents born in Sweden. By having several generations of Swedish Americans making up the community at the same time, the expressions of its "Swedishness" have varied greatly, both in terms of content and significance. To be Swedish in the Twin Cities in the 1910s for a Swedish-born maid obviously meant something quite different than to an American-born professional whose mother had immigrated from Sweden forty years earlier. A similar comparison can be made between a Swedish-born computer engineer who moved to the Twin Cities in the 1990s and his American cousin whose grandparents had come from Sweden in the 1910s but who had never been to Sweden herself.

The community's diverse complexity was not only related to generations. It was also subdivided according to social, religious, political, and gender lines. Scholars of ethnic life in America have argued that one important factor in assessing the strength of an ethnic community depends on how well it is able to address and fulfill the various needs its members may have. If the ethnic community was able to provide, for example, political influence, opportunities for employment, or religious satisfaction for its members, the likelihood that individuals would associate with the community increases. Obviously, an ethnic community needs both to be of a certain size and to have developed a fairly high degree of internal organizational life in order to be able to meet the needs of its members. The degree of "institutional completeness," to use the term coined by Canadian sociologist Raymond Breton, is an important factor in determining how viable an ethnic community becomes.[12]

Clearly, the Swedish American community in the Twin Cities developed a high degree of institutional completeness. Hundreds of Swedish American churches, lodges, clubs, mutual aid societies, and other organizations have existed in the Twin Cities since the beginnings of Swedish immigration. In 1910, the overall largest Swedish American institution in the United States, the Lutheran Augustana Synod, had twenty-two congregations in Minneapolis and St. Paul, while the second largest Swedish American denomination, the Swedish Evangelical Mission Covenant Church, counted six churches in the area. At least eighty-two Swedish-language newspapers and magazines have been published in the Twin Cities (many of them short-lived), and the cities have also been the home to several Swedish American institutions of higher learning. Today, a directory of Swedish American organizations in the United States lists more than twenty-five Swedish American groups in Minneapolis and St. Paul.[13]

The complexity of the Swedish American community in the Twin Cities is reflected in this book. The book begins with an introductory chapter on the overall history of immigration to the Twin Cities, past and present. Following that, the history of the Swedish American presence on a more general level is discussed, posing the question of why so many Swedes came to the area and explaining where and how they settled. More specific aspects of the community are examined next. We learn about the literary and creative life of the Swedish Twin Cities through discussions about the immigrant press, the community's reading habits, the language, its theater, and its artists. Religion was of great importance to the immigrants and the book explores the meaning of religion to both the immigrants and their children, as well as how the American host society viewed Swedish American religion. The rich Swedish American organizational life in Minneapolis and St. Paul is also addressed. One of the most visible landmarks, the American Swedish Institute, is discussed in one essay, and others focus on additional organizations of both a fraternal and an historical nature.

The book also explores ways in which Swedish Americans in the Twin Cities interacted with the surrounding American society. One essay discusses the struggle to introduce Swedish language into the curriculum of the Minneapolis public schools, and another utilizes the example of a prominent Swedish American philosopher to illustrate ways in which Swedish Americans entered into academic and public life. Other essays take up the rich participation and influence of Swedish immigrants and their descendants in the politics of the Twin Cities, as well as throughout Minnesota. There is also an essay that focuses on Winnipeg, which at the end of the nineteenth century was a rapidly growing settlement in the Canadian province of Manitoba, serving the northern fringe of Swedish America as a receiving and sending community from the Twin Cities and elsewhere on to the prairie provinces of the west. Its connection to and contrast with Minneapolis and St. Paul are revealing in many ways.

It is crucial to recall that the vast majority of people living in the Swedish American neighborhoods of Minneapolis and St. Paul were working men and women, struggling to make a living for themselves and their families. The social and economic circumstances are, therefore, of great importance. One essay delves into the neglected "underside" of the Swedish American community, namely the Swedes who found themselves inmates in the Minneapolis City Workhouse; another looks at working conditions for females in the textile industry.

There is, of course, further work to do in all the areas addressed in *Swedes in the Twin Cities*. Much more needs to be known, for example, about all the Swedish American neighborhoods in the Twin Cities, such as Northeast Minneapolis, the near-north-side, Camden, Powderhorn Park, as well as those areas of the east-side of St. Paul where immigrant communities moved over time. The shops and businesses of the commercial districts, as well as the companies begun by entrepreneurial Swedes, require attention. Labor and the trades, fraternal lodges and clubs, and the breadth of the Swedish American press are largely unexplored in all their complex fullness. Academic and literary life, festivals and public celebrations of ethnic memory and pride, education and religion, women and children, and music and athletics are topics for future scholars to mine. The continuing efforts to understand the interethnic and multicultural life of the Twin Cities, and the part played by Swedish Americans, will be crucial to a fuller picture of the life of this dominant ethnic group and how ethnic consciousness develops and changes through the generations.

The longevity of Swedish ethnicity in the Twin Cities demonstrates the persistence of ethnicity in American life. Ethnicity is malleable and takes on many meanings over time. By most measurements, the contemporary Swedish American community in the Twin Cities constitutes an example of a well-integrated ethnic group. Obviously, its sense of ethnic identity today is radically different from that experienced by Swedish Americans at the turn of the last century. One of its most salient characteristics is its elective or voluntary nature, a phenomenon that can be observed among other contemporary European-origin groups as well. The Twin Cities Swedish American community has changed fundamentally over the past century, yet its strong persistence constitutes an important way in which a significant group of people in the Twin Cities chooses to orient themselves within a gradually more diverse and multicultural environment. This context explains the continued interest in Santa Lucia celebrations at the American Swedish Institute (as well as at many churches and social organizations), the *Svenskarnas Dag* festivities at Minnehaha Park, and the visible presence of other social traditions, such as food and music, decorations and holidays. It is also demonstrated by the growing interest in genealogy and in the maintenance or creation of contacts with family or friends in Sweden.[14]

Given the long and sustained history of Swedish immigration to the Twin Cities, the group's experiences can provide answers to relatively unexplored questions. Why do ethnic groups survive, even flourish, in modern societies? And what are the conditions that make it possible for a sense of ethnic identity to continue through the generations, long after the immigrant experience itself of the first generation? Factors that play an important role in this process include dimensions of the internal life of the ethnic group, such as language use and retention, institution-building, settlement patterns, degrees of interaction with the host society and other minority groups, and ethnic political and cultural mobilization. Other determinants involve conditions within the host society, such as official ethnic and minority policies, language legislation, economic and social developments, experience (or lack of experience) with historical patterns of immigration within the host environment, and attitudes towards immigration and ethnicity among the population in the receiving area.

It is clear that the nature of ethnic consciousness among Twin City Swedish Americans today has changed radically from a century ago. Today, their identities are, as John Rice has argued, also powerfully shaped by factors such as class, gender, religion, and professions. Still, ethnicity does remain important for many in realized forms that are a mixture of the older and newer experiences. The way in which it functions today, both in the Twin Cities and elsewhere, is another unexplored field for future research.[15]

Swedish immigrants and their children had to work hard, and they often struggled as they established their lives in America. They experienced the difficulties and discrimination faced in varying degrees by most immigrant groups. Yet, it can also be argued that the Swedish Americans in the Twin Cities came to occupy, as a group, a privileged position within the local ethnic hierarchy. This is most likely one of the explanations for why a sense of contemporary Swedish ethnicity not only lingers but also remains patently visible in the Twin Cities. The question, however, remains largely unexplored, and further studies of the contemporary Swedish American community, or communities, in the Twin Cities, and in the United States in general, will no doubt furnish an opportunity to investigate what ethnicity means to a well-established and well-integrated group in the United States today.

* * * *

NOTES

1. Fredrika Bremer, *America in the Fifties: Letters of Fredrika Bremer*, Adolph B. Benson, ed. (New York: The American Scandinavian Foundation, 1924), 234f. The literature on Bremer and her journey to the United States is large. Some examples include Lars Wendelius, *Fredrika Bremers amerikabild. En studie i Hemmen i den nya verlden* (Uppsala: Svenska litteratursällskapet, 1985); Gunnar Sundell, *Med Fredrika Bremer i Amerika* (Stockholm: Carlssons, 1993); Laurel Ann Lofsvold, *Fredrika Bremer and the Writing of America* (Lund: Lund Univ. Press, 1999).

2. Quoted in Erik G. Westman, ed., *The Swedish Element in America*, 4 vols. (Chicago: Swedish-American Biographical Society, 1931–34), 1:139.

3. The figures for the top three groups in both cities are as follows. Minneapolis: Swedish Americans 16 percent, Norwegian Americans 10 percent, and German Americans 8 percent. St. Paul: German Americans 17 percent, Swedish Americans 11 percent, and Irish Americans 6 percent (U.S. Bureau of the Census, *Thirteenth Census of the United States 1910* [Washington, D.C.: U.S. Government Printing Office, 1913], 2:994). For Swedes in Chicago, see esp. Ulf Beijbom, *Swedes in Chicago: A Demographic and Social Study of the 1846–1880*

Immigration (Chicago: Chicago Historical Society, 1971), and Philip J. Anderson and Dag Blanck, eds., *Swedish-American Life in Chicago: Cultural and Urban Aspects of an Immigrant People, 1850–1930* (Urbana and Chicago: Univ. of Ill. Press, 1992).

4. For the establishment of the Minnesota Territory in 1849, see Anne R. Kaplan and Marilyn Ziebarth, eds., *Making Minnesota Territory 1849–1858* (St. Paul: MHS Press, 1999). Minnesota became a state in 1858. Westman, ed., *The Swedish Element in America*, 1:135, 139; A. E. Strand, ed., *A History of the Swedish-Americans of Minnesota*, 3 vols. (Chicago: Lewis Publ. Co., 1910), 2:496, 3:856; and Theodore A. Norelius, "The First Swede in Minnesota," *Swedish Pioneer Historical Quarterly* 8 (1957): 107–15.

5. State of Minnesota, *Census, 1905*, p. 120. At this time the Swedes were the largest foreign-born population in the state, followed by Germans (119,868) and Norwegians (111,611).

6. John G. Rice, "The Swedes," in June Drenning Holmquist, ed., *They Chose Minnesota: A Survey of the State's Ethnic Groups* (St. Paul: MHS Press, 1981), esp. 262ff. The essay by Professor Rice (p. 248–76) is the best demographic and critical survey of the Swedish experience in Minnesota, with much useful information on the Twin Cities.

7. U.S. Bureau of the Census, *Fourteenth Census of the United States 1920* (Washington, D.C.: U.S. Government Printing Office, 1922), 3:507; U.S. Bureau of the Census, *U.S. Census of the Population 1960, Minnesota: General Social and Economic Characteristics* (Washington, D.C.: U.S. Government Printing Office, 1961), 255.

8. U.S. Bureau of the Census, *1990 Census of Population, Social and Economic Characteristics, Minnesota* (Washington, D.C.: U.S. Government Printing Office, 1993), 81, 83, 407, 409. For a comparative analysis, see David E. O'Connor, "Who are We? The Swedish Americans and the 1990 U.S. Census," *Swedish-American Historical Quarterly* 48 (1997): 69–90. This was fifth in a series of periodic articles published by the *Quarterly* since the 1950s analyzing the category of Swedish ancestry in U.S. censuses.

9. Quotation from H. Arnold Barton, "Clio and Swedish America," in Nils Hasselmo, ed., *Perspectives on Swedish Immigration* (Chicago: Swedish Pioneer Historical Society, 1978), 3. In addition to the studies cited above on Chicago, see, for example, Dag Blanck and Harald Runblom, eds., *Swedish Life in American Cities* (Uppsala: Centre for Multiethnic Research, 1991); Dag Blanck, "Swedes and Other Ethnic Groups in American Urban Settings," in Ingvar Svanberg and Mattias Tydén, eds., *Multiethnic Studies in Uppsala: Essays Presented in Honour of Sven Gustavsson* (Uppsala: Centre for Multiethnic Research, 1988); Lars Wendelius, *Kulturliv i ett svenskamerikanst lokalsamhälle. Svenskarne i Rockford* (Uppsala: Centre for Multiethnic Research, 1990); and Charles W. Estus, Sr., and John F. McClymer, *gå till Amerika: The Swedish Creation of an Ethnic Identity for Worcester, Massachusetts* (Worcester: Worcester Historical Museum, 1994). On broader urban immigrant issues, see David Ward, *Cities and Immigrants: A Geography of Change in Nineteenth-Century America* (New York, 1971); Kathleen Neils Conzen, "Immigrants, Immigrant Neighborhoods, and Ethnic Identity: Historical Issues," *Journal of American History* 66.3 (1979): 603–15; and Conzen, "Ethnic Patterns in American Cities: Historiographical Trends," in Ulf Beijbom, ed., *Swedes in America: Intercultural and Interethnic Perspectives on Contemporary Research* (Växjö: Swedish Emigrant Institute, 1993), 24–32.

10. For articles and chapters, see, for example, selected essays in Hasselmo, ed., *Perspectives on Swedish Immigration*, such as Byron J. Nordstrom, "The Sixth Ward: A Minneapolis Swede Town in 1905," 151–65; Bruce L. Larson, "Swedish Americans and Farmer-Labor Politics in Minnesota," 206–24; and Janet Nyberg, "Swedish Language Newspapers in Minnesota," 244–55. See also the chapter on the Twin Cities in Byron J. Nordstrom, ed., *Swedes in Minnesota* (Minneapolis: T. S. Denison, 1976), 23–38, and Rice, "The Swedes," in Holmquist, ed., *They Chose Minnesota*, 248–76. Helge Nelson's chapters on the Twin Cities in his *The Swedes and the Swedish Settlements in North America* (Lund: C. W. K. Gleerup, 1943), 1:202–7, are also useful. Over the past half-century, much material touching on this subject

has appeared in the pages of the *Swedish Pioneer Historical Quarterly* (since 1982 the *Swedish-American Historical Quarterly*), as well as *Minnesota History*. The documentation included in the essays of this present volume covers much of the extant literature on Swedish Americans in the Twin Cities. For compilations, see, e.g., Alfred Söderström, *Minneapolis minnen. Kulturhistorisk axplockning från qvarnstaden vid Mississippi* (Minneapolis: published by the author, 1899); and Strand, ed., *History of the Swedish-Americans of Minnesota*, vols. 2–3.

11. Robert C. Ostergren, *A Community Transplanted: The Transatlantic Experience of a Swedish Immigrant Settlement in Upper Middle West, 1835–1915* (Madison: Univ. of Wisc. Press, 1988). See also Jon Gjerde, *The Minds of the West: Ethnocultural Evolution in the Rural Middle West, 1830–1917* (Chapel Hill: Univ. of N.C. Press, 1997), for a highly stimulating synthesis of migration patterns of different kinds to the Midwest.

12. Raymond Breton, "Institutional Completeness of Ethnic Communities and the Personal Relations of Immigrants," *American Journal of Sociology* 70 (1964): 193–205.

13. Cf. O. Fritiof Ander, *The Cultural Heritage of the Swedish Immigrant: Selected References* (Rock Island: Augustana College Library, 1956). *American-Swedish Handbook: Twelfth Edition* (Minneapolis: Swedish Council of America, 1997), 294f.

14. See, e.g., Mary C. Waters, *Ethnic Options: Choosing Identities in America* (Berkeley: Univ. of Calif. Press, 1990); Stanley Lieberson, *From Many Strands: Ethnic and Racial Groups in Contemporary America* (New York, 1988); and Richard D. Alba, *Ethnic Identity: The Transformation of White America* (New Haven: Yale Univ. Press, 1990).

15. Rice, "The Swedes," in Holmquist, ed., *They Chose Minnesota*, 271; Nordstrom, ed. *Swedes in Minnesota*, 65. For a comprehensive study of Norwegian American self-identity at the end of the twentieth century, see Odd S. Lovoll, *The Promise Fulfilled: A Portrait of Norwegian Americans Today* (Minneapolis: Univ. of Minn. Press, 1998).

Immigrants and the Twin Cities:
Melting Pot or Mosaic?

RUDOLPH J. VECOLI

Then they had names like Mattson, Oberhoffer, and Bjornson; now they have names like Yang, Gomez, and Abdirahman. Then they arrived by steamboat at the St. Paul docks or by train at the Minneapolis depot with immigrant trunks; now they arrive by jet airliner at the Minneapolis/St. Paul International Airport with leather luggage—or cardboard boxes. Radically different contexts, but do they share a common immigrant experience which transcends time and place? In what ways are their experiences similar? In what ways are they different? And what is the relationship between these two migrations to the Twin Cities, separated by almost a century?

As one considers the history of Swedish emigration to Minnesota, it is well to remember that the beginnings of the Twin Cities only go back some 150 years. We should also remember that these lands had long been the home of the Dakota and the Ojibwe and that what from the European American perspective is a saga of heroic pioneering is from the American Indian perspective a tragic tale of invasion and dispossession.

In 1850, the villages of St. Paul, St. Anthony, and Minneapolis numbered only a few thousand souls. But they were already a polyglot assortment of Yankees, French Canadians, and small numbers of British, Irish, and German immigrants. There were also thirty-nine African Americans. In the half century that followed, Minnesota became the chosen destination of many thousands of land-hungry peasants from Germany, Norway, Sweden, and a score of other countries. As the Twin Cities area emerged as the region's *entrepôt* and processing center, thousands of additional immigrants flocked to its mills, factories, and railroads. By 1910, the population of Minnesota had grown to over two million, and of these over 550,000 lived in Minneapolis and St. Paul.[1]

Who were these new Twin Citians? In terms of the percentage of their foreign-born populations, Minneapolis and St. Paul rivaled the great immigrant hives of the East. In 1910, almost 30 percent were immigrants and some 70 percent were, to use the U.S. Census's inelegant term, of "foreign stock." Two of three persons you might meet on Twin Cities streets would have been either immigrants or children of immigrants. Not only in homes but in public places you were more likely to hear German, Swedish, or Norwegian spoken than English. Henry James would have been just as shocked by the "alienism" of the Twin Cities as he was by that of the Lower East Side of New York City.[2]

The Twin Cities, however, differed from New York, Boston, or Chicago in terms of the ethnic mix of their population. Germans and Scandinavians were preponderant here, comprising over 75 percent of the foreign stock in 1910. In Minneapolis, Swedes were the most numerous, while Germans were the largest group in St. Paul. During the 1890s, the major sources of immigration to the United States had shifted from northern and western Europe to southern and eastern Europe, but, with the exception of the iron ranges, Minnesota did not attract great numbers of these Slavic, Jewish, and Italian newcomers. The population of Minnesota and the Twin Cities remained remarkably homogeneous for a half-century. This is not to say that other immigrant groups were absent. There were substantial numbers of Canadians and Irish, and one could find islands of Poles, Czechs, Slovaks, Jews, South Slavs, and Italians in this ocean of Germans and Scandinavians. Southern and eastern Europeans, for example, established communities near the railroads, flour mills, and meat-packing houses of "Nordeast" Minneapolis and South St. Paul.[3]

The Twin Cities, however, remained basically Nordic, and some Minnesotans did not think that such a bad thing. Albert Jenks, a sociologist at the University of Minnesota, in a 1909 essay had this to say about the ethnic character of Minnesota:

> The predominance of Teutonic foreign-born Minnesotans is an ethnic fact of great importance to our state. In the essentials of superior physique, dom-

Swedish American children and goat cart, taken by a roving photographer in North Minneapolis, 1915 (left to right, Edwin, Morris, Carroll, and Albert Anderson)

inance of will, industry, keenness and trustworthiness of intellect, high ideals and loyalty to the same, and, last, in ready and permanent adaptability to American environment, both physical and social, the Teuton has no superior.[4]

Although Jenks was voicing the current ideology of Nordic supremacy, not even Scandinavians were exempt from the prevailing racial bigotry. Writing to his parents in 1901 from a lumber camp, Horace Glenn, a St. Paul Yankee, made the following comments about Swedish lumberjacks:

> 9/10th of the men are Roundheads & the most disgusting, dirty, lousy repro-bates that I ever saw. . . . There are probably 15 white men here to 60 Swedes & those 15 keep them so they don't dare to say their soul is their own. . . . It is only evenings that I am forced to associate with these beasts they call Swedes that I get depressed. . . . Walking behind a string of Swedes is something im-possible to a person with a delicate nose. . . . It is an odor which could only come from generations of unwashed ancestors & no man can hope to ac-quire it in one lifetime without the aid of heredity.[5]

No immigrant group, it appears, has been spared its share of prejudice and dis-crimination. Too often, as in the case of Glenn, it has been the older established groups that have vented their anger and contempt upon the newcomers.

The two world wars, the immigration restriction laws of the 1920s, and the depression of the thirties interrupted immigration to the United States—and to Minnesota—for half a century. During these decades, small in-migrations of African Americans, Mexican migrant workers, displaced persons following World War II, and refugees from Communism during the Cold War did not al-ter the basic ethnic character of the Twin Cities, which remained staunchly northern and western European.[6]

The Immigration and Nationality Act of 1965, however, opened a new chap-ter in the history of immigration to the United States and to Minnesota. Abol-ishing the national origins quota system and opening the golden door to im-migrants from all over the world, this act resulted in a dramatic increase in the volume of immigration. From an average annual influx of some 250,000, the number of legal immigrants gradually increased to the current level of over 800,000. Since an additional several hundred thousand were entering the coun-try illegally, the total of about a million arrivals per year equaled the highs of the first decade of this century. Yet another consequence of the 1965 law has been a radical change in the sources of immigration. Historically over 90 percent of immigrants had come from Europe; in recent decades the overwhelming ma-jority has come from Asia and Latin America. Both the volume and the cultural and racial character of these new immigrants have aroused anxieties among many Americans and have incited a new spirit of xenophobia.[7]

How has this new immigration affected Minnesota and particularly the Twin Cities? Its impact may be highlighted by comparing a statistical profile of the non-European populations in the 1960s with one in the 1990s. By the 1960s, the American Indian population of the state totaled some 15,500, but of these only 2,500 were in Minneapolis and St. Paul. Meanwhile, the African American population had gradually grown to about 35,000, almost all in the Twin Cities. Also some 3,500 Mexican Americans were concentrated in St. Paul, while a few thousand Japanese and Chinese were scattered about the metropolitan area. In 1970, Minnesotans were still overwhelmingly of European origin.[8]

Thirty years of the new immigration—and intensified in-migration—have substantially changed the ethnic and racial composition of the Twin Cities. While the Twin Cities had been largely cushioned from the earlier "Great Migration" of several million African Americans from the rural South to northern cities, from the 1980s-on a growing number, among them refugees from the ghettos of Chicago, Gary, and other cities, have arrived in the Twin Cities. By 1990 African Americans in Minneapolis numbered 48,000 or 13 percent of the city's population, while in St. Paul they totaled 12,000 or 7.5 percent of the city's population. Meanwhile, migration from the reservations brought 12,335 Indians to Minneapolis (making up 3 percent the population) and 3,500 to St. Paul (1.5 percent of its population). Hispanics now numbered some 8,000 in Minneapolis (2 percent of its population) and 11,500 (4 percent) in St. Paul. Most were Mexicans or of Mexican ancestry from the southwest, but there were growing numbers of Puerto Ricans, Cubans, and Central and South Americans.[9]

Most dramatic, however, had been the increase in the Asian population. In 1990, some 16,000 Asian immigrants resided in Minneapolis (4 percent of its population) and 19,000 in St. Paul (7 percent). The majority were refugees from southeast Asia. Following the Vietnam War, millions of Vietnamese, Cambodians, Laotians, and Hmong fled on foot to Thailand or by boat to Hong Kong and other ports. Recognizing its complicity in their plight, the United States has admitted over a million of these refugees. Population estimates of 1995 placed the number of Hmong (most of whom resided in St. Paul) at 35,000, of Vietnamese at 18,000, of Cambodians at 7,600, and of Laotians at 7,200, for a total of 67,800. More recently, new streams of refugees from the former Soviet Union and eastern Europe, as well as Africans from Ethiopia, Somalia, and Sudan, have been arriving in the Twin Cities.[10]

Historically, Europeans for the most part had been economic immigrants who chose to migrate with expectations of a better life. By contrast, recent refugees have been forced to leave their homes, often fleeing for their lives. Their stories are heartrending tales of suffering and survival. Not surprisingly, they often arrive with physical and psychological scars. The Twin Cities area has been a major recipient of the Laotian Hmong who represent a classic example of the refugee. Recruited by the CIA to fight the Viet Cong, the Hmong became an object of retaliation when American forces left Vietnam. Fleeing to Thailand, many remained in camps for years before resettlement. A preliterate agrarian people lacking technical skills, theirs has been a particularly difficult adjustment to life in America.[11]

Why the Twin Cities? Refugees appear to have been initially drawn by the sponsorship of churches and social agencies. Finding a greater degree of tolerance and assistance here, they invited their kith and kin to join them. Other new immigrants, however, have not been refugees, but seekers of opportunity responding to Minnesota's expanding economy. These economic immigrants have included, among others, substantial groups of Koreans, Chinese, Asian Indians, Filipinos, Egyptians, Iranians, and Japanese. Those with professional education and entrepreneurial skills have quickly made their place in the urban economy. Once established, both refugees and economic immigrants initiated chain migrations of relatives and friends, as had the Germans and Scandinavians.[12]

Although conspicuous due to its visibility, this new immigration pales in comparison with that of the last century. While in 1910 some 30 percent of the population of the Twin Cities was comprised of immigrants, in 1990 only 6 percent of Minneapolis's residents and 7 percent of St. Paul's were foreign-born. While in 1910 Minnesota ranked second among the states in percentage of foreign-born population, it now ranked thirtieth (only 2.6 percent). Even including African Americans and American Indians, only 22 percent of the residents of Minneapolis and 18 percent of those of St. Paul qualified as "minority populations." Of the twenty-five largest metropolitan areas in the country, the Twin Cities had the lowest percentage of "racial minorities."[13]

Another indication of the continuing ethnic homogeneity of Minnesota can be found in the 1990 census data for ancestry. Of the ancestries claimed by Minnesotans, the top ten were European (African Americans ranked eleventh). The four leading ancestries were German, Norwegian, Irish, and Swedish. Together they accounted for over 90 percent of the state's population. A surprising finding is that over two million—or almost half of all Minnesotans—claimed German ancestry, while only 536,000 persons claimed Swedish ancestry.[14]

Still, the Twin Cities are once again a haven for tens of thousands of immigrants and refugees seeking new homes. Sometimes dark-skinned and colorfully garbed, worshiping in mosques and temples, these newcomers are conspicuous in a sea of blonde, blue-eyed Lutherans. Although much less so than California, New York, or Florida, Minnesota has been impacted by the global population movements of recent decades. Mayor Sharon Sayles Belton re-

cently observed: "Minneapolis, like our state and our nation, has become increasingly diverse. We are a multiracial, multicultural, multilingual city. We are
a kaleidoscope of skin colors, a tapestry of ethnic traditions, [and] a treasury of
spiritual beliefs." The Mayor concluded hopefully: "We are founded on a tradition of tolerance . . . nurtured by diversity. . . . Living peacefully and creatively
with diversity is the great American experiment."[15]

How fares the great American experiment in the Twin Cities? The returns are
mixed. We have been spared the pogroms against foreigners that have taken
place in cities in Europe and in the United States. However, expressions of racism
and nativism, including episodes of violence, have marred the image of "Minnesota nice." Newcomers have been subject to insult, stereotyping, discrimination, and, sometimes, physical attack, as were the immigrants of yesteryear.
The most significant response of older residents, however, has been an accelerated exodus to the suburbs as new people moved in. On the other hand, sympathetic and helpful responses to the needs of immigrants on the part of public agencies, foundations, churches, newspapers, and neighbors have not been
absent.[16]

Surprisingly, one often finds a lack of compassion for the newcomers among
those separated by only one or two generations from their immigrant roots.
A recent letter to the editor expressed this hostile sentiment:

> Both of my parents were immigrants. As were the parents and grandparents
> of many present-day Americans. But that was then and this is now. There are
> limits to population size . . . and we have reached those limits . . . Immigrants
> of the past did not have social services to rely on. They did it on their own.[17]

Most Minnesotans today are several generations removed from the immigrant experience. It takes a conscious act of empathy to place ourselves in that
painful status of being strangers in the land, to feel the wrenching homesickness, the deep loneliness of the immigrant. How many of us remember the old
ethnic neighborhoods created by Germans, Swedes, Poles, and Italians? Set
apart by language, culture, and poverty, feeling the disdain of others, immigrants
have always clustered together for comfort and mutual support. Here they
were not dumb, but could speak their native tongue. Here they could enjoy their
traditional foods, music, and religious observances without embarrassment.

Who remembers Swede Hollow, a ravine that was home to immigrant squat-
ters who built shacks along Phalen Creek? First came Swedes in the 1880s, followed by Irish, who in turn were succeeded by Italians, and finally Mexicans.
Other immigrant ports of entry into the Twin Cities were located on the river
flats, areas of cheap housing subject to flooding. Jews from Eastern Europe settled St. Paul's West Side, then were succeeded by Mexicans. St. Paul's Upper

Levee became an Italian village. Bohemian Flats, on the West Bank of the Mississippi River, was home to Slovaks, Irish, Germans, Swedes, and others. These immigrants literally began at the bottom and aspired to rise from these lower places to what they called "the Hill." Once on the high ground, they recreated their communities with their distinctive butcher shops and bakeries, saloons and ethnic halls, churches and synagogues. "Nordeast" Minneapolis epitomized the crazy quilt pattern of ethnic settlement with its concentrations of Germans, Poles, Ukrainians, Finns, Norwegians, Swedes, Lebanese, and Italians.[18]

Many of the old neighborhoods were obliterated by re-zoning or urban renewal; others were abandoned by "white flight" from an influx of newcomers of different races and cultures. Frogtown in St. Paul is an example of latter. Once home to Germans, Poles, Irish, Scandinavians, and French, its residents are now predominantly Hmong, African Americans, American Indians, and Hispanics. Old neighborhoods like Swede Hollow have been memorialized in nostalgic chronicles that, if romanticized, capture the quality of community that they embodied. As in the "ghettos" of the inner city today, their residents often suffered from wretched housing, poor public services, and deep poverty. But extended families and ethnic networks enabled the immigrants to cope with bad times and to enjoy good times. Current immigrants, such as the Hmong and Somali, have created such communities, often on the same grounds where similar communities of Germans, Swedes, Jews, and Italians existed not long ago. Yet today, the newcomers are often criticized for being clannish and failing to assimilate.[19]

Discussions of current immigration are often colored by a mythological view of the immigrant past. For a "nation of immigrants," we suffer from a curious amnesia regarding the real experiences of our foreign-born ancestors. In the retelling, too often one's family history becomes a saga of struggle and success, of how our forebears by dint of character and hard work pulled themselves up by their bootstraps (and the implication is: why don't *they* do the same?). Yet we know from historical records that the lives of immigrants often deviated from the myth. Many were defeated and crushed by the harsh conditions they encountered in America. Industrial accidents, unemployment, exploitation, alcoholism, familial abuse, crime, and vice were facts of immigrant life in the Twin Cities a hundred years ago, just as they are today. The rolls of Minnesota's relief agencies, charitable institutions, prisons, and lunatic asylums are replete with immigrant names. This is said not to denigrate our immigrant ancestors, but to remind us that they too were human beings with all the weaknesses and foibles to which human flesh is heir. Remembering this, we might be more compassionate as we witness the struggles of today's immigrants.[20]

A second historical distortion is the common assertion that the immigrants of the past, unlike those of the present, eagerly and easily assimilated. Nothing could be further from the truth. Authoritative studies, like those of Joshua Fishman's *Language Loyalty in America* and Sture Lindmark's *Swedish America*, have documented the tenacity with which many immigrants clung to their native languages and cultures. From their meager wages they built churches, schools, summer camps, theaters, fraternal organizations, cultural centers, libraries, and newspapers to sustain their sense of ethnic identity and to transmit their Old World heritage to future generations. The extent to which the immigrants succeeded or failed is a moot question, although the observance of the 1996 sesquicentennial of Swedish immigration in itself called into question the myth of the melting pot. In fact, the struggle to resist Americanization has been an integral element in the history of every immigrant group.[21]

One's native language is, we say, one's mother tongue. Yet nothing appears to infuriate neonativists more than the attachment of immigrants to their native languages. For several decades, the organization U.S. English has lobbied for a constitutional amendment that would prohibit the use of languages other than English in the conduct of public business. Nineteen states have adopted such measures—and it has been proposed in Minnesota. Recently in the state of California, the passage of Proposition 227 banned bilingual education. Proponents of such measures argue that immigrants in the past gladly gave up their mother tongues and readily learned English. Again, nothing could be further from the truth. Immigrant parents made financial sacrifices to have children taught their languages in parochial schools—or in public schools when they had sufficient political clout. Mother tongues were long used in religious services, and thousands of so-called foreign language newspapers have been and are still being published. The transition to English, which involved "linguicide" (Joshua Fishman's term), was neither easy nor natural. Rather, it was a traumatic process that tore congregations, societies, and families apart.[22]

Who among us has not known an elderly immigrant who could speak only a few words of English and thus was unable to communicate with her own grandchildren? If Anglicization won out in the long run, this should not dim our appreciation of the immigrants' struggle for language maintenance. Certainly an awareness of this struggle should make us more sympathetic to efforts of new immigrants to maintain their mother tongues. Considering the odds, there has been an amazing amount of language retention even among long established ethnic groups. In 1990, the most common mother tongue in Minnesota was not Spanish or Hmong; it was German.[23]

The title of this essay poses a rhetorical question. Were (and are) the Twin Cities a melting pot or a mosaic? The answer, of course, is neither. The question is too simplistic, the reality much more complex. Who would question that there has been a great deal of assimilation of immigrants and their descendants? Yet much of what has been labeled Americanization is in reality the result of a global process of modernization, a process that has affected those who stayed at home as well as those who left. My Italian cousins are in many ways as different from their grandparents as I am from mine.

Yet ethnicity has survived. The celebration of the Swedish Immigration Jubilee was itself evidence that Swedish American ethnicity is alive and kicking. Many thousands of persons of Swedish descent, often separated from their immigrant forebears by a century or more, were socially, intellectually, and emotionally involved in these events. The theory of the invention of ethnicity may help us understand this persistence of group consciousness based on a sense of peoplehood. In this conception, ethnicity is not an inherited identity based on blood or soil, but rather it is continuously being reconstructed out of old traditions and new experiences. As the realities of contemporary life change, our sense of what it means to be, say, Swedish American may change; the values, sentiments, and behaviors that make up the repertoire of Swedish Americanness may change. The fact that today's way of being Swedish American is different from that of previous generations does not make it any less real or authentic.[24]

Today's new immigrants are involved in this process of constructing their new identities as ethnic groups in this pluralistic America. They are, as we say, negotiating their ethnicity, deciding what they will give up, and what they will keep, from traditional ways of life. The Lao Family Community of Minnesota, a Hmong organization that seeks to facilitate adjustment to American life, consciously engages in just such discussions of what to retain and what to discard.[25]

Some Americans view the country's growing diversity with apprehension, fearing *The Disuniting of America*, to cite the title of Arthur M. Schlesinger, Jr.'s book. I do not share these fears. In our multicultural society, it is not only legitimate but healthy for those who are so inclined to affirm their ethnicities. Healthy because ethnicity provides a form of community, and we are very much in need of community in this postmodern society. True multiculturalism, however, should be inclusive of all ethnicities—Swedish American, Ukrainian American, Hmong American. As one who cherishes his Italian American ethnicity, I am troubled by the version of multiculturalism that defines only "people of color" as possessing ethnicity, all others being lumped together as Caucasian or white (i.e., persons of non-color). I am even more troubled by the fact that major institutions, universities, foundations, and public agencies have bought into this nonsensical formulation. Curricula, cultural programs, and research agendas are too often shaped by a definition of multiculturalism that excludes many of us.[26]

Certain population projections envisage that by the middle of the twenty-first century the majority of the population of the United States will no longer be "white." Such predictions are not only of dubious scientific validity, but are politically inspired, designed to mobilize "white Americans" in defense of their "race." While it is unlikely that Minnesota will be inundated by "people of color," there is little question that the presence of Asians, Hispanics, and Africans in the Twin Cities will become more accentuated in the next century, and correspondingly the Teutonic homogeneity, which Professor Jenks so valued, will continue to be diluted.[27]

How will we respond to this challenge of increased diversity? History and today's newspaper teach us that ethnicity is a two-edged sword, which can be used for ill as well as for good. Much will depend upon our capacity to mobilize the good will of all ethnic groups to address the serious problems of racism, nativism, and intergroup conflict that inevitably will confront us. The responsibility rests particularly upon those of us who belong to the established ethnic groups to reach out to the newcomers, to engage them in a dialogue in which we exchange experiences and understandings. We need to draw upon the best in our ethnic traditions and historical experiences to help each other make the Twin Cities a better place to live for ourselves and for our children.

* * * *

NOTES

1. While no comparative history of emigration to Minnesota has as yet been written, June Drenning Holmquist, ed., *They Chose Minnesota: A Survey of the State's Ethnic Groups* (St. Paul: MHS Press, 1981) is a valuable reference work. For population statistics see U.S. Bureau of the Census, *Thirteenth Census of the United States, 1910*, vol. 2, Population 1910, Alabama-Montana (Washington, D.C.: Government Printing Office, 1911) and subsequent census reports.

2. For a description of the polyglot character of early twentieth-century Minneapolis, see Ole E. Rølvaag, *The Boat of Longing* (New York: Harper Brothers, 1922); Henry James, *The American Scene* (first printed in 1907; Bloomington: Ind. Univ. Press, 1968), 121.

3. Calvin F. Schmid, *Social Saga of Two Cities: An Ecological and Statistical Study of Social Trends in Minneapolis and St. Paul* (Minneapolis: Minneapolis Council of Social Agencies, 1937). This neglected work is a basic source of data regarding ethnic and racial groups in the Twin Cities. For a more recent comprehensive study see John S. Adams and Barbara J. VanDrasek, *Minneapolis–St. Paul: People, Place, and Public Life* (Minneapolis: Univ. of Minn. Press, 1993).

4. Albert Ernest Jenks, "The People of Minnesota," *Papers and Proceedings of the Second Annual Meeting of the Minnesota Academy of Social Sciences* (Northfield, Minn., 1909), 204f. Jenks went on to say: "Though the state will have a certain share of peoples from eastern and southern Europe to absorb—as Slav, Italian, and Jew—yet because of the relative fewness of these as compared with many other states, Minnesota seems destined to remain

Teutonic in blood longer than many of our states . . . and to perpetuate as long as any other state the ideals which the transplanted Teuton has made American" (213).

5. Quoted in Peg Meier, comp., *Bring Warm Clothes: Letters and Photos from Minnesota's Past* (Minneapolis: Minneapolis Tribune, 1981), 194. Others also found the Swedes offensive: "The most troublesome and patience-exhausting fellow-creatures are undoubtedly the Swedes. They are an excellent class of people, and form excellent and most desirable citizens, but cause a great deal of trouble on their arrival. In the first place they smell of a compound of leather, salt, herring, onions, and perspiration, difficult to describe, but most apparent to the senses. . . . They are, moreover, though by nature rather suspecting and doubting, still made more so by parties in the old country who find it in their interest to guard them against the Castle Garden and its provisions, as if it were some terrible institution. Therefore they are very difficult indeed to deal with" (Louis Bagger, "A Day in Castle Garden," *Harper's New Monthly Magazine*, 42 [Dec. 1870–May 1871], 555). I am indebted to Joy Lintelman for this quotation.

6. Holmquist, *They Chose Minnesota*; Lowrey Nelson, *Town and Country in Transition* (Minneapolis: Univ. of Minn. Press, 1960), esp. ch. 3, "Of Kindreds, Tongues, and Peoples."

7. David Reimers, *Still the Golden Door: The Third World Comes to America* (New York: Columbia Univ. Press, 1992); Reed Ueda, *Postwar Immigrant America: A Social History* (Boston: St. Martin's Press, 1994); Elliott R. Barkan, *Asian and Pacific Islander Migration to the United States* (Westport, Conn.: Greenwood Press, 1992).

8. Nelson, *Town and Country in Transition*; Holmquist, *They Chose Minnesota*, Table 1, "Minnesota's Ethnic Populations in 1880, 1930, and 1970," 2.

9. Minnesota State Demographer, "Minnesota Minority Populations Grow Rapidly Between 1980 and 1990," *Population Notes* (Sept. 1991). The periodic reports from the office of the State Demographer are the best source for current changes in the ethnic composition of the state's population. Bob von Sternberg, "Beyond the Myth: Just who's moving to the Twin Cities," *Star Tribune*, Mar. 28, 1993. On migration of Hispanics to Minnesota and the tensions resulting from their arrival, see Wendy S. Tai, "A frosty welcome," *Star Tribune*, Jan. 3, 1994. For an updating of the statistics to 1997 for Minneapolis, see Dirk Johnson, "Ethnic Changes Tests Mettle of Minneapolis Liberalism," *New York Times*, Oct. 18, 1997, p. A1, 8; and "Minority Population Increases in Minnesota," *Star Tribune*, Dec. 19, 1997.

10. Wendy S. Tai, "Metro Area remains attractive to Asians," *Star Tribune*, Apr. 18, 1993; Minnesota Department of Education, "Asian Americans in Minnesota," *Aware: Celebrating Diversity* (May 1994), n. 5; Amherst H. Wilder Foundation, "Many Faces, Many Voices: New Americans in the Twin Cities," *Community Matters* 5 (Fall 1998): 3; Refugee Studies Center, Univ. of Minn., "Migrants from Ethiopia, Sudan, and Somalia," *Refugee Review* (Spring 1996).

11. Douglas Olney, "The Hmong and Their Neighbors," *CURA Reporter* 13 (1983): 8–14; Saint Paul Foundation, *Voices and Visions: Snapshots of the Southeast Asian Communities in the Twin Cities* (St. Paul: Saint Paul Foundation, 1996) includes personal accounts as well as profiles of the groups. The Twin Cities press has carried in-depth coverage of the Hmong. See esp. "Dreams in Exile: The Hmong in St. Paul," *St. Paul Pioneer Press*, Nov. 26, 1989, and "Hmong of Minnesota: Lost in the Promised Land," *Star Tribune*, Apr. 21, 1985; for a first person account by Bee Yang Her, a Hmong woman, see Northwest Area Foundation, "Unheard Voices: An Introduction to Colors," *Northwest Report* (July 1994), 32.

12. The Twin Cities press has carried frequent stories of the reunification of immigrant families, e.g., Mary Lynn Smith, "Resettlement brings tears of joy and sorrow," *Star Tribune*, Oct. 4, 1996. On the dramatic differences among Asian immigrant groups in their educational background and economic adjustment, see Wendy S. Tai, "Metro Area Remains Attractive to Asians," *Star Tribune*, Apr. 18, 1993.

13. Minnesota State Demographer, *Minnesota Minority Populations*; Peter Leyden, "Facing the Facts: Twin Cities rank high in rent and low in diversity," *Star Tribune*, Apr. 21, 1992; Wendy S. Tai, "Change of Face in Minnesota," *Star Tribune*, Sept. 23, 1994.

14. Bob von Sternberg, "Nordic roots hold true," *Star Tribune*, Dec. 18, 1992; Bureau of the Census, U.S. Department of Commerce, *Census '90: Supplementary Reports, Detailed Ancestry Groups for States* [1990 CP-S-1–2] (Washington, D.C.: Bureau of the Census, 1990).

15. Sharon Sayles Belton, "It's time for all to take an oath," *Star Tribune*, Jan. 5, 1994.

16. Johnson, "Ethnic Change Tests Mettle of Minneapolis Liberalism"; Tai, "A frosty welcome"; Bob von Sternberg, "Trail led into core Cities in late '80s, not just out," *Star Tribune*, Apr. 12, 1993; Peter Leyden, "Racism Growing in Minneapolis," *Star Tribune*, Apr. 16, 1993. On an incident of blatant ethnic insult in the 1990s, see Leslie Brooks Suzukamo, "'We are sorry,' KQRS says to Hmong," *Saint Paul Pioneer Press*, Nov. 6, 1998. On positive initiatives taken by organizations and institutions, see *Minnesota Ethnic Resources Directory* (St. Paul: International Institute of Minnesota, 1995).

17. *Star Tribune*, Oct. 20, 1996; a second letter commented: "Many northeast Minneapolis residents had foreign-born parents and grandparents, and some are vocal opponents of American immigration policies.... My parents came to the United States from Poland in the early 1900s.... They did not come expecting a handout; they came to make a better life for themselves and were proud of the opportunity to do so" (July 14, 1997).

18. On various neighborhoods see "The Cities' Backyard: History from the Neighborhood Viewpoint," *Common Ground* (Minneapolis) n. 1 (Spring 1974) and subsequent issues; also Richard Wolniewicz, *Ethnic Persistence in Northeast Minneapolis: Maps and Commentary* (Minneapolis: Minnesota Project on Ethnic America, 1973); and Federal Writers' Program, Work Projects Administration, *The Bohemian Flats* (1941; reprint, St. Paul: MHS Press, 1986).

19. For a sympathetic portrait, see Wing Young Huie, *Frogtown: Photographs and Conversations in an Urban Neighborhood* (St. Paul: MHS Press, 1996); and, on Northeast Minneapolis, Mike Kaszuba, "A hardy community bows to change," *Star Tribune*, Dec. 26, 1985. One can recapture the feel of the old neighborhoods best by reading the memoirs of persons who grew up there. On the Jewish neighborhood of West St. Paul, see William Hoffman, *Those were the Days* (Minneapolis: T. S. Denison, 1957) and *Tales of Hoffman* (Minneapolis: T. S. Denison, 1960). On Swede Hollow, see the Gentile Yarusso Papers, Immigration History Research Center, Univ. of Minn., and Nels M. Hokanson, "I Remember St. Paul's Swede Hollow," *Minnesota History* 41 (1969): 362–71. Efforts of Hmong to adapt through creating communities are described in *The Saint Paul Foundation, Voices and Visions*; Jean Hopfensperger, "Growing Up Hmong," *Star Tribune*, Oct. 2, 1998. On the Somali, see Wendy S. Tai, "A profound animosity," *Star Tribune*, Oct. 24, 1993, and Paul Gustafson, "Far from home, Somalis mark nation's independence," *Star Tribune*, June 28, 1999, and Chris Tomlinson, "Somalis Adapt to Life in [Minnesota] the U.S.," Associated Press, Nov. 17, 1997.

20. For an egregious example of this "amnesia," see Georgie Ann Geyer, *Americans No More* (New York: Atlantic Monthly Press, 1996). Geyer, who reports that her grandparents were immigrants, indicts the failings of current immigrants by gross exaggerations of the successes of earlier immigrants. Recent historical literature is replete with studies that document the dark side of the immigrant experience. For Minnesota Swedes, see Chapter 4, below, and the unpublished paper by Roger McKnight, "Night Pails and Trick-or-Treaters: The Story of Swedish Immigrants in Stillwater Prison."

21. Joshua Fishman, et al, *Language Loyalty in the United States* (The Hague: Mouton, 1966); Sture Lindmark, *Swedish America, 1914–1932* (Stockholm: Läromedelsförlagen, 1971).

22. On the language issue, see Margaret A. Lourie and Nancy F. Conklin, eds., *A Pluralistic Nation: The Language Issue in the United States* (Rowley, Mass.: Newbury House, 1978), and Nancy F. Conklin and Margaret A. Lourie, eds., *A Host of Tongues: Language Communities in the United States* (New York: Free Press, 1983); Susan J. Dicker, *Languages in America: A Pluralist View* (Philadelphia: Multicultural Matters, 1996).

23. Office of Human Resources Planning, Minnesota Department of Energy, Planning and Development, Population Notes (Mar. 1983); "German top foreign language spoken by

Minnesotans," *Star Tribune*, Apr. 28, 1993. Spanish was a close second, while Hmong was fourth, following Norwegian.

24. Kathleen Neils Conzen, et al., "The Invention of Ethnicity: A Perspective from the USA," *Journal of American Ethnic History* 12 (1992): 3–63; Dag Blanck, *Becoming Swedish-American: The Construction of an Ethnic Identity in the Augustana Synod, 1860–1917* (Uppsala, Sweden: Acta Universitatis Upsaliensis, 1997).

25. Douglas P. Olney, "We Must Be Organized: Dual Organizations in an American Hmong Community" (Ph.D. diss., Univ. of Minn., 1993).

26. Arthur M. Schlesinger, Jr., *The Disuniting of America: Reflections on a Multicultural Society*, 2nd ed. (New York: W. W. Norton, 1998). For an extended critique of exclusive multiculturalism, see my "Italian Immigrants and Working-Class Movements in the United States: A Personal Reflection on Class and Ethnicity," *Journal of the Canadian Historical Association* 4 (1993): 293–305, and "Are Italian Americans Just White Folks?" *Italian Americana* 13 (1995): 149–61.

27. Minnesota Planning State Demographic Center, *Faces of the Future: Minnesota Population Projections, 1995–2025* (St. Paul: State Demographic Center, 1998). Noting the rapid growth of non-European origin populations in recent years, the report projects high rates of increase of those groups in coming decades. Still, over 80 percent of Minnesota's residents will be "white" in 2025. Hispanics are not included in the "non-white" category, since persons of Hispanic origin "may be of any race." See also Bob von Sternberg, "Minnesota's Face in 2020," *Star Tribune*, Aug. 3, 1993.

Why Minnesota, Why the Twin Cities?

H. ARNOLD BARTON

Minnesota is proverbially regarded as America's most "Swedish" state, both in this country and in Sweden, and with good reason. At their height in 1910, Swedish Americans of the first and second generations—who alone were counted as the "Swedish stock" by the United States census—numbered nearly 270,000 persons in Minnesota. This amounted to almost 13 percent of the state's total population or close to one-fifth of its "foreign white stock." The distant second place was shared that year by Nebraska and Washington state, where the Swedish element came to a little under 5 percent. One out of five Swedish Americans lived in Minnesota.

Including the third and later generations, those with some Swedish blood in their veins come to a much larger proportion of Minnesota's present population. By 1930, Helge Nelson estimated that "far more than half" of the state's inhabitants were immigrants or descendants of immigrants. Including the slightly larger Norwegian element and the smaller Danish and Finnish groups—many of the latter Swedish in language—the Scandinavian element in Minnesota is generally estimated to amount to at least a third of the population. Its impact upon the character and history of the state can hardly be overestimated, as witnessed, for instance, by its prominence in state and national politics. Moreover, Minnesota's distinctive dialect, now nationally recognized largely thanks to Garrison Keillor's "Prairie Home Companion," bears an unmistakably Scandinavian stamp.[1]

Enough of statistics. The point is made. But why was it that Swedes found their way to Minnesota, and to the Twin Cities, in such numbers? The question has received no small amount of attention over the years and deserves a closer look.

The most widely held popular view, on both sides of the ocean, is that Swedes were drawn to Minnesota because its nature and climate most closely

resembled those of their homeland. This idea was stated in memorable fashion
at the very beginning of Swedish settlement in the territory by the celebrated
Swedish author Fredrika Bremer, who noted at the beginning of her excursion
down the Mississippi River in 1850 that Minnesota might well become a "glorious new Scandinavia."[2]

This sentiment has reappeared in a variety of forms down to the present. In
an early compilation on the history of the Swedes in Minnesota from 1910,
A. E. Strand declared:

> Like Sweden itself, the state of Minnesota is especially adapted to provide
> all the natural conditions for the development of a race of Swedish Americans who are hardy and active, both physically and intellectually. The North
> Star State—the very name speaks of sparkling waters, a clear, bracing climate, and all that stands for a life of purity and high endeavor! The Swedish
> Americans of Minnesota have, in truth, fixed their habitation in the very section of the United States which is most perfectly adapted to preserve the
> massive, intense traits of the old Northmen, and yet to modify and electrify
> them with a distinctively American spirit.[3]

In this same regard, the Swedish geographer Helge Nelson stated somewhat
more soberly in 1925:

> Time and time again one is surprised, in studying the distribution of the
> Swedes in America, by how the Swede has chosen the beautiful and from
> his viewpoint the most agreeable location, instead of that with the best soil.
> So often he has chosen the occupation he had at home in Sweden, whether
> it was lumbering, fishing, farming, or the like, but with this his way out there
> has led to areas, whose nature and possibilities for a livelihood have in some
> degree recalled those of his own home place.

In 1943 Nelson brought out what still remains the most detailed study of the
Swedish settlements in North America, in which he emphasized Minnesota's
resemblance to Sweden. The climate, he held, was "suitable only to a hardy race,"
thus it was natural that Swedes should prefer it, just as it was for folk from
Småland and Dalarna to settle in Chisago and Isanti Counties, with their "forests,
the abundance of their water-courses in fish and lumbering, to all of which
they were accustomed in their native country." Nelson's lyric description of his
first visit to Chisago County in 1921 heightens the effect:

> It was a softly rolling landscape with forests and fields alternating and with
> lakes, fringed by deciduous forests, popping out here and there. . . . At the
> wide waters of Chisago lake—a picturesque lake with sounds and islets and
> inlets but not a single crag—the farms were most frequently situated out on

the tongues [of land] and were reflected in the water. It was as if you should
have come into a South-Swedish lake-studded landscape with oak-hills and
maple-groves and a small fat Scanian piece of plain between.[4]

"Even while there was still fertile land to be had at a good price in Illinois," the
Swedish scholar, Albin Widén wrote in 1937, the Swedes "preferred the more
distant Minnesota, clearly because it most reminded of Sweden."[5]

Vilhelm Moberg in his novel *Unto a Good Land*, first published in Swedish
in 1952, does not state that his immigrant group chose in 1850 to go to Minnesota
for reasons of nature and climate; they went because Fina-Kajsa, an old woman
on their ship, had a son already living there. Moberg does, however, describe
how strange and repellant they found the "sea of grass" they crossed in northern Illinois on their way to the Mississippi. It was rich and fertile, but "the peasants from the forest regions passed over the prairie and shrank from the land
opening before their eyes in all its incomprehensible vastness." Later, making
their way through the Minnesota woods north of Stillwater on the St. Croix,
the immigrants from Ljuder parish "were in a foreign forest, yet they had arrived home: No longer were they the lost ones of this world."[6]

Still, one cannot but wonder about all of this. One may well suspect that
Americans, including Swedish descendants, tend to assume that Sweden *must*
be like Minnesota because so many Swedes came there, while Swedes take for
granted that Minnesota *must* resemble Sweden, for the same reason.

But *how* similar is Minnesota to Sweden in nature and climate? The southeastern and east-central areas of the state, near the Mississippi and St. Croix
Rivers—in Goodhue, Washington, Chisago, and Isanti Counties—where Swedes
first settled in the 1850s, bear even today a certain resemblance to parts of southern Sweden, even though such forest as still remains there consists mainly of
hardwoods. Nevertheless, I remember how I myself was rather surprised that
this area—"Mobergland"—did not look more "Swedish" when I first visited it.

Moreover, as the Swedes moved west along the expanding railroads, out to
the Red River Valley, they settled in areas of open prairie that did not look
Swedish at all. Already a bit west of Litchfield in Meeker County—in what was
by then an area of growing Swedish settlement—the Swedish journalist Hugo
Nisbeth encountered in 1874 "the endless *prairie*. Not a tree, not even a bush
met the eye wherever one turned. Everywhere emptiness, deathly silence. One
felt oppressed by this great, overwhelming emptiness."[7]

The area most reminiscent of much of Sweden was actually the coniferous
forest region of northeastern Minnesota—the *last* part of the state where Swedes
settled in sizable numbers. They came there, however, mainly to cut timber

and above all to work in the mines, with the exploitation of the Vermillion and Mesabi iron ranges beginning in the 1880s and '90s.[8]

As for climate, although Minnesota lies at a far more southerly latitude than Sweden—around the latitude of France—its continental climate is much more extreme in both summer and winter than Swedish immigrants were accustomed to at home. Winter temperatures in southern Minnesota compare with those in Haparanda in northernmost Sweden, while summer temperatures are higher than anywhere in the Old Country.[9]

What, meanwhile, do contemporary sources tell us about the early settlers' concern with landscape and climate? Almost nothing, at least not directly. So far as I have been able to determine, the numerous emigrant guidebooks of the 1850s do not concern themselves with Minnesota's alleged similarities with Sweden. Interestingly enough, *Beskrifning öfwer Nord-Amerikas Förenta Stater* from 1853, probably the most detailed of them, which so greatly impresses Vilhelm Moberg's fictional emigrants, says virtually nothing at all about Minnesota. But then, its author, the Småland parson Johan Bolin, had never actually been in America.[10]

Nor do the preserved letters or recollections of the early Swedish settlers in Minnesota shed much light in this regard. A letter from the pioneer Per Andersson, from Chisago Lake, dated September 7, 1851, to his fellow immigrant from Hälsingland, Eric Norelius, evidently aroused much interest in the area. Andersson speaks of the "good and fertile soil," the "good forest, useful for all the farmer's needs," with "no dry prairies" but meadowlands with an "excellent growth of grass." There was plentiful hunting and fishing. The climate he considered healthful. "In a word," Andersson concludes, "we have, in my opinion, the most favorable place I have seen for Swedes to settle." But judging simply by what he wrote, it would seem he was considering only down-to-earth, practical advantages. Peter Cassel's celebrated description of southeastern Iowa in 1846 had been no less enthusiastic, as were many immigrant letters from northwestern Illinois in the 1840s.[11]

Reminiscences of Swedish pioneer life in Minnesota during the 1850s published by the early pioneers Hans Mattson, Eric Norelius, and Trued Granville Pearson likewise say nothing of any similarities to Sweden. In 1890, Eric Norelius would, to be sure, write in his history of the early Swedish settlements that Per Andersson, coming from the "Finn-forests" of Hälsingland, naturally considered it essential that he live in a area of woods and lakes and that he thus could not have thrived in Illinois. But this comment was made long after the event, at a time when, it would appear, such speculations based on hindsight were becoming commonplace. Most of the early immigrant letters from Minnesota that I have seen dwell, indeed, more on the *differences* between the new land and the old than upon their similarities.[12]

Meanwhile, although Minnesota drew increasing numbers of Swedes from the older settlements in northern Illinois and Indiana during the expansive decade of the 1850s, its attractions did not go unrivalled. Kansas in particular was already arousing a good deal of interest, as shown by a lively exchange of letters appearing in the Chicago newspaper *Hemlandet* during 1859 between the Swedish boosters of the two states. Again the emphasis is upon essentially practical advantages, with Minnesotans attributing particular importance to their region's allegedly more healthful climate. One Louis Lybecker, who claimed to have been on a surveying team there, did however urge his countrymen not to settle in Kansas, whose "endless prairie with its eternal monotony" he considered repellant to Scandinavians. He confessed he had not seen Minnesota, but continued, "No, we only feel at home amidst a glorious nature, amidst our evergreen forests, by a lake or river. Only then can we say: New Sweden!"[13]

Still, if Kansas did not attract any large number of Swedes prior to the Civil War, this may be largely attributed to turmoil in the "Bloody Kansas" of those years. By the later 1860s and '70s, following the war and as the transportation network spread westward, growing numbers of Swedes from the more wooded areas of early settlement did move out to the prairies of Kansas, of western Iowa and Nebraska—and, indeed, of central and western Minnesota.[14]

There is meanwhile another explanation for the great influx of Swedes and other Scandinavians into Minnesota that has nothing to do with landscape or climate. It maintains that this was simply the result of *timing, opportunity, transportation*, and *promotion*. This view has generally been endorsed by scholars.[15]

Swedish emigration to America began on a modest scale during the 1840s and '50s, and the same was true of Swedish settlement in Minnesota. The census of 1850 showed 6,077 white inhabitants in the territory, of whom only four were Swedes. By 1860 they had increased to a modest 3,200, still outnumbered by the Germans and Norwegians. The situation changed radically during the 1860s. Between 1867 and 1869, Sweden suffered disastrous crop failures, quickly resulting in a vast increase in the emigration of Swedish peasants. The majority naturally went to places where Swedes, often relatives or friends, were already settled in America. By now, most of the good land in Illinois and southeastern Iowa—where their earliest settlements lay—was already taken, so most of the new arrivals moved on to where land was available on terms they could manage.[16]

They arrived just in time to cash in on one of the most remarkable offers ever made: the American Homestead Act of 1862, which provided 160 acres of free government land to any citizen (or person who declared his intent to become one) who effectively occupied his claim. Few homesteads were taken in Minnesota at first, during wartime and following the Sioux uprising that same year, but after the Civil War ended in 1865 the frontier advanced rapidly. When the great wave of Swedish immigration reached these shores in the later 1860s, the state lay open to settlement.

The end of the Civil War opened the way for the rapid conversion from sail to steam in Atlantic passenger traffic, making ocean travel far faster, more convenient, and cheaper, while the American railroad network spread across the continent. The railroads played a key role in the settlement of the region. They received support from the federal government in the form of extensive land grants along their rights of way. Their construction called for armies of laborers, providing them with earnings that often in turn were used to purchase railroad lands. In this way strings of Swedish settlements extended westward and northward along the advancing tracks. Lumbering in the northern forests during the winter provided further sources of income. Thus Minnesota, in this crucial phase of Swedish immigration, offered both land and the earnings to acquire and settle it.

The state's self-promotion was meanwhile particularly effective. In the decades following the Civil War, many midwestern states competed vigorously in attracting settlers, both from the eastern states and from Europe. Minnesota established an Emigrant Bureau in 1867 and appointed the Swedish American Hans Mattson, the early pioneer and celebrated Civil War colonel, as its secretary—in effect, its director. Mattson was particularly concerned with attracting his own countrymen to the state and to that end he visited Sweden in 1868–69. In 1870–71 he served as Minnesota's secretary of state, which also included overall responsibility for promoting settlement.

Returning to private life in 1871, he became the emigrant agent for the St. Paul & Pacific Railroad. More astutely aware than his competitors of the importance of using the existing Swedish settlements in the state as magnets to

Foreman's office for the Great Northern Railroad's rip track workers, Westminster Street, St. Paul, 1915. Foreman Ole Swanson, seated to the left, had lived in Swede Hollow.

attract further immigration from Sweden, he began by inducing Swedish settlers to write home about the advantages of Minnesota and their communities,
providing free paper, envelopes, and not least postage—no small item at that
time! He spent most of the years from 1871 to 1876 in Sweden, promoting Minnesota and the lands of the Lake Superior & Mississippi Railroad, and each time
he returned he was accompanied by large groups of immigrants. He was also
involved in land transactions. Mattson was probably the most famous Swedish
American of his day. No doubt, more than any other, he succeeded in "selling"
his state to his own people.[17]

In a promotional booklet, published in Sweden in 1872, Mattson confidently
predicted that Minnesota would become the heart of Scandinavian rural settlement in America. "Besides its great abundance of fertile land," he wrote, "it
has many attractions for the sons of the North, such as a landscape with hills
and vales, forests and plains, lovely lakes teeming with fish, and rushing rivers,
but in particular a healthful and invigorating climate." Its winters were, to be
sure, severe—a point the promoters of other states constantly alluded to. But,
Mattson rejoined, Scandinavians had always thrived best in the North and many
who had sought to avoid winter in more southerly climes "grievously found instead sickness and untimely death." Mattson's booklet meanwhile concerned
itself above all with Minnesota's "abundance of fertile land" and other material advantages.[18]

Meanwhile, why have Swedes settled in such numbers in the Twin Cities?
A few were there almost from the start, including the proverbial "first Swede
in Minnesota," the fur trapper and later Methodist preacher Jacob Falström,
who had drifted down from Canada around 1818 and lived, with his Chippewa
wife and numerous children, as a squatter at Fort Snelling already in 1836–37.
Others arrived during the 1850s. But with the great influx beginning in the later
1860s, the Twin Cities' Swedish population grew rapidly, with its centers in St.
Paul's "Swede Hollow" and Minneapolis's Cedar-Riverside district.[19]

By the 1880s, the Minnesota land boom promoted by the Homestead Act
and the railroads was running dry. Most of the good land out to the Red River
was taken and it became ever more expensive to acquire. Land-seekers moved
further west: to the Dakotas, to the Pacific Northwest, and, after the turn of the
century, up to the Canadian prairie provinces.

By this time, too, arriving immigrants from Sweden came increasingly from
the poorer classes of the countryside—those who earlier had lacked the means
to emigrate or establish themselves as farmers—thanks to better wages, lower
transportation costs, and above all prepaid tickets or money sent to them by
relatives or friends already in America. These newer immigrants were in im-

mediate need of cash, and the Twin Cities provided the readiest opportunities for most of them to earn it. The men often worked much of the year outside the cities—in logging, in railroad construction, or by following the wheat harvests—but returned periodically to their boarding houses in town. The women found plentiful employment as domestics in American households. Duluth and the new mining towns on the Iron Range also drew their share of the later arrivals.

To be sure, residence and work in the cities was often a way station to acquiring a farm. But as time passed, many found permanent employment in town and settled down. Helge Nelson claimed, moreover, that the early Swedish immigrants' tendency to acquire relatively small farms in forested areas, requiring back-breaking labor for only modest returns, caused many of them and their children in time to move to the cities, in particular Minneapolis and St. Paul, which lay close to the areas of old Swedish settlement. By the turn of the century, over half of Minnesota's Swedish element—like that of the country as a whole—was living in urban, rather than rural areas.[20]

What are we to make of the two schools of thought as to why Minnesota became the most "Swedish" of the states? There are, certainly, plenty of good, practical reasons for this, as we have seen. But does this in itself mean that landscape and climate had little to do with the case? Certainly the opinions, for instance, of such authorities as the late Helge Nelson and Albin Widén are not to be taken lightly.

That Swedish peasant farmers, as well as those who sought to attract them to Minnesota, were not inclined to write about the appeal of Minnesota's landscape to the Swedish soul should not be surprising. However poets and intellectuals might rhapsodize about communion with Nature, peasants, who actually lived close to the soil, were essentially concerned with what it produced and the livelihood it gave them. My friend, the late Sigvard Cederroth of Uppsala, made this point in striking fashion in an essay in which he compared descriptions of the spring of 1827 on the Uppsala plain in the diaries of a poet and of a peasant farmer. But, as Cederroth also maintained, concern with mundane matters need not exclude unexpressed and largely unconscious reactions to natural surroundings, feelings which it would take the imaginative insight of the novelist, like Vilhelm Moberg, to put into words. From real life, Robert Nisbeth, who visited western Minnesota in 1872, gave a deeply moving account of a newly arrived Swedish pioneer wife whom he visited at her dugout. She gave good reasons for her family's settling in the area. "We could never have had it so good back home," she said. But then she admitted, "However that may be, you never really feel at home here." He asked if she was happy. "'Happy,' she said, bursting into tears, 'No, I am not as happy and thankful as I ought to be, but, you see, it is hard to be so alone. You see how desolate it is here, and then comes the long, cold winter.'"[21]

There is another aspect that needs to be taken into consideration. When the *Swede* Helge Nelson, in the collaborative work *Svenskarna i Amerika*, argued in 1925 that Swedes were strongly drawn to settle in those areas that most resembled their old homeland, the *Swedish American* journalist Ernst Skarstedt, in the same volume, maintained the opposite.

Upon his arrival in America in 1878, Skarstedt had at first worked on a farm near Litchfield, Minnesota, but soon moved to Lindsborg, Kansas. In his memoirs he indeed described how depressing he found the Kansas prairie on first encounter, but he soon discovered the charm of the prairie flowers and the big sky. He later tried his hand at farming in the Northwest and in California's San Joaquin Valley.[22]

In Wisconsin, the Pacific Northwest, and, above all, Minnesota, Skarstedt wrote in 1925, Swedish immigrants found natural and climatic conditions most similar to Sweden's. "One ought therefore to be able to assume," he wrote, "that the Swedes should thrive better in these states than in others, but experience teaches that they thrive and succeed just as well in those areas that least resemble their native places.""The Swedish settler," he went on, "does not appear inferior to the Americans in his ability and willingness to adapt to new conditions." Indeed, Skarstedt held that those who had settled on the open prairie had done far better than those who had felled trees and grubbed stumps in the wooded regions.[23]

Does this conflict of views between the Swedish professor and the Swedish American journalist and veteran pioneer farmer *in itself* tell us anything about the nature of the Swedish immigrant experience, not only in Minnesota, but in North America? To me, it suggests a deeper psychological significance. For patriotic homeland Swedes, both at the time and since, it has been hard to admit that emigrants from Sweden could ever really feel at home anywhere else. Thus, in their view, their emigrated compatriots naturally sought to settle in those parts of North America that offered the nearest equivalents to what they had left. In Minnesota, even though she would never get over her homesickness, Moberg's Kristina could find a "New Duvemåla." For Swedes in Sweden, assumed similarity thus offers a certain consolation over those they have lost to the "Great Land to the West" and a reaffirmation of their homeland's unique qualities. It has been a way of somehow holding on to those who left.

For proud Swedish Americans, like Ernst Skarstedt, it was meanwhile altogether natural and justifiable that they should have emigrated to America when it offered them better opportunities. It was, therefore, essential to make people back home understand that they had no regrets and could feel perfectly at home wherever they settled. To assert their independence from physical environment meant to seek freedom from the constraints of the past and from any lingering feelings of guilt over their emigration. They were thus naturally skeptical toward the idea that nostalgia had been important in deciding where they went.[24]

How much was the choice of Minnesota as the immigrant's new home determined by the head? How much by the heart? We may only conclude that *both* played their part and that *neither* ruled out the other.

* * * *

NOTES

1. Helge Nelson, *The Swedes and the Swedish Settlements in North America*, 2 vols. (Lund: C.W.K. Gleerup, 1943), 1:186ff.; Lars Ljungmark, *Den stora utvandringen* (Stockholm: Sveriges Radio, 1965), 190–98, esp. 192.
2. Fredrika Bremer, *The Homes of the New World*, 2 vols. (New York: Harper Bros., 1853), 2:56f.
3. A. E. Strand, ed., *A History of the Swedish-Americans of Minnesota*, 3 vols. (Chicago: Lewis Publ. Co., 1910), 1:iiif.
4. Nelson, *Swedes and Swedish Settlements*, 1:56f., 184, 190f. Cf. Helge Nelson, "Svenskar och svenskbygder i Nordamerika. Deras geografiska utbredning," in Karl Hildebrand and Axel Fredenholm, eds., *Svenskarna i Amerika*, 2 vols. (Stockholm: AB Historiska förlaget, 1925–26), 1:358ff. An excellent survey of Swedish settlement in the state is provided by John G. Rice, "The Swedes," in June Drenning Holmquist, ed., *They Chose Minnesota: A Survey of the State's Ethnic Groups* (St. Paul: MHS Press, 1981), 248–76.
5. Albin Widén, *Svenskar som erövrat Amerika* (Stockholm: Nordisk Rotogravyr, 1937), 77.
6. Vilhelm Moberg, *Unto a Good Land*, trans. Gustaf Lannestock (1954; reprint, St. Paul: MHS Press, 1995), 3, 85f., 136.
7. Hugo Nisbeth, *Två år i Amerika (1872–1874). Reseskildringar* (Stockholm: Aftonbladets aktiebolags tryckeri, 1874), 59. Cf. Byron Nordstrom, ed., *The Swedes in Minnesota* (Minneapolis: T. S. Dennison, 1976), 14.
8. See Nelson, *Swedes and Swedish Settlements*, 1:233–38.
9. Ibid., 1:179.
10. Johan Bolin, *Beskrifning öfwer Nord-Amerikas Förenta Stater. Jemte Upplysningar och Råd för utwandrare* (Wexjö: Tryckt hos A. G. Deurells enka, 1853). Cf. Märtha Ångström, "Swedish Emigrant Guide Books of the Early 1850's," *Yearbook of the American Swedish Historical Foundation, 1947* (Philadelphia, 1947), 22–48.
11. Eric Norelius, *De svenska Luterska Församlingarnas och Svenskarnes Historia i Amerika*, 2 vols. (Rock Island, Ill.: Augustana Book Concern, 1890, 1916), 2:543f. Cf. Nelson, *Swedes and Swedish Settlements*, 1:191f.; Emeroy Johnson, "Per Andersson's Letters from Chisago Lake," *Swedish Pioneer Historical Quarterly* 24 (1973): 3–31; H. Arnold Barton, ed., *Peter Cassel and Iowa's New Sweden* (Chicago: Swedish-American Historical Society, 1995), 91–96; H. Arnold Barton, *Letters from the Promised Land: Swedes in America, 1840–1914* (Minneapolis: Univ. of Minn. Press, 1975), esp. 28–33.

12. Hans Mattson, *Reminiscences: The Story of an Emigrant* (St. Paul: D. D. Merrill Co., 1891); *The Early Life of Eric Norelius (1833–1862)*, trans. Emeroy Johnson (Rock Island, Ill.: Augustana Book Concern, 1934); Arvid Bjerking, ed., *En skånsk banbrytare i Amerika. Trued Granville Pearsons självbiografi* (Oskarshamn: A-B. Axel Melchiors Bokhandel, 1937); Norelius, *De svenska Luterska församlingarna*, 1:541. Cf. Barton, *Letters*.

13. George M. Stephenson, "'Hemlandet' Letters," *Yearbook of the Swedish Historical Society of America*, 1922–23, esp. 87–91.

14. On the spread of Swedish settlement, see, above all, Nelson, *Swedes and Swedish Settlements*.

15. See, for instance, Florence E. Janson, *The Background of Swedish Immigration, 1840–1930* (Chicago: Univ. of Chicago Press, 1931), 143; Lars Ljungmark, *For Sale—Minnesota: Organized Promotion of Scandinavian Immigration, 1866–1873* (Chicago: Swedish Pioneer Historical Society, 1971); Nordstrom, ed., *Swedes in Minnesota*, 14–22; Rice, "The Swedes," esp. 248f.; Barton, *Letters*, 114. Cf. Carlton C. Qualey, *Norwegian Settlement in the United States* (Northfield, Minn.: Norwegian-American Historical Assn., 1938), ch. 5. Qualey does, however, state that Minnesota's resemblance to parts of Norway was mentioned in publicity in Norwegian American newspapers and "was often noted in the America letters," but he provides no documentation (114).

16. Nelson, *Swedes and Swedish Settlements*, 1:181; Alan Kastrup, *The Swedish Heritage in America* (Minneapolis: Swedish Council of America, 1975), 196.

17. Mattson, *Reminiscences*; Ljungmark, *For Sale—Minnesota;* "Come to the New North West: Immigration Promotion among the Swedes in America and in the Old Country, 1869–1873," in Nils Hasselmo, ed., *Perspectives on Swedish Immigration* (Chicago: Swedish Pioneer Historical Society, 1978), 109–20; and *Swedish Exodus*, rev. ed. (Carbondale: Southern Ill. Univ. Press, 1996), 58–68; H. Arnold Barton, "Hans Mattson. Ett emigrantöde i vidare perspektiv," *Sverigekontakt* (Dec. 1995), 10ff.

18. Hans Mattson, *Den nya Svenska Kolonien i Minnesota—Nordamerika* (Kristianstad: K. J. M. Möllersvärd, 1872), esp. 4.

19. Emeroy Johnson, "Was Oza Windib a Swede?" *Swedish-American Historical Quarterly* 35 (1984): 207–20; Nordstrom, ed., *Swedes in Minnesota*, 23–47.

20. Nelson, *Swedes and Swedish Settlements*, 1:57, 188f.

21. Sigvard Cederroth, "Professorn, bonden och naturkänslan," in his *Hemma i det fattiga. Uppländska strövtåg och utsikter* (Stockholm: L Ts förlag, 1982), 77–85; Nisbeth, *Två år i Amerika*, 61–66.

22. Ernst Skarstedt, *Vagabond och redaktör. Lefnadsöden och tidsbilder* (Seattle: Washington Printing Co., 1914), 18ff. Cf. Emory Lindquist, *An Immigrant's American Odyssey: A Biography of Ernst Skarstedt* (Rock Island, Ill.: Augustana Historical Society, 1974), esp. 44f.

23. Ernst Skarstedt, "Svenskt nybyggarliv i Amerika," in Hildebrand and Fredenholm, eds., *Svenskarna i Amerika*, 1:327, 358ff.

24. Cf. H. Arnold Barton, *A Folk Divided: Homeland Swedes and Swedish Americans, 1840–1940* (Carbondale: Southern Ill. Univ. Press, 1994), 279. Such differences in perception are the basic concern of this book.

Swedish Neighborhoods of the Twin Cities: From Swede Hollow to Arlington Hills, From Snoose Boulevard to Minnehaha Parkway

DAVID A. LANEGRAN

It is estimated that nearly 60 percent of the Swedes who came to the United States settled in the cities of the upper Midwest and Pacific Northwest. Chicago, Minneapolis, St. Paul, Duluth, and Seattle all had sizable Swedish populations. The immigrants moved into cities whose forms and functions were determined by the industrializing mass society of the late nineteenth century. The industrialized culture produced urban landscapes that contained little evidence of the European cultures of the immigrants occupying them. Nonetheless, the urban neighborhoods occupied by Swedes in the Twin Cities are quite interesting. They ranged from some of the rawest slums to fine pastoral suburbs adjacent to luxurious parks.

Beginning in the 1880s, Swedish emigration to the Twin Cities grew dramatically. John Rice reports that, by the end of the decade, Minnesota became the state with the largest Swedish population, approximately 60,000 immigrants. Of that number, 26,000 or 45 percent settled in the Twin Cities. The migration continued at a rapid rate until the outbreak of World War I. Minnesota's Swedish population peaked in 1905 at about 126,000, of which 38,000 lived in Minneapolis and St. Paul. Chicago had a much larger population of Swedes, but about 7.5 percent of the population of the Twin Cities was Swedish. No other large city had such a high percentage.[1] The large number and high proportion of Swedes made it possible for them to create their own neighborhoods. Although the majority of the Swedes lived in a few neighborhoods, for reasons that will become clear in this chapter they cannot be considered a ghettoized population.

The Twin Cities attracted immigrants for one primary reason: they offered employment for people with limited ability to speak English. The Swedish neighborhoods in both Minneapolis and St. Paul, as well as the much smaller community in South St. Paul, shared many common features. The overwhelming majority of the immigrants were of common origins with few skills. They were willing to work, however, and many had strong backs. Given their status, they could most readily find jobs in the developing industrial sector. The railroads, lumber mills, flour mills, slaughterhouses, construction firms, cabinet shops, garment factories, and breweries all welcomed good workers. The first residential communities were located within walking distance of the factory zones. In those days walking distance was up to three miles. Another very important form of employment was domestic service, though no permanent community of domestics developed.

St. Paul

Although no great Lutheran church dominates the skyline of St. Paul, Swedes and their descendants have made up a significant portion of the city's population for most of its history. From the time of the city's first land boom in 1857 until the end of the great European migration around 1920, St. Paul's manufacturing and transportation industries attracted immigrants from both northern and southern Europe. Germans were the largest single ethnic group until 1920, when their decline over the next decade, combined with the increase of the Swedish population, made Swedes the largest group of foreign-born residents in the city.

Swedish immigrants came to the Twin Cities along the same route that carried their compatriots to the Chisago Lakes area northeast of St. Paul. Instead of heading up the St. Croix to claim the wooded farmland, however, they disembarked at St. Paul. Many of the immigrants lacked the capital to begin farming and hoped to make quick money in town. St. Paul was the leading port of the Upper Mississippi. It was located on the north side of a great curve in the river where the valley formed by Phalen Creek and Trout Brook joins that of the Mississippi. This tributary valley, the largest break in the 80- to 100-foot cliffs that wall the river, was selected by the founders of the city because it allowed them to develop a wagon road with a gentle grade to the uplands away from the river. The main section of the city developed to the west of the marshy creek mouth on the heights, where the warehouse district and Union Depot would be constructed.

Founded by New Englanders and others from the mid-Atlantic states, St. Paul soon became known for its fur trade, port activities, wholesaling, and healthful climate. Together with Minneapolis, it dominated the Upper Midwest, processing the products of the region and distributing the manufactured goods, news, and people from further east. Although Stillwater was the largest city in the area when the Territory of Minnesota was created in 1849, by 1850 St. Paul had become Minnesota's largest city.

The Swedes came to St. Paul when transportation was slow and expensive. Most people walked to work, to shop, and to attend social functions. They generally tried to live close to their jobs because people worked long hours for five and often six days a week. All residential communities, commercial districts, and places of employment in St. Paul during the early years were located close to the river landing. Nearby were the main commercial, financial, entertainment, and warehouse districts of the city. When the railroads replaced steamboats and began to dominate transportation in the region after the Civil War, their tracks and repair shops were located in level creek beds. Soon the railroad landscape almost surrounded the city core. Further away from the city center, in the small stream valleys, mills and breweries were established. Swedes lived near all these sites.

The wealthy first lived to the north and east of downtown in an area known as Lafayette Park, but later, particularly in the 1870s and '80s, moved to St. Anthony Hill and Summit Avenue, to the west of the city. Some Swedes lived in the monumental Victorian mansions west of the city center as domestic servants. Many a "Swede Girl" got her start in America, living in a cramped garret room and waiting on the elite families of the Hill district.

The East Side

This configuration of housing and employment opportunities determined the location of the Swedish and Scandinavian community in St. Paul. Throughout the nineteenth century, Scandinavians generally lived east of the railroad tracks from downtown and on the other side of town from the Hill district. The Swedes were highly concentrated on the East Side, as it became known (Figure 1). The map understates the Swedish dominance in that area because it shows only the foreign-born and ignores the children of Swedish immigrants born in this country. By 1930, after the period of greatest migration from Sweden had ended, over half the Swedish-born population was still on the East Side. During the late 1930s and after, however, new residential areas in the western portion of the city attracted increasing numbers of the more affluent. In these new middle-class neighborhoods, Swedes made up a very small fraction of the total population and lost most of their Swedish identity.

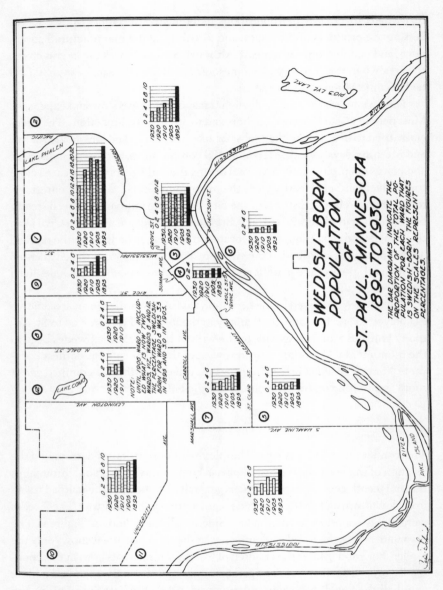

Figure 1: Swedish-born population of St. Paul, Minnesota, 1895–1930. This map indicates the concentration of Swedish-born living in the East Side neighborhoods that grew up around the manufacturing sites developed during the railroad era. From Calvin F. Schmid, *Social Saga of Two Cities: An Ecological and Statistical Study of Social Trends in Minneapolis and St. Paul* (Minneapolis: Bureau of Social Research, The Minneapolis Council of Social Agencies, 1937).

The several reasons behind this marked concentration of Swedish immigrants are relatively clear. Although there was no concentrated effort to ghettoize Swedes, there were several reasons for them to cluster on the East Side of their own accord. First, several places of employment for unskilled and semiskilled labor were located on the East Side. Because people walked to work, a home in the area was very convenient. Second, the Swedes knew about this area because it was on the way to the major cluster of Swedes in the Chisago Lakes area. All immigrants going to and from the river landing and rural community would pass through the East Side. Those moving to town tended to locate on the side of the city closest to their rural home area. Third, once the first group had become established, it attracted others by the typical chain immigration process. Most immigrants came to St. Paul on the advice of a friend or relative who had come before them. The newcomers naturally sought out his or her relatives or friends and tried to live near them. Fourth, ethnic areas attracted newcomers because these places functioned as transition zones in which people could gradually move from their own culture to the dominant Anglo-American culture. In such areas, shopkeepers spoke the languages of the immigrant community and sold traditional items. Swedish American churches were also present. These ethnic enclaves were havens of comfort from the pressures of acculturation. Immigrants often felt threatened by the diversity around them, and many of their fears were indeed justified. For example, Gust Nygren—a six-foot-five former lumberjack—felt it necessary to carry a cheap .25-caliber pistol in his pocket when he went to work in the slaughterhouses in South St. Paul during the first decade of the twentieth century. Other Swedes working there carried dirks in their boots, which they had customized from the butcher knives supplied by the company. A fifth reason was the lack of opportunities to settle elsewhere in the city. In the third quarter of the nineteenth century, there were few places in the city where unskilled or semi-skilled laborers and their families could live. New immigrants could go to Frogtown, the marshy area to the north of University Avenue and west of the capitol, but Frogtown was occupied by German-speaking people. They could have settled along West Seventh Street to the southwest of downtown, but this area was also occupied by Germans and Bohemians, and did not offer extensive employment opportunities.

All of these factors worked together to create the East Side settlement. Once it was established it gained a positive reputation, reflecting the images the immigrants had of themselves, and was never called a ghetto. Most Eastsiders could not imagine a better place to live. It was a large and diverse section of the city, ranging from inner city manufacturing and housing to suburban residential areas and parks. Swedes lived in all parts from the worst to the best.

Svenska Dalen

Undoubtedly the most famous part of the East Side was Swede Hollow or *Svenska Dalen*. The hollow is actually the lower portion of Phalen Creek Valley, a narrow ravine about three-quarters of a mile long with sides 60 to 80 feet high. A railway line ran through the valley on its way to Duluth. The Swede Hollow community was first occupied by people other than Swedes. Trappers, lumbermen, and casual laborers squatted in the Hollow in the 1840s. The Swedes began to occupy the shacks in the 1850s, and their presence dominated the valley for about a half century. The creek attracted industry very early: the North Star Brewery (1855); Brainard Mills (1856); City Mills (1860); Excelsior Brewery (1863); Union Mills (1864); St. Paul Mills (1867); and North Star Mills (1872). These establishments, together with the railroad and business in the city's center, provided jobs for the early settlers and later the Swedish immigrants.

During the last years of the nineteenth century, Swede Hollow served as a funnel through which many Swedes entered the East Side. Swede Hollow was a "stepping stone" neighborhood, a temporary home where immigrants stayed only until they could afford to move up the hill. It was a place where impoverished newcomers could find cheap housing while they got started. It also

Swede Hollow, ca. 1910

served as a refuge for people who had fallen on hard times and needed a place to stay while they pulled themselves together again. It was a slum. Unlike the residential areas surrounding it, the Hollow was not divided into a regular grid pattern of streets and alleys. In fact, the one street in the Hollow was much more like a country lane, meandering along the side of the creek. The steep walls and narrow valley prevented the laying out of neat town lots as occurred in the rest of the city. Instead, the houses were crowded and were clustered close to each other wherever space was available. Residents got their water from a natural spring and used the creek as their sewer. Of course, each house had its outdoor privy and some residents even built theirs on stilts out over the creek. The houses were small, largely homemade, with a variety of additions and modifications made over the years. Most families had gardens and barnyard animals out of necessity. The slum in the valley was in the shadow of the Hamm's brewery and the mansion of Theodore Hamm, its owner. In those days the captains of industry were proud of their accomplishments and liked to look at their factories, though it meant residency near a slum. We do not know, however, if Mr. Hamm looked at the Swedes down in the Hollow.

In 1881, Swedes in the Hollow were joined by Irish immigrants. The newcomers lived in a portion of the valley between the Seventh Street and Fourth Street bridges. This community was called Conamara Patch. Living in that area downstream from the privies of Swede Hollow was unpleasant year-round, but it was made worse in the spring when the rising creek encouraged a massive neighborhood clean-up. Anything that was unwanted was thrown in and pushed off downstream with poles.

According to Nels M. Hokanson, who lived in the Hollow during these years, there was friction between the groups. He wrote vividly about the coming of the Irish in very personal terms:

> Some were Irish, and their numbers grew steadily along with their chickens, ducks, pigs, goats and other animals. Once the young men even brought some wild western horses, whose kicking and neighing disturbed our sleep for several nights. The combative Irish boys, whom father called the "damnable Irish," threw stones at the drum during Salvation Army services; they picked fights with Swedes and harassed me at every opportunity.

Other Hokanson reminiscences of family life in the Hollow provide a comparatively idyllic picture:

> Winter interfered with the arrival of the vegetable wagon because the only road was often closed by snow drifts. Father would be called out to help clear the tracks when heavy snow and freezing halted streetcar operations. Between jobs he cut wood and kept close to the stove where he liked to read

the Swedish paper. Sometimes he sang folk tunes accompanied by his dragspel [accordion] which he kept under the bed. In the evenings friends would often come to share the warmth, drink coffee, take snuff or smoke their curved Swedish pipes. Mother spun wool or knitted and listened to the talk from her place in a corner under a picture of King Oscar II of Sweden. Sister was put to bed early. I liked to sit in her little rocking chair and watch the reflection from the wood fire while I listened to the news the visitors reported: a Swede found dead—probably from a heart attack—another beaten by a drunken Irish, a Swedish couple hauled off in the paddy wagon after a fight.[2]

Conversations in the Hokanson household also dealt with politics, economics, and better places to live and work. The family left the Hollow for Aitken, Minnesota, and in so doing they were typical of many other families who passed through on their way to a better future. Although Hokanson and many other former residents of the Hollow interviewed in the 1970s looked back on their childhood in Swede Hollow with nostalgia, public health workers who visited the area remembered the numerous cases of whooping cough, pneumonia, undernourishment, and other childhood diseases.

Although the community continued to be called Swede Hollow, a series of immigrant groups followed the Swedes through *Svenska Dalen*. After 1900, Italian became the dominant language on the lower East Side, and the Hollow was known for the smell of fermenting grapes each fall. The Italians' place in the Hollow was taken over by Mexicans after World War II.

Arlington Hills and The Greater East Side

When families became established, they left the Hollow and moved up the hill into Arlington Hills or further out toward Lake Phalen. In the first decades of the twentieth century a strong residential community developed on what was then the fringe of the city. It was subdivided by real estate speculators who sold lots to individuals who then built modest middle class homes and planted neat lawns and gardens.

The configuration of the neighborhoods was controlled by the grid-pattern streets and topography. The hills were occupied by wealthier people; the lowest areas were avoided because of the high water table. The community developed a distinctive pattern of detached wooden or stucco houses in a few basic styles: the St. Paul eclectic cube, the bungalow, the story-and-a-half Cape Cod, or the duplex. There were only a handful of apartment houses. The community wholeheartedly adopted the "own your own home" mentality. The builders used plan-book designs for these houses. Lumberyards in the city made available the resources; contractors, along with their clients, chose basic plans and modified them according to taste and budget. The dimensional lumber needed to build the house was then delivered to the site. A basement was dug and the foundation laid, though in early years homes were frequently built without basements in order to save money. The climate and culture, however, dictated that basements would be added as soon as possible. The added space was also welcome in relatively small homes. Many, if not most, of the carpenters who built the East Side were Swedes or Scandinavians.

Several churches representing the Swedish American denominations were established and social organizations were formed. Here the children went to school, people shopped, banked, and worked, and when they died they were buried in the nearby cemetery. Throughout the twentieth century, the neighborhood remained a safe place. Children, young people, and women customarily walked to school, to the shops, to the beaches of Lake Phalen, to church, and to friends' homes for a visit. Of course, there were many residential eyes watching this area. Women generally did not work outside the home, and the older generation was not institutionalized. People lived in their houses long after retirement and took an active interest in everything around them. When asked to name their neighborhood, they most often responded with "the East Side." They would, when pressed, produce street names, but to a remarkable extent they maintained an identity with the entire area.

The success of the East Side community has stemmed from its diversity. As families increased in wealth they could adjust their housing conditions and neighborhood status by moving further out toward Lake Phalen and the edge of the city. Thus, even though the Swedes abandoned the Hollow and much of lower Payne Avenue, they remained on the East Side and maintained their institutions and the positive image of the area for over a century.

Payne Avenue

All thriving residential areas were served by local shopping streets. The East Side had two, Payne Avenue and Arcade Street. Arcade was also Highway 61 heading north to Duluth. Although it had many establishments that served the community, its role was that of a thoroughfare. Payne Avenue had a more local function and earned the epithet "Snoose Boulevard."

This was the main street of the Swedish community in St. Paul, and, according to Wilfred Anderson, a store owner on the avenue for over three decades, if you could not speak Swedish, you had no business on Payne Avenue.

The Avenue developed in response to the needs of the people on the East Side for goods and services. It was a commercial strip development of a sort that emerged along streetcar lines before the automobile became common. Commercial development began in the late 1880s on the corners of Bradley, Bedford, and Decatur near the manufacturing district associated with Phalen Creek and the railroads. The first stores sold groceries and meats. They shared the street with saloons, barbershops, and professional offices. The expansion of the commercial district northward began in earnest in 1893 when the bridge over the railroad tracks was completed. The streetcar line that ran along Minnehaha and then north on Payne spurred the rapid growth.

From the turn of the century until the late 1940s, the street was characterized by long-established merchants who had been in business on Payne Avenue for several decades. Jacobson's bakery provided the usual daily fare plus "melt-in-your-coffee" cinnamon rusks beloved by young and old. There were several butcher shops like Westlund's and Charlie Olson's. Charlie had big barrels of herring in his store and, in the winter, stacked lutefisk like cord wood outside the door. Swenson Brothers sold furniture, the Rylanders appliances, the Borgstroms drugs, and the Setterholms groceries. A few Swedes bought their furs from Leafgren. Everyone bought coal and firewood from the Petersons, who delivered to basement coal bins. A few had their pictures taken in Erickson's Photo Studio.

Although the local and national economies slowed during the 1930s, Payne Avenue and the East Side prospered after 1934 when Prohibition was repealed and Hamm's Brewery could return to full production. Through political pressure Wilfred Anderson acquired a Swedish liquor license after the repeal of Prohibition. He was fond of telling of how representatives from the various immigrant communities lobbied the City Council to make sure that each ethnic group got its own liquor license. They did not want to deal with outsiders. Because the number of licenses was severely limited, owning a license guaranteed its possessor a good income. Anderson's Liquor Store was adjacent to his merchandise market.

The Avenue thrived until the early 1950s when nearly 165 establishments—small groceries, craftsmen shops, dry goods stores, and professional offices—usually operated by local residents were in operation. Some of the shopkeepers cemented the older community together. Most sold goods on credit to the residents and this bond of trust seems to have been very important. The merchants not only fetched desired items from the shelves, they also delivered them to homes in the area. These services were crucial during the Depression and war years.

The 1950s brought dramatic changes, however, because residents began to abuse the credit provided by smaller merchants. When they had money, residents shopped for bargains at the "cash and carry supermarkets." When their check was gone, they returned to the neighborhood and ran up large bills in the local stores. Grocers like Setterholm rewarded promptness and gave children bags of candy when their mothers settled their monthly accounts. But not everyone settled up, and some households owed the grocer as much as $1,500 by the middle 1950s. Nearly all the small grocers and meat markets saw their customers switch to the cash and carry stores. None of the neighborhood markets survived the 1960s.

After the 1950s, the Avenue provided a place for neighborhood residents to have casual meetings and a place where community celebrations, such as a Salvation Army parade or the Harvest Festival, might occur. These once-a-year events were but faint expressions of the multiple bonds that had once tied residents to merchants during the early years of the community.

The St. Paul Swedish Community Today

The lure of increased living space, new homes, modern schools, churches with parking lots, and increased status pulled many of the successful families of Swedish or mixed descent out of the East Side. The younger generations, Americanized in public schools, lost most of their distinctive Swedish culture and no longer felt the need to live in the Swedish community. Although many remained on the Greater East Side, others moved to other parts of the Twin Cities metropolitan area. The population of St. Paul's East Side decreased and grew older. There was a 16 percent decline between 1940 and 1970. The Scandinavian churches that had changed to English language services during the 1930s began to follow the general movement to the suburbs, and the historic community began to break up. By the 1970s, the majority of the immigrant generation had sold, or was in the process of selling, their homes. Thirty years later, they are all gone. Their place was not necessarily occupied by other Scandinavians. With the passing of the immigrant generation and the dispersal of the second and third generations into newer, middle-class neighborhoods in the suburbs, there is no longer a recognizable geographical core of the Swedish population in St. Paul. There are still many people of Scandinavian ancestry living on the East Side, however, who continue to celebrate holidays in a traditional manner. But, while some churches maintain a Scandinavian flavor, there is not one Scandinavian restaurant on the East Side.

The third and fourth generation descendants of Swedish immigrants have forgotten the necessities of life in Swede Hollow or Payne Avenue. They are not threatened by other groups and do not require a special spatial community

other than one defined by social and economic status. They are a part of the
Twin Cities. For them and their descendants, Swede Hollow and the East Side
are places through which people, who are seen only in old photos, passed on
the journey toward Americanization.

Minneapolis

The pattern of Swedish neighborhoods in Minneapolis is significantly different from the relatively few highly concentrated neighborhoods of St. Paul. The
earliest Swedish immigrant appears to have come to Minneapolis in 1851. He
emigrated from Skåne and was a shoemaker. He established a shop in the earliest core area for Swedish settlement in the city—on the river flats north of St.
Anthony Falls. It took many years, however, before any significant influx of
Swedes occurred. The 1860 Federal Census showed no Swedes in the city. But
by 1870 there were 2,676 native-born Swedes in the city, and by 1900 this figure
had grown to 20,035. The Swedish population peaked in 1920 at 26,515. The total population of the city was about 375,000. It must be noted that these figures
do not include the children and grandchildren of the first-generation immigrants. Of all the ethnic groups that settled in Minneapolis, the Swedes were
the largest. In 1930 they comprised 17 percent of the population of the city.[3]

There were many more Swedes in Minneapolis than in St. Paul. There were
so many Swedes in Minneapolis that they constituted the largest foreign-born
group in every section of the city. This pattern reflects both the greater employment in the industrial sector of the city and the lack of competing ethnic
groups. By 1910 Minneapolis was home to 70 percent of all the Swedes living in
the Twin Cities.

The Swedish population in Minneapolis grew dramatically after 1870, settling in several neighborhoods (Figure 2). The city's two "Swede Towns" developed on the north side of the Mississippi River in the Second and Ninth wards
and south of the river along Washington Avenue, east of the Milwaukee Railroad Depot. This second area became the most highly concentrated Swedish
and Scandinavian section in the city. It was not exclusively Swedish, but included a significant mixture of Norwegians and Danes. From these two central
cores the Swedish population spread north and northwest up the river, cross-
ing it at Twenty-fourth Avenue. They moved east and south from the depot
area into the Cedar-Riverside and Seward sections of the city. At the turn of
the century, 25 percent of the population in this area was Swedish, the
strongest concentration in the city. In the northern areas, 9 to 15 percent had
come from Sweden. The largely self-contained Cedar Riverside neighborhood
had low income housing on the river flats in an area known as Bohemian Flats

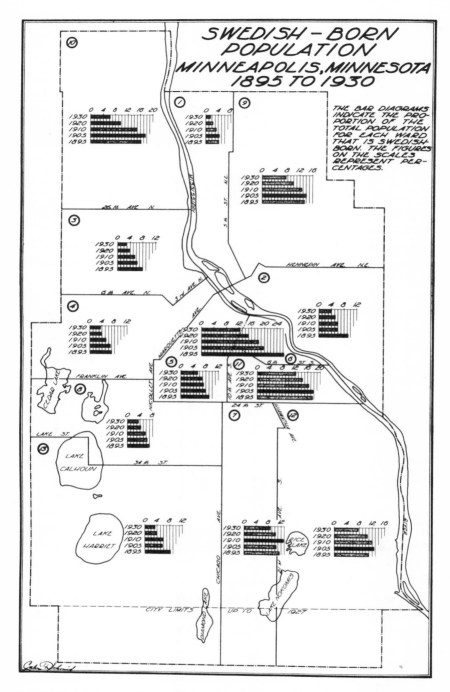

Figure 2: Swedish-born population of Minneapolis, Minnesota, 1895–1930. Minneapolis Swedes lived in all parts of the city but during the early years settled in inner neighborhoods near employment opportunities. From Calvin F. Schmid, *Social Saga of Two Cities: An Ecological and Statistical Study of Social Trends in Minneapolis and St. Paul* (Minneapolis: Bureau of Social Research, The Minneapolis Council of Social Agencies, 1937).

and more substantial homes further south toward Franklin Avenue. There were two Snoose Boulevards here: Washington Avenue, which had become the district where lumberjacks, farmhands, and other seasonal workers, as well as the homeless or unemployed, hung out; and Cedar Avenue, which was lined with Scandinavian businesses, saloons, and theaters.

By the turn of the century, the population was rapidly pushing southward across the level neighborhoods of South Minneapolis. In this large area, laid out in a grid of rectangular blocks, single-family houses were developed by builders in a manner similar to that described earlier. The major difference was that neighborhoods were defined by arterial streets, and the generic term "South Minneapolis" was used to refer to large areas of middle-class housing districts occupied by Swedes and others. Schmid's map of European ethnic groups dramatically illustrates how dominant Swedes were in the newer communities of South Minneapolis along Minnehaha Creek. Almost 44 percent of the immigrants in the Twelfth Ward were born in Sweden. In addition, 32 percent of the Seventh Ward and 20 percent of the Thirteenth Ward were also born in Sweden. The same was true of the northern areas outside the city limits. About 25 percent of both the Ninth and Tenth wards were Swedish immigrants.

Another concentration of blue-collar Swedes lived near the industrial zone of Northeast Minneapolis. This area, more commonly known for its Slavic population, was home to Swedes from the 1880s until World War II. Many second- and third-generation Swedish Americans still reside in the old neighborhood or have moved to northern suburbs. Swedes also dominated the Maple-Hill-Columbia neighborhoods and the area south of Broadway called Dogtown. Neither of these areas housed many Scandinavians after 1950. On the west side of the river, a concentration of Swedes was located after the turn of the century in the Camden area near Shingle Creek. In addition to newly arrived immigrants, many families moved further north from the older neighborhoods on the north side. This working-class area was home to the greatest concentration of Swedes outside of the Cedar-Riverside core.[4] In most respects this neighborhood resembled the middle class areas of South Minneapolis and the East Side of St. Paul. Families owned their own homes, worshipped in nearby churches, and frequented the Swedish shops and businesses in the area. By this time, as in South Minneapolis, Camden was linked to downtown Minneapolis by the streetcar system, providing residents employment and commercial opportunities.

Minneapolis as a whole offered a variety of employment opportunities for the immigrants, many of whom were young, single, poor, and unskilled. They often resided for a time in the ubiquitous boarding houses on the periphery of the downtown industrial and commercial sections. The railroads, timber mills, flour mills, construction companies, cabinet shops, and foundries employed thousands. The C. A. Smith Lumber Mill (Smith himself was a Swedish immigrant) on Washington Avenue North employed 700 men. Equally as important as the employment prospects were the opportunities to advance. As skills were acquired, the early immigrants moved upwards and their places were taken by new immigrants and new ethnic groups. The aggressive and assertive had ample opportunity to establish their own businesses and large numbers of immigrant entrepreneurs emerged. At the same time, there were significant numbers of professionals who immigrated. Minneapolis had its share of Swedish lawyers, doctors, and the like who settled in the city.

In the last quarter of the nineteenth century, a significant proportion of the individuals who emigrated to America's cities from Sweden were young women. They too found employment in the growing industries of Minneapolis, particularly in the garment sector. But more importantly, they were hired by the thousands as domestics, to clean, cook, and care for children in the homes of the upper class "Americans." In the Kenwood district of Minneapolis, many homes had their "Swede girl." Such opportunities often enabled these girls to enter the mainstream of American life more rapidly than those who were employed in industry, and many swiftly reached a much higher social level through marriage. Another major employer of immigrant women was the downtown office section of the city. Here, cleaning women were in great demand. Evelina Månsson's *Amerika minnen* is a superb statement of the conditions in such employment, as well as a portrait of the Cedar-Riverside Swedish community during the first decade of the twentieth century.

Social, cultural, and spiritual life revolved around the core areas. Until well into this century these communities provided these aspects of life in the native language. In the Cedar-Riverside/Washington Avenue district, one finds the best example of such a community. Washington and Cedar avenues served as the business, service, and entertainment bases for the residential community that spread out from these streets. Along the avenues were the shops, bars, meeting halls, and theatres that served the Swedish, Norwegian, and Danish immigrants. The Southern Theater, Samuelsons, Holtzermanns, and Dania Hall were only a few of the important establishments in the neighborhood. Knowledge of Swedish or another Scandinavian language was imperative for shop employees.

Virtually any kind of entertainment or activity could be found along the avenues. Drama clubs, singing organizations, debating clubs, gymnastics clubs, temperance societies, and the like sponsored innumerable events. The coarsest to the most cultural of entertainment could be found. Dania Hall's upstairs theatre and the Southern Theatre featured performances that ranged from Strindberg's *The Father* to the ever-popular *Värmländingarna* to the immigrant vaudeville comedy of Olle i Skratthult. Special musical programs were the fare at Christmas and Easter, featuring serious music as well as folk music and dancing. Although some performances of both plays and concerts were held outside the ethnic community, the majority took place within the confines of the neighborhood. Like other aspects of the community, the entertainment accentuated the ethnic character of the area while inhibiting contacts with other sections of the city.

Since the 1950s it has become increasingly difficult to determine the extent of the Swedish or Swedish American population in Minneapolis. Gradually, the ethnic community of the Swedes in Minneapolis proceeded outward. They moved first to Franklin Avenue, then to Lake Street, later to Minnehaha Parkway, and, finally, to the suburbs. Those elderly who chose not to leave the core have now passed away and few signs remain of the once exuberant community

Charles Samuelson in front of Samuelson's Confectionery,
Seven Corners, Minneapolis, 1890

along Cedar and Riverside. Today, Mount Olivet, the largest Lutheran Church in the world, located near the southern edge of Minneapolis, and dozens of suburban Lutheran churches give testimony of the modern blended Scandinavian community of the metro area.

Conclusion: Redevelopment of the Historic Cores

In 1956, the spring that provided water for Swede Hollow residents for over a century was declared unfit for human consumption, and the fourteen Mexican families living in the Hollow were consequently evicted. Their houses were burned down by the fire department. The following year, vandals torched the unoccupied Hamm mansion. For a while, the remains of Swede Hollow were neglected; then the valley became a site for dumping rubble from demolished buildings. Plans were made to fill in the Hollow to support a new highway toward Wisconsin. That proposal failed, however, and, in the early 1970s, the sorry-looking valley was selected as a site for a park to commemorate the success of the immigrants. The plan was adopted by the St. Paul Garden Club under the leadership of philanthropist Olivia Dodge. The club worked with the city government, the Neighborhood Youth Corps, and the Park Department to clean the area and develop some amenities. The site of the old Hamm mansion was incorporated into the park and an overlook was developed. After a long struggle, the railroad right-of-way was paved for a recreational path, and the Hollow is now accessible to bikers and other sports enthusiasts. Today the area surrounding the Hollow continues to attract new arrivals to the city. The Swede Hollow neighborhood remains home to low-income households living in single-dwelling residences.

Cedar-Riverside, on the other hand, is the site of one of the area's largest public housing projects. The twenty-story apartment complexes overwhelm the old commercial structures on Cedar Avenue. This is what remains of the bold 1960s plan to build a new "town-in-town" on the fringe of the University of Minnesota. This new community was to be built in accord with the principles of urban planning developed in Sweden during the 1950s. Minneapolis in the late 1960s and early 1970s, however, was very different from Stockholm in the 1950s, and the plan failed. Today, rather than a vibrant mixed-income community supporting a flourishing artistic scene, there exists one of the city's highest concentrations of low-income households.

Although the landscapes of the two most historic Swedish neighborhoods in the Twin Cities are now quite different from each other, they are still home for new arrivals. Their residents are immigrants from inner cities elsewhere in the United States, or from war-torn areas in Southeast Asia or East Africa. A new ethnicity gives character to these places. Thus, the processes of immigration and urbanization continue to determine the culture of Swede Hollow and Cedar-Riverside long after the Swedes have gone.

✳ ✳ ✳ ✳

NOTES

1. John G. Rice, "The Swedes," in June Drenning Holmquist, ed., *They Chose Minnesota: A Survey of the State's Ethnic Groups* (St. Paul: MHS Press, 1981), 262.

2. Nels M. Hokanson, "I Remember St. Paul's Swede Hollow," *Minnesota History* 41 (1960): 363–71.

3. David A. Lanegran, "The Twin Cities," in Byron J. Nordstrom, ed., *The Swedes in Minnesota* (Minneapolis: T. S. Denison, 1976), 32.

4. Rice, "The Swedes," 263f.

"Unfortunates" and "City Guests": Swedish American Inmates and the Minneapolis City Workhouse, 1907

JOY K. LINTELMAN

"WILL HOE CORN" read a story line in the "City News" section of the *Minneapolis Tribune* on June 29, 1907. The story continued: "Swan Holmberg drew a straight workhouse sentence when he was arraigned before Judge Smith in police court. He will spend the next 30 days at the Shingle Creek institution." What do we know of "city guests" and "unfortunates" (terms often used by journalists and officials for inmates in the local workhouse) such as Holmberg who found themselves serving time? Why was he arrested? Was he a criminal or just down on his luck? How frequently did Swedish immigrants land in the workhouse?[1]

Scholarship on Swedish immigration has not often addressed the "underside" of Swedish immigrant life. Individuals who experienced difficulties left few records. People were unlikely to write home about arrests or other problems with the law. Ethnic newspapers also were not likely to stress the negative elements of immigrant society, and family stories passed down through generations would undoubtedly leave out chapters about criminal activity. This study examines the inmate population of the Minneapolis City Workhouse with particular attention given to Swedish American inmates. The findings indicate that despite varied ethnic backgrounds, workhouse inmates were a relatively homogeneous population. At least in terms of committing minor offenses, membership in the working class rather than ethnicity seemed to be more of a determining factor in receiving workhouse sentences.

Official records of correctional institutions can provide some answers to the questions posed above. A look at the published annual reports of the Minneapolis City Workhouse reveal that if Swan Holmberg was Swedish, he was one of 360 Swedes out of 3, 223 persons admitted to the workhouse in 1907. But to find out more about individual inmates, the manuscript ledger books for the workhouse provide much more detailed information. For example, a look at the 1907 ledger book reveals that Swan Holmberg was indeed a Swede, and had been arrested for drunkenness. At the time of his arrest he was forty-one years old. He was married with children, worked as a stonecutter, and listed himself as a Protestant. He could read and write, had been sentenced to the workhouse twice before, was in good health, stood five feet, eight-and-one-half inches tall, and weighed 144 pounds.[2]

This study is based primarily upon an examination of workhouse data, such as that provided about Swan Holmberg, and includes a quantitative analysis of the population of the Minneapolis City Workhouse for the calendar year 1907. A number of ledger books from the workhouse have survived to the present day. The ledger books contain entries for every workhouse inmate, with data on age, sex, occupation, ethnicity, and a variety of other factors that allow one to make observations about the social origins and demographic characteristics of the inmates, as well as information regarding their treatment by the legal system.[3]

The 1907 ledger is chosen because it was one of the few ledgers that had no lapse in entries (many of the surviving ledgers were missing entries for a number of weeks or months) and because 1907 is close to the 1910 census year, for which population statistics are available for comparison to the workhouse population. For the years 1900 to 1907, the Minneapolis City Workhouse published annual reports, which included comments made by the superintendent as well as some aggregate statistics about the inmate population. A comparison of these reports verified that 1907 was not an atypical year for the workhouse, at least in terms of aggregate numbers.[4]

This essay will begin with a brief overview of the Minneapolis City Work-house. The main section of the study will describe findings regarding the characteristics of workhouse inmates, and the final section will draw some conclusions regarding Swedes and other inmates in the Minneapolis City Workhouse.[5]

Historical Background

On July 10, 1878, the Minneapolis City Council adopted an ordinance establishing a "city workhouse . . . providing for the keeping of male prisoners at work in such workhouse or upon public improvements." At its inception, no physical structure called the "workhouse" was constructed. Prisoners sentenced to the workhouse were kept in the city jail and released during the day to repair and maintain the streets of Minneapolis. Although no separate building existed, workhouse prisoners slept in a separate wing of the jail; a belief in the separation of minor and major offenders was evident in Minneapolis, as it had been in other cities in earlier years.[6]

During its first three years, 1878 to 1880, only males who had been arrested for vagrancy were sentenced as workhouse inmates. In 1881, the City Council passed an ordinance that permitted workhouse sentences for persons convicted of drunkenness as well as vagrancy. Maintaining the tradition of other nineteenth-century workhouses, the Minneapolis City Workhouse was from its inception designed for the confinement of persons committing offenses of a minor rather than serious nature, usually crimes against public policy. For example, ordinances allowed sentencing for disorderly conduct and petty larceny, among a host of other minor crimes, including barbering without a license, gambling, and reckless driving.[7]

In 1884, the City Council finally agreed upon the desirability of a separate building to house workhouse inmates. Completed in 1886, the Minneapolis City Workhouse was located in North Minneapolis near Camden Police Station. The new building held up to 150 inmates and included six special cells for solitary confinement of prisoners who disrupted discipline. The new site offered new types of work for the prisoners. A turn-of-the-century history of the Minneapolis Police Department stated:

> During the first two years [of the Camden workhouse's existence] most of the "city guests" were largely employed in grading roads, farming and gardening, repairing the building, improving grounds and making clothing and bedding, as well as general routine work. Cutting ice, working at the Northside Pumping Station and working on bridges and in the city cemetery were additional means resorted to later.

It is unclear from the surviving records the exact year in which the workhouse began to accept female inmates. An educated guess, however, would place the date at 1895. In that year the annual report first listed "laundry" as work "performed by inmates." Women were certainly placed in the workhouse by 1900, as one writer then observed that "for women who are committed to the workhouse there is work in the clothing room and laundry."[8]

The Minneapolis City Workhouse was first placed under the jurisdiction of the Minneapolis Police Department, with the chief of police acting as workhouse superintendent. In 1898, the Minneapolis Board of Charities and Corrections took over administration of the workhouse, and a superintendent was appointed annually by the board. Additions to the building were constructed in 1887 and 1910, evidencing a growing inmate population.[9]

Haven, Hospital, or Hell?

The preceding historical sketch generally describes the functions that the Minneapolis City Workhouse was designed to serve. It provided for the punishment and possible redemption of persons convicted of minor crimes through physical labor and stern discipline within a restricted environment. The existence of these institutions indicates that those who designed penal systems made definite distinctions between persons deemed more or less capable of reform and successful re-integration into society. But how were inmates to be reformed or redeemed? Were the workhouses successful in this endeavor? Were people consistent in their views of the workhouse? How did inmates themselves view the institution and its purpose?

On November 17, 1907, the *Minneapolis Tribune* ran a story entitled "Call of Winter Fills Workhouse Cells." The workhouse population had reached 238

"Call of Winter Fills Workhouse Cells,"
article from the Minneapolis Tribune, *November 17, 1907*

inmates, an all-time high. The article included discussions with the workhouse superintendent and several inmates. The news story suggested that the workhouse served a variety of functions for inmates, from "an institution of punishment and an object of dread" to "a haven for the homeless and sometimes regarded as 'home sweet home.'" For some individuals, the workhouse could indeed be a haven. The *Tribune* had earlier in the year related the story of Peter Nilson, a Swedish immigrant who had been arrested for vagrancy. The article was entitled "Nilson Given a Home" and noted that Nilson had "been sleeping in dry goods boxes all winter in the rear of 1309 Washington Avenue South." He was destitute and unemployed, and it is likely that the warm bed and adequate food provided in the workhouse were a welcome relief to homelessness.[10]

For other inmates as well as administrators, the workhouse was seen as a treatment center for alcoholics and drug addicts. A 1916 *Minneapolis Tribune* article related the story of an alcoholic who asked to be arrested and sent to the workhouse for treatment. His request was granted, and he was, at the time the article was written, taking "the cure." For a number of inmates it appears that the workhouse served as a "free hospital," a place where persons could obtain treatment for drug and alcohol addiction at no cost other than arrest, confinement, and work at some type of daily labor. Administrators recognized this workhouse function and encouraged it through sentencing procedures, as well as treatment within the workhouse. In 1904, the workhouse superintendent had asked for funding to purchase a new medicine, a "liquor cure" to treat alcoholics.[11]

The 1907 superintendent's opinions were expressed in some detail in the "Call of Winter" article. His views of the workhouse tended toward haven or hospital. He saw inmates positively, making clear that workhouse inmates should not be considered hardened criminals. He believed that most inmates were average people who were just a bit down on their luck. He even regarded the name "workhouse" as a poor one for his institution, suggesting the name "Minneapolis Conservatory for the Criminally Inclined" instead. It was also noted in the article that most sentences in the workhouse were for drunkenness, a result of both boom and bust times for workers:

> When times are good, work is plentiful and money flows freely, the honest laborer gets drunk, loses his money and lands on Shingle Creek [the location of the workhouse]. Then again when times are hard, there is no work and little money, and the laboring man gets discouraged, gets drunk on general principles or something stronger and lands in the workhouse. Either extreme prosperity or hard times contribute to filling the workhouse cells.[12]

Some inmates, while not referring to the workhouse as a hell, did complain that their sentences were unjust and suggested that a class bias existed in arrest

and sentencing patterns. One inmate indicated that the only difference between himself and others outside the workhouse was that he lacked the money
to purchase transportation home when drunk. He correctly pointed out that
individuals who had to walk home in a drunken state were much more likely
to be arrested than those who were transported home by butlers or friends.[13]

Annual reports submitted by workhouse superintendents reveal additional
purposes of the workhouse, and also offer some insight regarding the workhouse's organization and administration. Several superintendents emphasized
the workhouse as an institution for moral and spiritual reform. One superintendent, while applauding a group of Christian missionaries who held worship
services for workhouse inmates, wrote in 1902 of the excellent work being done
"to save wandering boys and girls." The statement indicates an attitude of su-
periority on the part of the administrators with its reference to the inmates as
juveniles. The theme of redemption is also evident: the inmates were perceived
as persons who had wandered off the "appropriate" path and could be re-
directed with the proper guidance. Just as a child is schooled in the ways of the
adult world, the inmates were to be schooled in acceptable social behavior. Religious overtones are even more visible in later comments by the superintendent. He praised inmates who attended worship services and showed interest
in "those subjects which lead their thoughts above themselves and to a higher
understanding of life." The services also allowed inmates "to investigate and
learn more of the truth which makes men free."[14]

Moral and spiritual reforms are also obvious in a 1903 statement to the
Board of Charities and Corrections. A superintendent emphasized the need to
provide clean clothes for outgoing prisoners: "After being corrected of their
faults, no chance was given them to better their condition and any good resolutions formed during their confinement were dissipated in the shame of their
condition." For this superintendent the workhouse apparently fulfilled a variety of roles: it punished criminals through hard physical labor, but it also attempted to reform their behavior so that "good resolutions" would be made.
Prisoners were to recognize the error of their ways, feel ashamed of their behavior, and reform. The superintendent in 1903 also criticized a past administrator for being satisfied with being a "mere jailer." Workhouses were obviously
perceived by some persons as much more than penal institutions.[15]

One theme appeared consistently in each superintendent's report: the inmates were viewed as somehow below the acceptable standards of respectability, but they were seen as objects of pity rather than of disdain. Inmates were frequently referred to as "unfortunates." The offenders were
thought of as misguided rather than corrupt, as "led astray" rather than innately
evil. Inmates were "victims," and the workhouse was a helping institution pro-

vided to assist them. Unfortunately, few persons were capable of questioning just what made these persons victims. The emphasis was on the individual; unacceptable behavior, it was believed, must be because of some fault in the moral and spiritual being, a fault that could be remedied by the proper treatment. Neither administrators nor members of the judicial system were willing to question the structure of society and the modern capitalist economic system as sources for these faults.

Gender attitudes added another hierarchical level to the social and moral categories established between inmates and administrators. Males and females alike were considered misguided persons in need of discipline and advice. But females, aside from this pitied status, were also to be protected. A 1907 news story suggested that judges were less likely to sentence women to the workhouse than men. The article stated that "judges are lenient with womankind and there are many forgiveness' [sic] before the first workhouse sentence." This also meant that women who were sentenced to the workhouse were worse than the average male inmate. The writer stated: "Most of the women who land at the workhouse are reasonably bad characters. . . . With the men it is different."[16]

While opinions of its proper role and functions varied widely, all were in agreement that the workhouse was not a hellish institution. Prisons and jails such as Alcatraz or Devil's Island, although members of the same family of penal institutions as workhouses, were distant cousins. Inmates' views of the workhouse varied from seeing it as a temporary refuge from the struggles for economic survival to seeing it as a free hospital. Administrators supported the institution's function as a treatment center for the chemically dependent, but also emphasized the workhouse as a place for spiritual, moral, and the consequent behavioral reform of unenlightened and misguided persons. The Minneapolis City Workhouse was in all cases seen as a correctional rather than a punitive institution, and in many instances it served as a quasi-welfare organization. These functions were applied to all inmates, regardless of their ethnic background. There was no evidence of Swedes or other immigrant groups being singled out in the comments made in newspaper accounts about workhouse inmates. But what do the statistics in the workhouse ledger reveal about the Swedes and others?

Profile: Swedes and the Workhouse Population

First-generation immigrants made up a sizable proportion of the workhouse population—57 percent of the inmates were native-born and 43 percent foreign-born. Most of the immigrants were northern Europeans, who were termed by contemporaries as "old immigrants." The "new immigrants," persons from southern and eastern Europe, had not emigrated to Minneapolis in significant numbers at that time, although the workhouse did admit a few inmates who had been born in Syria, Italy, Poland, Palestine, and Russia. The five immigrant groups with the largest representation within the workhouse population were Swedes, Norwegians, Irish, Germans, and Canadians.

Table 1 shows the major ethnic groups represented in the workhouse population compared to the proportion of the general Minneapolis population they comprised (using statistics from the 1910 Federal Census). The Irish show the greatest difference between the two relative percentages—almost 7 percent. The Swedes and Norwegians show about a 3 percent difference between the workhouse and the city population, with the Canadians and Germans showing only a 1 percent difference. One should not necessarily interpret the differences as indicating a propensity toward crime, however. While that may indeed be the case, these findings also point to the need to examine the arrest procedures of the Minneapolis Police Department. Did the policemen have biases regarding those persons they arrested for misdemeanor crimes? Did they tend to arrest men and women of particular ethnic groups more often than others?

Age

The majority of the inmates (55 percent) were between the ages of twenty and forty at the time of their admittance. The youngest person sentenced to the workhouse in 1907 was seventeen and the oldest eighty-four. The mean age of

Table 1
Major Ethnic Groups in Workhouse Compared to the Proportion of the Minneapolis Population They Comprise, 1907

	Percent of Minneapolis Population	Percent of Workhouse Population
Canadian	2.49	3.23
German	2.87	3.44
Irish	0.95	7.23
Norwegian	5.44	8.59
Swedish	8.78	11.17
Other Foreign	7.97	9.56
Native-born	71.50	56.78

Source: Minneapolis Workhouse, 1907 Ledger, Minneapolis City Courthouse, Archives Division; and U.S. Department of Commerce, Bureau of Census, *Thirteenth Census of the United States, 1910, Abstract of the Census* (Washington, D.C.: Government Printing Office, 1913), 604–5.

the prisoners was thirty-eight. The Swedish inmates ranged in age from nineteen to sixty-seven, with the mean age of prisoners at forty-one. The diagrams presented in Graph 1 show the age structure of the five ethnic groups that comprised the largest number of workhouse inmates. The Swedes did not exhibit a unique pattern. The Canadians, Irish, Swedes, Norwegians, and "Other Foreign" all show the highest number of inmates between the ages of forty and fifty, while the Germans show a peak in their thirties and forties. The native-born inmates peaked in their twenties and thirties.

The differences between the native and most foreign-born inmates might be explained by differences in social mobility between the groups. While young native-born males were often able to obtain better-paying jobs and greater economic security as they grew older, immigrant groups may have been less likely to do so. Trapped within the lower working class, facing limited opportunities for advancement and few avenues for personal entertainment and recreation, Swedes and other immigrants may have found themselves in the workhouse more frequently as difficulties increased over their life course.

Offenses

For what offenses were Swedes sentenced to the workhouse? How did these offense patterns compare with other immigrant and native groups? The four most-often committed crimes were public drunkenness, vagrancy, larceny, and

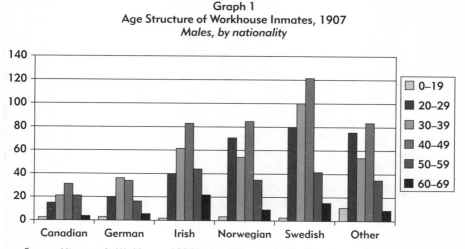

Graph 1
Age Structure of Workhouse Inmates, 1907
Males, by nationality

Source: Minneapolis Workhouse, 1907 Ledger, Minneapolis City Courthouse, Archives Division.

disorderly conduct. The vast majority of Swedes in the workhouse were sentenced there for a crime of drunkenness. Eighty-seven percent of Swedish arrests were for drunkenness, 7.2 percent for vagrancy, 2.5 percent for larceny, and
1.4 percent for disorderly conduct. The remaining crimes considered together
comprised 2.2 percent. Public drunkenness accounted for 71.2 percent of all individuals sentenced to the workhouse. Vagrancy and larceny were the next two
most common crimes overall, comprising 12 percent and 5.2 percent of the
population. Disorderly conduct was the cause of 3.5 percent of the sentences,
while a wide variety of other minor offenses accounted for the final 8.1 percent.
Table 2 compares crime categories between the major groups in the workhouse. The native-born showed a tendency to be arrested for larceny, vagrancy,
and disorderly conduct. The Germans also showed a slight tendency toward
disorderly conduct arrests, and the Swedes, Norwegians, and Irish a propensity
for arrests for drunkenness.

Occupation

For the purposes of analysis, occupations of the inmates were separated into
seven major categories, corresponding to those categories used by the U.S.
Census Bureau. These categories are as follows: 1) agriculture, forestry, animal
husbandry, and trade; 2) manufacturing and mechanical industries; 3) transportation; 4) professional services; 5) clerical occupations; 6) domestic and personal service; and 7) mineral extraction and all other occupations.[17]

Most of the Swedes were employed in the manufacturing and mechanical
industries sector (88.3 percent), with a few individuals in transportation
(4.4 percent), clerical (4.5 percent), professional services (2.2 percent), and agri-

Table 2
**Four Most Common Crimes Committed: Percentage Proportion of Ethnic Groups
Committing Those Crimes, 1907 Workhouse Population**

	Percent Of Total	Drunkenness	Vagrancy	Larceny	Disorderly Conduct
Canadian	3.23	3.30	2.33	2.34	3.54
German	3.44	3.64	2.58	2.92	5.31
Irish	7.23	8.28	7.24	4.09	3.54
Norwegian	8.59	9.50	5.43	7.02	7.96
Swedish	11.17	13.53	6.72	5.26	4.42
Other Foreign	9.56	9.71	7.75	9.36	10.62
Native-born	56.78	52.04	67.95	69.01	64.61

Source: Minneapolis Workhouse, 1907 Ledger, Minneapolis City Courthouse, Archives Division.

culture (0.6 percent). None of the Swedes serving in the workhouse were employed in domestic and personal service or mineral extraction. Trends were similar for the workhouse inmates as a whole, with 72.5 percent of inmates falling under the manufacturing and mechanical industry category. Most of these prisoners were unskilled workers—52 percent of the inmates listed "common laborer" as their occupation. Unlike the Swedes, the second largest occupational category overall was that of domestic and personal service, whose members totaled 10.3 percent of the inmates. Transportation industry occupations made up 8.2 percent of the total, and all other occupations made up the remaining 9 percent. Swedes sentenced to the workhouse tended to be members of the working class in wide-ranging areas from bakers and blacksmiths to stonecutters, steamfitters, and wireworkers.

"Habits of Life"

Ledgers from the workhouse included information regarding the "habits of life" of the inmates—a euphemistic term for behavior related to alcohol consumption. Inmates were classified as intemperate, moderate, or temperate. It is unclear from the records whether these notations in the ledgers were the result of a verbal response by the inmates to a clerk's question, or a judgment call on the part of the workhouse staff. (Given the column's placement in the ledger, however, the former seems more likely.) Most of the Swedes were listed as moderates (83.1 percent), with 16.7 percent listed as intemperate, and only one Swedish immigrant (0.3 percent) listed as temperate. Similarly, most of the inmates overall were listed as "moderate drinkers" (80.7 percent) with 16.6 percent of the prisoners listed as intemperate, and only 2.6 percent as temperate.

Marital Status

About three-quarters of the Swedes sentenced to the workhouse were single (76.1 percent). Smaller numbers of Swedish inmates were married with children (15.6 percent), married with no children (5.8 percent), or widowers with children (1.7 percent). One Swede was found in each of the following categories: widow with no children, widower with no children, and single with child. Again the Swedes followed the general pattern of other workhouse inmates. Three-fourths of the workhouse population was single, and nearly 20 percent was married. Of those who were married, only 6.7 percent had children. Widows and widowers, with or without children, and unmarried individuals with children comprised the remaining 5.2 percent of the population.

The lower numbers of married individuals is not surprising. Qualitative

evidence suggests that a workhouse sentence was often a "last resort" in attempting to reform a drinking father or husband. A *Minneapolis Tribune* story
from January 9, 1907, illustrated this tendency. The article focused on the plight
of a fifteen-year-old Russian immigrant boy, George, whose stepfather was a
heavy drinker. The family was having difficulty making ends meet. The boy was
quoted as stating that he "sold papers after school but . . . can't make enough to
take care of the family and he [the stepfather] don't keep work more'n a week
because he drinks all the time." His mother did laundry in other people's
homes but was unable to support the family on her meager wages. The judge
responded by telling the boy that "[I have] made your father promise to quit
drinking and go to work and take care of you. If he doesn't, the first time he
fails I am going to report him and he goes to the workhouse. I'm going to
look after him for you." The writer went on to praise the courts for supporting families. He stated that the judges frequently gave men such as George's father "a workhouse sentence with a stay of one year, in order to give him a
chance to brace up and take care of his family. . . . One false step lands them in
the workhouse."[18]

Profile: Female Inmates

Of the 360 Swedes sentenced to the workhouse in 1907, only twelve were
women. While one can not draw many conclusions from such a small number,
their characteristics do provide a glimpse into a seldom-viewed area of
Swedish immigrant women's lives. Although twelve sentences were served by
Swedish females, they involved only eight women, as the remaining four sentences were repeat offenders. Swedish women represented 5.4 percent of all
females sentenced to the workhouse. Ethnic composition of the female inmates overall varied considerably from that of the males. While only 56 percent
of the men were native-born, 76 percent of the women had been born in the
United States. Fewer foreign-born women in the workhouse may indicate that
these women remained in the home for cultural reasons and enjoyed less
personal freedom with regard to spending leisure time in public places than
native-born women or foreign-born males.

Only 43 percent of the women in the workhouse were single, compared to
77 percent of the men. Among the Swedish female offenders, one was married
with children, one married without children, one widowed with children,
three single, and one single with children. The Swedish women ranged in age
from 27 to 43 years, while the whole female population ranged from 17 to 63.
The Swedish women showed a greater similarity to the male's age range with

a mean age of 38, while the female population as a whole had a mean age of 29.9 years.

As was the case with males, drunkenness was also the most common crime for females, both Swedish (9 of 12 arrests) and all others (40.3 percent of all females in the workhouse were arrested for this offense). The crime of prostitution accounted for 20 percent of the females arrested and for the remaining three Swedish female arrests. Since prostitutes are likely to be young rather than middle-aged women, it may be that this group of inmates accounts for the lower average age for females as opposed to males. A detailed analysis of women arrested for prostitution would allow one to form a collective portrait of the prostitute. Also of interest for further research would be an analysis of the arrests of males listed before and after female arrests in the ledgers. Such an examination would reveal whether males who visited houses of prostitution tended to be arrested along with females and, if so, whether males and females received similar fines and sentences.[19]

Four of the eight Swedish women were listed as in "poor" health. These four had been arrested for drunkenness, three of the four had prior arrests, one of them with twenty priors! Clearly alcohol abuse was a problem for some turn-of-the-century immigrant communities.

Occupational statistics for females were radically different from statistics for the male inmates. For the Swedish women, five listed "housekeeper" as occupation, and one each listed "inspector," "dressmaker," and "cook." Only one female in the entire 1907 workhouse population listed unskilled labor as an occupation. Sixty-six percent of women overall listed "housework" as their occupation. It is likely that "housework" meant that these women worked days or nights cleaning other persons' homes or office buildings. Women working as domestics (probably differentiated from housework by having "live-in" employment) accounted for 16.7 percent of the females; a total of 82.7 percent of the women thus spent most of their time at housework in their own or someone else's home. A few of the women overall worked as laundresses (5 percent), cooks (2.3 percent), and waitresses (2.3 percent). The remaining 7.7 percent of the women worked in a variety of other occupations, almost all of which were occupations traditionally filled by women (for example, dressmaker or telephone operator). When placed within the census occupational categories explained above, 93 percent of the female's occupations fall into the domestic and personal service category. Workhouse statistics suggest that the existence of a "separate sphere" for women, centered primarily upon home and family rather than more public places probably decreased the likelihood of women being arrested for misdemeanor crimes that might land them in the workhouse.

Seasonality of Crime

The ledger books may also be used to look at arrest patterns of the workhouse inmates over the course of a year. High or low rates in certain months may indicate that crimes were resorted to only in specific situations (e.g., theft or vagrancy in times of unemployment, drunkenness when jobs—and therefore wages—were plentiful).

Graph 2 lists the average number of prisoners received in the workhouse each month, spanning the years 1886 through 1918. October and November have the highest rates, followed by June and July. In the period from February through May, lower numbers of inmates were received. How might these patterns be explained? If large numbers of inmates chose a sentence in the workhouse as a way to assure adequate board and room during the winter months (as was provided for Peter Nilson), one would expect a large increase of inmates during or just preceding the coldest months of the year. While December and January rated in the top three months a few different years, they still

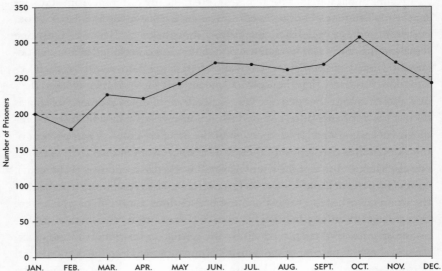

Graph 2
Average Number of Prisoners Received Each Month, 1886–1918

Source: *Annual Reports, Department of Charities and Corrections, Poor Department, City Hospital, and Workhouse, City of Minneapolis* (Minneapolis: Heywood Manufacturing Company, 1900–1907); and Frank R. McDonald, *Annual Report of the City Workhouse of the City of Minneapolis for the Year Ending December 31, 1918* (Minneapolis: Elander-Winkler Co., 1919), 18.

lagged considerably behind the fall and summer months in numbers of inmates received. The workhouse was obviously not a "winter haven" for a majority of the inmates.

Large numbers of prisoners in June and July may simply reflect seasonal weather changes. Most of the inmates were arrested for drunkenness, vagrancy, and disorderly conduct—crimes that usually took place out-of-doors and that would be less likely to occur in the coldest months. Employment opportunities in jobs subject to seasonal variation often increased in the summer (industries such as construction or food processing). Wages from these jobs might have allowed the person who had previously been unemployed or employed part-time to have extra money to purchase liquor.

The data examined did not reveal a clear-cut explanation for the highest rates occurring in October and November. One reason may be that it was in those months that the possession of additional money from seasonal work coincided with a decrease in work hours (as the harvest season ended and weather became less conducive to outdoor construction work), providing more leisure time and a resulting increase in the number of persons publicly drunk, disorderly, or vagrant. A news piece in October 1907 supports this theory. The *Minneapolis Tribune* ran an article about the police court dismissing cases of disorderly conduct because the workhouse was filled to capacity. The police had apparently been arresting a high number of individuals for drunkenness. When questioned about these arrests, the chief of police indicated that he did not think that there was more liquor available, but rather that men had returned to the city with "rolls" [of money] they had "saved up in the harvest fields."[20]

Examining arrest patterns according to nativity (Graph 3) reveals no major deviations in the general patterns. Each group showed a tendency toward increased arrests in late summer and early autumn. An analysis of patterns of arrests according to nativity on a daily basis might prove to be a more valuable approach to the question. Ethnic holidays might coincide with increased arrests for drunkenness, or the reverse might occur, depending upon particular ethnic practices. The same type of analysis focusing upon occupation rather than nativity might reveal distinct employment patterns relating to propensity to commit particular crimes at certain times of the year.

Cross-tabulations of the four most common crimes with the date of entrance to the workhouse allow an investigation of variations in seasonality of specific crimes. Results of the cross-tabulations for the 1907 data are included in Table 3. The most common crime, drunkenness, shows the highest rate in October, November, and August, respectively, following the more general pattern discussed above. Vagrancy also peaked in the autumn and early winter months, as did larceny. Frequency of crimes including disorderly conduct and other offenses did not fall quite so exclusively in October and November, but showed a general tendency to increase in late summer and early fall.

Graph 3
Monthly Arrest Patterns of Ethnic Groups in Workhouse, 1907

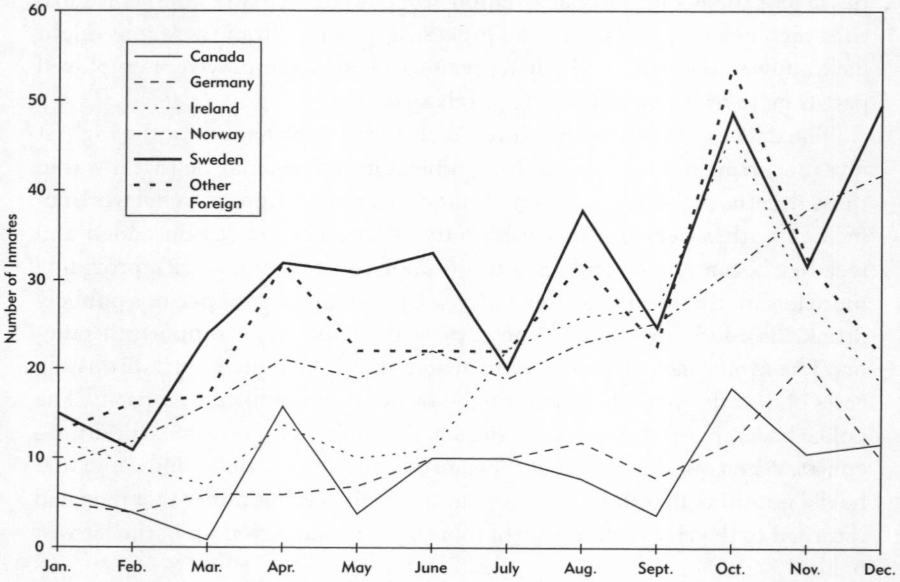

Source: *Annual Reports, Department of Charities and Corrections, Poor Department, City Hospital, and Workhouse, City of Minneapolis* (Minneapolis: Heywood Manufacturing Company, 1900–1907).

Table 3
Monthly Arrest Totals for Most Frequently Committed Crimes Resulting in Workhouse Sentences, 1907

	Jan.	Feb.	Mar.	Apr.	May	Jun.	Jul.	Aug.	Sept.	Oct.	Nov.	Dec.
Drunkenness	111	95	109	142	155	199	194	237	212	387	257	196
Vagrancy	10	15	11	40	21	30	24	42	26	42	52	73
Larceny	12	10	9	13	10	9	13	8	9	23	23	28
Disorderly Conduct	2	4	5	14	4	17	5	10	15	22	6	9
Other Crimes	16	12	8	36	17	28	17	36	18	30	21	24

Source: *Annual Reports, Department of Charities and Corrections, Poor Department, City Hospital, and Workhouse, City of Minneapolis* (Minneapolis: Heywood Manufacturing Company, 1900–1907).

The female inmates show a slightly different pattern of arrest seasonality. As depicted in Table 4, the arrest rate for women was considerably higher in August than any other month. The second and third highest concentrations occurred in December, July, and October, respectively, following the trend of the whole population. The high rate in August may relate to the types of crimes for which women were most commonly arrested—drunkenness and prostitution. Both activities (drinking and soliciting) were more likely to take place out-of-doors in the summer months and were therefore more often in the public eye and more likely to lead to arrest. Without an examination of the female arrest patterns of other years, it is difficult to generalize from the 1907 data. The high rate in August might reflect a crackdown by the police against prostitution, making the year examined atypical.

Variations in arrest patterns represent an important area for further study. Detailed information on unemployment and inflation in Minneapolis and the surrounding regions should be obtained. Comparisons between these economic indices and arrest patterns within specific years as well as over a period of several years may reveal important relationships between unemployment and minor criminal offenses, suggesting that the propensity toward certain offenses may relate to one's economic status rather than to age, ethnicity, or sex.

Conclusions

Who were those Swedes in the Minneapolis City Workhouse? This analysis has pointed out a variety of characteristics of the Swedish population in the workhouse. They tended to be young to middle-aged single males. Most were employed in occupations at the lower end of the wage scale. Most were Protestant, could read and write, and were in good health. How did these Swedes compare to other workhouse inmates? When the total workhouse population is considered, the inmates appeared to be mostly white, single, literate males in

Table 4
Male and Female Arrest Patterns, by Month, 1907 Workhouse Population

	Jan.	Feb.	Mar.	Apr.	May	Jun.	Jul.	Aug.	Sept.	Oct.	Nov.	Dec.
Males	143	125	133	227	195	263	230	289	269	481	343	304
Females	8	11	9	18	12	20	23	44	11	23	16	26
Total	151	136	142	245	207	283	253	333	280	504	359	330

Source: *Annual Reports, Department of Charities and Corrections, Poor Department, City Hospital, and Workhouse, City of Minneapolis* (Minneapolis: Heywood Manufacturing Company, 1900–1907).

their twenties, thirties, and forties who worked as unskilled laborers. Although they considered themselves only moderate drinkers, they were very likely to be arrested for public drunkenness. While some minor differences were discovered between the Swedes and various other groups, the workhouse was overall a rather homogeneous population. In fact, the findings suggest that those who committed crimes resulting in workhouse sentences shared a membership in the working class. One can form a picture of single young to middle-aged men, who, after working at hard physical labor all day or all week, desired relaxation, fellowship, recreation, or an escape from the everyday work world. Living in small apartments or in boarding houses, these men were likely to meet with other co-workers and friends at saloons or parks rather than in an individual's home. Their activities were thus by nature public. If they happened to drink to excess, make a little too much noise, or become involved in a brawl, the police were called and arrests made. Even if given the opportunity to pay a fine rather than serve a sentence, because of the low wages they earned they probably chose to enter the workhouse. Propensity to commit misdemeanor crimes appears likely to be related to social class rather than ethnic, age, or gender differences.[21]

The qualitative sources examined in this study reinforce the idea that the workhouse was not a penal institution of the same nature as a jail. It focused upon correction rather than punishment. The workhouse was also a welfare institution. Treatment of chemical dependency was available for those prisoners who desired it. Some inmates chose to spend time in the workhouse as a relief from unemployment.

Monthly arrest patterns over a period of about thirty years showed an increased tendency toward arrests in the late summer and fall. While a number of explanations for this occurrence were suggested, the evidence did not allow any conclusive comments to be made. Seasonality of crimes remains an interesting topic and one that demands further research.

The information presented within this study represents only a beginning in researching the "darker" side of Swedish immigrant life and immigrant life in general. Suggestions have been made throughout the essay for directions in which further study of workhouses and ethnicity should be aimed. Such studies will contribute to the growing body of knowledge that helps to answer questions about ordinary people in their everyday lives. Whether viewed as "unfortunates" or "city guests," Swedish and other inmates in the Minneapolis City Workhouse experienced what was in theory and, at least to some degree, in practice a benevolent institution that attempted to play a helping role in their lives.

* * * *

NOTES

1. "Will Hoe Corn," *Minneapolis Tribune*, June 29, 1907, p. 6. The paper did not identify Swan Holmberg as a Swedish immigrant, but his name suggests that he was.

2. Minneapolis Workhouse, 1907 Ledger, Minneapolis City Courthouse, Archives Division.

3. Workhouse Ledger, 1907.

4. These reports have been published in book form: *Annual Reports: Department of Charities and Corrections, Poor Department, City Hospitals and Workhouse, City of Minneapolis* (Minneapolis: Heywood Manufacturing Company, 1900–1907). I have been able to locate only one other annual report, that for the year 1918 (a particularly interesting report, as the workhouse population was much smaller then because of the effects of World War I): *Annual Report of the City Workhouse of the City of Minneapolis for the Year Ending December 31, 1918* (Minneapolis: Elander-Winkler Co., 1919), 18.

5. Historical literature regarding workhouses is limited, and that about immigrants and workhouses non-existent. See Blake McKelvey, *American Prisons: A Study in American Social History Prior to 1915* (Chicago: Univ. of Chicago Press, 1936), which provides the most information about workhouses, tracing their development since colonial times. Some brief discussion of workhouses may be found in local records of cities. A history of the Minneapolis Police Department published in 1899 provided some information about the Minneapolis workhouse (see Note 6 below). Recent works on crime have focused upon local police departments, crime rates in the past, and the relationship between crime and social class. See Roger Lane, *Policing the City, Boston 1822–1855* (Cambridge: Harvard Univ. Press, 1967); James Richardson, *The New York Police* (New York: Oxford Univ. Press, 1970); J. J. Tobias, *Crime and Industrial Society in the Nineteenth Century* (Harmondsworth, England: Penguin, 1972); and Eric Monkkonen, *The Dangerous Class: Crime and Poverty in Columbus, Ohio 1860–1885* (Cambridge: Harvard Univ. Press, 1975). The research outlined within this essay represents a step toward filling this gap in our knowledge of crime, ethnicity, and penal institutions by offering some tentative answers to questions surrounding immigrants, workhouses, and workhouse inmates. Because this study is one of the first to focus on the workhouse, the findings presented cannot be considered applicable to all workhouses or immigrants in major cities. They do, however, help to adumbrate a general framework within which further research may be carried out.

6. Quotation from *Community Crossroads: A Study of the Minneapolis City Workhouse* (Minneapolis: Community Welfare Council, 1957), 9; Alix J. Muller, *History of the Police and the Fire Department of the Twin Cities* (Minneapolis: American Land and Title Register Association, 1899), 45ff.

7. Muller, *History*, 45ff.

8. Ibid., 131, 132.

9. *Community Crossroads*, 9.

10. "Call of Winter Fills Workhouse Cells," *Minneapolis Tribune*, Nov. 17, 1907, p. 27; "Nilson Given a Home," *Minneapolis Tribune*, Apr. 10, 1907, p. 7.

11. "Trip to the Workhouse Sought by Many," *Minneapolis Tribune*, Jan. 23, 1916; *Annual Reports*, 1904 Report, 52f.

12. "Call of Winter."

13. Ibid.

14. *Annual Reports*, 1902 Report, 6.

15. *Annual Reports*, 1903 Report, 53, emphasis mine.

16. "Call of Winter."

17. U.S. Department of Commerce, *Bureau of the Census, Thirteenth Census of the United States, Occupational Statistics, 1910*, vol. 4 (Washington, D.C.: U.S. Government Printing Office, 1914), 73–98.

18. Quentin, "George Kostik Faces Judge in the Courtroom," *Minneapolis Tribune*, Jan. 9, 1907, p. 5.

19. It may be that those women who were married (44.8 percent) were also those who were arrested for drunkenness, and that they were arrested along with their husbands as they drank liquor together. But until further investigation of these arrests is undertaken, such an assertion remains unfounded. (The 1907 data collected does allow for such analysis. It is, however, a very time-consuming undertaking to examine a large number of individual arrests.)

20. "Is Lenient to Drunks," *Minneapolis Tribune*, Oct. 27, 1907, sect. 2, p. 14.

21. A study of St. Paul police arrests in the late nineteenth century noted this, as well. See Joel Gorden Best, "Police Work in the Nineteenth Century City: Arrest Practice in St. Paul, 1869–1874" (master's thesis, Univ. of Minn., 1979).

5

Evelina Johansdotter,
Textile Workers, and the Munsingwear Family:
Class, Gender, and Ethnicity in the Political Economy
of Minnesota at the End of World War I

LARS OLSSON

In the year 1901, young Evelina Johansdotter from Västergötland (Sweden) traversed the Atlantic Ocean with her maternal uncle in order to seek work in America. A paternal uncle was to meet her in New York and help her to find a job. He never materialized, however, so instead Evelina accompanied her maternal uncle to his farm in Minnesota. After a short period with her uncle's family, Evelina left in order to earn her own living and to stand on her own two feet. She started work as a maid in an English-speaking family of Swedish descent who did not live far from her uncle's family. Since Evelina did not speak a word of English, however, and the family did not want to speak Swedish any longer—not even with Evelina—she did not tolerate them for very long. Through the exchange of letters with childhood friends who worked at a laundry in Minneapolis, she was led to believe that she might gain employment there and be able to work with Swedish-speaking co-workers.[1]

Evelina met with a second disappointment as soon as she arrived in Minneapolis. Her childhood friends were not very well informed as to the employment opportunities at the laundry, and it had no need for yet another young Swedish girl. Through Mrs. Lindqvist's employment agency Evelina was instead offered a cleaning job at a boardinghouse, but after washing dishes for three hours, scrubbing the floor, and then washing dishes for three more hours, she had had enough. Instead, she took an appointment as a housekeeper for an old Swedish couple. Here she both enjoyed the work more and was paid better than in the first Swedish family. The old woman's suspicions that Evelina was flirting with their son, however, caused her to quit that job as well. "No thank you. 32 year old widowers at that time—when oneself was only 22, and all of life smiled, despite that as a poor servant girl one had to move at a safe distance from haughty mistresses and suspicious old ladies!" wrote Evelina in her America memoirs.

After having failed to master both a sewing machine at Carlson Manufacturing Company and a manual washing machine at a laundry, Evelina took a job as a cleaning woman. Actually, a childhood friend of Evelina's was supposed to get the job, but the Swedish foreman allowed them to share the work while they waited for full-time employment for the both of them. After a while, Evelina began cleaning in another building where virtually all of the workers were of Swedish descent. After eighteen months she had earned enough money so that she could return to Sweden. But after only a half-year at home in Sweden she had spent almost all of her savings without having settled down. As a result of this she returned to Minneapolis.

In November 1905, Evelina began work as a sewing girl at Sterling Manufacturing Company, but she had not forgotten the friendly atmosphere and the stable income from her cleaning jobs. For a short time she tried to hold down two jobs. She wrote: "Thus, I first cleaned in Fenix in the morning and then, after in all haste eating breakfast at a restaurant, showed up at the 'factory,' where one must absolutely be present before 8 o'clock. After finishing my sewing time at 5 o'clock P.M., I drank one cup of coffee only, before hurrying back to Fenix for the afternoon work."

Evelina reconsidered her situation, however, and eventually chose the fellowship of the Swedish work place, a certain degree of free time in the middle of the day, and the stable, but lower, income. However, when her new roommate, an eighteen-year-old girl, came home with higher earnings from her job as a sewing girl with Weum Watt Company, Evelina left her cleaning job and began sewing again. This time it was only men's clothes. She was put to work among over a hundred other women. Most of them, but not all, were young. Some were married, and some were

Evelina Johansdotter (right) and her sister Augusta, Minneapolis, ca. 1905

widows. Half of them were of Scandinavian descent, while the rest were of other nationalities. German, Irish, and Jewish girls were also there. She worked with these women for two years.

Just before Christmas, 1907, Evelina left America with the man she had married three days before her return to Sweden. This time, as Mrs. Månsson, she would stay in her old homeland. In Minneapolis, however, the manufacturing of men's clothing would develop into a large industry, and many women of Swedish origin would come to work there with women of other nationalities. Their story is the focus of this essay. Through it, insight into the working conditions of Swedish women will be gained using class, gender, and ethnicity as organizing principles. They were workers in a large capitalistic production, women in a sexually segregated work place, and Swedes in a multicultural environment—at a time when national identity was put to the test in American society during World War I.

The Immigrant Working Woman

More than twenty years ago, in a brief article about Evelina, the Swedish American historian Byron Nordstrom pointed out that very little had been written about the conditions of the urban Swedish working class in America. This was particularly true for Swedish working women. Nordstrom's observation was already embarrassing in 1980. It is still of great concern in that there is little that has been written since, despite extensive research concerning Swedish immigrants. Historical writing surrounding the Swedish men and women who settled in America has tended to follow an international pattern of interpretation. This is where largely male scholars, as Kathie Friedman-Kasaba expresses it in a book about Jewish and Italian women in New York, "treat the category 'women' solely as a synonym for one who is unproductive and dependent, and see women as only functioning within the framework of the family, and as with children, are seen only as passive followers to 'the real emigrant,' the male working wanderer or the political refugee." The story about Evelina indicates how misguided this picture of the immigrants is in reality.[2]

Just like Evelina, millions of women came from Europe to America in order to find work. Some came alone and unmarried, as Evelina did, and had only themselves to look after. They had no one else to provide for their needs. They might even have been expected to send money to those who had remained in the homeland. Others came with their families, and most were forced to contribute to the family's income whether they wanted to or not. Teresa Wolfson points out in her classic study, *The Woman Worker and the Trade Unions*, that, regardless of what social ideas the immigrant women brought with them, they were forced to work for wages. If they did not belong to the proletarian classes before leaving Europe, they soon came to belong to them in the Promised Land. Not even marriage gave any certain guarantee that the women immigrants in America would escape a life of selling their labor. "Some of them—German, Swedish, Polish, Bohemian, and French Canadian women—arranged childcare and domestic service and worked in factories and as maids even after they had gotten married," emphasizes Alice Kessler-Harris in another classic study of women's work in the United States.[3]

Minneapolis: An Industrial Center in the Swedish Settlements

From the end of the nineteenth century, Minneapolis grew from a little trading center to a major industrial city, which in 1920 harbored more than 380,000 inhabitants. One quarter of these were new immigrants from several European countries, with Scandinavians being the largest group, while a large number of the newly arrived came from the surrounding countryside as part of an accelerating proletarization and urbanization process. Others moved in from other cities in conjunction with the secondary migration of an expanding western frontier.[4]

A growing number of industrial goods were manufactured in Minneapolis, but the production of machines for the expanding agricultural sector and the refinement of agricultural products dominated. The transportation network was built both for transportation to and from the city as well as within the city limits. With a well-developed streetcar system, workers could be transported to and from their jobs. All of this was controlled by the capital of older American institutions and people, and by the beginning of the 1910s Minneapolis had become the largest banking center west of Chicago.

It was men who worked within the leading industrial branches of the city, while women primarily earned their livings within the service sector. But, concurrent with the increasing bureaucratization of the fast growing industrial businesses, the number of women working outside of the home increased. Several of them drew attention to themselves within the city's bourgeois public sphere when 1,200 telephone operators were bold enough to strike and demonstrate for their demands on city streets in November 1918, just when World War I came to an end. Other women worked assiduously and in a less visible manner. This was the case, for example, with all of the many Swedish domestic servants who cleaned, cooked, cared for children, and waited on the predominantly Anglo-Saxon bourgeoisie in the city. This was also the case for the quickly growing number of female textile workers of various nationalities who tried to earn their livelihoods, and maybe a bit more, through working, as did

Evelina for example, at Weum Watt Company, or, even better, at Northwestern Knitting Company.

The Largest Female Workplace

George D. Munsing was one of the many Anglo-Saxons from New England who saw the opportunities for establishing themselves as businessmen in the newly colonized areas of the northern Midwest. In 1886, Munsing and two colleagues from Massachusetts Institute of Technology started a company for the manufacturing of knitted underwear, the Northwestern Knitting Company. Munsing himself constructed the machines and supervised the work of the newly hired women. The company remained, however, relatively small until several of the city's established leading citizens—the mill-king Charles A. Pillsbury, the banker and industry owner Clinton Morrison, and the streetcar magnate Thomas Lowry—opened their eyes to its expansion possibilities. They invested large sums of money in new buildings and machines and additional workers. From the nineteenth century's final years up until the outbreak of World War I, the company grew into one of the city's largest workplaces for women. In 1914, it occupied an entire city block in the northern part of Minneapolis' industrial area on the western side of the Mississippi River, and the highest part of the complex rose eight stories above ground. Every morning, 200 men and 1,500 women walked through the company's impressive front entrance at 217 Lyndale Avenue to work for the three finance and industrial capitalists and a few shareholders. They earned their own livelihoods at this work, and it was said that one out of every forty households in the city had had some family member on the company's payrolls.[5]

In the beginning, the women made underwear for both men and women. Later, the production was concentrated on men's underwear alone, branded Munsingwear, and enjoyed a high status. These developments accelerated during World War I. When the United States entered the war in April 1917, Northwestern Knitting Company became the main supplier of underwear to American soldiers. It was no wonder that, as opposed to Minnesota's Swedish-born Senator Charles Lindbergh, for example, the company's management were big supporters of American involvement in the war. It was a profitable attitude, and the management could develop production even more. In 1917, 2,000 people were employed in the factory, and in 1918 their numbers had grown to 3,000, of which 2,500 were women of thirty different nationalities. Over 400 of them were born in Sweden, or in the United States to parents with Swedish citizenship. Still other women were born in the U.S. and had American citizenship but claimed a Swedish heritage.

At the turn of the century, as Swedish and other women moved to Minneapolis in order to try to earn a living, they could, in the best of cases, be hired through an acquaintance who was already employed at a workplace. Sometimes these promises could not be fulfilled, however. Evelina had evident problems in finding employment, at least under conditions that she could accept. She did not mention searching for work by reading the want ads in the daily newspapers, but many other Swedish women probably did so. This was the most common method of gaining employment at the beginning of the century. Others used the federal employment agency or, as Evelina did, for example, went to one of the thirty-three private employment agencies that existed in Minneapolis during the 1910s. Still others put their faith in private relief organizations, such as The Salvation Army, The City Mission, or the Women's Cooperative Alliance, where they could hope to find accommodations as well as physical and spiritual nourishment.[6]

Those women who would come to work for the three wealthy men who headed Northwestern Knitting Company did not, however, make use of any of the above-mentioned opportunities. As a large-scale, modern business, Northwestern Knitting Company had its own hiring department. At end of World War I, all of the women (and a smaller number of men) who applied for jobs in the manufacturing of men's underwear would have been met by Miss Frances Little. Her job was to welcome applicants and to show them around the enormous factory complex so that, as it was so nicely put in an advertisement brochure for the company, they could have a little tour of "the Home of Munsingwear." The purpose of this tour was so that every newly employed man or woman could be "placed in the department where he or she was best suited." No doubt it was not the job applicants who decided this, but Miss Little, or perhaps even someone who was her supervisor.[7]

In any case, the job applicants could, in their wanderings through the large factory building, observe a strict sexual segregation in the division of labor. Most male workers were skilled. According to Charles Pillsbury, "these men are nearly all especially trained in our work and vitally necessary to it, especially in view of the fact that most of our regular operatives are girls, the men are filling positions where men and trained men are essential." Most of the preparatory and finishing work was done by men, while women between the ages of sixteen and sixty (that is, not just girls) manufactured the underwear or were involved in the production in some other manner. There was no even distribution of workers in the various departments by age or nationality; instead, there was a definite age and ethnic division that could be seen by every job applicant who was guided through the different departments.[8]

Ethnic Division of Labor

The first phase of the work after the yarn had been delivered to the factory was winding it onto the bobbins. This was a job for very young immigrant women. Most of them were between sixteen and twenty years old, and Polish women were clearly over-represented, while comparatively few Swedes and only a few American women worked in this department. This work was viewed as being so simple that it was not even referred to in the previously mentioned brochure that was meant to interest women in working for the company.

From the yarn-winding department, the production continued at three different knitting departments. Here the work was mechanized, and the women workers were machine assistants. They changed spools, threaded needles, and supervised the proper function of the knitting. Alert eyes and manual dexterity were an asset in this work. Even though the women had to call on male repairmen if something happened to the machines, this was still seen as a high status job. The women were somewhat older than those in the yarn-winding department, most of them between the ages of eighteen and twenty-five, and the majority of them were Americans. Only eight Swedish and seven Norwegian women, in addition to an occasional few of other nationalities, had managed to land jobs at these machines. That the immigrant women did not have alert eyes or dexterous fingers is hard to believe. Rather, the obvious division of labor according to nationality in this woman's job is a social construction that American women helped to uphold through collaboration with the management.

From the knitting departments, the products were transported to the laundry department in order to be bleached, a job that required great expertise. Despite the fact that this was traditionally a female area of competence, only one woman worked there, a twenty-year-old Swedish woman.

The bleached, tube-formed knitted goods were then napped and turned inside-out, all of which was done by machine and with male machine super-

Woman managing machine at the Munsingwear Knitting Mills, 1920s

visors. Next, mostly American women between the ages of eighteen and twenty-five folded the sections, after which they were sent to the cutting department, where approximately 270 women cut up the pieces of cloth. It was hard work and demanded great skill because of the elasticity of the material. Those women who worked with scissors were therefore somewhat older than those in the earlier departments, indicating that they were trusted and that perhaps they crowned their careers in this department. A large number of the women were over thirty years old, but surprisingly few of them were Americans. Only a third of them were born in the United States and were American citizens. Swedish, Norwegian, Finnish, and German women were clearly over-represented, something that cannot be explained by saying that immigrant women remained with the company longer than Americans. It was instead just the opposite. Only continued research can elucidate the reasons for this division of labor among the women.

The manufacturing process then continued in two large sewing departments where the work, according to the advertisement brochure, was marked by "the girl's wonderful dexterity in handling the sewing machines." The author said that he was led to think of a pianist when he watched the women working. The comparison, however, became dubiously weak when he added that it is actually not very difficult to learn the tricks of the trade. Neither did he mention anything about working at the machines being dangerous. Evelina herself experienced this: "Only once did I sew over my finger so that the needle broke into several pieces. I stayed calm however, quickly wrapped my finger tightly in a handkerchief, put in a new needle, and continued sewing as if nothing had happened. It was not until lunch break that I could examine my finger—luckily I discovered no pieces of needle in my finger, but it was seriously injured and very much in the way during the time when I had to keep it wrapped." It was worse for many others around her: "Some . . . were in such a bad way that they came near to fainting and often had to get a doctor to remove the bits of needle from their fingers." According to Evelina, it was "quite common that especially the beginners sewed over their fingers, very likely because of the speed of the machines which were electrically powered."[9]

Just as in Evelina's case, the women at Northwestern Knitting Company were paid for the number of garments they produced, and that required an intensive working pace in order to achieve a fairly reasonable earning. This was particularly the case since they did not get paid for those garments that did not pass inspection by one of the many supervisors, preferably American women, who controlled and approved or disapproved of the work they had done. It was extremely trying to sew buttonholes day in and day out. Approximately

1,100 women were employed solely to sew together the pieces of material for what was referred to as "the unmentionables." The number is worth repeating: 1,100 women working monotonously at the factory's many clattering sewing machines.

The social context around the different machines varied with regard to the mixture of seamstress nationalities. At one type of machine, almost three quarters of the women were Americans, while Swedish women were clearly over-represented by a little over 20 percent at another type of machine. To a certain extent, the same was true for Norwegians and Germans, although around twenty different nationalities were represented in the work. Many languages were spoken (if they were able to converse with one another during the intensive work). They all shared in common, however, an abhorrence for the twenty-three-year-old "time and motion study" man who not only supervised their work but also doubtlessly forced them to increase their pace in order to maintain the daily earnings.

The finished underwear was controlled by no fewer than 200 women, the majority of whom were Americans. This position of responsibility, which was most likely not paid by the piece, was obviously not work for immigrant women. More than half of these inspectors were women of, at most, twenty-five years of age, so the work was not a top step on a career ladder for American women at the company. The packaging of the inspected underwear, however, was done by many Swedish, Norwegian, and German women.

To sum up, we can now establish that there was a clearly pronounced ethnic- or nationality-based division of labor at Northwestern Knitting Company near the end of World War I. The inspecting and supervising women were preferably American citizens. They were hired within the conceptual framework that American women had priority to the more qualified jobs. That several Swedish women were hired for such jobs indicates that the Swedes—seemingly more than Norwegians and Germans, for example—were on their way to being admitted into the American society.

Swedish, Norwegian, and German women were preferably hired to work certain machines, while Americans dominated at other machines. Among the larger groups of nationalities, the Polish women had a more difficult time than the Scandinavians and Germans being hired for work in the actual production phases. They were instead clearly over-represented within the reproductive sphere by working in the large kitchen and accompanying restaurant and as cleaners. Other women, Russian Jews, for example, who were quite numerous in Minneapolis and whose colleagues worked in the textile industry in New York, did not manage to gain employment at the company. It is possible that

the difficulties that Polish, Russian, and Jewish women had in finding employment in the Minneapolis textile industry were a result of their belonging to a
later generation of immigrants than the Scandinavians and Germans. It could
also be that they were placed at the bottom of a not only a sexually coded but
ethnically coded labor market. Minneapolis was no melting pot, in any case not
for women within the textile industry during World War I. Rather, it was a city
where many women of different nationalities knew their place in a hierarchical labor market.[10]

Among the cleaning women and cafeteria personnel there was, however, an
unexpectedly large group of American women, which upsets the unequivocal
picture of an ethnic-national hierarchy within the labor market, where management preferred American women for the more qualified jobs with higher
status and higher wages. The conditions at Northwestern Knitting Company
certainly give support to this picture, but they also point to a clear differentia-
tion and pauperization among native-born American women, demonstrating
that some of them had to be satisfied with jobs that otherwise went to those
who were lower in the hierarchy.

The Patriarch and the Multitude of Women

Northwestern Knitting Company was a very fast growing, large-scale, capitalistic business in the beginning of the twentieth century, characterized by a significant and constantly upheld division of labor. For women of different nationalities, this may have provided on-the-job social support and made it easier
for women of certain nationalities, just as Evelina, to be hired by a company
through her fellow countrywomen's efforts.

A far-reaching division of labor, however, also risked bringing about mo-
notonous work, a fast working pace, and, as we have seen within the textile industry in Minneapolis, a great risk for injuries. These circumstances could lead
to high worker absentee rates and problematic worker turnover rates. This was
indeed the case at Northwestern Knitting Company, and the board of directors
discussed these problems exhaustively and regularly throughout the 1910s.[11]

Around 1915, just when the large factory complex opened, a comprehensive
plan of action was begun, aimed at decreasing the turnover rates and instead
tying the workers to the company. It was not enough that the majority of employees could eat their lunches and other meals in the company's modern
restaurant and cafeteria, which, according to Charles Pillsbury's own account,
was served by "one of the best equipped kitchens in the whole of Minneapolis" and where the work of the many Polish women was supervised by a male
"expert." The company had, in addition, also hired a full-time trained nurse,

while doctors with various specialties made regular visits. One of the most important tasks the nurse performed was probably removing bits of broken needles from women's fingers.[12]

In order to help employees with more serious sicknesses and injuries, a mutual help fund was also started in 1915, the Employee's Mutual Benefit Association of the Northwestern Knitting Company. It was established so that no one would have to pay an admittance fee but everyone who worked at the company longer than one month could, after applying, become a member. After admittance, twenty-five cents per month would be drawn out of one's wages as a monthly membership fee, except during illnesses that lasted longer than two weeks, when the fee would be waived. This benefit could only be received six weeks in a row and a total of eight weeks during one year. But it was not just an easy opportunity to stay at home. It was the duty of a special committee to visit the sick or injured employee at least once a week, and thereafter report to the secretary of the association as to the condition of the sick or injured person.[13]

Every now and then the internal newspaper, *Munsingwear News*, was distributed free of charge to all employees, and those who were receiving sick benefits were listed. Perhaps this was done in order to control abuse of the system or to create an atmosphere of concern on the part of the management. Thus, for example, all the munsingites could read in the March 1918 edition that Eva Hedberg from Department K had met with the misfortune of falling and breaking her ankle. She was, therefore, forced to remain at home for several weeks and would not be back on the job for some time. The author maintained that all of her colleagues missed her smiling face and hoped that she would soon be back "with us" again.

Reports about women employees' birthdays, marriages, and visits to family in Minnesota and other parts of the country all give the same impression that management wanted to create a feeling of intimacy among the female workers. The high turnover rate of women employees, which in internal discussions among the directors was a serious problem, was denied in the official rhetoric and was turned into its opposite instead. *Munsingwear News* wished those who quit their jobs at the company for one reason or another "Good luck" in the future. Terms such as "munsingites" and "The Munsingwear Family" were meant to emphasize solidarity within the company, not only between the management and the workers, and between men and women, but, perhaps even more so, solidarity between women of thirty different nationalities.

Within the framework of family ideology, the national diversity of the company was affirmed. For example, Selma Isacson could report on "A Trip to Sweden," which she made in August 1916, accompanied by Eva Warmgren, who had previously worked in Department H, and Anna Norberg, who was also a "mem-

ber of The Munsingwear Family." When the United States entered the war in
April 1917, however, the contents of the management's ideological and political message changed.

America! One Nation Made from Many Peoples

One week after the United States declared war on Germany, Governor Joseph
Burnquist appointed the Minnesota Public Safety Commission, whose job it
was, using all means necessary within the limits of the law, to guarantee Minnesota's full support for the war efforts. The commission's activities were aimed
not only at people of German descent, and along with them the closely related
Swedes, but also at every person who did not give his or her full support to the
American entrance into the war. Thus, the commission had both an ethnic and
a class-conscious edge, and the Anglo-American bourgeoisie could kill two birds
with one stone, both national diversity and the socialistic worker's movement.
Women would come to participate in the activities of the commission as well
as be subjects for the commission's actions.[14]

A women's committee was established within the commission under the
leadership of Mrs. Francis Buel Olson and Miss Agnes Peterson, the latter from
the Minnesota State Department of Labor and Industry. It was this committee
that, in conjunction with the Departments of Labor and Industry, performed
a mapping of all women (with the exception of domestic servants) who worked
outside of the home. In Minneapolis alone, some 3,100 workplaces, which together employed a little over 19,000 wage-earning women, were surveyed. One
objective of the survey was to investigate the extent to which working women
had replaced men who had been mobilized for the war. An effect of these activities is that we now have an enormous amount of source material about
women's work that American historians have not yet utilized.

Nevertheless, the commission's main function was to guarantee political
loyalty in Minnesota. This occurred through a comprehensive Americanization program. A large number of pamphlets were printed with the aim of re-
shaping the mindsets of a large number of individuals. In one pamphlet issued
by the women's committee, it was maintained that the outbreak of war caused
people in America to realize that there were many nationalities populating the
country and that there were many languages being spoken, through which traditions from many countries were being preserved. With the outbreak of the
war, it was time to come to terms with this diversity and instead create One
Nation.[15]

The women's committee considered immigrant women to be in a strategic
position, especially mothers. The committee even believed that the word

"mother" was more important than "nationality." Each American mother was therefore encouraged to "Americanize" one immigrant woman. Every American woman should teach a foreign-born woman to speak English, and American women were encouraged to involve foreign-born women in all sorts of patriotic activities. At many workplaces, evening courses in English were arranged, and these language courses were linked with the issue of citizenship. This is what took place at Northwestern Knitting Company, for example, and quick-to-learn students were rewarded in the customary manner through personal recognition. In *Munsingwear News*, all of the students in English and Citizenship were listed. Many Swedish women were among these: Hilda Bloomquist, Ida Anderson, Emma Hanson, Elna Broman, Olga Karlson, Inga Sundgren, Margaret Nordin, Emma Peterson, Agnes Mattson, Ellen Nelson, Mait Erickson, Hulda Anderson, Selma Franzén, Anna Johnson, Lena Olson, Lydia Gustavson, and Anna Törnquist, just to name a few. They had not only shown themselves to be worthy members of the Munsingwear Family, but were now also considered to be American Women. They were women workers in a middle-class hegemonic Anglo-American environment, where class identity was opposed and where the national identity was being transformed so that women from European countries would be liberated from their cultural heritage.

This endeavor was not completely successful, and Swedishness, in any case, survived, if only to our eyes, in a picturesque style. It is important that we remind ourselves, however, of the visible and invisible larger political situation into which women, men, and children are thrust when they leave one society in order to participate in the building of another. This is true of the past, as well as of our own day and age. Through more research about the destiny of Swedish immigrants from an ethnic, as well as a class and gender perspective, an increased understanding of the present may be gained, as Sweden is a completely different society than it was in Karl Oskar's and Christina's day.

* * * *

NOTES

1. Evelina's story is based on Evelina Månsson, *Amerika minnen. Upplevelser och iakttagelser från en 6-årig vistelse i U.S.A.* (Hvetlanda: Svenska Allmogeförlaget, 1930).
2. Byron J. Nordstrom, "Evelina Månsson and the Memoir of an Urban Labor Migrant," *Swedish Pioneer Historical Society* 31 (1980): 182–95; Kathie Friedman-Kasaba, *Memoirs of Migration: Gender, Ethnicity, and Work in the Lives of Jewish and Italian Women in New York, 1870–1920* (New York, 1996).
3. Teresa Wolfson, *Woman Workers and the Trade Unions* (New York, 1926), 35ff.; Alice

Kessler-Harris, *Out to Work: A History of Wage-Earning Women in the United States* (New York: Oxford Univ. Press, 1982), 124.

4. The survey of Minneapolis is primarily based on Mildred L. Hartsough, *The Twin Cities as a Metropolitan Market* (Minneapolis, 1925), and Elisabeth Faue, *Community of Suffering & Struggle: Women, Men, and the Labor Movement in Minneapolis, 1915–1945* (Chapel Hill: Univ. of N.C. Press, 1991).

5. The story of the company is primarily based on *The Story of Munsingwear, 1886–1961* (Minneapolis, 1964); and Munsingwear, Inc. Corporate Records, MHS.

6. Hartsough, *Twin Cities as a Metropolitan Market*, 57; William B. Taylor, "The Labor Market for the Northwest: A Study Based Chiefly upon the Records of Minneapolis Private Employment Agencies for the Period 1919–1922" (master's thesis, Univ. of Minn.), 8, 17.

7. *The Success of Well Doing,* an undated booklet published by the Munsingwear Corporation, copy in MHS collections. The management of the company publicly called it "The Home of Munsingwear"; see, for example, the cover of the first issue of *Munsingwear News* (1916), a journal for all "Munsingites," that is, all employees of the company.

8. Charles Pillsbury to John S. Pardy, June 13, 1917, Minnesota Commission of Public Safety Records, MHS. The analysis of the ethnic division of labor is based on Minnesota Commission of Public Safety Records, Women's Commission, Women in Industry Survey Forms, 1918–19, microfilm roll 3, MHS.

9. Månsson, *Amerika minnen.*

10. See Friedman-Kasaba, *Memoirs of Migration.*

11. "Extracts of Minutes of the Stockholders' and Directors' Meetings, 1887–1925," Munsingwear, Inc. Corporate Records, MHS.

12. Charles Pillsbury, *Munsingwear—Its Ideals and Development* (Minneapolis, 1923), 3.

13. There is a copy in Munsingwear, Inc. Corporate Records, MHS.

14. Carl Crislock, *Watchdog of Loyalty: The Minnesota Commission of Public Safety During World War I* (St. Paul: MHS Press, 1991); John G. Rice, "The Swedes," in June Drenning Holmquist, ed., *They Chose Minnesota: A Survey of the State's Ethnic Groups* (St. Paul: MHS Press, 1981), 270f.

15. This pamphlet was published by the Women's Committee, Minnesota Division of the Council for National Defense, and the Women's Auxiliary Committee of the Minnesota Commission of Public Safety, n.d., Minnesota Commission of Public Safety Records, MHS.

The Northern Neighbor:
Winnipeg, the Swedish Service Station in the "Last Best West" 1890–1950

LARS LJUNGMARK

The Swedish immigrant communities that emerged on the North American continent in the nineteenth and early twentieth centuries existed within a network of contacts and connections. These networks were important for continued association and exchange of people and ideas with Sweden, as well as with other Swedish immigrant communities in the New World. By 1900, several such communities had emerged, including the Twin Cities and Chicago in the American Midwest.

Swedish immigrants did not only settle in the United States; Canada also became an important North American destination, although Swedish immigrants settled there in substantially smaller numbers than in the United States. The leading Swedish Canadian settlement was Winnipeg, Manitoba, which began receiving immigrants in the 1870s. At this time, Winnipeg was really a part of Swedish America, situated on the northern Swedish American frontier of settlement, an extension of the Swedish settlements in the United States. Most of the city's Swedish inhabitants were secondary migrants from the United States, forming part of an extended network of Swedish immigrants in North America with strong and important connections to areas in Minnesota such as the Twin Cities.[1]

Even though the ties to the Twin Cities Swedish American community were important for the Winnipeg Swedes—especially during the formative period— the Winnipeg experience differed in several ways from that of the Swedes in Minneapolis and St. Paul, a fact which became increasingly marked during the decades after the 1870s. Four aspects in particular should be noted: the long-lasting pioneer situation; the comparatively late immigration directly from

Sweden; Canadian nationalism; and the feelings of inferiority in the community in relation to other immigrant groups and to Swedes in the Twin Cities. These aspects present interesting similarities and differences between the communities of Winnipeg and the Twin Cities, both of which were important parts of the growing network of Swedish immigrants.

Background

Where the Red River and the Assiniboine River merged, and the western and southern merchant routes met, the Hudson's Bay Company had a stronghold at Upper Fort Garry. A small town developed north of the fort during the 1860s. The town was named Winnipeg—"muddy water" in the native Indian language— for a lake some forty miles to the north.

Winnipeg soon became the gateway to one of the most rapidly expanding farming regions in the world. The Canadian prairie made up one pillar in Winnipeg's economic life. A second was its role as a central, fast-growing railway junction through which all three transcontinental railroads passed, beginning with the Canadian Pacific Railway in 1882. From Winnipeg, new arrivals were spread out to homesteads and jobs in western Canada. Winnipeg had 42,000 inhabitants in 1901. Then followed a boom period between 1901 and 1911 during which Winnipeg grew to 150,000 inhabitants and became the third largest city in Canada. To this census figure one must add a floating population made up mostly of single men searching for jobs.

Winnipeg's rapid growth during the boom years led to significant ethnic transformation between the Anglo-Saxon charter groups from Great Britain and Ontario and the newly arrived "foreigners," of which the majority were Slavs and Jews from eastern Europe. They were spoken of as "strangers within our gates."

The newcomers segregated themselves in foreign ghettos in the North End, an area just north of the giant yard of the Canadian Pacific Railway. The British-Canadian majority withdrew into a solid, isolated group in the South and West Ends. During World War I, intolerance and hatred increased. As pro-British feelings grew among members of the charter group, everyone who was not obviously British was placed under suspicion. Feelings of hostility and hatred generated by the war did not subside immediately after the war ended in 1918. Unemployment met the returning soldiers, who now saw Germans and Ukrainians holding their old jobs. And the great Winnipeg General Strike in 1919 was believed by many in the charter group to have been led and supported by those who had been disloyal during the war.

There is no doubt that by 1920 Winnipeg was a city of isolated and frequently bitter ethnic groups. One can speak of a divided city. But from 1920 to 1950, tension eased as the city grew less rapidly (from 180,000 to 265,000), immigration slowed, and natural increase played a greater role. Finally, during World War II the demand for manpower knew no ethnic limits.

The first Swedes arrived in the 1870s. They came from Swedish America, south of the border. Most of them wanted land, and so did the Swedes that arrived after them, directly from Sweden. To Swedes, Winnipeg now became the major "service station" for all who arrived and went further. It also served those who had settled on the prairie but wanted equipment, or those who needed a short rest between jobs as farmhands, lumberjacks, or navies—jobs that for most of them were intended to furnish the necessary money for a start out on a homestead. During the booming years, Winnipeg was a ready source of money for labor. Many immigrants also dropped their farming plans and started businesses in the city or remained in their works in the factories, shops, Canadian households, or the Canadian Pacific Railway's railroad yard and associated shops.

The Scandinavians (who in the statistics included the Icelanders, Swedes, Danes, and Norwegians) were according to the 1901 census 8 percent of Winnipeg's population and the second largest ethnic group after the British, whose dominance was complete. In 1911, the Scandinavians were only 3.6 percent of Winnipeg's population and ranked fifth among the ethnic groups. These numbers remained stable, and in later years the Scandinavians ranked as either fifth or sixth among the census population.

During the 1880s and 1890s, Swedes formed an enclave of their own in the district around Logan Avenue near the North End slum on the opposite side of the Canadian Pacific Railway yard. Logan Avenue was soon described as "Snoose Boulevard," the customary name for Swedish-dominated streets all over North America.

By 1914, on Logan Avenue there were two Swedish and one Norwegian newspapers; three Swedish churches (Lutheran, Baptist, and Mission Covenant), and a Scandinavian branch of the Salvation Army; about a dozen Swedish restaurants, cafes, boarding houses, and hotels; and a number of well-stocked Swedish shops carrying everything from snuff and Swedish food to equipment for life out on the farms or in the lumber camps.

Swedish activities, however, were more concentrated around Logan Avenue than was Swedish habitation. Many families lived in the West End, or northeast in Elmwood, on the other side of the Red River. So, even when Swedish commercial life on Logan Avenue was at its height from just before World War I through the late 1920s, it was not a "Little Sweden" like the Chicago Avenue area in Chicago or some Swedish neighborhoods in the Twin Cities. But almost all social events among the Swedes in the city took place in the different societies belonging to the churches or the secular societies that met in the restaurants, cafes, and dancing halls in the Logan Avenue district. Swedish was the dominant language.

Above all, Logan Avenue was a service district for all Swedish prairie farmers and for immigrants who arrived at the Canadian Pacific station nearby. It was also a place of rest during the intervals between different jobs for Swedes who worked on the farms, in the woods, or along the railroads. It was a place where Swedes belonging to the two typical parts of Winnipeg's population—the established "census people" and the "floating population"—met. Up to the 1940s, Logan Avenue could be described as a central place for all Swedish Canadians in the prairie provinces, that is, for about 85 percent of all Swedes in Canada.

Logan Avenue was most important as a center for benevolent work and a place for rescue in times of destitution. And those times were many. The World War I period was most difficult, but the following two years and the depression years from the 1920s through the "Dirty Thirties" were also trying for Swedish Canadians in Winnipeg. The district was in decline during the 1930s. Chinese, Ukrainians, Jews, and other groups from the North End were on their way into the region. Established Swedes were, at least with regard to living in the district, definitely on their way out. Poor, worn-out people gave Logan Avenue the impression of a Scandinavian "Skid Row." But through the hard times of the Depression the street enjoyed a final period of greatness as the center of both organized and spontaneous aid to the poor. In many ways, the 1930s were Logan Avenue's best period. When the crisis subsided at the end of the 1930s, however, Swedish Logan Avenue was clearly in decline. The restaurants and cafes were closed or changed hands, and drew new customers. The churches moved out in the 1940s and 1950s and merged with Canadian congregations.

Logan Avenue became a Swedish "Snoose Boulevard" thanks to the fact that it was situated in Winnipeg, the "Tollgate to the Prairies," and thus close to the center of immigrant communication—the Canadian Pacific Railway Station and the Immigration Hall. In the same way, the Swedish enclave in Winnipeg was directed outwards, to the Swedish immigrant stream, to the Swedes all over western Canada who visited the city to shop, rest, meet, or seek employment. This lively Swedish Canadian *immigrant* life, not an established Swede Town, gave the Swedish enclave in Winnipeg its unique profile. This was a profile and status that disappeared along with Swedish emigration to the Canadian prairies at the end of the 1930s.

As already pointed out, the differences in experience for Swedish immigrants in Winnipeg as compared to the Twin Cities was not as visible during the early days of the immigration, as the Swedish enclave then was really a part of the Swedish immigrant community in the United States. Strong connections to this community in the Twin Cities are especially noticeable in the early history of the Swedish churches in Winnipeg.

The Swedish congregations in Winnipeg started in two different ways. Swedish America was involved in the establishment of the two oldest churches. The Swedish Mission Covenant Church was first, beginning as immigrants met privately to worship in the home of M. P. Peterson, who had arrived in 1874 from Michigan. In 1876 Peterson managed to get a Swedish American pastor to extend his ordinary mission field in the Red River valley and North Dakota to Winnipeg. One year later, Guds Skandinaviska Församling i Winnipeg was founded. Soon it changed its name to Skandinaviska Kristna Missionsförsamlingen.[2]

As for the Lutherans, Canada belonged to the mission field of the Minnesota Conference of the Augustana Synod, which sent pastors on visits to work among the Swedish settlers on the Canadian prairies during the 1880s. In 1889, a Lutheran congregation was formed in the first Swedish settlement—New Stockholm, Assiniboine, Northwest Territories. This action was influenced by the fear that the Swedes in this settlement would join the Mission Covenant. The same concern was behind the formation of the next and more important Lutheran congregation in Canada, Zion Lutheran Church, in Winnipeg in 1890. Later, and similarly influenced by close contact with Swedish America, a Baptist church was founded. As in early Swedish America, from the beginning all the congregations embraced a broader Scandinavian people, as the Swedes were too few to form churches of their own. In time, all became Swedish and centers of immigrant social life, following the same pattern as Swedish America. After these initially strong connections between Midwestern U.S. and Canadian Swedish immigrants, however, the development of Winnipeg's immigrant community was often in direct contrast to that of the Twin Cities.[3]

Winnipeg, a Pioneer City

Winnipeg remained a pioneer city well into the 1940s because it was the entry point into the last region of Swedish immigration in North America. This pioneer situation also put its mark on the life of the Swedish enclave during the whole period. This can be illustrated by Canada's first Swedish newspaper, *Den Skandinaviske Canadiensaren*, started by Emmanuel Öhlen as a monthly in 1887. Öhlen was the founder of New Stockholm, the first Swedish colony in the Northwest Territories. Before he started the paper, Öhlen presented his plans to Ottawa's Department of Agriculture, which was in charge of immigration policy. He stated that the newspaper would "contain several letters from Scandinavian farmers in Manitoba and the Northwest in order to induce the Scandinavians to settle there." He secured the department's support and it promised to buy 1,000 copies of every number for distribution to emigration agents. Obviously, the immigration promoters found the newspaper valuable for their interests, as evidenced by the purchase of 10,000 copies in a single month of 1891, which were distributed widely throughout Scandinavia and the United States.[4]

Den Skandinaviske Canadiensaren was one of the precursors of *Svenska Canada Tidningen*. It was a weekly that changed names several times during the 1890s, receiving its final name in 1907, *Canada Tidningen*. During the 1920s, the paper appeared in either a twelve- or sixteen-page format; throughout the western Canadian provinces, it competed successfully with the largest Swedish papers in the United States. The stiffest competition came from the Twin Cities, where *Svenska Canada Tidningen* managed to recruit almost all of its editors. In 1970, the paper amalgamated with *Svenska Amerikanaren Tribunen* in Chicago. The background of *Svenska Canada Tidningen* is very typical for Winnipeg's role as a pioneer center with a great interest in the promotion of immigration. Other newspapers had regarded the Twin Cities to be at the very center of Swedish immigrant life and news, while Winnipeg remained on the periphery, a town of presumptive immigrants.

The pioneer environment was problematical for the Swedish societies in Winnipeg. The city's role as a stop on the immigrant's way west made it difficult to keep together an organization, even if from the beginning it was backed by enthusiastic charter members, when soon both the leaders and the members were scattered all over western Canada. The churches had a better situation, as pastoral leadership was less inclined to move and therefore anchored the community. Moreover, the charter group consisted of more established families that remained in the city.

Also typical for Winnipeg's pioneer situation—and a difference from the Twin Cities—were the many Swedish residents in Winnipeg who owned farms. Some of them were on their way to a chosen homestead but stayed in Winnipeg for a time to earn money necessary to begin farming. Other farmers left their families in Winnipeg during the first year, often one of hardship, while the land was cleared and a home built on the homestead. Then there were established farmers, who left the farm during the winter months for the more comfortable city life. And finally there were also those who were established city dwellers, yet owned a farm to which they went for some time during the summer months.

Above all, Winnipeg's predominant role as a "service station" for Swedes rested on a pioneer situation, with a constant immigrant stream up to 1930 passing through the railway stations and the Immigrant House in Winnipeg. It was the city with the land office, the launching point for prospective farmers making their way to their homesteads. It had the labor exchanges that distributed the newcomers to jobs out on the prairies or in the woods. Farmers then got their supplies in Winnipeg, and, if destitute, they returned to the city and their Swedish compatriots for aid.

The Twin Cities never comprised such a central role for the Swedish pioneers. When the heavy Swedish emigration to the frontiers of settlement in Minnesota, and then further west, began in the 1860s, St. Paul and Minneapolis were burgeoning cities without much close contact with the arriving Swedes. The established farmers away from the Twin Cities did not look to them as needed sources of supplies. For these pioneers, small towns closer to the frontier of settlement—such as St. Peter, Alexandria, and Litchfield—served as service stations. The Twin Cities were separated from the pulse of Swedish immigration in a way quite different from Winnipeg. Winnipeg and the Twin Cities had one service role in common, however. Whether in prairie Canada or in the American Midwest, the two "Snoose Boulevards" (Logan Avenue in Winnipeg and Cedar Avenue in Minneapolis) were commercial gathering places and centers of entertainment.

Later Immigration, from a Modern Sweden

Those who came directly from Sweden to Canada represented a later stage of migration when compared to the United States. Consequently, the immigrant enclave in Winnipeg had a quite different character than the Swedish ethnic neighborhoods in the Twin Cities. This is especially noticeable in the history of the Swedish societies in Winnipeg.

From the beginning, most of these societies were dominated by Swedish Americans who had gone north. Many came from the Twin Cities. The ideals of these earlier immigrants were based on a nostalgic view of the old country's heroic history, beautiful nature, and the reputed high work ethic of the Swedes. They took pride in what were considered special Swedish virtues, ones that, for example, made the Swedes law-abiding (in contrast to Americans), hardworking (many times mentioned in contrast to British immigrants), and prone to self-effacing humility (often in contrast to Norwegians).

After World War I, when Swedish emigration to Canada was at its height, the newcomers (the great majority now came direct from Sweden) had left an industrialized home country with more mobility, more internal migration, more non-religious people, and more people with radical political views than before the war. This made these new Canadians less interested in Swedish nationalism and nostalgic homesickness. They rejected the earlier rhetoric of Swedishness, the dominance and cliquishness of the societies' first generation, as well as the old-fashioned social forms. Instead, they asked for a more Swedish Canadian profile and desired more realistic and practical programs, especially dur-

ing the hard times of the late 1920s and 1930s, that would address poverty, unemployment, the need for English-language education, and appropriate cultural
activities that would address the issues of the day. Esse W. Ljung, editor of
Canada Tidningen, was the strongest proponent of these demands. He wrote
in 1933: "The struggle for the piece of crisp bread forces people to a realism that
gives no time for the honor of the forefathers, a glorious history, a beautiful
mythology, etc. etc."[5]

Representative of the new cultural environment is the life of Swedish theatre in Winnipeg during the 1930s. The earlier popular plays in "Swinglish," such
as *Yon Yonson* or *Man from Sweden*, played by Swedish American troupes with
stars such as Gus Heege or Knute Nelson, had disappeared. They were exchanged for a radical theatre of social protest, with plays written in Winnipeg
and addressing the situation in Winnipeg. A leading example of these new plays
was *Paria's Son*, which in 1934 was played by the leading amateur theatre group
in the city, Skandinaviska Arbetarklubben. According to the advertising, the
play dealt with the fight between the capitalistic master and the enslaved
worker. The topic reveals a major difference between the common political
views among the Swedes in Winnipeg and those in the Twin Cities. In Winnipeg,
radical political views dominated, especially during the 1920s when most newcomers were recruited from the working class in northern Sweden.[6]

Contact with the modern Sweden that the newcomers had left was also be-
hind the new tone of Swedishness in Winnipeg toward the end of 1930s, when
Sweden's surprisingly fast recovery from the Depression came into focus.
In 1937, the Swedes in Winnipeg gathered around a new gospel: "Sweden the
Middle-way." The climax was the Swedish Festival on St. Vital's Fairgrounds in
July with 1,200 participants. Here a glorious history was no longer the proof of
Swedish virtues. Now the Swedes in Winnipeg were representatives of the
country that, through cooperation between different classes, had created a
state with more "solid democratic principles and better social, economic, and
political security" than Canada. A year later in Minneapolis, however, the glorious Swedish history was still alive and well when on *Svenskarnas Dag* a huge
auditorium of proud Swedish Americans, together with the Crown Prince of
Sweden, celebrated the 300th anniversary of the founding of the New Sweden
Colony on the Delaware River.[7]

Canadian Nationalism

In the American Midwest, the Swedes in the nineteenth century had arrived
together with other European immigrants into a sort of nationalistic vacuum,
which they gradually helped to develop into a society as well as part of a na-

tion. Similarly, in Canada the Swedes populated new regions, but they were part of a young Dominion of the British Empire with a strong nationalistic spirit that now and then could cause trouble for the immigrants. This is also a part of the differences between the Swedes in Winnipeg and those in the Twin Cities.

During the Boer War, at the turn of the century, when Canada for the first time entered a war side by side with its Mother Country, nationalism rose to hysterical heights. Most Swedes did not join in support, as they were pro-Boers. This time their disloyalty with Canadian war aims did not, however, cause much trouble, but during World War I it turned out to be different. Now everybody who was not openly British came under suspicion. This included the Swedish Canadians, since they came from a country with a foreign policy that was considered pro-German.[8]

During the first years of the war, this negative view caused many Swedish Canadians to escape to the United States. Mostly, it was a return to the American Midwest that they had left earlier. For many it meant a return to the Twin Cities. The Swedish newspaper asserted that the accusations of disloyalty were false, and the Swedes in Winnipeg expressed in open meetings their loyalty to their new country. The war years were, nevertheless, a difficult time for the Swedes, who were used to being regarded positively but now by many Canadians were seen as "undesired aliens." In Winnipeg, there was also a distinctively Canadian nationalism that included help for the Swedish assimilation into the new country. Behind this was the reality that this Canadian nationalism in peacetime included an anti-British sentiment shared by the Swedes.[9]

In the West, the first Canadian immigration promotion in the 1860s had resulted in a stream of unwanted poor Englishmen from the cities. Before and after World War I, too many of the English immigrants were still badly suited to life as farmers on the Canadian prairies. Added to this were the arrogant attitudes of the arriving Englishmen. Many behaved like English colonialists in African colonies. "They would refuse a job but want a position," was a comment from Winnipeg's Anglo-Saxon charter group. The Swedes had also met English arrogance, as well as their favored situation during the war, because they were seen as sons of the Mother Country and war comrades. After the war, the negative Canadian view of English immigrants was again openly shown, a view shared by the Swedes. In the Swedish Winnipeg newspapers and private discussions, the English were often cast in dark contrast to the Swedish farmer, farmhand, or lumberjack.[10]

The editor of *Canada Tidningen*, Esse W. Ljung, started a campaign in the 1930s for a more active Swedishness, whereby alert Swedes would fight against all injustice suffered by the immigrants. This campaign increasingly targeted the English. Toward the end of the 1930s, the campaign against English bullying and lack of understanding changed to a critique of Great Britain's sovereignty over Canada. Behind this initiative, no doubt, was a fear that close ties to Britain could draw Canada into a new war. This would only result in a repetition of the hard times the immigrants had suffered during World War I. The campaign's critique was, however, quite in keeping with the policy of Prime Minister Mackenzie King, and the broadening of a Swedish anti-British attitude quickened Swedish assimilation into Canadian society, including Winnipeg. There is no doubt that this critique of the British, along with the fact that Swedes in Winnipeg formed such a small minority in the city compared to the Swedes in the Twin Cities, explains the more rapid incorporation of the Swedes into Winnipeg and Canada, when compared with Swedish immigrants in the Twin Cities.[11]

Number and Status

The Swedes in Winnipeg also developed a sense of inferiority as a consequence of being so few in number, an experience that had no counterpart in the Twin Cities. This feeling was even present in relation to another Nordic group in the city, the Icelanders. The immigrants from Iceland enjoyed a unique position among the Nordic people in Winnipeg. They had arrived in the 1870s as part of a Canadian immigration program and were viewed by British Canadians as an "adopted people." In the 1891 census, there were almost seven times as many Icelanders in Winnipeg as Swedes. And in 1901 no less than 75 percent of the Nordic group were Icelanders. As immigration from Iceland decreased during the following years and the overall numbers declined, Icelanders nevertheless remained the largest single Nordic group in Winnipeg.

Swedes envied and admired the smooth progress in Canada experienced by Icelanders, especially their cultural and political contribution to the new country. The Icelandic situation in the Nordic world in Winnipeg may best be described as a splendid isolation by virtue of their status. In the Swedish newspaper they were referred to as "our distant relatives." This inferiority relative to another Nordic group was unknown to Swedes in the Twin Cities.[12]

The Winnipeg Swedes also developed a feeling of inferiority when comparing themselves to the Swedes in the United States. For many Swedes in Canada, Swedish Americans were very close relatives, since so many of them had arrived from areas south of the border. These ties were especially close out on the prairies, where most Swedish Americans had settled after their arrival from the American Midwest. In Winnipeg there were also many Swedish Americans, especially within the leadership circle of the Swedish enclave. They had had, of course, no reason at the beginning for feeling inferior to the Swedes in America. But this developed in time, primarily because the Winnipeg Swedes remained such a small group in their own city. Subscribing to Swedish American newspapers, mostly from the Twin Cities, aspiring immigrants read of the numerous success stories in the American world.

These feelings of inferiority toward their numerous southern relatives were demonstrated in connection with two important initiatives from Swedish America in the 1930s. One was when the Vasa Order of America held its first Grand Lodge meeting outside the United States in Winnipeg in 1935. When the decision was made known, *Canada Tidningen* rallied Swedes to the importance of this opportunity to host a successful event, thus showcasing their abilities to their wealthy American cousins. When the weeklong gathering proved to be a triumph, everyone was jubilant and the newspaper noted every word of praise.[13]

The other initiative from Swedish America was an invitation to participate in the Delaware Jubilee in 1938. This event demonstrated the need for the Swedes in Winnipeg and all of Canada to shed this inferiority complex and enter the grand stage beside the Swedish Americans. *Canada Tidningen*, however, maintained its inferior tone by stressing that Swedish Americans are so numerous and have climbed so high on the social ladder that Swedish Canadians "have to look hard at their countrymen in the U.S. to see them as their relatives." But soon the paper highlighted the opportunity of Swedish Canadians finally to develop their own identity in America and Sweden, as well as in Canada. Swedish Canadians were not merely a subdivision of Swedish Americans, but a group in their own right. In fact, "there is a great difference between the Swedes north and south of the border." Following the American festivities in Wilmington and Philadelphia, the newspaper was convinced that Canadian participation had been a success. At last Swedish Canadians had developed an identity of their own.[14]

Only a few weeks later, however, the inferiority of the Swedish Canadians was once again demonstrated by the report of the huge *Svenskarnas Dag* celebration in Minneapolis, with "royal guests, gigantic audience, and radiant summer weather," compared to the Swedish festival in Winnipeg with "not many participants" and rain.[15]

A City Apart

From the beginning, the Swedish enclave in Winnipeg was part of Swedish America. The contacts with the Swedish immigrants in Minnesota and especially with its largest Swedish American enclave, the Twin Cities, were natural and close. Religious life provides a good example of this. All three Swedish congregations in Winnipeg had their origin in Swedish American churches.

After the earliest period, however, the social and cultural differences between Winnipeg Swedes and their compatriots in the Twin Cities became obvious. Important in this distinction was that Winnipeg remained a pioneer city
right up until World War II, an ongoing center for the emigration to western
Canada. Thus, life in the Swedish enclave in Winnipeg became dominated by
the city's role as a service station for newly arrived Swedes. The Twin Cities never
played that dominating role in Swedish emigration to Minnesota or further
west.

Immigration from Sweden was much later to Canada than to the United
States, and that is a clear point of contrast between Winnipeg and the Twin
Cities. An example was the reaction of these later Winnipeg Swedes to any
Swedish American filiopietism of the earlier sort, so often expressed by the first
Swedes in the city, who had been part of a secondary migration from the
United States. The radical views of the newcomers were also visible in the sub-
ject matter of the plays that the Swedish amateur theatre groups performed.
The societal tensions and the dominating radical amateur theatre had no par-
allel in the Twin Cities.

Canadian nationalism, much stronger than the kind of nativism or nationalism encountered by Swedes in America, also resulted in differences between
the situation in Winnipeg and in the Twin Cities. During World War I, their status as "undesired aliens" caused Winnipeg Swedes to return to the United States.
Many relocated in the Twin Cities from which they had come.

A sense of inferiority was often present among the Swedes in Winnipeg in
relation to their more numerous countrymen in America. In this regard, the
comparisons with the Twin Cities were omnipresent and inescapable. Winnipeg Swedes read about it all the time. Newspapers from both Minneapolis
and St. Paul were readily available, and *Canada Tidningen* regularly reported
on Swedish American news in Minnesota. Swedish America was vast and envied. And the Twin Cities were full of cousins.

NOTES

1. For a full treatment of Swedish life in Winnipeg, see the author's *Svenskarna i Winnipeg. Porten till prärien 1872–1940* (Växjö: Emigrantinstitutets vänner, 1994).
2. *Minnesskrift Första Skandinaviska Kristna Missionsförsamlingen, Winnipeg, Canada.
Femtio år 1885–1935* (n.p., n.d.).
3. Ferdy E. Baglo, *Augustana Lutherans in Canada: Canada Conference of the Augustana
Lutheran Church* (1962). *Grant Memorial Baptist Church 1894–1869* (n.p., n.d.).

4. Öhlen to Agricultural Department, Feb. 3, 1887, Letters Received, 58293; Åkerlind to Agricultural Department, May 28, Letters Received, 787549 and July 27, Letters Received 79574 (1891)—all in RG 17:1, National Archives of Canada, Ottawa.

5. *Canada Tidningen*, July 6, 1933.

6. Ibid., Nov. 22, 1934.

7. Ibid., July 1, 1937.

8. On the Swedish Canadian reactions to the Boer War, see Ljungmark, *Svenskarna i Winnipeg*, 84–87.

9. Cf. *Svenska Canada Tidningen*, Sept. 16 and 23, 1914.

10. G. F. Chipman, "Winnipeg: The Melting Pot," *The Canadian Magazine* 33 (1909).

11. Important in E. W. Ljung's campaign were the following leaders in *Canada Tidningen*, July 6, 1933; Aug. 24, 1933; Oct. 11, 1935; Apr. 13, 1938; May 4, 1938; and May 18, 1939.

12. *Canada: The Swedish Weekly*, June 29, 1899.

13. *Canada Tidningen*, June 13 and 20; July 4, 1935.

14. Ibid., Oct. 14, 1937; Nov. 25, 1937; 1937; July 7, 1938.

15. Ibid., July 21 and 28, 1938.

The Swedish Historical Society of America: The Minnesota Years

BYRON J. NORDSTROM

Historical societies have been important within the complex of organizations established by a number of ethnic groups in this country, not least of all among the Scandinavians. Their purposes have been several. In general, they have provided a basis for the work of professional and amateur historians concerned about the preservation of resources and the communication of immigrant history; created archives, libraries, and artifact collections; acted as vehicles by which changing views of the immigrant past have been formulated and conveyed through publications and programs; nurtured expanded contact with the homeland; and provided a variety social functions. The earliest of these societies among the Swedish Americans was the Swedish American Historical Society, founded in Chicago in late 1889. Little is known about this group beyond its founding. It has left behind only a few brief notices in the Swedish American press and a couple of documents on file with the State of Illinois. More important were the Swedish Historical Society of America (1905–1934), the Swedish Colonial Society (1908–), the American Swedish Historical Museum (1926–), and the Swedish Pioneer Historical Society (now the Swedish-American Historical Society) (1948–). The focus of this essay is the Swedish Historical Society of America during the "Minnesota years" (1921–1934), when the group first seemed to flourish but then faltered and disappeared.[1]

After many months of discussion and planning among a diverse group of Swedish American academic, business, church, and professional leaders from across the Upper Midwest (including Aksel Josephson, Johan A. Enander, C. G. Wallenius, G. A. Andreen, G. N. Swan, David Nyvall, and Charles A. Smith), the Swedish Historical Society of America was founded on July 22, 1905, in Chicago. From the outset, its stated purposes were "to promote the study of the Swedes in America and their descendants," to "collect a library and museum illustrating their development in America," to "issue publications relating to their history," and to "encourage the study of Swedish history and literature." Pursuant to those goals, the leaders of the Society organized annual meetings that were informational and social; recruited a national membership of over 400; collected funds almost entirely through memberships ($2.00 per year) sufficient to support their activities; published a yearbook through 1926 and a quarterly journal (of sorts) from 1928 to June 1932; and coordinated the development of a considerable monograph, periodical, clipping, and manuscript collection.[2]

For the first fifteen years of its history, the Society remained in Chicago. It held its last meeting there on April 9, 1920, however, and moved its base of operation to the Twin Cities the following year. University of Minnesota professor and historian A. A. Stomberg, who became president of the Society after the move, said that the decision was based on a number of factors, including the observation that "the Twin Cities are, and in an increasing degree will continue to be, the center of Scandinavian studies and culture in America." Probably more important in precipitating the change was an arrangement reached in January 1921 with the Minnesota Historical Society, which solved for the leaders the ongoing problem of the organization's growing library. Under the terms of this agreement, the Society's collection would be housed and cared for by the Minnesota Historical Society. The books would be classified, shelved, and possibly merged with the larger collection. Each SHSA book, however, was to contain a special identifying bookplate and could not be loaned out. Finally, it was agreed that duplicates or materials "not pertinent" could be sold or exchanged.[3]

The organization carried on its activities in the Twin Cities for thirteen years, and for a time appeared to prosper. Membership stayed at around 400 for much of the 1920s. (See Table 1.) Finances seemed sound, given the group's limited expenses. (See Table 2.) Annual meetings, often at the Minnesota Historical Society and usually in December, were held from 1922 to 1934 (except in 1932). These typically involved a lecture or two, a business meeting, and a dinner at a local hotel such as The Francis Drake or The Nicollet. Program lecture speakers and titles or topics included:

1923 Rev. J. J. Daniels (Lindsborg), "The Commission of the Swedish People in America"
Dr. A. A. Stomberg, "Early Efforts at Scandinavian Church Union in America"
1924 T. W. Anderson, "Swedish Pioneers in Kansas"
V. E. Lawson, "Early Settlements in the Kandiyohi County Region and Their Fates in the Indian Uprising of 1862"

1925 Adolph Olson (Bethel Seminary), "Educational Work among
        the Swedish Baptists in America"
      T. Blegen, "Minnesota's Campaign for Immigrants"
1926 G. M. Stephenson, "The Founding of the Swedish Augustana
        Synod"
      C. G. Wallenius, "William Henshaw"
1928 Levin Faust on the Swedes in the industrial development of
        Rockford, Illinois
      C. G. Wallenius on Swedish Americans in Illinois
      A. A. Stomberg on attitudes in Sweden towards emigration
1929 G. A. Lundquist, "Tendencies among the Swedish Population
        of Minnesota"
      Rev. J. W. Johnson, "The Immigrant Pathfinder"
1930 Dr. L. G. Abrahamson, "Svenska Historiska Sällskapet och dess
        uppgift"
      Professor David Swenson, "The Uses of Historical Study"
1931 Dr. T. Blegen, "Leaders of People in Dispersion."
      Dr. G. A. Hagstrom (Bethel Seminary), "Conserving the Treasures
        of the Past"
1932 No annual meeting was held
1933 The program was dedicated to recognizing the contributions
        of Eric Norelius
1934 G. A. Lundquist and Amandus Johnson, no titles[4]

Precisely how many people attended these meetings was not recorded. The
secretary's reports usually said something to the effect that the lectures were

---

Table 1
**SHSA Membership Compared with the
Norwegian-American Historical Association**

Year	Number	NAHA membership
1906	60	
1911	c.200	
1913	c.300	
1921–22	434 (137 in Minneapolis and St. Paul)	
1922–23	404	
1923–24	506	
1924–25	504	200
1927		842
1930	292 (c.80 in Minneapolis and St. Paul)	
1934	c.40	527
1941		929
1975		c.1000

"very interesting" or "deeply appreciated," and that the audience was "larger than usual" or the meeting was "enjoyable and interesting and well attended." In reporting the 1931 annual meeting, Secretary Conrad Peterson wrote: "The usual general spirit prevailed at the meeting which was again felt to be a suc-

Table 2
SHSA Finances

Year	Income	Expenses	
1913–14	945.59	588.78	
1914–15	649.37	588.51	
:			
1920–21	928.68	418.47	
	184.13 from Chicago	144.99 to A.S.*	
	819.87 in dues	227.76 to move	510.21 in bank
1921–22	408.89	312.84	
		264.44 to A. S.	806.16 in bank
1922–23	922.53	799.66	
	839.00 in dues	442.95 to A.S.	929.03 in bank
1923–24	218.22	623.71	
	194.00 in dues	94.79 to A.S.	
		50.00 to C.P.	523.54 in bank
1924–25	288.00	586.62	
	267.00 in dues	98.03 to A.S.	
		100.00 to MHS	
		224.92 in bank	
1925–26	467.67	537.80	
	419.00 in dues	190.69 to A.S.	91.79 in bank
	35.00 in donations		
1926–27	926.08	745.33	
	545.35 in dues	93.98 to A.S.	
	335.00 in donations to	80.96 to C. P.	272.54 in bank
	Swendsen Drive		
1927–28	547.00	565.87	
	290.00 in dues	73.75 to C.P.	253.67 in bank
1928–29	388.75	533.42	
	363.75 in dues, etc.	90.00 to C.P.	109.00 in bank
1929–30	603.75	588.76	
1930–31	350.92	468.48	117.53 deficit
1931–33	307.50	288.39	
	257.50 in dues		
	50.00 in donations		
1933–34	95.61	102.00	
	85.00 in dues		

* A. S. is Alfred Söderström; C. P. is Conrad Peterson.
Figures are based on the Secretary-Treasurer's ledger and published reports in the Society's *Yearbook* or *Bulletin*.

cess." Only for the 1925 meeting do we have numbers. Then the secretary noted that about "fifty members and friends" took part.[5]

In terms of publications during the Minnesota years, five editions of the *Yearbook* appeared between 1922 and 1926. Each contained articles and/or primary source materials related to Swedish American history. In an effort to expand this aspect of the Society's activities, the quarterly *Swedish-American Historical Bulletin* replaced the yearbook series in 1928. Secretary Peterson described the change:

> The Yearbook of the Swedish Historical Society of America, published annually, has now been replaced by the Swedish-American Historical Bulletin, to be published quarterly. One or more issues every year will be more pretentious and scholarly, and somewhat on a par with the former Yearbooks. The remaining issues will be smaller and less pretentious, and more in the form of News-Letters.[6]

In fact, two issues each year were often dedicated to scholarly articles or printings of primary sources, and ran up to a hundred pages in length. The remaining issues were only a few pages long and amounted to little more than newsletters. The hope, of course, was that eventually every issue would be lengthy. Finally, the Society's library collection continued to grow.[7]

Judging from the public face presented in the Society's activities, problems were few and none threatened the very existence of the group. Similarly, any difficulties are either missing or carry little emphasis in the records of the Society. In fact, aside from some concern with budget shortfalls, there appears to have been no sense that matters were becoming serious in the early 1930s and no clues that the group would fail in 1934. Everything seemed to be going splendidly.

In 1930, discussions about changing the name of the group to The Swedish-American Historical Society (the name first chosen in 1889) began, and a decision to do so was reached in January 1931. The leaders inserted the new name in the logo of the Society on the cover of the *Bulletin*, but did not change the name with the State of Illinois. The last issue of the *Bulletin* appeared in June 1932 and contained articles by Gunnar Westin and Amandus Johnson—but not a word about problems. The final annual

Alfred Söderström, treasurer of the Swedish Historical Society of America, 1912–27, and editor of Svenska Folkets Tidning

meeting, held at The Union at the University of Minnesota on December 1, 1934, appears to have taken place without a hint of impending doom. New governing council members were elected for terms ending in 1937. State senator and Society president Victor Lawson acted as a congenial toastmaster. Consul General Hellström greeted the group in Swedish. G. A. Lundquist and Amandus Johnson spoke. But Secretary-Treasurer Conrad Peterson knew the truth. Membership was now fewer than fifty and the Society was insolvent. His last entry in the minute book read: "This was the last meeting of the Society." There still remained an unpaid bill of $116.94, owed to Minneapolis Veckoblad Company, which the Society was unable to pay. The Veckoblad Company later went into receivers' hands.[8]

Why did the Swedish Historical Society of America cease existence? How do we account for its demise? Why was its fate different from that of the Philadelphia-based American-Swedish Historical Museum or The Swedish Colonial Society, which remain vital to the present; or of the Norwegian-American Historical Association (founded in 1925), which has a history of remarkable success in striving for virtually the same goals as the SHSA; or of the Swedish-American Historical Society (1948), which celebrated its fiftieth anniversary in 1998? There are no clear or simple answers to these questions. None of the leaders are alive to interview. The personal papers of the leaders seem to be silent. The Society's publications say next to nothing. As is so typical of organizational records, the papers of the Society are frustratingly miserly in yielding information, although they do contain indications of problems and some understanding of their causes. To an extent, we have waited too long to ask. Still, some tentative answers can be proposed.[9]

One explanation may lie in the composition of the leadership: too many academics and too few practical-minded businessmen. This view was first expressed in a series of letters from June and July 1905 between Society founders Aksel Josephson and C. A. Smith. Smith appears to have initiated the "conversation" when he suggested on June 30 that the new society should have among its founders and governing board a number of prominent and well-known Swedish Americans, such as Minneapolis judge N. O. Warner, whom Smith described as "intensely Swedish." A prominent figure in the Minneapolis business community (C. A. Smith Timber Company), he believed such persons could best direct the affairs of the society and attract other members and money. In a letter dated July 4, Josephson disagreed. He believed the first governing board of the new society should be composed of historians—to get things going and to inspire confidence among bankers, lawyers, and businessmen who were not trained to carry on the activities of a historical society. Smith appears to have been willing to compromise. He replied to Josephson saying that the affairs of the society should not be entirely in "the hands of 'writers and professors'" and that a couple of businessmen would help. (See Table 3.) In general, Smith's hopes went unfulfilled in so far as there were relatively few of those practical-minded businessmen among the Society's officers.[10]

A. A. Stomberg (academic), George M. Stephenson (academic), H. P. Linner (dentist), Theodore W. Anderson (educator/church leader), J. A. Jackson (politician), Conrad Peterson (academic), Viktor Lawson (editor/politician), and all the others who directed this group from 1921 to 1934 should not be faulted for a failure of leadership. They were volunteers with busy lives. (The only "compensated" officer was the corresponding secretary.) As professors, pastors, political leaders, businessmen, physicians, and other professionals, they lacked the time to do more, and few had the financial resources to do so.

Although the ongoing presence and assistance of more "practical" leaders may have helped, membership was more crucial, and this was also recognized from the beginning. An undated letter among the early correspondence of the Society included the seemingly prophetic statement that "unless the efforts of our Society are seconded by the Swedish Americans at large our efforts will be in vain." Secretary Conrad Peterson expanded on this in the June 1928 edition of the *Bulletin*:

> If the work of our Society is ever to compare with the work that is accomplished by other nationalities, not to mention state and even local historical societies, we are in need of a great increase in membership and general support. A vast amount of work must be done if the record of the contributions of millions of Americans of Swedish descent is to be preserved. Only a very small part of that field, the early colonial period, is adequately taken care of through the Swedish Colonial Society and the John Morton memorial. The

Table 3
SHSA Officers

Year(s)	President	Secretary	Treasurer	Corresponding-Secretary
1921–23	A.A. Stomberg	Andrew G. Johnson	C. J. Swendsen	A. Söderström
1923–26	A.A. Stomberg	Erik Dahlhielm	C. J. Swendsen	A. Söderström

	President	Vice President	Secretary-Treasurer	Editor
1928	T. W. Anderson	J. A. Jackson	Conrad Peterson	G. M. Stephenson
1929	H. P. Linner	J. A. Jackson	Conrad Peterson	A. A. Stomberg
1932	Victor Lawson		Conrad Peterson	A. A. Stomberg

N.B.: J. A. Jackson is Vice President through the entire period.

larger field of the nineteenth and twentieth centuries should receive proportionate recognition. When we reach the goal of one thousand Associate Members, each paying two dollars per year, we shall be able to do many things, now left undone, and to do things we are now doing better.

Four years later he repeated this and added two other observations when he wrote:

> In short, the Norwegian-American Historical Society is accomplishing what the Swedish-American Historical Society would have been able to accomplish if it had enjoyed wholehearted and united support from the beginning, and if the work had never been weakened by founding later organizations which are also interested in some phase of Swedish-American history and without co-ordinating these organizations.[11]

Certainly, membership was the most important and immediate problem facing the Society. Support from what was a fairly loyal membership of over 400 was present for over twenty years. This is a strikingly low figure, however, and one wonders if it was the best Swedish America could do to sustain a society dedicated to the preservation of its history. Similarly, money to support the group's activities did not pour unsolicited into its treasury. Membership and sound finances were inseparable, and in the long run both were lacking.

Still, there should have been enough people and money in Swedish America to support this group. In 1920, there were 625,580 Swedish-born and 888,497 American-born of Swedish parentage in the United States. In 1930, these numbers were 595,250 and 967,453, respectively. "Swedish stock" in Minneapolis numbered 70,463 in 1930, with 25,430 in St. Paul. Even a casual glance at the Society's financial records reveals how relatively inexpensive its operations were. For most of its history, the members' annual $2.00 dues provided funds sufficient to meet the costs of printing the periodical, subsidizing a librarian at the Minnesota Historical Society, and supporting the recruiting efforts of a corresponding secretary (see below). A stable membership of 500 or so would have been adequate; the hoped for 1,000 would have been divine.[12]

From the outset, the Society's leaders knew a stable membership and secure annual income were needed if the organization was to succeed, and they consistently hoped for more. When numbers declined, they

George M. Stephenson, director of the Swedish Historical Society of America and Professor of History, University of Minnesota, ca. 1918

responded with what they believed would be sufficiently energetic campaigns and appeals to recruit new members or raise funds. Repeatedly, the corresponding secretary was encouraged to do more. Based on a personal challenge from C. J. Swendsen, a fundraising effort among the leadership was begun late in 1926 that yielded several hundred dollars. All these attempts were conservative and limited, however. For example, as the curtain was falling in 1932, the governing council drafted a plan to identify fifty "patrons," each of whom would "pledge himself to pay any sum, not to exceed ten dollars, which might be necessary to cover any deficit due to publishing four quarterly *Bulletins.*" This sort of myopia was not unique to this Society.[13]

The problems of competing groups and lack of coordination among them are also very important—they haunted Swedish America then, and they continue to do so now. Recognizing these issues, Society leaders considered establishing a cooperative association with the American Sons and Daughters of Sweden in 1928, but dropped the idea, without explanation. What both reflect is the diversity and heterogeneity of Swedish America. Swedish American history dates to 1638 (or even earlier, if we are to believe the Kensington Runestone). Swedish America has been divided by the differences in geographic origins of the immigrants, regionalism in terms of settlement, social class, religion, political outlook, interests, age, and generation. Perhaps the very idea of a single historical society was chimerical.[14]

Other factors affecting the viability of the Society include the decline of Swedish immigration during the 1920s and 1930s, assimilationist sentiments and pressures within American society, the changing demography of the Swedish American population with growing numbers in the second and third generations who were less interested in ethnicity and the Swedish American past (or in the versions of that past portrayed by the Society), and the worsening national economic situation after 1929. The Norwegian-American Historical Association experienced similar problems during this period and again in the 1950s. Odd Lovoll partially explained these when he wrote that they were the result of "lagging interest in national diversity caused by the political and social pressures of the times."[15]

The very nature of the Society may also have worked against it. An historical society may have, in almost any context, a limited pool of potential members. Its publications may be seen as esoteric; its library collections as uninteresting and useless; it leaders as stuffy academics; its activities as dull or irrelevant.

In a similar vein but from a slightly different perspective, there may have been problems with what the Society had to offer—or did not offer. There was really only one activity, the annual meeting. The publications were not aimed at a general audience. They were for specialists and interested lay readers. Furthermore, the Society had no home, no stable or visible base of operations. Its library collection may have been at the Minnesota Historical Society, but this was not a gathering place for members. Most Swedish Americans probably wanted a good deal more than the Society had to offer and preferred activity-focused clubs. While belonging to the Society was easy and inexpensive, without regular activities and other membership reinforcements it was also easily forgotten.

For much of its history, the Society supported a policy whereby the corresponding secretary, whose principal duties were to recruit members, collect dues, and solicit donations to the library, received a "commission" of as much as 25 percent of all dues collected and was compensated for supplies and travel expenses. The officers of the Society might be faulted for this arrangement. From 1912 to 1927, Alfred Söderström held this position, and the annual financial reports reveal the hundreds of dollars he received in compensation for his efforts. (See Table 2.) Paying a person to perform similar tasks in a profit-making enterprise is one thing. Doing so in a nonprofit, volunteer organization the size of the Swedish Historical Society of America is another, especially if the drain undermined the financial viability of the group. Furthermore, if the dues were not sent in regularly or the accounts carefully kept, which became the case, a cash-flow problem could develop.

Questions about Söderström's work became increasingly frequent in the minutes of the Council meetings from 1924, and a crisis was reached in 1926–27. The questions focused on his failure to submit regular reports or send in dues received, problems probably caused by advancing age (he was in his late 70s) and declining health. At first, the secretary was asked to write to Söderström and request better reports, but the tone quickly turned cooler. In 1925, he was informed that the Society expected "regular" monthly reports, wanted the names of members who had not paid their dues, and "reserved the right to send out statements" of its own and collect dues directly. In 1927, Söderström was sacked and replaced by Professor Conrad Peterson of Gustavus Adolphus College, a man who was younger, more energetic, and incredibly thorough. To justify and facilitate Söderström's removal, the constitution of the Society was revised, collapsing the positions of secretary, treasurer, and corresponding secretary into a single office. Interestingly, the Society only solved the problems of Söderström's declining energies and efficiency with these changes. Peterson, too, received a commission on dues collected. As the Society's financial problems worsened, however, he stopped asking for his share.[16]

Did the commission policy and Söderström's decline bring down the Society? No. However, they did undermine its viability, which became increasingly fragile. Also, the conflicts with Söderström may have cost the Society members it could hardly afford to lose. The cantankerous old journalist, freelance writer, author, and publisher had many friends in Swedish America. He had been modestly successful in the Midwest in recruiting members and in securing donations of books and other materials for the Society's library. He complained bitterly about his treatment to the Council, and one cannot help think that he told others about what he took as insults. (See Table 1.) Between 1925 and 1930, membership in the Society had declined by more than 200 persons.

The personality factor that is evident in the Söderström case raises another question, the answer to which may provide other clues about the Society's collapse. Were there serious conflicts among the leaders of the group? Here the organizational records are mute. Only the resignation of George Stephenson as a member of the Council in late 1930 and his disappearance as editor and writer from the pages of the *Bulletin* arouse suspicions of deepening troubles. It would be very surprising, however, if there were no conflicts. The Society, its officers, and its governing board were microcosms of an eclectic Swedish America. They included Lutherans, Baptists, Mission Covenanters, Republicans, Democrats, professionals, academics, older and newer generations. Conflicts growing from this diversity certainly could have eroded the group's cohesiveness and contributed to a collapse at its core. It would not have been the first or only Swedish American organization to be pulled apart by the heterogeneity of Swedish America.

In the broader scheme of Swedish American life, with all its complexities in America and the Twin Cities, the Society must have occupied a very small space, its membership and activities overshadowed by larger, more active, and more popular groups. Clearly, however, we are left with more questions than answers about its demise. We know the membership of the Swedish Historical Society of America fell below a critical point capable of sustaining its limited activities. We know the general environment was unfavorable and there were too many organizations trying to do similar things nationally. We know that capable and well-meaning leaders lacked forcefulness, practicality, time, or the willingness to contribute significant amounts from their own resources to sustain the Society. We know the financial situation could have been improved and a possible loss of members avoided by an earlier response to the commission question and Alfred Söderström's decline. In general, one can say that circumstances, location, mistakes, and accidents combined to bring about the Society's collapse. Beyond these explanations we have, so far, only suspicions and conjecture.[17]

* * * *

NOTES

1. Notice of this founding appeared first in *Gamla och nya hemlandet* on Oct. 12, 1889. A longer article appeared on Nov. 2, 1889. The group was incorporated in Illinois under the name Swedish American Historical Society in Nov. 1889. Neander N. Cronholm, John A. Enander, O. G. Lange, P. A. Sundelius, Jakob Bongren, Samuel A. Freeman, Herman Lindskog, Charles J. Sundell, and Hans Mattson were listed as the founders. In July 1902, state authorities cancelled the group's charter for failing to file an annual report and pay a $1.00 fee, but the charter of incorporation was not revoked nor was the name removed from the records. In June 1937, State authorities dissolved the corporation.

2. The Swedish Historical Society of America was incorporated on Apr. 10, 1908, and dissolved by the State of Illinois on June 9, 1937. For a survey of its history, see Roy Swanson, "Our Predecessors," *Swedish Pioneer Historical Quarterly* 1 (1950): 12–21. The founders first chose to call their organization The Swedish-American Historical Society. When they went to incorporate the society in Illinois, however, they discovered that name was already taken by a group founded in 1889, hence they chose the name The Swedish Historical Society of America. The revised constitution appears in *Swedish-American Historical Bulletin* 1 (1928): 94ff.

3. Quotation from A. A. Stomberg in the "President's Report," *Yearbook 1921–1922* (Minneapolis: Minneapolis Veckoblad Publishing Company, 1922), 99. Much of the Society's collection had been housed at the Swedish Methodist Seminary in Evanston during the Chicago years. Part of it, however, found its way to Denkman Library at Augustana College in Rock Island, Ill. Following what Stomberg describes as lengthy negotiations resulting from a "misunderstanding," Augustana College directors agreed to transfer this portion of the Society's holdings to St. Paul (*Yearbook 1921–1922*, 101). The agreement was signed by A. A. Stomberg and Andrew G. Johnson for the SHSA, and by Frederik A. Fogg (President) and S. J. Buck (Secretary) for the MHS. For a copy, see Swedish Historical Society of America, Records and Collected Papers, minutes, vol. 31, MHS.

4. Swedish Historical Society of America, Records and Collected Papers, minutes, vol. 31, MHS.

5. Ibid., Secretary's minutes, vol. 32, Dec. 7, 1928, and Dec. 5, 1930, respectively; Secretary's minutes, vol. 32, Dec. 12, 1931; Secretary's minutes, vol. 31, Dec. 2, 1925.

6. *Swedish-American Historical Bulletin* 1 (1928): 2.

7. For a discussion of the subjects and contents of these publications, see Byron Nordstrom, "Swedish America: Changing Perspectives," in *Nordics in America: The Future of Their Past*, ed. Odd Lovoll (Northfield, Minn.: Norwegian-American Historical Association, 1993), 90–99; *Yearbook, 1922–1927*; *Swedish-American Historical Bulletin*, vols. 1–5 (1928–32). On the development of the library, see the accession records, Swedish Historical Society of America, Records and Collected Papers, vol. 1–4, MHS.

8. Swedish Historical Society of America, Records and Collected Papers, minutes, vol. 32, Jan. 5, 1931, MHS; Conrad Peterson, Secretary-Treasurer records.

9. For a brief history of the Norwegian-American Historical Association, see Odd Lovoll and Kenneth Bjork, *The Norwegian-American Historical Association 1925–1975* (Northfield, Minn.: Norwegian-American Historical Association, 1976). The stated goals of this group have been "to collect and disseminate information about the people in the United States of Norwegian birth and descent and to preserve the same in appropriate forms as historic records" (17). Although the group has experienced two periods of membership decline, its financial position has been sound and its record of publication remark-

able. To date I have only explored the papers of Conrad Peterson, the Society's Secretary-Treasurer from 1927 and long-time history professor at Gustavus Adolphus College. They are meager, indeed, on this subject. Those of A. A. Stomberg, G. M. Stephenson, Victor Lawson, and others may contain additional information.

10. Swedish Historical Society of America, Records and Collected Papers, correspondence, MHS.

11. "Dear Sir," unsigned and undated letter, ibid.; quotation from *Swedish-American Historical Bulletin* 1 (1928): 7f.; quotation from Conrad Peterson's report on the annual meeting of the Society in the *Swedish-American Historical Bulletin* 5 (1932): 5.

12. Sture Lindmark, *Swedish America 1914–1932: Studies in Ethnicity with Emphasis on Illinois and Minnesota* (Stockholm: Läromedelsförlagen, and Chicago: The Swedish Pioneer Historical Society, 1971), 28, 31.

13. *Swedish-American Historical Bulletin* 5 (1932): 7.

14. Swedish Historical Society of America, Records and Collected Papers, minutes, vol. 32, MHS.

15. Lovoll and Bjork, *Norwegian-American Historical Association*, 31.

16. Swedish Historical Society of America, Records and Collected Papers, minutes, vol. 31, MHS. See the Secretary's minutes of the meetings of the Council for Mar. 5, 1924; Feb. 6, 1925; May 25, 1925; and Jan. 28, 1926.

17. Support among Minnesota Swedish Americans for an historical society reemerged in 1948 with the founding of The Swedish Pioneer Historical Society (since 1982 The Swedish-American Historical Society). Throughout this organization's history, many members, leaders, advisors, contributors to its publications, and participants in its conferences have come from the Twin Cities.

Swan Johan Turnblad and the
Founding of the American Swedish Institute

NILS WILLIAM OLSSON & LAWRENCE G. HAMMERSTROM

Swan Johan Turnblad typified the alert, industrious, and clever Swedish new-comer who arrived in the United States with little money but by dint of pluck, ability, and industry was able to rise from his Swedish peasant background and eventually reach a pinnacle of material success. This essay will describe his life and highlight his career, which ultimately was to benefit the Swedish American community in the Twin Cities well beyond the donor's initial dreams.

Sven Johan Olofsson, who sometimes may have used his father's patronymic of Månsson, was born in Tubbemåla in Vislanda Parish, in the county of Kronoberg on October 7, 1860, the son of Olof Månsson, a farmer, and his second wife, Ingegerd Månsdotter. Sven Johan was the youngest of the eleven children born in Olof Månsson's two marriages. Peter Olofsson, a half-brother of Sven Johan, born in Brohult, Vislanda Parish, on June 1, 1839, had emigrated to the United States in July 1864 with his wife, Catharina Jonsdotter, and had settled in Vasa Township of Goodhue, Minnesota, where he assumed the surname Turnblad.[1]

In 1867 Sweden suffered a period of unseasonably cold weather, which extended into the summer and autumn and virtually eliminated the chance of the farmers being able to harvest even enough to supply seed corn for the following year. The weather did an about-face in 1868, providing a summer of scorching heat that dried up any semblance of a crop. Famine became prevalent and entire families took to the highways and byways seeking their sustenance by begging.

The resultant scarcity of food caused thousands of Swedes to look westward to America, where free land was available thanks to the recently enacted Homestead Act of 1862, which was to provide the magnet in attracting Swedish immigrants to the Middle West. Olof Månsson in Vislanda was one of thousands of Swedish farmers who left famine-ridden Sweden for a better life across the sea. He arrived in New York, together with his family, on September 25, 1868, aboard the *S. S. City of New York* out of Liverpool. Some of the names of the children and their ages are garbled and both Sven Johan and his sister Anna Catharina are missing on the manifest. Nevertheless, there is no doubt that it refers to the emigration of Olof Månsson Turnblad (on the manifest spelled Tunbbad) and his family. Of some interest is the fact that among the passengers traveling in the cabin class was Ole Bull, the noted Norwegian violin virtuoso.[2]

Olof Månsson Turnblad and his family settled in Vasa Township, Goodhue County, Minnesota, where Peter Olofsson Turnblad had settled four years earlier. Vasa was a thriving Swedish community founded by Eric Norelius, one of the prominent church leaders in the Augustana Lutheran Synod. Sven Johan now Americanized his first baptismal name, calling himself Swan. Very little is known of his early life, except that he was confirmed in the Swedish Lutheran church in Vasa in May 1876. A year later, at the age of seventeen, he obtained a printing press and printed a book on arithmetic for his teacher, P. T. Lindholm.[3]

Swan Johan Turnblad left Vasa in 1879 and moved to Minneapolis, which was to be his home until his death. The 10th Federal U. S. Census of 1880 lists him as a boarder living with his brother-in-law, Charles Fridlund, and his wife, Mary. The following year, the *Minneapolis City Directory* lists him as a compositor at *Minnesota Stats Tidning*, a Swedish American newspaper published in Minneapolis. On April 28, 1883, Swan Johan married Christina Gabrielsdotter, born in Offerdal Parish in Jämtland on February 25, 1861. A daughter, Lillian Zenobia, was born in Minneapolis on September 2, 1884, and on November 1 of the same year Swan Johan filed his intention of becoming a citizen of the United States.[4]

On January 31, 1885, articles of incorporation for the Swedish American Publishing Company were filed with the Minnesota Secretary of State by a group of eleven men interested in furthering the cause of temperance. The first issue of *Svenska Amerikanska Posten* appeared on March 10 of the same year, devoted "to the promotion of temperance, good morals, and the elevation of society." The founders, however, were inexperienced in business, and for a while it appeared as if the newly organized newspaper

Swan Johan Turnblad with his wife, Christina Gabrielsdotter, and daughter, Lillian Zenobia, ca. 1890

would have to cease operations. About this time, Swan Johan appeared on the scene, and, by purchasing ten shares of stock in the venture, he was elected manager. He had now entered a career that was to occupy his time, efforts, and energy for the next forty years—first as manager, then editor, and finally publisher.[5]

Turnblad was an innovative and aggressive business manager and was the first in the annals of the Swedish American press to use the Linotype machine and the rotary press. He expanded the newspaper and hired editors who were strong personalities, including Gustaf A. Wicklund and Emil Meurling. By 1894 he had altered the politics of the paper from prohibitionist to independent Democratic, and under his leadership the circulation increased from 1,400 to 40,000 by the end of the century. It was to keep climbing, and by the early twentieth century reached an all-time high of 55,000, thus emerging as the largest and most successful of all Swedish American newspapers. Turnblad was the first to introduce color in its pages, and even attempted for a brief while to publish a daily Swedish American newspaper.

Despite the paper's success, Turnblad reported to the board of directors that it was in financial straits, thus prompting some of the directors to forfeit their stock or to sell their shares at depressed prices. The buyer was Turnblad, who by 1888 had become the principal stockholder. On October 19, 1897, *Svenska Amerikanska Posten* had been sold to Christina Turnblad, who in turn transferred it to her husband on February 5, 1901.

Meanwhile, Turnblad turned his attention to real estate. In 1892 he purchased property at 1511 Stevens Avenue; three months later he acquired a building permit for $22,000 to construct a three-story brick block of flats. He bought the last remaining lot in Loring Park in 1899 for $25,000, hoping to build a fine residence, but his hopes were dashed when the Minneapolis Park Board threatened to condemn the property and offered to redeem it for $15,000. After three years of litigation, Turnblad lost in the Minnesota Supreme Court and was awarded $13,465.83, which he accepted. In 1903, Turnblad bought six lots at 2600 Park Avenue for the purpose of building a residence, paying $10,000 for the land. He obtained a building permit in the amount of $50,000, as well as an additional $10,000 for the construction of a carriage house. He now began to construct the mansion that eventually was to become the home of the American Swedish Institute. The construction proceeded by fits and starts, frequently interrupted by liens filed against Turnblad by various contractors and suppliers. The residence was finally ready for occupancy in 1908.[6]

The magnitude of Turnblad's real estate holdings (he had bought various plots in townships 43 and 44 in Pine County, Minnesota, for $54,150) reached the ears of disgruntled shareholders. Having been informed of the fragile economy of the newspaper, they had sold their shares or forfeited them for non-payment of the stock assessment. They came forward in 1908, one after the other, claiming fraud and chicanery on the part of Turnblad, suing for amounts varying from $6,000 to close to a million dollars. Though the Minnesota Supreme Court dismissed the largest claim, Turnblad lost some of the other suits. By 1911 he had become quite discouraged, writing to his brother Magnus that there was a possibility of his losing everything. By the end of the year, he finally was able to reach agreement with the plaintiffs: Turnblad was to turn over the property in Pine County and pay $20,000. Additional suits totaling more than $100,000 were also settled.[7]

The next decades comprised a period of relative calm in the turbulent life of Turnblad. He was appointed to the Minnesota State Board of Visitors by Governor Adolph Eberhardt and served as a colonel on the staffs of governors John Johnson, Eberhardt, and J. A. Burnquist. In 1920, he sold the newspaper to Magnus Martinson for the sum of $150,000. Apparently the new owner was unable to carry on the publishing of the paper to the satisfaction of Turnblad, and in 1927 the former owner was back as president, general manager, publisher, and editor of *Posten*.[8]

As Swan Johan grew older, he began to think more and more about the future of his newspaper and the mansion on Park Avenue. Between 1925 and 1929, he consulted frequently with the Swedish consul, Nils Leon Jaenson. Turnblad suggested at first that he donate the mansion to a Swedish institution, provided an amount of $100,000 could be raised. The consul reported to the Swedish authorities that raising such a large sum was unrealistic, particularly since "Turnblad was not popular, and the cloistered life of the family did not help." As time went on, Turnblad became increasingly restless and offered the building to Odin, a local Scandinavian club, for a reputedly low cost. The club, however, was financially fragile and therefore declined. When a Jewish club offered to buy the residence for a considerably higher price, Turnblad turned down the offer. This demonstrates that it was not purely a financial need that motivated the sale, but that he wanted the building to be used by a group that shared his filial pietistic ideals. Turnblad's next move was to find a Swedish organization capable of raising $100,000; in turn, he would donate both the building and the money to that organization. His advisors attempted to convince him that even this would not work. There simply was not that kind of money available.[9]

In 1926 the Crown Prince of Sweden visited the United States to participate in the cornerstone laying of the John Morton Museum in Philadelphia. At this time, the Swedish minister in Washington, D.C., Wolmar F. Boström, visited Minneapolis in the company of the Crown Prince, at which time Turnblad hinted that he might donate the building without any conditions attached.

Later that year, Consul Jaenson hosted a party at his residence in honor of Turnblad, on which occasion he bestowed on Turnblad the Order of the North Star,
partly in recognition of his role in raising $20,000 in famine relief for the peo-
ple in Norrland back in 1902. However, Turnblad remained coy and no progress
could be reported until 1927–28. He still insisted that the donation could not be
made until money had been raised to ensure the maintenance of the building,
even though it was pointed out to him that it would be far easier to raise the
cash after the donation, rather than before.

Another matter occupying Turnblad's mind at this time was the financial
mess that Magnus Martinson had created at *Posten*. The newspaper had gone
bankrupt and was purchased by Turnblad and a few others. He then bought out
the co-owners and once again became the sole proprietor. This, plus his efforts
to redeem the sullied name of the paper, was all consuming and prevented any
pursuit of the terms of donating the mansion, his foremost dream.

By the end of 1928, Turnblad seemed to have recovered from the trauma of
the *Posten* crisis and could redirect his attention. He appeared at the Swedish
consular office in February 1929 and offered to donate the residence on Park
Avenue—its contents consisting of expensive rugs and a library of 10,000 volumes—to the Swedish government, without conditions. Jaenson was non-
plussed, but thanked Turnblad, on behalf of his government, for the generous
offer. He believed, however, that Sweden's *Riksdag* would be unwilling to finance the cost of its maintenance. Moreover, Turnblad's name would disappear
from the donation, since once the Swedish government took possession of the
building, it could do anything with the building, including arranging for its subsequent sale. In a letter to the Swedish minister in Washington, dated May 9,
1929, Jaenson referred obliquely to the Turnblad offer and its difficulties. He
did, however, add that a compromise plan had been worked out with the assistance of Turnblad's advisor, Gustaf Lindquist, which had Swan Johan's full
approval.[10]

The proposed agreement stated in essence that Turnblad would turn the
residence and its contents over to a Swedish American foundation that would
have "a moral guarantee from the Swedish State recognizing the valuable assistance Swedish Americans have shown in the peopling and the development
of the American nation, thereby honoring the land of their fathers." Furthermore, the Swedish Crown Prince would serve as a patron of the new organization. The Swedish government, once the organization had been incorporated
and sufficient funding had been assured, would loan the fledgling institution
works of art, preferably Swedish, and lend a hand in providing assistance and
advice to create an awareness of Swedish cultural life in general. Finally, referring to Turnblad's impatience and frustration, the consul suggested that a let-

ter of encouragement from the Crown Prince be sent to Turnblad. Through the instrumentality of the Swedish Foreign Ministry, as well as the Prince's adjutant, the Crown Prince wrote Turnblad on July 22, 1929, and expressed his pleasure at hearing of Turnblad's intended donation. He also promised to become patron of the new organization, provided that two conditions were met. First, Turnblad must put his commitment in writing; second, sufficient funding must be raised to guarantee the future of its maintenance and operations.[11]

Nothing could have pleased Turnblad more than the receipt of the royal letter. He soon paid a visit to the consulate to set in motion the mechanics of the donation. J. A. Burnquist, the former governor of Minnesota, was asked to draft the charter documents for the founding of the "American Institute of Swedish Arts, Literature and Science. Founded by Swan J. Turnblad." (This name would be changed at a later date to the American Swedish Institute.) Once again the discussions among Turnblad's advisors and the consulate were stalled because he insisted that the $100,000 be raised within six months to a year before the donation of the new institute to the board of directors would actually occur. Negotiations also almost came to a stop because of Christina Turnblad's much lamented illness and death in the fall of 1929.

Several weeks after his wife's funeral, Turnblad again paid a visit to the consulate, this time prepared to drop any conditions attached to the donation. He asked the consul to communicate with several influential Swedish Americans

The American Swedish Institute, 2600 Park Avenue, Minneapolis

on a national basis for the purpose of signing the charter. This correspondence naturally took time, and it was not until November 30, 1929, that the charter document was finally registered with the Minnesota Secretary of State.

Meanwhile, detailed negotiations concerning a reasonable solution to the maintenance and operation of the donated property continued. Turnblad indicated that he might be willing to make a second donation, this time including not only the newspaper, *Svenska Amerikanska Posten*, but also the valuable real estate in downtown Minneapolis housing the printing plant. After additional difficult negotiations, Turnblad agreed to consolidate it all into a single donation, which was made public on December 9, 1929. The real credit in this four-year period of sporadic yet intense negotiations belongs to Turnblad's advisor, Gustaf Lindquist, and the Swedish consul, Nils Leon Jaenson. They charted the way to make the American Swedish Institute a reality, based on the generosity of one family's philanthropic gift and love of Swedish culture.

✳ ✳ ✳ ✳

NOTES

1. Vislanda parish, Kronoberg län, birth records, Church of the Latter-day Saints, microfilm, roll 144620.
2. Passenger lists of vessels arriving at New York, Sept. 8–25, 1868, Church of the Latter-day Saints, microfilm, roll 175657.
3. Swedish-American Lutheran Church Records, Minnesota Conference, Vasa Lutheran Church, ASI, microfilm, roll 20.
4. Minneapolis city directories 1881–1933, Minneapolis Public Library; Offerdal parish, Jämtland län, birth records, Church of the Latter-day Saints, microfilm, roll 134854.
5. Swedish American Publishing Company, Articles of Incorporation, Book K, 531–34, Minnesota Secretary of State's Office.
6. Proceedings 1901–1902, Board of Park Commissioners, Minneapolis; Deed Book 569: 329, Public Records Division, Hennepin County; Permit D37421, Inspector of Buildings, City of Minneapolis.
7. Deed Book 25:408 and 27:8f, Register of Deeds, Pine County; Cases 16844–16857, files 49.A6.8F and 49.A6.9B, Minnesota State Supreme Court, MHS.
8. Report of the Swedish Vice Consul Nils L. Jaenson on the founding of the American Swedish Institute, Dec. 31, 1929.
9. Ibid., 3–4.
10. Ibid., 10–13.
11. Ibid., 11, 14.

Brothers Whether Dancing or Dying:
Minneapolis's Norden Society, 1871–198?

WILLIAM C. BEYER

On a Wednesday evening in late January 1873, the Norden Society was gathered for its weekly meeting in a rented hall above Vanderhorck's Grocery on Bridge Square in downtown Minneapolis. The nine members present were listening to twenty-five-year-old Alfred Söderström, who had emigrated from Stockholm four years earlier. Söderström was reading aloud in Swedish his committee's draft of the procedures for the Society's new sick benefit fund. After Söderström finished reading, A. P. Anderson turned Norden's attention from illness to dancing: he proposed a motion that the Society place an advertisement in the local paper announcing that the Norden Society would host a masquerade ball in the middle of the following month. N. N. Ringdahl, who had been the first to propose the sick benefit fund the previous April, seconded dancing, and Anderson's motion for the masquerade ball passed. Minutes of the Norden Society over its one-hundred-plus-year history are filled with these juxtapositions of support and sociability. Here are three more from 1874, 1932, and 1951.[1]

At a regular Wednesday evening meeting in July 1874, Andrew G. Krogstad proposed that the Society hold a ball the following week as the only appropriate way to show appreciation to its soon-to-be past-president, C. M. Reese. As the members spiritedly discussed the ball, according to the minutes, they were interrupted by:

> a musical outburst in the vestibule; the door opened, and in paraded 20 or 25 ladies in party dress. After having bowed to the society's president, Mr. C. M. Reese, for whom the surprise was intended, they were immediately swept up by the members to dance a spirited waltz. . . . the dancing continued energetically, speeches were raised [periodically], and the food and drink on the bountiful tables were consumed readily. The meeting was adjourned in good order *at 4 in the morning.*

After an identical surprise by eighteen young women two weeks later at a Monday night meeting (the effects of this surprise lasted until 3:00 A.M.), most of the twenty members present "expressed their intention to attend faithfully the regular business meetings of the Society in the future." During an uninterrupted business meeting not long after, Norden's members changed their bylaws to establish a "Relief Komite" of three. The committee was charged to "investigate and report to the society all cases of illness [among members] and attempt to provide help to each and every one in need."[2]

Almost a half-century later on February 21, 1932, in the midst of the Great Depression, some thirty representatives convening as the Grand Lodge of all four (by that time) local Norden lodges, considered the case of a member who died, leaving his family in "difficult circumstances." After rejecting a proposal to loan the family $100 indefinitely, the representatives decided that Norden as a whole would sponsor a dance to raise money for the family. And, as a final example, at the end of 1950 through most of 1951, the minutes show the men of Norden receiving regular reports on the health of their "brother," Herman Johnson. They took up a collection as a Christmas gift for Johnson; heard the Society's president urge them to "visit Herman and all the other sick brothers[,] for that matter[,] because time is heavy on their hearts;" learned that Johnson was worried about his worsening finances; and finally, when "Br.[other] Johnson" died before Norden members could hold a benefit dance they had been discussing, the members took up a collection for his widow.[3]

For over a hundred years, Norden's meeting minutes record such humble entries in United States social welfare history. They show business meetings routinely beginning with a report on sick or dead members and then turning to planning dances, theatrical evenings, and singing performances; debates, fairs, and a lending library; picnics, crawfish parties, and turkey raffles; softball games, bowling teams, and fishing trips—and dances, almost to the end in the 1980s, dances.

The historical literature on mutual aid organizations, including Swedish American mutual aid societies, is not extensive. Without looking at Norden specifically, Ulf Beijbom has portrayed in several publications the Swedish American secular organizational life of which the Norden Society was a part. Timothy J. Johnson has sketched the history of the Independent Order of Svithiod, much larger than Norden but similarly motivated, that was founded in Chicago in 1881. Wesley M. Westerberg used Norden specifically in 1976 to illustrate the relationship between Swedish American religious and secular organizations, as well as to set a visionary agenda for those secular organizations.[4]

The purpose here is to link the experience of Norden, and by implication organizations like it, to the history of social welfare in the United States. Like

the incidents just glimpsed, Norden's history shows United States social welfare history from the bottom up, as well as from the inside out. Both of these
perspectives have been too seldom employed, according to Clarke Chambers's
essay, "Reflections on the Course and Study of Welfare History," delivered in
1992 as the sixteenth annual *Social Service Review* lecture at the University of
Chicago. Chambers finds "historical writing on welfare themes" too similar to
"military history tradition—analyses of battles and wars with little reference to
company commanders, platoon leaders, and common soldiers." According to
Chambers, historians have consistently undervalued the "informal systems of
kith and kin" as well as "formal mutual and self-help societies." The resulting
written histories, he argues, contribute to the "persisting belief" in the United
States that:

> the needy are somehow different from "the rest of us." They are perceived
> not to share the dedication to work, thrift, prudence, self-reliance, and other
> characteristics that define an American middle-class ethic and standard. Po-
> tential recipients of assistance appeared to be not only of different habits
> and life-styles but different as well in religion, nationality, and race. . . . In ob-
> jective fact, of course, the poor were often merely persons down on their
> luck, persons who shared mainstream values with those who enjoyed higher
> and more secure income, just as today the "new poor," who have suffered a
> decline in their living standards owing in substantial part to systemic changes
> in technology and global competition, continue to cling to middle-class ideals
> and goals.

When the predominantly working- and lower-middle-class men of Norden had
to cope with economic uncertainties or began to slip toward poverty through
illness or hard luck, these men reached out to one another. Amid the uncertainties, they first dignified each other with "Herr" (Swedish for "mister") and
then, from approximately 1890 onward, they drew closer rhetorically and
claimed each other as "Brother." When sick and dying, and often when poor,
these men ministered to each other.[5]

   The Norden Society is one expression of the shift in work and demograph-
ics that emanated from Europe to immigrant receiving countries beginning in
the 1700s. Primarily urban workers throughout Europe, and the new countries
to which the workers emigrated, responded to industrialization and population
increases by creating safety nets for themselves. John Bodnar looks to American conditions in the nineteenth and early twentieth century as responsible for
mutual self-help in the United States; both Günther Sollinger and Torkel Jansson, however, see capitalism and industrialization stimulating mutual self-help
wherever they appeared. Opportunities to succeed also entail risks of failure,
which in turn engender efforts to minimize the risks.[6]

Ulf Beijbom's characterization of Swedish American social organizations in the nineteenth and early twentieth centuries fits Norden almost exactly: urban, male, secular, benefit giving, and small. As unmarried immigrants were attracted to the expanding labor markets of American cities, Beijbom explains, they included large numbers of young men who were not especially religious or who felt excluded from family-centered church activities. They faced sickness and unemployment without familial or church support. These men, then, formed many different organizations with relatively few members and with mutual aid, most often sickness and burial benefits, as a response to their vulnerability as well as a recruiting tool for wider membership.[7]

Norden, like many similar organizations, began with cultural activities, added sickness and burial assistance, and then expanded that assistance to include a death benefit for members' wives. These hedges against disaster, however, seem to have been far from the minds of the founders, five young Scandinavians, both men and women, who began what they called the Minneapolis Skandinavisk-Dramatiska Förening (Minneapolis Scandinavian-Dramatic Society) on August 22, 1870. These young people set out to further education and enjoyment among members, as well as among the larger Scandinavian American population of Minneapolis and its twin city, St. Paul. Theatre performances, as the Society's name suggests, were the primary means for spreading the enjoyable education that the members sought. Within four months of the Society's founding, forty-three men and twelve women had performed in Norden's name two different Norwegian plays, one in Minneapolis and the other in St. Paul. Six months after the first meeting, the members incorporated on February 23, 1871, as Föreningen Norden (The Norden Society). The name is shrewdly taken. As the most inclusive name for Denmark, Finland, Iceland, Norway, and Sweden, "Norden" welcomes widely all who would claim a grand Viking heritage.[8]

By 1872, the majority of the membership was men, and their reasons for gathering had gone beyond performing plays, which would remain a mainstay for some time but not be the defining activity. The women withdrew as members, and Norden remained all male for the rest of its existence. Norden acknowledged this shift, and its membership becoming wholly Swedish, as stipulated in a new constitution in 1877, when it restricted the Society to men of Swedish descent.[9]

From the 1880s to World War I, membership held at 100 to 150, with anywhere from twenty to forty members at each meeting. In 1903, a group of Norden members living on the north side of Minneapolis organized a second lodge, "Vega," to meet nearer their homes, and the other members on the east side of Minneapolis continued to meet but now saw themselves as local lodge "Norden #1." From 1903 to 1951, the Norden Society consisted of local lodges and a "Grand Lodge" made up of representatives from the locals. Eventually there were four locals spread around the city: "Norden" on the east side, "Vega" to the north, "Klippan" in the southwest suburb of Hopkins, and "Friendship" on the south side of Minneapolis, organized in 1936.[10]

At its peak membership in 1930, Norden's four lodges numbered 711 paid-up members (a total of 805 were on the rolls). Even at this high-water mark, Norden ought to be seen as a local of locals in contrast to the three biggest Swedish American "fraternal benefit societies" in 1930: The Independent Order of Vikings and The Independent Order of Svithiod each had 15,000 members throughout the United States, and The Vasa Order of America counted 72,000 members in both the United States and Sweden. The scale of the Vasa Order meant that it could exhibit many of the features of the most successful fraternal societies, whatever their ethnic origins: a national board, multi-million dollar assets, a monthly newspaper, a youth division, even an old-age pension product to supplement sick and death benefits.[11]

By 1942, the Norden Society perceived itself to be in difficulty, with merely fifteen new members the previous year and $50 in the Grand Lodge treasury. By January 1946, the Grand Master of the Grand Lodge was talking officially about "putting all [Norden] Lodges into one big Lodge." In fact, Norden had considered mergers in the past—in 1883 with Svenska Bröderna, in 1886 and 1891 with Gustavus II Adolphus Lodge, and in 1931 with Svithiod—and it again would consider merging in 1954 with Gustavus II Adolphus Lodge. Each of these possible external mergers was set aside. In April 1946, however, the smallest Norden lodge, Klippan, whose members came from the southwest part of the metropolitan area, joined together with those in the south-side local Friendship, because Klippan's membership had dropped, seemingly irrevocably, to fifteen by 1946 from twenty-five in 1938. The other three lodges would consolidate for the same reason in 1951. In 1978, Wesley M. Westerberg reported Norden to have seventy-five members. Thirty-one were over eighty years old, averaging more than eighty-six, and the other forty-four averaged sixty-six. Meeting twice monthly, they held together, Westerberg observed, "for built-in camaraderie and the sick benefits." The minutes deposited in the archives of the American Swedish Institute in Minneapolis end abruptly on September 8, 1980. Norden seems to have disappeared shortly afterward.[12]

Westerberg's observation holds true for the whole of Norden's long life: Norden's papers at the American Swedish Institute demonstrate again and again that the social aspect of the members coming together was every bit as important as the modest financial benefits. The meeting minutes show ample discussion of planning for a dance club, Grand Lodge picnics, card parties with dance, the baseball team, a chicken dinner ("if some difficulty about dancing can be ironed out"), fishing trips, and signs of simple good fellowship: "As there was no more business," the Friendship lodge's minutes for June 12, 1939, record, "the members entertained themselves telling stories." In the papers, tavern keepers' bills for beer at meetings are mixed with physicians' certifications of illness.[13]

While these men enjoyed each other's company, they also took seriously the misfortunes of their brothers. In 1873, for example, Norden's president called an extra meeting the day after a "Herr Bargman" died, and, since Bargman had no family or relatives in Minneapolis or St. Paul, Norden assumed responsibility for his burial. Members organized, financed, and attended the funeral—and they sent to his parents back in Europe his pocket watch and several other small belongings. The minutes of the Friendship lodge in the 1940s provide other examples:

> Åhlen was present. He is getting better but very slowly. He hopes to get work again soon. He was paid two weeks sick ben.[efit] in the 2nd class, Sept 10 to 24.

> Howard Johnson was severely burned in a blow torch explosion. . . . Members urged to visit Johnson.

Brother Johnson's slow recovery was aided by visits from Norden members, and, during the six months after the accident, they sold tickets throughout the Swedish American community in Minneapolis and St. Paul for a benefit that raised $396 to send Johnson to a warmer climate when released from the hospital. When necessary, these brothers were as adept at showing circumspect concern as they were at organizing big fund-raising events:

> Bro.[ther] Mike Olson reported in bad financial condition. Motion made, 2nd & carried to make check for $10 & leave it with Bro. Cha[rle]s Lind, with discretion to him as to whether or not [to] deliver it.

Norden members were prepared to help, but also were careful not to embarrass Mike Olson and thereby add to his difficulties. The thoughtfulness shown to lodge brothers Åhlen, Johnson, and Olson is not unusual: several thank-you notes from families appreciative of kindnesses on the occasion of a father's or husband's death are extant in Norden's papers.[14]

Norden's sociability and support, however, were not without limits. These limits were drawn first in 1872 between genders, as already noted, and then variously along lines of nationality, resources, conduct, and over-arching values. After 1877, the Society emphasized its Swedishness despite its pan-Nordic name. While the Swedes, Norwegians, and Danes who began the Minneapolis Skandinavisk-Dramatiska Förening in 1870 and reformed it into Norden in 1871 had much in common, meetings could be cumbersome. Presenting a new constitution in 1875, for example, required reading aloud alternately in Swedish and Norwegian all twenty-seven paragraphs. Meeting minutes until 1877 were kept:

one period by a Norwegian, the next by a Swede, and the third time by a Dane, which meant that when a Swedish acting secretary should read aloud the minutes written by his Norwegian brother, it sounded as if a child were beginning to learn the first lines of his ABC book.

After Norden became an exclusively Swedish organization, things were at once simpler and richer.[15]

Norden could eventually become, for example, a dependable supporter of Swedish American institutions such as *Svenskarnas Dag* (Swedish Day), which has demonstrated Swedish American solidarity across organizational lines in a day-long celebration each summer since 1934, and the American Swedish Institute, which since 1929 has been one of the most important expressions of Swedish American life in the Twin Cities. The 1877 constitutional provision restricting membership to men of Swedish descent stood until 1950, when the Society voted to extend membership to "non-Swedes married to Swedish women." The change was justified by pointing to declining immigration from Sweden since the 1920s and to increasing intermarriage with other nationalities by second- and third-generation Swedish Americans. The change, however, did not alter the Swedishness of Norden. When the last three local lodges consolidated in 1951, for example, one adjourned its final meeting with the Swedish national anthem, "Du Gamla, Du Fria," and, at *Svenskarnas Dag* in June 1980, Norden's 110th anniversary was celebrated by having the Society's seal appear on the front of the *Svenskarnas Dag* program book at that most public of Swedish American events in the Twin Cities.[16]

Monetary resources defined Norden at least as much as national identity. The Society, for example, set aside *ålderdomsfrågan* (the question of the aged) in 1930 because "the size of the membership and of the treasury do not allow us to take too large a handful." The Depression placed severe strains on all financial institutions, and mutual aid societies were not exempt. Grand Lodge Master Frank Peterson, struck somber notes in his annual report for 1932:

> The past year has left deep tracks. Both in a social and an economic respect the so-called Depression has stretched over fraternal life. A large number of members have been suspended because of unpaid quarterly fees, no fewer than fifteen deaths have occurred, and merely sixteen new members have been inducted during the year.

Small, cautious Norden seems to have bounced like a small boat atop the sea swells of the Depression, taking water, sinking a bit, but staying afloat.[17]

A scandal that rocked the five-year-old Society in 1875 is a most vivid illustration of the members' eagerness to guard Norden's and their own respectability. At Norden's January 6, 1875, meeting, Andrew G. Krogstad, a Norwegian who clerked at McConnell & Company dry goods store, was elected president of the Society. The outgoing president included Krogstad among Norden's four members who had done the most to ensure the Society's progress. Two weeks after Krogstad's election, Martha Amondson, "a respectable young Scandinavian maiden," brought charges of "bastardy" against Krogstad in municipal court. Within days, before she could give a deposition to the court, Amondson was dead and her child stillborn. Although the criminal case against Krogstad was dropped when Amondson died, the following week a packed meeting of twenty-seven members (ten usually attended ordinary weekly meetings) voted to ask "five of the city's best men outside the Society" to serve as a jury for "Mr. Krogstad's private trial" before the Society.[18]

Two weeks later, with the jury still to meet and with another full house of members present, Norden voted to ask Krogstad to resign. Although Krogstad at first refused to step down, the membership voted to depose him, prompted by a petition from five Swedish members for Krogstad's dismissal because of the "serious charges against his morality" and because of his unwillingness to comply with the members' initially friendly request for his resignation. It is impossible to determine how much of Norden's effort to dismiss Krogstad stems from the members' outrage and how much from their discomfort with the coverage by Twin City newspapers at each step of the case of "the poor Scandinavian girl who was debauched by Krogstad," president of the Norden Society. Although the private jury could find no evidence against Krogstad, he nonetheless disappeared from Norden and from Minneapolis during 1875. Brotherhood stretched to dancing but not to debauchery.[19]

If poor Miss Amondson and the discredited Mr. Krogstad set negative limits on the expression of Norden's values, the rituals of Norden provided positive presentation of them. From at least 1874 onward, the rituals helped define what was expected of members, and they dramatized those expectations against a historical backdrop that had contemporary appeal. Norden operated from 1874 to 1885 with a ritual no more elaborate than a password, which the treasurer provided every six months to paid-up members and which the watchman asked for at the door prior to each meeting. In 1885, five members wrote (how much they borrowed from other societies is unclear) a Swedish-language ritual peopled with a chieftain, warriors, and thralls who performed in supposed Viking clothes, helmets, and spears. Apparently, in the 1930s this ritual was revised and translated into English.[20]

Both versions of the ritual open with the president asking the guards if all in attendance have a right to be present, and then, in the Swedish version, the *Ordets Kämpe* (literally, The Word's Champion) concentrates the brothers' attention on their responsibilities during meetings:

Att hava vördnad för våra förordningar lydnad för vår Hövding och de tjän-
stgörande bröderna, undvika tvister och otillbörliga yttranden, men på samma
gång ej frukta att oförbehållsamt framhålla våra uppriktiga tankar.

[To respect our regulations [and] obey our Chieftain and brothers in office,
avoid disagreements and unseemly comments, but at the same time, not fear
to put forward unreservedly our sincere thoughts.]

Broader goals of sociability and support are clearly at the center of the charge
by the master of ceremonies in the English-language revision from the 1930s:

The general purpose and plan of this society shall be to promote and improve the morals, education, benevolence and fraternal spirit of its members,
assist them in case of sickness or personal injury, and to provide a funeral
benefit in the event of death.

Even after the chieftains and thralls, the helmets and spears, exit from the revised text, the frame of reference is still exalted, as in the admonition in the
English-language closing:

The Norden Society, posed in Viking costumes, ca. 1910

Do not forget the founders of this organization, our forefathers, who so many years ago left their homes in Sweden, and founded this organization, in order that they might promote good fellowship amongst those Vikings who were willing to assume the duties that devolve upon Norden members.

The Viking heroes of a distant, glorious past are overtly equated with Norden's founding heroes of recent international migration. At one point in both versions, the officers recite in turn the Society's watchword virtues, which in the English version are clearly the attributes of a citizen of the industrial age rather than those of a warrior in an age of conquest: loyalty, honesty, quality, efficiency, justice, orderliness, and punctuality.[21]

The Norden Society never grew beyond four lodges and never became an insurance company, as did some societies that offered sick and death benefits. The men of Norden, however, did sustain each other through migration, unemployment, injury, illness, and death. The hundreds of men who comprised the Society over its more than a century of existence offered each other a mix of material assistance and social acceptance. The informal aid of their companionship was as available according to the laws of fellow feeling as the formal benefits for the sick and the deceased were readily dispensed according to the bylaws. The working- and middle-class men of Norden recognized each other as brothers, even when battered by misfortune—which challenges us to recognize them, and our contemporaries like them, as brothers, too—whether dancing or dying.

* * * *

NOTES

1. I use "Norden Society" rather than "Society Norden," which is a formulation influenced by Swedish language conventions, because the former is the reference members and others have used most commonly in English. The papers of the Norden Society, which include minutes, membership rosters, ritual books, financial records, correspondence, and photographs, are in the collections of the ASI. The four local lodges were: Norden #1, Vega #2, Klippan #3, and Friendship #5; why Friendship was numbered "5" rather than "4" is unclear from the Norden papers and secondary sources. References to the papers in these notes cite date, document with the lodge noted, if any (e.g., 1942–1951 Vega #2 Minutes), and page or file folder (ff.).

May 28, Jan. 2, and Jan. 22, 1873, 1872–73 Minutes, n.p.; Algot E. Strand, ed., *A History of the Swedish Americans of Minnesota*, 3 vols. (Chicago, 1910), 2:678; [Apr.] 1872, 1872–73 Minutes, n.p. N. P. Nelson's Treasurer's Report in 1930 (Feb. 23, 1930, 1928–37 Grand Lodge Minutes, 60) states that Norden first paid a sick benefit in 1883. Alfred Söderström, however, dates the beginning of the sick fund from Feb. 1873 (*Minneapolis minnen. Kulturhistorisk axplockning från qvarnstaden vid Mississippi* [Minneapolis: published by the author, 1899], 272) and the Norden Society's meeting minutes for Jan. 2, 1873, record passage of a motion to

(a) establish a sick benefit fund "för föreningens medlemmar" with $75 from the treasury, plus that month's dues of 25 cents per person, and (b) appoint a committee of five to draft procedures (1872–73 Minutes, n.p.).

2. July 15, 1874, 1873–77 Minutes, 45–46; July 27, 1874, 1873–77 Minutes, 50; Sept. 2, 1874, 1873–77 Minutes, 56. All translations and emphasis are mine.

3. Feb. 21, 1932, 1928–37 Grand Lodge Minutes, 118; Dec. 15, 1950, Jan. 5, 1951, Jan. 19, 1951, Feb. 16, 1951, and Mar. 2, 1951, 1942–51 Vega #2 Minutes, 319, 327 (quotation), 329, 333, 335; June 11, 1951, June 25, 1951, and Sept. 24, 1951, 1951–58 Minutes, 162, 165, 177.

4. Ulf Beijbom, *Svenskamerikanskt. Människor och förhållanden i Svensk-Amerika* (Växjö: Emigrantinstitutets vänner, 1990); *Swedes in Chicago: A Demographic and Social Study of the 1846–1880 Immigration* (Stockholm: Läromedelsförlagen, 1971); and "Swedish-American Organizational Life," in Harold Runblom and Dag Blanck, eds., *Scandinavia Overseas: Patterns of Cultural Transformation in North America and Australia* (Uppsala: Centre for Multiethnic Research, 1990), 47–67; Timothy J. Johnson, "The Independent Order of Svithiod: A Swedish American Lodge in Chicago," in Philip J. Anderson and Dag Blanck, eds., *Swedish-American Life in Chicago: Cultural and Urban Aspects of an Immigrant People, 1850–1930* (Urbana and Chicago: Univ. of Ill. Press, 1992), 343–63; Wesley M. Westerberg, "Swedish-American Religious and Secular Organizations" in *Perspectives on Swedish Immigration: Proceedings of the International Conference on the Swedish Heritage in the Upper Midwest, April 1–3, 1976, University of Minnesota, Duluth*, Nils Hasselmo, ed. (Chicago: Swedish Pioneer Historical Society and Univ. of Minn., Duluth, 1978), 199–205. Cf. Lawrence G. Hammerstrom, "Norden Society Members in Minneapolis 1903–1906," *Swedish-American Genealogist* 10 (1990): 60–72.

5. Clarke A. Chambers, "'Uphill All the Way': Reflections on the Course and Study of Welfare History," *Social Service Review* 66 (1992): 495f., 500. Throughout Norden's existence, most of its members were tradesmen, salesmen, and laborers. In 1953, for example, Norden's president was a barber, its vice-president a machinist, its recording secretary a salesman, its financial secretary a factory-hand, and its treasurer a city highway equipment operator. Edwin Eklund listed himself as "Secretary, Society Norden," an unpaid position in the 1952 Minneapolis city directory, after bouncing from one laboring job to another since 1944. See *Society Norden Directory 1953* (Minneapolis: Norden, 1953), 2; Minneapolis city directories for 1944 (p. 321); 1948 (p. 390); 1950 (p. 351); 1952 (p. 347); 1953 (p. 76, 378, 553, 994, 1315).

6. Torkel Jansson, *Adertonhundratalets associationer. Forskning och problem kring ett språngfullt tomrum eller sammanslutningsprinciper och föreningsformer mellan två samhällsformationer c:a 1800–1870* (Uppsala: Historiska Institutionen vid Uppsala Universitet, 1985), 12–21; John Bodnar, "Ethnic Fraternal Benefit Associations: Their Historical Development, Character, and Significance," in *Records of Ethnic Fraternal Benefit Associations in the United States: Essays and Inventories* (St. Paul: Immigration History Research Center, 1981), 6; Günther Sollinger, *Sjuk-och begravningskassor och andra understödskassor in Kungl. Bibliotekets Samlinger* (Stockholm: Fälths Tryckeri, 1985), 23f.; Jansson, *Adertonhundratalets associationer*, 13f. Bodnar's essay is the best survey of the characteristics of fraternal benefit societies in the United States; the most comprehensive collection of essays on immigrant fraternals is Matjaz Klemencic, ed., *Ethnic Fraternalism in Immigrant Countries* (Maribor, Slovenia: Pedagoska fakulteta, 1996). The volume edited by Professor Klemencic includes my essay, "Fraternal and National: U.S. Ethnic Fraternal Benefit Societies and World War II" (185–95), on which I have drawn for this essay.

7. Beijbom, "Swedish-American Organizational Life," 48ff., 55.

8. Söderström, *Minneapolis minnen*, 270; cover page, 1873–77 Minutes, 45f.

9. Söderström, *Minneapolis minnen*, 271.

10. Apr. 3, 1903, 1903–9 Vega #2 Minutes, 1; Feb. 5, 1936, 1936–42 Friendship #5 Minutes, 3.

It is unclear from the Norden papers and secondary sources when the Klippan Lodge was organized.

11. Feb. 22, 1931, 1928–37 Grand Lodge Minutes, 85; Beijbom, "Swedish-American Organizational Life," 62; *American Swedish Handbook* 1 (1943), 23–27; *American Swedish Handbook* 2 (1945), 34ff.

12. Jan. 14, 1942, 1937–49 Norden #1 Minutes, 208; Apr. 11, 1946, 1937–49 Norden #1 Minutes, 385 (quotation); Mar. 12, 1951, 1951–58 Norden Society Minutes, 148; Söderström, *Minneapolis minnen*, 275; Nov. 12, 1931, 1928–37 Grand Lodge Minutes, 103; Jan. 10, 1954, 1951–58 Norden Society Minutes, 296; Westerberg, "Swedish-American Religious and Secular Organizations," 203 (quotation); Sept. 8, 1980, 1967–80 Norden Society Minutes, back page. The final extant minutes tell of no organizational demise but rather recount the usual absences, hospitalization, hall rent, funeral flower bill, and checking balance, which suggests that the final book of minutes has been lost.

13. To the sick benefit fund in Jan. 1873, members paid 25 cents a month for the assurance that, if sick, they would receive $3 per week, and, if severely ill, they could count on visits and even direct care from fellow members. By 1883, ten years later, the benefit had risen to $4 per week but was restricted to eight weeks per year. In 1901, Norden began paying a funeral benefit. By the beginning of the 1930s, at the height of Norden's strength, the sick benefit had risen to $6 per week for "Class I" membership and $12 per week for "Class II" membership up to twelve months; the death benefit was $100 for a member and $25 for a member's wife. Fifty years later, as Norden drew to a close, the sick benefit had not changed appreciably—$12 per week for all members up to $150 per year and a $100 death benefit (plus flowers or $20 cash) for members only (Söderström, *Minneapolis minnen*, 270ff., 275; Feb. 26, 1933 and Mar. 11, 1931, 1928–37 Grand Lodge Minutes, 92, 150; Sept. 26, 1977 and June 9, 1980, 1967–80 Minutes, 242, 297). Feb. 2, 1876, 1873–77 Minutes, 179; Feb. 13, 1939 and Jan. 8, 1940, 1936–42 Friendship #5 Minutes, 137, 184; Oct. 23, 1939, 1936–42 Friendship #5 Minutes, 166; May 12, 1949 and July 28, 1949, 1949–51 Norden #1 Minutes, 3, 12; Mar. 10, 1941, 1936–42 Friendship #5 Minutes, 229 (quotation); July 9, 1951 and July 22, 1957, 1951–58 Norden Society Minutes, 166, 466; June 12, 1939, 1936–42 Friendship #5 Minutes, 152 (quotation).

14. Feb. 17, 23, and 26, 1873 and Mar. 12 and 26, 1873, 1872–73 Minutes, n.p.; Sept. 28, 1942, 1942–47 Friendship #5 Minutes, 7; May 12, 1941 and July 28, 1941, 1936–42 Friendship #5 Minutes, 236, 246; Aug. 11, Aug. 25, Oct. 13, and Nov. 24, 1941; Jan. 26, 1942, 1936–42 Friendship #5 Minutes, 250, 252, 259, 264, and 274; Apr. 28, 1943, 1936–42 Friendship #5 Minutes, 266.

15. Apr. 14, 1875, 1873–77 Minutes, 137; Söderström, *Minneapolis minnen*, 271, trans. mine.

16. Cf. Irma Morrison to Member of *Svenskarnas Dag* (Swedish Day), n.d. [1939], following inserted material from Norden Minutes 1937–49; Jan. 8, 1941, 1937–49 Norden #1 Minutes, 154; Nov. 8, 1954, 1951–58 Norden Society Minutes, 335; Jan. 2, 1948, 1942–51 Vega #2 Minutes, 227; untitled resolution to be presented Jan. 8, 1950, Miscellaneous Papers (quotation), ff. unmarked; Oct. 27 and Dec. 8, 1949, 1949–51 Norden #1 Minutes, 18, 19; Feb. 22, 1951, 1949–51 Norden #1 Minutes, 63; June 23, 1980, 1967–80 Norden Society Minutes, 298.

17. Feb. 23, 1930, 1928–37 Grand Lodge Minutes, 65; Feb. 26, 1933, 192837 Grand Lodge Minutes, 137.

18. For other instances of sanctioning members, see Dec. 31, 1873, 1872–73 Minutes, n.p., and July 21, 1875, 1873–77 Minutes, 155; Jan. 27, 1875, 1873–77 Minutes, 99; *Minneapolis City Directory for 1874* (Minneapolis: Campbell & Davidson, 1874), 246; "A Sad Case," *St. Paul Pioneer*, Jan. 20, 1875, p. 3 (quotation); *St. Paul Pioneer*, Jan. 22, 1875, p. 3; *St. Paul Pioneer*, Jan. 24, 1875, p. 3; Jan. 27, 1875, 1873–1877 Minutes, 99 (quotation, trans. mine). I am indebted to Professor James E. Erickson for sharing with me information about the Krogstad affair.

19. Feb. 9, 1875, 1873–77 Minutes, 107; Feb. 10, 1875, 1873–77 Minutes, 111 (quotation, trans. mine); *St. Paul Dispatch*, Jan. 25, 1875, p. 4; "Krogstad," *St. Paul Pioneer*, Mar. 14, 1875, p. 3 (quotation); *Minneapolis City Directory for 1875* (Minneapolis: Campbell & Davidson, 1875).

20. Sept. 2, 1874, 1873–79 Norden Minutes, 56f.; Jan. 7, 1885, 1879–85 Norden Minutes, 239; *Ceremonier för Föreningen Norden* (n.p., n.d.); *Rituals for Society Norden* (n.p., n.d.).

21. *Ceremonier för Föreningen Norden* (n.p., n.d.), 2, trans. mine; *Rituals for Society Norden* (n.p., n.d.), 1, 11, trans. mine; *Ceremonier för Föreningen Norden* (n.p., n.d.), 4; *Rituals for Society Norden* (n.p., n.d.), 1.

Pictures from a New Home:
Minnesota's Swedish American Artists

MARY TOWLEY SWANSON

A symbiotic network of events, organizations, patrons, and content connected the careers and art of Minnesota's Swedish American artists to their ethnic heritage. Not only did research reveal these connections, but an examination of the thirty-three artists whose work comprised the exhibition "Pictures for a New Home, Minnesota's Swedish-American Artists," at the James J. Hill House Gallery, sponsored by the Minnesota Historical Society from May 1 to October 27, 1996, also disclosed visible characteristics shared by the artists as a composite group.

Most works by immigrant artists dated from the years of the artists' artistic maturity in America, coinciding with the years of heaviest emigration to the New World (1880 to 1930). Both living and deceased artists used subject matter that was either landscapes, genre pieces, or portraits and the human figure — typical content at the time in both European and American art. Few artists depicted memories of Sweden. Instead, most recorded American subjects, paralleling content in national Swedish American art exhibitions held between 1905 and 1964. The work of immigrant artists served as visual records of acculturation to their American environment, while second-, third-, and fourth-generation Swedish American artists showed minimal and elusive ethnic images and ties.[1]

Historically, the earliest and most important influences on these artists were three official exhibitions of Swedish art that toured the United States between 1887 and 1916. Reactions to, and receptions of, these exhibitions laid the foundation for a collection of Swedish art in Minneapolis and a positive climate for Swedish American artists in the Twin Cities.

Minneapolis hosted the first official exhibition of Swedish art sent to America. Sweden shipped fifty-three paintings to the second Minneapolis Industrial Exposition in 1887, including work by noted Swedish artists Ernst Josephson

(1851–1906), Bruno Liljefors (1860–1939) and Oscar Björk (1860–1929). A reporter for the Minneapolis-based *Svenska Folkets Tidning* of September 7, 1887, proudly listed each Swedish, Norwegian, and Danish work in the exhibition but scolded Swedish American artists for not following the lead of the Norsk Konstförenin-gen, which had exhibited work from its own Norwegian American community. He wrote: "for us less active Swedes, the exhibition organized by the Norsk Konstföreingen is a beautiful example of the energy and interest for artistic en-deavors that is possible with such an organization." The reporter revealed the actual reason for his concern, explaining that an exhibition would "raise our status in American eyes." Although the Norden Society had held a series of ear-lier temporary art exhibitions in Minneapolis between 1885 and 1889, these ex-hibitions probably reached out only to their own ethnic community. The soci-ety, a fraternal benefit organization of (primarily) Swedish American men, raised money by holding raffles of drawings and paintings on exhibit in their club rooms.[2]

When in 1877 Minneapolis Industrial Exposition officials purchased Swedish artist Alfred Wallander's (1834–1906) painting, *On Their Way to Church*, from the Scandinavian section of the 1887 exposition for its own collection, they pro-vided the cornerstone for the first professional Scandinavian art collection in the Twin Cities. With the demise of the art exhibitions as a part of the indus-trial expositions in 1890, the painting was transferred to the collection of the Minneapolis Society of Fine Arts. It hung in the Minneapolis Commercial Club as early as 1909, and occasionally in the Minneapolis Public Library and the Min-neapolis Society of Fine Arts' official exhibition space until 1915. It now resides in storage at the Minneapolis Institute of Arts, a very beautiful painting in poor condition, without funds for restoration.[3]

Swedish paintings by Gustav Fjaestad (1868–1948) and Hjelmer Mas-Olle (1884–1969) were added to the Minneapolis Society of Fine Arts collection in 1916 on the initiative of the Scandinavian Art Society of Minneapolis. The paintings were purchased, however, as a result of an initial setback in 1912. That year Scandinavian American cultural leaders in the Twin Cities attempted to find gallery space for a large exhibition of noted Scandinavian artists that toured to five major American cities from 1912 to 1913 under the auspices of the Amer-ican Scandinavian Association, drawing 168,000 visitors. Although an exhibi-tion of Scandinavian design, organized through the Swedish Club of Chicago, came to Minneapolis and St. Paul during March and April 1913, the larger exhi-bition of Scandinavian paintings and sculpture did not. Disappointed that adequate space was not found in either of the Twin Cities for this important exhibition, Scandinavian Americans met to organize and raise money at a well-publicized and -attended town meeting. Headlines on the front page of the

December 7, 1912, *Sunday Journal* read: "Scandinavians Plan Gallery in Art Museum." Within the same article, a reporter quoted the enthusiastic response of John R. Van Derlip, vice president of the Minneapolis Society of Fine Arts: "It is felt by the promoters of the institute to be fitting that the first move for a permanent collection should come from the Scandinavian Americans." A prominent booster for the Scandinavian gallery, University of Minnesota president George Vincent warned, "one of the greatest dangers is that these cultural influences may disappear from America. Our effort here should be to make this city a cultural center for Scandinavians of America." The resultant Scandinavian Art Society, incorporated in February 1915, pledged over $5,000 for the support of a gallery to be placed in the future Minneapolis Institute of Arts. By 1916, *Minneapolis Journal* headlines read: "Minneapolis as Scandinavian Art Hub of U.S. Predicted."[4]

Because of the Scandinavian Art Society, Hjelmer Mas-Olle's *Dalecarlian Peasant* and Gustav Fjaestad's *Summer Evening on the River* joined Wallander's painting in 1916 to form the foundation of the Scandinavian collection. They had been a part of the Swedish segment of the San Francisco Panama Pacific Exposition, which toured American museums in 1916, opening at the Minneapolis Institute of Arts to large crowds on September 3, 1916.

Swedish art met a receptive public in the Twin Cities that fall. Headlines in the *Minneapolis Journal* reported that "Thousands Attend Swedish Exhibition at Museum." An article in the *American Scandinavian Review*, moreover, praised Minneapolis's Scandinavian cultural leaders for their initiatives, writing, "the Scandinavians in Minneapolis are keeping alive that fresh current of impulse from the Old Country without which the waters of Scandinavian culture in America would soon turn brackish."[5]

Only the first of many Swedish and Scandinavian exhibitions to tour Minneapolis and St. Paul museums and galleries, these exhibitions encouraged artists within a society that found little practical use for the fine arts. They fostered a favorable cultural climate for Swedish American artists that cannot be precisely quantified. It is interesting to note that there is no record of any other group that raised monies for an ethnic collection at the Minneapolis Institute of Arts.

Although the Mas-Olle and Fjaestad paintings were purchased by Minneapolis's Scandinavian Art Society, it is not clear from the records of the Minneapolis Institute of Arts that they were shown continuously as a unit at the Minneapolis Institute of Arts. The October 5, 1917, issue of *Allsvensk Samling* reported that Osvold Sirén, professor of art history at Stockholm University, traveled to Minneapolis that year to encourage the founding of a permanent exhibition of Swedish art in Minneapolis, having observed that the Minneapolis

Institute of Arts already had a fine collection of Scandinavian art. The Swedish works, in fact, continued to be owned by the Scandinavian Art Society and loaned to the Institute through May 1937. At that time, the remaining officer of the Scandinavian Art Society, William Mattson, asked that they be placed in the recently organized (1929) American Institute of Swedish Arts, Literature, and Science, later renamed the American Swedish Institute.[6]

These paintings were a visual influence on Minneapolis Swedish American painters, several of whom were studying at the Minneapolis Institute of Arts as early as 1915, when the school opened. Dewey Albinson (1898–1971), who began his studies in 1914 and completed them in 1918, for example, would have seen Mas-Olle's portrait of the *Dalecarlian Peasant*. Although he used coloring in his portrait of *Charles O. Roos*, 1926 (Minnesota Historical Society collection), that drew on French modernist styles of Fauvism and Cubism, the setting and posture of figures in both portraits are similar. The wooden tankard in Mas-Olle's painting is echoed in a Pueblo pot held by Roos, describing the interests of the painter's sitter.[7]

Besides the exhibitions, altar paintings in early immigrant churches were another shared visual legacy for Swedish American artists in the early twentieth century. They were often the first works of fine art that an immigrant or even second- and third-generation Swedish American would view. Most altar paintings in Lutheran churches in Sweden were of the Crucifixion or the Last Supper. These themes followed to New World churches. Church jubilee books in the archives of Gustavus Adolphus College, for example, cite and often illustrate altar paintings, but rarely name the artist. The altar painting of *Christ on the Sea of Gallilee* in the Cokato Lutheran Church, however, is an unusual example because of both its subject and the depiction of the lake, which resembled a northern Minnesota scene.

Periodicals distributed by official church publishing houses often illustrated their pages with the art of immigrant painters or well-known Swedish artists, thereby unofficially sanctioning the visual arts among the immigrant communities. Two artists in the exhibition "Pictures for a New Home: Minnesota's Swedish-American Artists," Birger Sandzén (1871–1954) and B. J. O. Nordfeldt (1878–1955), had several of their

Charles O. Roos,
portrait by Dewey Albinson, 1926

paintings and etchings illustrated in issues of *Prärieblomman* and *Ungdoms-vännen*. Both periodicals were publications of the Augustana Book Concern, the publishing arm of the Lutheran Augustana Synod.[8]

Swedish-language papers published in the Twin Cities provided additional encouragement and evidence of ethnic artistic success within its community. Their editors often printed small articles on Swedish immigrant artists who had held exhibitions in various states. For example, the front page in the January 17, 1900, edition of *Svenska Folkets Tidning* included a short article on the painter B. A. Wikstrom, who lived in New Orleans. The reporter concluded, "when the history of art in the South will be written, his name shall be at the front."

It is possible to trace a modicum of ethnic contact with every immigrant artist and most second-, third-, and fourth-generation artists in the exhibition, "Pictures for a New Home, Minnesota's Swedish-American Artists." Alfred Sederberg (1830–77), for example, left little trace of his Swedish background in Minnesota records. Probably born in Värmland, Sederberg was actively painting in Winona by the 1860s and died in Red Wing, where he had worked as a landscape and portrait painter until 1877. Sederberg probably lived and worked within that city's sizeable Swedish immigrant population. The artist had studied in Dusseldorf sometime in the late 1850s or early 1860s, as evidenced by the panoramic idealism and golden glow of his landscape, *Fort Snelling*, ca.1870 (Minnesota Historical Society collection). Similar to Sederberg in its absence of

Fort Snelling, *Alfred Sederberg, ca. 1870*

Swedish content, Otto Norquist's painting *Minnesota State Fair*, 1890 (Minnesota Historical Society collection), reflects an American scene, but the painter lived and received commissions from the Swedish American community in the heavily Swedish section of the east side of St. Paul, near First Lutheran Church and Swede Hollow.[9]

Fritiof Colling (1863–1944), in contrast, exploited his ties to the Swedish immigrant community in Minneapolis. He regularly advertised his paintings of Swedish farmsteads, American landscapes, and his three books on Swedish American life in area Swedish-language newspapers, although *North Oaks*, 1886 (Minnesota Historical Society collection), typified the more numerous American subjects painted within his *oeuvre*. Colling and Andrew Stenstrom (1880–1953) were both examples of, and had possibly been inspired by, *gåra-målare*, Swedish farmstead painters who appeared in rural areas of Sweden in the late nineteenth century.[10]

Dewey Albinson also made choices throughout his career that sporadically included ethnic content. He chose to portray *Charles O. Roos*, for example, a member of a prominent Swedish immigrant family in Taylors Falls. In 1922, Albinson painted *Shacks and Snow*, a visual recreation of the famous Swede Hollow in St. Paul, which toured Sweden in 1930 under the auspices of the

Minnesota State Fair, *Otto Norquist, 1890*

American Federation of the Arts and the American Scandinavian Society. Like Albinson, Art Institute of Chicago-trained immigrant painter Elof Wedin often chose familiar Swedish immigrant subjects when he returned to settle in Minnesota in the late 1920s. He repeatedly portrayed his wife or her grandmother, immigrant farm wife *Kaisa Johnson*, 1927 (Minnesota Historical Society collection), who lived near Waverly, Minnesota.[11]

A number of paintings in the exhibition "Pictures for a New Home: Minnesota's Swedish-American Artists" reiterate the necessity of ethnic patronage in the careers of the more nationally known Swedish American artists in Minnesota collections. For example, Chicago's Swedish community provided an environment for B. J. O. Nordfeldt's portrait of his sister *Clara* (Weisman Art Museum, University of Minnesota), painted in 1911 when the immigrant artist, who had studied in New York and England, came back to his closely-knit family in Chicago in order to find patronage for his work. Arvid Nyholm (1866–1927), who had studied at the Royal Academy of Art in Stockholm under Anders Zorn before emigrating in 1891, painted numerous portraits of prominent Swedish immigrant leaders throughout his career, including one of Minnesota governor A. O. Eberhardt (1916, Minnesota Historical Society collection). Nyholm's portrait of his wife in *The Letter*, 1915 (American Swedish Institute), however, is more freely painted than the artist's official portraits.[12]

North Oaks, *Fritiof Colling, 1886*

Not only did Swedish American artists create images from their ethnic American environment; they often chose definite American subjects that resembled views the immigrant artist had known in the Old Country. These works subconsciously provided a sense of security. New York painter John F. Carlson (1874–1945) painted scenes in Woodstock, New York, such as *Winter Landscape*, 1920 (Minnesota Museum of American Art), but admitted that he made choices that resembled his childhood home in Kolsebro, Småland. Henry Holmstrom's (1900–1981) paintings of cold Minnesota backyards such as *Zero Morning*, 1940 (Minnesota Historical Society collection), resemble areas in his native Småland. David Ericson (1869–1946), born in Östergötland but raised in Duluth, often illustrated harbor scenes that resembled Nordic ports such as *Full Moon*, 1925 (Minnesota Historical Society collection).[13]

Inspired by the activities of Swedish immigrant lumberjacks in Maine, Carl Sprinchorn (1887–1971) painted a series of fantasy scenes, including *Northern Spring*, 1921 (American Swedish Institute collection), which toured to the New Gallery in New York and the Worcester Art Museum in 1922. Like Sprinchorn, Gustaf Tenggren (1898–1970) brought memories of Swedish objects into his art. He painted Arabian sailors in a Viking ship for his illustration from *Golden Tales from the Arabian Nights*, 1957 (Kerlan Collection, University of Minnesota).[14]

While there are no records in letters or exhibition catalogs, interviews with Henry Holmstrom indicate that a group of Swedish American artists often painted together in Twin City backyards during the Depression, possibly drawn by a common ethnic heritage. Holmstrom, who shared a studio with immigrant artist Elof Wedin, worked alongside Dewey Albinson in the 1930s, then was joined by B. J. O. Nordfeldt, who taught at the Minneapolis School of Art in 1934 and became the group's leader during that short period. Nordfeldt's strong Cezannesque-influenced forms, which flattened and geometricized landscape shapes, are seen in Albinson's *Minnesota Farm*, ca. 1935 (Minnesota Historical Society collection), as well as landscapes by Wedin and Holmstrom.

Although their subject matter is purely American, the work of second-, third-, and fourth-generation Swedish American artists in Minnesota has been influenced by peripheral connections to their Swedish American heritage. Ruth Mattson Oseid Johnson (b.1939), for example, first exhibited work professionally in an exhibition of student work from Gustavus Adolphus College at the American Swedish Institute in 1958. Her paintings are collected by Richard Hillstrom, a significant patron of Swedish American and American art in the Twin Cities, and a Swedish American clergyman who at one time has owned work by at least twelve of the thirty-three artists in the exhibition "Pictures for a New Home."

Participation in Swedish American art exhibitions, based in Chicago, provided psychological and monetary support for a significant number of Swedish American artists nationally, but only a few of the Swedish American artists from Minnesota participated in the exhibitions. The Swedish-American Artists Association organized thirty-four exhibitions between 1905 and 1964 in Chicago's Swedish Club. The exhibitions toured to Minnesota in 1936, 1940, 1941, 1947, 1949, 1951, 1955, 1957 and 1961. Minnesota's Swedish immigrant artists Knute Heldner (1886–1952), along with Robert Robertz and his wife, Erna Palm, from Duluth, were the first Minnesotans to show work in 1921. Dewey Albinson exhibited in 1923 (*Mrs. Tamarack*, now owned by the Minnesota Historical Society, and *Indian Abode*); Peter Wedin in 1936; his brother Elof in 1946.[15]

Swedish American or Swedish artists with nationally-based reputations whose work resides in Minnesota collections, such as Birger Sandzén, Arvid Nyholm, John F. Carlson, Anders Zorn, and B. J. O. Nordfeldt, participated in the early Swedish American exhibitions, often winning prizes. Nyholm, Sandzén, and Zorn, for example, showed paintings in the first exhibition of 1905; John F. Carlson, Arvid Nyholm, Sandzén, and B. J. O. Nordfelt showed in the second in 1911, and the third in 1912. Carlson won first prizes in both the 1911 and 1913 exhibitions; Nyholm in 1912 and 1916; Sandzén in 1921; and Knute Heldner in 1924. Carlson, Nyholm, Sandzén, and Sprinchorn participated in the exhibition of Swedish American art that toured Swedish galleries in 1920. Works by Carlson, Sandzén, Sprinchorn, Albinson, David Ericson, Nordfeldt, Nyholm, and Heldner were chosen to travel to the Gothenburg Tercentenary Exhibition in 1923.

Representative of their gender in the early part of this century, few women exhibited with the Swedish American artists in Chicago, and there were few known women artists in Minnesota at the time. The lives of Hilma Berglund (1886–1972) and Florence Olson-Kennedy (1902–87) represent women's choices and possibilities during the first half of the twentieth century. Olson-Kennedy's story is perhaps most typical. She took a correspondence course from the Federal Art School (later the Bureau of Engraving) from 1918 to 1924, then moved to Minneapolis where she worked in commercial art establishments and as a fashion illustrator until after World War II, when she stopped to raise a family of three children. Her daughter, Pat Kennedy Crump (b.1936), a landscape painter, recalls coloring drawings her mother would make to entertain her.

Hilma Berglund, on the other hand, followed the path of women artists who decided to pursue a career, which always precluded a single life. She studied at the St. Paul Institute, then the Handicraft Guild, then the Minneapolis Institute of Art, earning a master's degree in art education from the University of Minnesota. Although she attended weaving school in Sweden and retained

Swedish influences in her work, she returned home to teach art and weaving at the University of Minnesota.

Like one's verbal and intimate behavior, an ethnic group reveals itself in visual images. The canvases of second-generation Swedish American Jack Youngquist (1918–93), who taught many years at Moorhead State University, and Swedish-born but Minneapolis-based Eric Austen Ericson (b.1920), who studied at New York's Art Students League and taught at the Minneapolis School of Art and Macalester College, would appear to show few indications or connections to their Swedish background. Upon visiting the exhibition "Pictures for a New Home: Minnesota's Swedish-American Artists" in September 1996, however, an Irish American art historian looked at their work in comparison with others in the gallery. He exclaimed: "When placed together, there's a bluish overall hue and a cool, contemplative stillness in all of the art. I'd say, cool, blue and quiet—is that Swedish American?"

* * * *

NOTES

1. In a survey of the twenty-nine extant catalogs of the thirty-three Swedish American art exhibitions held in Chicago between 1905 and 1964, only 3.8 percent of the works of art have Swedish titles.

2. The 1887 exhibition had thirty-six works by Danish artists and thirty-one by Norwegians. See *A Complete Catalogue of the Art Department of the Second Minneapolis Industrial Exposition* (Minneapolis, 1887), unpaginated. Alfred Söderström, *Minneapolis minnen. Kulturhistorisk axplockning från gvarnstaden vid Mississippi* (Minneapolis: published by the author, 1899), 266, lists the years that the organization exhibited art as 1887–93; *Svenska Folkets Tidning* printed at least four articles on the exhibition, beginning Aug. 31, 1887, through its weekly edition of Sept. 21, 1887, numbered i–iv and titled "Den skandinaviska konstutställningen vid Minneapolis Exposition." This quotation was found in the second article, Sept. 7, 1887; "Fair Organized for Purpose of Creating a Building Fund for the Society," unidentified Minneapolis newspaper clipping, dated Nov. 22, 1885, Norden Society scrapbooks, ASI. Fritiof Colling contributed a crayon portrait of the Swedish singer Christian Nilsson; N. Larson contributed a crayon drawing of Tegner and Svea; and M. Norgren "has several large and spirited marines in oil." A second unidentified article in Norden's scrapbooks was dated Oct. 30, 1889.

3. Letter dated Dec. 25, 1909, Archives of the Minneapolis Institute of Arts, requesting that the painting remain in the Commerical Club until a suitable fine arts museum would be built. The painting was donated by Mrs. F. B. Semple, Mrs. William Donaldson, B. V. Nelson, and J. B. Janney.

4. "The Art Exhibit," *The American Scandinavian Review* 1 (1913): 21. The exhibition opened in New York on Dec. 9, 1912, and was shown in the following venues: Buffalo Fine Arts Academy (Albright Art Gallery), Jan. 4–26; Toledo Museum of Arts, Feb. 1–16; Art Institute of Chicago, Feb. 22–Mar. 16; Museum of Fine Arts, Boston, Mar. 24–Apr. 21. See also Mary Towley Swanson, *Konsten och fäderneslandet. Om svensk-amerikansk konst*, exhibition catalog (Stockholm: Riksutställningar och Millesgården, 1996), 56; exhibition catalog, "Min-

nesota State Art Society, Annual Art Exhibition, Assembled and Shown in St. Paul under the Auspices of the St. Paul Institute, March 1–8; Given in Minneapolis under the Auspices of the Minneapolis Society of Fine Arts, March 21st to 31st; Given in Owatonna under the Auspices of the Trustees of the Free Public Library, April 12th to 21st," MHS collections. The painter Alfred Wallander contributed designs to many of the porcelain pieces manufactured by the Rorstrand factory; "Hundreds Join in Promoting Scandian Art," *Minneapolis Journal*, Feb. 23, 1914, p. 1; *Minneapolis Journal*, Oct. 1, 1916, p. 1.

5. *Minneapolis Journal*, Sept. 3, 1916, p. 1; "Art Loving Minneapolis," *The American Scandinavian Review* 5 (Jan. 15, 1917).

6. Files of the registrar, Minneapolis Institute of Arts.

7. Born into a Swedish immigrant family active in the Minneapolis business community and Swedish Mission Covenant Church, Albinson decided in his teens to become an artist. He began his studies at the Minneapolis Institute of Art, then went on to the Art Students League in New York. During the 1920s he spent several stints in Europe, including one period of study with Cubist painters in Paris. Albinson returned to the United States to participate in the WPA Federal Art Project, directing art centers in Minnesota from 1935 to 1937. He painted landscapes in Minnesota and New Jersey in the 1940s, then moved to Mexico where he worked until his death.

8. Sandzén immigrated from Blidsberg in Västergötland in 1894 and taught French and art at Bethany College in Lindsborg, Kansas, until his retirement in 1950. He helped found the Swedish American Artists exhibitions in Chicago, beginning in 1905. B. J. O. Nordfeldt, born in Tullstorp, Skåne, emigrated with his parents to Chicago in 1891. He studied at the Art Institute of Chicago, then in Paris, returning to paint and exhibit his work in New York galleries, finally settling in Taos, New Mexico, and Lambertville, New Jersey.

9. Otto Robert Landelius scrapbook of Swedish American cultural leaders, p. 667, Archives of the Emigrantinstitutet, Växjö, Sweden.

10. Colling lived in Kallinge in Helleberg parish, Småland, until he emigrated in 1879 to join his sister in Minneapolis. Promoting himself as the "traveling artist," he made eight trips to Sweden between 1885 and 1902, painting the childhood homes of Minnesota's Swedish immigrants for the sum of $5 per image. He returned to Sweden for good in 1904, editing *Hjo Tidning* until his death. Stenstrom emigrated to Mora, Minnesota, in 1888, learning to paint farmstead scenes from his father Louis.

11. Wedin immigrated from Harnasend, Angermanland, at age nineteen. After studying at the Art Institute of Chicago, he studied at the Minneapolis School of Art and supported his family as a steamfitter, painting evenings and weekends.

12. For Nordfeldt and the Swedish American art community in Chicago, see Mary T. Swanson, "Chicago and Swedish-American Artists," and Rolf Erickson, "Swedish-American Artists and Their Chicago Exhibitions," in Philip J. Anderson and Dag Blanck, eds., *Swedish-American Life in Chicago: Cultural and Urban Aspects of an Immigrant People, 1850–1930* (Urbana and Chicago: Univ. of Ill. Press, 1992), 150–60, 161–77. Nyholm emigrated to Chicago in 1892. Upon the recommendation of Zorn, Nyholm specialized in portraits of Chicago's wealthy industrialists as well as those of young women in Swedish costumes. He was one of the founders of the Swedish American artists' exhibitions in Chicago, beginning in 1905, and his work toured Sweden in the Swedish American exhibitions of 1920 and 1923.

13. Carlson emigrated with his mother and siblings to New York in 1884, joining his father in the Scandinavian section of Brooklyn. He studied at the Art Students League in New York City and the Byrdcliffe art colony in Woodstock, New York. Carlson then taught in Woodstock and in Colorado Springs, and had his own John F. Carlson School of Landscape Painting from 1923 to 1945.

Holmstrom immigrated from Nybro in Småland at fifteen, eventually settling in Waseca. He studied at the Minneapolis School of Art under Cameron Booth and at the Art Institute of Chicago, where he met Elof Wedin.

Ericson, born Axel David Eriksson, emigrated with his family to Duluth in 1873. By age fifteen, he had won a gold medal at the Minnesota State Fair. He left Duluth in 1887 to study at the Art Students League in New York, then went to England to study with James McNeill Whistler. Over the next fifty years Ericson painted and taught in New York, Buffalo, Provincetown, Venice, and Paris, returning to Duluth in 1943.

14. Sprinchorn emigrated from Broby, Skåne, at age sixteen to New York to attend classes at the New York School of Art under Robert Henri. Sprinchorn exhibited his work in the Armory Show of 1913 and in numerous New York galleries. He was also included in two collections of works by Swedish American artists that toured Sweden in 1920 and 1923. Born in Magra, Västergötland, Tenggren emigrated to America in 1920 to do commercial illustration. Hired by the Walt Disney studios to supply inspirational sketches for the films *Snow White and the Seven Dwarfs* (1937) and *Pinnochio* (1938), Tenggren illustrated stories for Golden Books after 1942.

15. After immigrating from Vederslöv, in Småland, Heldner settled in Duluth where he lived until 1934, when he moved to New Orleans. Self-taught as an artist, he won a gold medal at the 1915 Minnesota State Fair for the first painting he ever exhibited. Since Heldner and both Robertzes were from Duluth, they may have formed a small immigrant artistic community there.

Performing Ethnicity:
The Role of Swedish Theatre in the Twin Cities

ANNE-CHARLOTTE HARVEY

When discussing Swedish theatre in the Twin Cities between 1880 and 1930, one could focus on what was performed, where, when, by whom, and for whom; on its relationship to theatre in Sweden; on venues, theatre groups, and touring. All of this deserves investigation, especially since very little has been written about Swedish theatre in the Twin Cities. But it is more illuminating—and at this point more feasible—to look at its function, which is reflected in the title of this study. But what does the title mean? Does it mean "to perform ethnicity," as opposed to something else, say "morality"? And if so, how is that done? Or is it about "ethnicity that performs"? The title is admittedly—and intentionally—ambiguous. It certainly would have confounded Swedish audience members in the Twin Cities a century ago; if you had asked them about "the role of theatre" or why they went to the theatre, they probably would have simply replied, "To have a good time."[1]

Theatre can have many functions, not necessarily consciously invoked. Besides being a vehicle for artistic expression, it can provide escape, intellectual stimulus, and emotional release. It can teach, inform, persuade, and create community. Likewise, it may criticize, promote social change, even incite revolt. Theatre can correct social ills through laughter, observe and process reality, generate and maintain a collective memory of shared images, reiterate central myths, and so on.

As an ethnic expression, Swedish theatre in the Twin Cities did this and much more. It promoted fellowship and communal bonding, boosting the ego of the group (often by putting other groups down), and defined and promoted an image of itself to the rest of the world (including the Old Country). It helped preserve the Swedish language, heritage, and culture, and created ethnic personae, which also maintained a viable link to the Old Country. In doing this,

Swedish American theatre facilitated an accommodation with urban mainstream culture, as well as concretized and validated the group's origin and history. It accomplished all this by ringing variations on certain well-worn and familiar themes and images, such as the lost homeland/childhood home, the
crossed Swedish and American flags, and (most powerfully) certain character
types vested with Swedishness: the heroic Viking, the romantic *dalkulla*, and
the comic peasant.[2]

This essay will discuss one specific function among the many served by the
Swedish theatre in the Twin Cities, namely the role it played in creating, refin-
ing, and maintaining a Swedish identity. What was its role in the incorporation
of the Swedes in America and the articulation of their own ethnic consciousness? Though my specific examples are from the Twin Cities, the general pattern emerging from this study applies also to theatre in other urban areas in
Swedish America. (In their specifics, however, the Twin Cities differed, not only
from the larger and older metropolitan centers of Chicago and New York, but
also from each other. Only New York and Chicago—the only American city to
have been documented as far as Swedish theatre goes—had a critical mass of
educated Swedish immigrants for a long enough time to provide a base for sustained theatre activity. Minneapolis had quickly overtaken St. Paul in size, and
was dominated by new money and Scandinavian immigrants, as compared to
old-moneyed St. Paul, with its German and Irish, later Czech and Polish, immigrant populations.) And, insofar as it can be seen to have contributed to the
creation of a Swedish identity, this discussion will also include references to
non-Swedish mainstream theatre attended by Swedes in the Twin Cities.[3]

In order to understand the theatre's role in creating a Swedish identity
in the Twin Cities, it is helpful to know something about that theatre. I will
give a quick sketch, in very broad strokes, of the time around the turn-of-the-
century, then dive into the stream of time for certain specific years in a kind of
"connect-the-dots" exercise. The major source for my survey is the Swedish-
language press in America, a rich source but one requiring interpretation. Reading the theatre ads in the Twin Cities Swedish papers is a little like reading a secret language, a code for which you need a key. Such a key is knowledge of the
various venues and their intended audiences. There is theatre and then there is
theatre.[4]

In the decade around 1900, for the purposes of this discussion, four types of
theatre can be distinguished in the Twin Cities: the elite mainstream theatre,
the popular mainstream theatre, the elite ethnic theatre, and the mainstream
ethnic theatre. The elite mainstream theatre had two Metropolitan Opera
houses, one in St. Paul and one in Minneapolis, as flagship venues. The managers of these theatres booked New York–produced touring productions with

international stars or first-class American actors, like *A Glass of Water* starring Sarah Bernhardt, Ibsen's *A Doll's House* with Alla Nazimova, John Barrymore's *Hamlet*, and *The Count of Monte Cristo* with James O'Neill. The companies usually stayed for one or two days only, sometimes for a week. The Twin Cities were considered a cultural and geographical backwater, so the managers had to entice or cajole the stars to stop there on their way to the West Coast. The plays: touring shows, a new one as often as the market would bear. Selling points: money, status, and culture. Patrons: moneyed elite. Price: twenty-five cents up to one dollar or more.

The second kind was middle- and lower-class mainstream theatre, with the Grand Opera House in St. Paul and the Bijou in Minneapolis as main venues.

The Metropolitan Opera House,
320 First Avenue South, Minneapolis, ca. 1898

These two houses also bought commercially produced touring shows from New York. As the two theatres were under the same management, transportation costs to the Twin Cities were shared and the shows were booked for a full week in St. Paul followed by one in Minneapolis. Two enormously popular plays on the repertoire in these theatres were *In Old Kentucky* and *Yon Yonson*, closely followed by *Under the Gaslight* and *Shores Acres* (*Svenska Folkets Tidning*, January 2, 1895). Through the 1890s, these theatres also booked more and more variety and vaudeville shows, magic shows, etc. The plays: touring shows, a new one each week. Selling points: money and entertainment. Patrons: lower and middle classes, many women at matinees, families. Prices: ten to fifty cents.[5]

The third kind was the elite ethnic (in this case, Swedish) theatre, booked into ethnic halls and only occasionally into the larger commercial theatres. The German Mozart Hall in St. Paul and Harmonia Hall in Minneapolis, as well as the Danish Dania Hall in Minneapolis, were prestigious and well-equipped all-purpose venues. They would house sporadic ethnic guest performers, like Carl and Anna Pfeil from the Swedish theatre in Chicago in the 1880–90s, and the Swedish actor August Lindberg in *Gengangere* (Ghosts) in 1912. Dania Hall was the site of choice for occasional ambitious productions like Strindberg's *Fadren* (The Father) by Minneapolis's Svenska Dramatiska Sällskapet in 1916. This is where one would go to see serious Scandinavian drama, historical drama, and professional caliber comedy. Performances were sometimes given in the "teater, visafton och bal" (theatre, song-evening, and dancing) format (hereafter abbreviated TVB), which could include a bit of folk-dancing, some singing, some recitation, a play, and then (after the chairs had been cleared) *bal*, dancing for everyone. Selling points: prestige, patriotism, and fun. One production each fall or spring season was the average. (Some seasons there were more, other seasons none at all.) Each play would run for one or two performances. Patrons: if the event was written up well in the Swedish press, even a Swede totally uninterested in theatre could be persuaded to attend by an appeal to his patriotic duty or pride. Prices: twenty-five to fifty cents, depending on venue and occasion.[6]

The fourth kind, the lower- and middle-class Swedish theatre, was housed in the lesser ethnic halls, like Norrmanna Hall in Minneapolis and Vasa Hall in St. Paul. The productions were always produced by local talent—amateurs in the best sense of the word—and sporadic, usually one or two per season, each playing one performance only. The repertoire consisted of short comedies, farces, or Swedish folk-plays, such as *Tre förälskade poliskonstaplar* (Three Constables in Love) and *Hon både sparkas och bits* (She Kicks as Well as Bites). This was inconsequential fluff from the European Continental repertoire translated into Swedish for the smaller theatres in Stockholm and later imported to Swedish

America. The short plays were usually incorporated into a larger whole, like a New Year's soiree or full-length variety performance of TVB format, or (less often) as a curtain raiser or after-piece for a longer play. Selling point: fun for everyone, including the children. Price: affordable.

This fourth kind of theatre was participatory, lively, and greatly enjoyed, but without the pretension of being great art. No one involved was passionate about theatre as theatre. It was more a legitimate way of socializing informally with people speaking the same language, but of the opposite sex. Imagine men and women, not married to each other, embracing, gazing into each other's eyes, making love, and beating each other up! There was no end to the emotions one could safely vent in the context of play rehearsal and performance, and no end to the merriment in the audience, seeing friends and neighbors making fools of themselves on stage.

A fifth kind of theatre in Minneapolis should be mentioned, namely the professional touring productions of Hjalmar Peterson (better known under his stage name "Olle i Skratthult"). After arriving in Minneapolis—first in 1906, for good in 1911—he began touring as a *bondkomiker*, a stand-up peasant comedian, first in Minnesota, then the Midwest, and finally nationwide. During his hey-day in the late 1910s and 20s, his shows were rehearsed, produced, and opened in Minneapolis, and then went on tour. The format was always variety, but in the mid-1910s Peterson began to use a TVB format including one-act plays. Eventually, he moved on to full-length plays, the peak being reached in 1928 with an ambitious *Värmlänningarna* (The People of Värmland). His shows were performed in local halls (except *Värmlänningarna*, which was booked into Pence Auditorium). Peterson's choice of plays was very much like that of the local Swedish amateurs, but his shows were professionally produced. He toured nationwide in an efficient and American-inspired manner with full-time performers contracted per season. Ticket sales were supplemented by sales of Olle i Skratthult's songbooks and scripts.[7]

Now to the "connect-the-dots" exercise, or a brief chronological survey of Swedish theatre in the Twin Cities. To set the scene, I will go back to the early 1870s in St. Paul and an advertisement typical of the pretheatre era in *Svenska Monitören*, dated June 14, 1871. The event publicized is a "stor Skandinavisk Pic Nic" on Sunday, June 19, 1871, arranged by the Scandinavian Sharpshooters As-sociation of St. Paul. The program includes folksongs, sack races, dancing, games, refreshments, and prizes for the three girls voted most beautiful. No hard liquor will be served, and the strictest order will prevail. "Come and breathe the fresh, beautiful, and delightful air in the green outdoors!" the planning com-mittee invites. Note, first, the pan-Scandinavian emphasis; second, the legitimized courtship play in the guise of folk games; and, third, the need to reassure that the event will be orderly and beneficial, reflecting the pervasive church prejudice against idleness and pleasure.

The first public theatre performances in Swedish in the Twin Cities took place in the early 1870s, under the aegis of the pan-Scandinavian cultural Norden Society. (Compare with the date 1868 for Chicago.) One such early performance, on November 6, 1874, was *Söndagslejonen eller Resan efter äventyr* (The Sunday Lions, or The Trip to Adventure) at Pence Opera House, advertised as part of "theater och bal" in *Svenska Nybyggaren* on October 29, 1874. The play is a light comedy with song in seven acts; doors open at 7 P.M., the performance begins at 8 P.M., and the *bal* continues until 4 A.M. (!). The date of the event—November 6, the date of the battle of Lützen in 1632—suggests that the Gustavus Adolphus craze had not yet hit the Twin Cities or that the group was predominantly Dano-Norwegian. The week after the performance, a brief— and discerning—review reported that "the play kept [the audience's] interest fairly well and would have done so even more if all the participants had been able to carry their roles as well as Mr. Reese and Mr. Söderström" (*Svenska Nybyggaren*, November 12, 1874). The wording of the review makes it clear that *Söndagslejonen* was not the first play produced by Norden, though it was the first one reviewed in the press.

The first half of the 1880s is, like the 1870s, characterized by pan-Scandinavian and sporadic performances. On January 23, 1882, at Harmonia Hall one could see "the old familiar light comedy *Abekatten* (The Monkey)," performed by the local Scandinavian dramatic society. The play was very well received. The reviewer noted that the rest of the evening was tastefully arranged and ended around midnight "after a merry and innocent turn around the floor" (*SFT*, January 24, 1883). Note the Dano-Norwegian title of the play, the Scandinavian name of the producing society, the fact that the play had been produced before, and the format concluding with *bal*. And again there was the need to downplay the lure of dancing, calling it an innocent turn around the floor!

In the mid-1880s, the pace picked up with the arrival from Sweden of some experienced actors. The Twin Cities now had more able theatre leaders and a larger pool of actors. In the late 1880s, the new leadership and the larger Swedish population began to move the theatre away from pan-Scandinavianism toward Swedishness. Swedish actors from Chicago were invited to perform in the Twin Cities. The audiences were also growing, unfortunately not only in size but also in rudeness. Hjalmar Cassel, who attended the Chicago-produced *Värmlänningarna* in St. Paul on April 26, 1888, dismissed Swedish theatre in America summarily, both the visiting actors from Chicago and the Twin Cities audiences:

The subject is soon exhausted. During all my time in St. Paul there was no more than a single theatre performance and that was given by a touring company, consisting of two true artists, an actor and actress from Sweden [Carl and Anna Pfeil] and several more or less dilettantish amateurs from Chicago. . . . About the play and the singing I merely wish to note [that it was all] . . . fairly enjoyable. But the audience! It was far more impossible than either the singing or the Värmland dialect of the Chicago amateurs. The audience stomped and whistled so that it was hard to catch what was being said, and during the most moving scenes one was disturbed by raucous laughter. The well-known scene in which Anna steps out of the boat and sings her deeply melancholy farewell song was greeted by persistent lunatic laughter, the reason for which I, for my part—despite a well-developed sense of the comic—found very hard to see. Of all that is fine and poetical in *Värmlänningarna* this audience seemed not to catch much.[8]

Also in 1888, ads began to appear in the Twin Cities Swedish-language press for the mainstream national touring shows coming through Minneapolis and St. Paul, plays like *Our American Cousin* and *Under the Gaslight*, playing a week in St. Paul and a week in Minneapolis. These regularly occurring informational ads were in Swedish, but one column wide and only about an inch high, compared with the bigger, often illustrated, ads for the sporadically scheduled Swedish-language entertainment. The 1890s also witnessed some increase in theatre offerings generally, less so in Swedish-language performances. Swedish-language play scripts, published or imported primarily by Anders Löfström in Chicago, were advertised throughout Swedish America, indicating a growing interest in play readings and amateur theatre.

Actual production efforts in the Twin Cities were erratic, however. For example, in all of 1892, *Svenska Folkets Tidning* mentioned no Swedish-language theatre performance at all. Instead, other entertainments dominated the ads in the Swedish press: *prismaskerader* (prize-awarding masked balls), concerts, the famous Lutteman sextet, and *snus* (snuff).[9]

In part, the still on-going public debate between church and theatre can be blamed. One pastor moaned: "The bad influence from the saloon, the theatre, and the ballroom . . . these are the three main causes of young men's ruination" (*Vårt hem* [Minneapolis], March 1, 1895). In a good season, the Swedish theatre group would typically produce one play in the fall and one in the spring, in St. Paul at Turner Hall, in Minneapolis at the People's Theatre or Harmonia Hall. Popular offerings continued to be *Värmlänningarna* and *Anderson, Petterson och Lundström*. As Ernst Lindholm dryly remarked, "Swedish audiences approve of no plays other than *Värmlänningarne* and *Andersson, Petterson och Lundström,* unless it should be *Andersson, Petterson och Lundström* and *Värmlänningarne.*"[10]

Judging from the Swedish press, the biggest attraction for the Swedish audiences in the 1890s appears not to have been a Swedish play at all but a play in English about a Swede, namely the dialect comedy *Yon Yonson* (1890). The second such play by the German American professional actor Gus Heege (his first effort was the less polished *Ole Olson* [1889]), *Yon Yonson* had premiered in Minneapolis some time in the late fall of 1890. It had then been produced for nationwide touring by the powerful New York–based theatre owner Jacob Litt, who later brought it back to his theatres in the Twin Cities, the Bijou (Minneapolis) and the Grand (St. Paul). Though the ad copy is generic—the identical wording about "*underbar mekanism*" (fabulous special effects) is used for both *Yon Yonson* and the next play booked into the venue—*Yon Yonson* is unusually heavily advertised, not only in the Twin Cities Swedish newspapers, but also in the local French, German, Danish, Norwegian, and American papers. This play about an immigrant Swede was a hit nationwide, but became especially firmly established in the Twin Cities, where it was to return over the next fifteen years—to begin with, every season.[11]

In the 1890s, some "bleed-through" between the ethnic and mainstream theatres began to occur. The celebrated Swedish actress Ullie Åkerström and the singer Arthur Donaldson, who had "made it" on the tough competitive American stage, hit the Twin Cities on their national tours. In the decades around the turn of the century, Donaldson appeared in roles representing the whole spectrum from Swedish to American: as Birger Jarl in *Bröllopet på Ulfåsa* (The Wedding at Ulfåsa) and Erik in *Värmlänningarna,* as the title character in *Yon Yonson,* and as the lead in the mainstream operetta *Prince of Pilsen.* In the early 1900s, *Yon Yonson*—by then a tradition—was still coming through town each season. New actors replaced each other in the title role, some American, like Ben Hendricks, some Swedish American, like Arthur Donaldson, and some "Swedish," like Knut Ericson, who was billed as "straight from Norrköping in Sweden" (although he really was not).[12]

In a significant change, the repertoire of the Swedish theatre in the Twin Cities, responding to current trends in Sweden and following the lead of Chicago, began to reflect an intense interest in folklore and *bondkomik,* folk-inspired rural comedy, "traditional" and "genuine." In 1901, a performance of *Småland-sknekten* (The Soldier from Småland), highly praised for its genuine Småland characters, was followed by a "genuine Swedish Christmas feast" (*SFT,* December 25, 1901). Two devoted and talented theatre leaders, Richard Rosengren and Emma Nilsson, emerged in the Twin Cities, and under their leadership activity picked up. In 1902, Rosengren played the lead in *Per Olsson och hans käring*

(Per Olsson and His Wife), produced by Svenska Dramatiska Sällskapet, and also performed Swedish *visor* (folksongs, ditties) collected by the folklorist August Bondeson. For a while there was a Swedish play almost every month, mostly comic and folksy plays like *Tosingar* (Crazies) or *Tratt och Bratt* (Tratt and Bratt). In 1904, Rosengren also appeared as the heroic Fridthjof in scenes from the recent Viking opera *Fridthjof and Ingeborg* (1898), by Swedish American composer Charles Hanson of Worcester, Massachusetts. On the same bill, however, was the short play *En svartsjuk tok* (A Jealous Fool). In early 1905, Rosengren—apparently inspired by a recent trip to Sweden—even appeared as an outright *bondkomiker* under the name Lars i Jöljeryd (Lars from Jöljeryd) on a TVB variety program that also included art songs and the one-act play *Bagarns fästmö* (The Baker's Fiancée). The conservative Lindstrom newspaper was very critical of the coarse *bondkomik* repertoire Rosengren had picked up in Sweden (*Medborgaren*, March 16, 1905). Unlike Hjalmar Peterson (Olle i Skratthult), Rosengren did not understand that Midwestern Swedish American audiences were still wary of the smell of brimstone emanating from the sinful stage. Peterson, on the other hand, upon returning to Minneapolis in 1911 after a two-year visit to Sweden, carefully cleaned up the new repertoire he had acquired there.[13]

As late as 1912, the deeply embedded church-theatre conflict was still rearing its head. In response to a complaint that more people were going to the theatre than to church, *Svenska Folkets Tidning* reassured its readers that while St. Paul had nine theatres and seventeen moving picture houses, it also had (thank goodness) 182 churches. This meant, according to the paper, that the 40,000 people going to the theatre on any given Sunday were more than outnumbered by the 103,639 churchgoers (*SFT*, December 11, 1912). The statistics, however, revealed another development that was a cause for concern: moving pictures were taking over. Legitimate theatre suffered doubly: vaudeville and variety shows had already begun to invade its regular venues, and now its audiences were further shrunk by the lure of such exciting fare as movies of the Stockholm Olympic Games.

On New Year's Day in 1912, the Swedish theatre group produced the typical short comedy *Det skadar inte* (Can Do No Harm) at Dania Hall. It was also at Dania that Olle i Skratthult opened his fall 1912 season as he had done the previous year, with a varied program of stories, songs, and guest artists. After giving one more performance, at Vasa Hall in St. Paul, he disappeared from the Twin Cities newspapers for that season; he was on tour in the Midwest. The major Twin Cities theatre event of the year was the visit by the famous Swedish actor August Lindberg in *Allt för Finland* (All for Finland) and Ibsen's *Gengangere* (Ghosts). There was extensive publicity, and the farewell performances were scheduled into the elite mainstream venue Metropolitan Opera House, Minneapolis (*Allt för Finland*), and the prestigious ethnic Mozart Hall, St. Paul (*Gengangere*). There was no more Swedish theatre in the Twin Cities that season.

The pattern, then, up to World War I was an increasingly steady diet of American fare sporadically laced with Swedish ethnic theatre offerings. Like the social season, the theatre season began the first week of September and ended the first week of June. A production was typically heralded by ads in the American and ethnic press one to three weeks in advance, sometimes followed by a report after the opening performance. True reviews, however, were rare, except in the American press of elite mainstream performances. The popular mainstream theatres paid for ads in the press with sought-after complimentary tickets. As the papers did not want to alienate their advertisers and lose these free tickets, they rarely criticized a performance. In the ethnic press, few reporters were qualified theatre reviewers, and reviewing ethnic plays as consumer information was not relevant since most plays ran for only one or two performances. Reporting on their success as ethnic events, on the other hand, was important and fairly standard procedure. (Instead of describing, analyzing, and evaluating the work performed, the "review" would discuss how many Swedes attended, whether there were any non-Swedes there, how Swedish the performance was, and so on.)[14]

At the end of World War I, the entertainment climate had changed markedly. In 1918, numerous ads in the Twin Cities papers reflected a growing mass market for cultural technology in the form of Swedish-language moving pictures and phonograph recordings on Victor and Columbia. The recordings featured primarily *bondkomik* material, reassuringly ethnic and backward in nature, or sentimental-nostalgic songs, "the dear old Swedish, Norwegian, Finnish, and Danish songs that bring tears to the listener's eyes" (*SFT*, January 9, 1918). Anything Swedish was sold with the aid of pictures of genuine folkdancers or pretty *Rättvikskullor* (women from Rättvik in traditional costume). There were Swedish concerts, lectures, singers—but no Swedish theatre. And no Olle i Skratthult performance was mentioned in the press, possibly because he did not need to advertise to fill his season openers, possibly because metropolitan Twin Cities by then thought him passé. When Ibsen's *Master Builder* came to the Twin Cities, interestingly—and symptomatically—it was not clear from the ad whether it was a touring stage play or a film.

In 1922, more ethnic recordings and films were offered through large ads. The big ethnic event of the year was the showing at the Minneapolis Auditorium of the Swedish movies *Herr Arnes Penningar* (Herr Arne's Money) and *Sveriges städer och natursköna bygder* (Sweden's Cities and Picturesque Countryside). The Swedish female folksinger and *bondkomiker* Lydia Hedberg ("Bergslagsmor") visited the Twin Cities, but the reviewer lamented that her "charming concert of genuine Swedish folk songs" was not as well attended as one might have wished. During that year, there was not a single Swedish theatre ad, nor any ad for an Olle i Skratthult performance, though he was now in the midst of his most successful decade. When a rare live theatre performance was announced, as with *Värmlänningarna* by the Svenska Dramatiska Sällskapet in Minneapolis for September 5–6, 1925, the poster proclaimed "not a Moving Picture, but the Real Play!"[15]

What this "connect-the-dots" exercise suggests is that, except for occasional periods of creative energy under strong leaders, Swedish theatre in the Twin Cities had a rather marginal existence. At first it was hampered by religious prejudice and the lack of a critical mass of Swedish audience members, and then later it suffered along with mainstream theatre from overwhelming competition from vaudeville and moving pictures. Over the years, Twin Cities Swedes saw more performances of *Yon Yonson* than of all the Swedish-language plays taken together. Generally favorable conditions and strong leadership existed only in the decade around the turn of the century. And no Swedish theatre group in the Twin Cities had the broad support and talent base found in Chicago or New York for ongoing theatre efforts. Nor were there any local professional theatre material culture resources—like Schoultz's costume house in Chicago or the scene painting studios in New York—which was one reason for the popularity of revivals in the Twin Cities Swedish theatre.

Let us now return to the question of how theatre helped promote a sense of Swedish identity. Who created this identity? Certainly not "theatre," but individuals: the promoters (initiators, sponsors, fundraisers, cultural leaders, critics, editors, and enthusiasts) and the providers (playwrights, seamstresses, producers, directors, actors, and singers), those who stood on stage in makeup and costume, declaimed, danced, and sang. But it was also the audiences, the nameless masses who absorbed, adopted, consumed, followed, were impressed, and clapped and cheered and laughed in the wrong places. There was a complicity implied in attending: unless you left a performance, you were tacitly approving what was being shown and told. Your presence, even if you sat on your hands, indicated some sharing in the values and images presented.

This was a two-way process, a contract of sorts between the audiences and the men and women whose personality, creative talent, and opportunity combined to make them theatrical leaders. These leaders, *eldsjälar* (literally, "spirits of fire"), like Richard Rosengren, Gus Heege, and Hjalmar Peterson in Minneapolis, and Anna and Carl Pfeil in Chicago, accomplished what they did by making choices. One important choice was that of venue with an attendant outreach mechanism (playbills? handbills? newspaper ads? which ticket outlets? special promotion?). In the absence of a permanent Twin Cities venue for Swedish theatre, the support structure for each new production had to be reinvented, which was time-consuming, laborious, and expensive, but also offered opportunities for shaping the event and steering audience response. The wrong choice could be disastrous, since each venue had its own built-in public.

Other choices to be made concerned repertoire, casting, staging (*mise-en-scène*, acting, costuming), directing, timing, schedule, budget, and programming of the entire evening. Of these, the choice of repertoire was key. (It is also the area best documented, hence most easily researched.) The choice of repertoire is illuminating: it tells us what the leaders had chosen, but also what the collaborators supported and what the followers accepted. We get a triple portrait of the parties involved in a sensitive negotiation, one desiring cultural prominence and support, one pleasure and self-expression, one entertainment and self-esteem.

Repertoire choices were based on a number of factors, including practical constraints like cost of script, rights and royalties, availability, suitability for the performers available, the time of year and occasion, and the overall fit with the season. But there was also the fun quotient, patriotism quotient, nostalgia quotient, potential as a moneymaker, recognition value (familiar play), and revival value ("we have the sets and the original cast is still around").

What was the repertoire? When Swedish archivists came to the United States in the late 1970s looking for the "old Swedish song heritage," they found to their surprise that it seemed to consist of nothing but *bondkomik* and nostalgia. The same thing can be said of the theatre repertoire. The two most performed Swedish plays in Swedish America were *Värmlänningarna* (1846) and *Anderson, Petterson och Lundström* (1866), both of which harkened back to a pre-industrial world peopled by comic and romantic characters.[16]

In terms of genre, the Swedish American theatre repertoire encompassed melodrama, farce, and all types of comedy from satire to romance. Almost entirely missing was serious drama and tragedy. We find many more romantic and comic characters than heroic ones, and the few heroic ones tend to be romantic-heroic or melodramatic-heroic, not tragic-heroic. When Charles Hanson of Worcester created his Viking opera *Fridthjof and Ingeborg* in 1898, for example, he was working in a romantic-melodramatic-heroic mode. Operating here—in part at least—was class differences. The tragic genre and the heroic character were perceived as high culture, upper class, and elitist. The melodramatic, farcical, and comic genres and characters were seen as popular. The romantic character was an interesting "swing" or "pivot," since it could function equally well in a tragic-serious and a comic-light mode.

From the repertoire, one may draw the conclusion that Swedish theatre's main function in America was to entertain. "A good time" may indeed have been the only thing the audiences were aware of wanting, and it was certainly deliberately provided, since the primary item on the leaders' agenda was to "get bodies into seats" to guarantee their own survival. But the leaders were also consciously working to educate, uplift, ennoble, and in the process ethnicize their audiences. In retrospect, Swedish theatre can be seen to have worked its magic and accomplished its mission, even beyond the conscious aspirations of its leaders, teaching what one might call "subliminal lessons in Swedishness."

How did this actually happen? What elements were particularly effective in this process? The leaders—actors, producers, managers—made choices among available formats (short play in TVB format? two or three short plays? full-length play?) and titles available in print. In exceptional cases—mostly in the bohemian circles of turn-of-the-century Chicago—they would "commission" a new script from some talented local Swede. In the Twin Cities, revivals of previous "hits" were popular choices with organizers and audiences alike, for financial, administrative, and psychological reasons.[17]

The TVB format was ideal for promoting a sense of ethnic identity, combining a variety of folkloric performances—dancing, singing, monologues, short plays—with audience participation in the concluding *bal*. Unlike a regular theatre evening format, TVB reinforced ethnicity through all the senses, including taste (refreshments) and touch (public dancing). It was also far more practical and economical. It is not surprising that full-length regular theatre evenings were rare, except when the beloved six-act musical folk drama *Värmlänningarna* was on the repertoire.

The plays chosen, in whatever format and of whatever length, varied in their overt "Swedishness," from those with completely non-Swedish subject matter, to those with Swedish topics, settings, and characters. There were also some set in Swedish America, most of them light-hearted comedies like *Anna Stina i Chikago* (Anna Stina in Chicago) (1899). A few were serious treatments of Swedish American life, for example, Gustaf Malm's Kansas-based *Härute* (Out Here) (1919). In the Twin Cities, the talented columnist Otto Anderson made an impassioned contribution to the dual allegiance debate with *Smålänningarna* (1919), set in Småland and Minnesota. Of course, any performance by an ethnic group in a dominant, mainstream culture can be considered "ethnic," whatever the topic, issues, setting, characters, or intention. In that sense, all Swedish-language theatre in America was ethnic. Swedish-language plays, however non-Swedish their topics, were ethnically charged merely by being performed in America in Swedish. In this category belonged most of the plays produced in Swedish America, from the numerous one-act farces originally translated from the French or German for the nineteenth-century Swedish stage and later imported to Swedish America, to the occasional Swedish-language *Hamlet* or *HMS Pinafore*. The result was always "ethnic" even if the group producing it had no such intention.

Beyond the Swedish language, which was a given, what element of a play's performance could most powerfully convey "Swedishness"? Of Aristotle's six dramaturgical elements—plot, character, thought, diction, music, and spectacle—the Swedish language spoken on stage represents diction and music (the sound of the language). Of the remaining four, it is tempting to rank spectacle, or setting, as the most important element. Setting can certainly provide powerful images of the old homeland, but a setting is static and (literally) only a backdrop for the action. As for plot, character, and thought, it is important to realize that *there are no Swedish plots, only Swedish characters*—and, through them, the potential for Swedish thought. In the theatre, character—the recognizable semblance of a human being—is *the* most powerful communicator of Swedishness, because it sets up a live bond with the audience in a shared time and space, creating strong empathy/identification, kinesthetic response, and a two-way communication. A character is what we feel with and absorb "in our bones."

As suggested above, the Swedish characters adopted by and adapted to Swedish America to signify Swedishness can be reduced to three essential types: the heroic (the Viking), the romantic (the *dalkulla*), and the comic (the rural yokel, the peasant). These types populate the visual arts, performing arts, and literature, but—I am suggesting—have the greatest potential impact in live performance. Whatever character a Swede in the Twin Cities saw on stage—Richard Rosengren dressed as a Viking singing *Fridthjof and Ingeborg*, a pretty young girl dressed as a *dalkulla* singing Swedish folksongs, Olle i Skratthult

performing some of Fröding's "paschaser," Olga Lindgren Peterson as Stella in *Gubben Månssons testamente*, or Gus Heege as Yon in *Yon Yonson*—there were traits to discern, qualities to respond to, and perhaps a lesson to be learned.

By far the most widely known and pervasive stage representations of Swedishness in all of Swedish America were the comic characters of the greenhorn "Yon Yonson" and the Swedish peasant "Olle i Skratthult." Interestingly, both were felt to "belong" in the Twin Cities, and it can be argued that they had a greater impact on their audiences there than anywhere else

Olle i Skratthult (Hjalmar Peterson, right), with accompanist Gustav Nyberg, ca. 1919

in Swedish America. Hjalmar Peterson, Olle i Skratthult, came to Minneapolis in 1906, used it as a base of operations for most of his career, and died there in 1960. Gus Heege had worked as a journalist in Minneapolis before he created *Yon Yonson*, the play had its "out-of-town tryout" in Minneapolis before it was picked up and copyrighted by Jacob Litt, and it played in the Twin Cities from 1890 until at least 1905.[18]

It is illuminating to compare these two central characters with respect to their Swedishness. Swedish folk characters like the *kulla* from Rättvik and *bondkomik* characters like Olle i Skratthult and Lars i Jöljeryd, presented object lessons in Swedishness without accompanying commentary. No one challenged their ethnicity, no one analyzed the traits they embody or personify. They spoke for themselves: one picture said more than a thousand words. Nor did anyone question the performers' ethnicity—Hjalmar Peterson's or Richard Rosengren's right to portray these *bondkomik* characters, to wear these signs of Swedishness. If they were discussed at all in terms of ethnicity, it was to note how genuinely Swedish they were, authenticating them by tracing their Swedish pedigree. (No one strove to be a poor ethnic, so it was understood to be bad form to quibble about inauthentic costumes, poorly pronounced Swedish, or other evidence of falls from ethnic grace—so long as ethnicity could be claimed by blood, that is.) And very, very few reviewers were so curmudgeonly as to apply the criteria of mainstream art to ethnic performances. Hanson's opera *Fridthjof and Ingeborg* was one of the exceptions, but though it was dismissed as music it was still hailed as an ethnic event by Chicago mainstream critics.

The American stage Swede Yon Yonson, on the other hand, was accompanied from the beginning by detailed questioning in the Swedish-language press about his Swedishness; whether the author/actor Gus Heege had any Swedish blood in him, and, if so, through which parent; whether his Swedish dialect was convincing; whether he had ever been to Sweden; and so forth. Because Swedish American reviewers of this American-created character were forced to verbalize what he stood for, however, Yon Yonson (taken together with the press discussion of his and Heege's Swedishness) serves better than Olle i Skratthult to spell out for us today what was seen at the time as the essence of Swedishness—by Swedes and Americans alike.

Thus, there is ample evidence of what was apparently considered "typically Swedish." Yon is praised for his "kindheartedness and slow, calm and thoroughly honest way that wins the undivided sympathy of the audience" (*Svenska Amerikanaren*, August 27, 1891), as well as his "unshakeable calm and composure at times when all around him lose theirs" (*SFT*, March 30, 1893). "The author has shown much courtesy to us Swedes," explained the press, "for Yon is presented as honest and intrepid next to some Yankee scoundrels and a couple of caricatured Englishmen" (*Skandinavia*, March 30, 1893). Yon is praised for "initiative, courage, and honesty" (*Vestkusten*, November 6, 1891) and "mechanical aptitude and enterprising spirit" (*Svenska Kuriren*, November 29, 1892). According to one reviewer, Yon is "noble, goodhearted, and honest" (*Skandinavia*, March 31, 1892); and another commented on "the honesty, kind heart, lack of ostentation, and industry" (*Nya Pressen* [Moline], January 30, 1895) in Yon's character. Overall, he is described as kind, hardworking, honest, slow (here a positive quality, the opposite of "rash"), even-tempered, plain, strong, and enterprising. One reviewer even praised Heege for having created Yon expressly for the purpose of showing Americans what Swedes are like and how wonderful they are (*Skandinavia*, March 13, 1891). The reviewer also summed up female Swedishness in his remarks about the character of Grace, who turns out to be Yon's long-lost sister: "In her, the Swedish woman's modest, noble, and mild traits shone through along with filial piety and respect, but also a determined and firm stand against injustice and betrayal" (*Svenska Amerikanaren*, August 27, 1891). The same reviewer also characterized this Swedish paragon by saying what she is not when he criticized the American girl's "enterprising spirit as well as frivolity" and "the pushy Irish traits" exhibited by another of the female characters.

The author/actor Gus Heege, however, was criticized by several reviewers for exaggerating Yon's struggle with the English language and his poor taste in clothes: "A Swede who comes to this country as an adult may many times be bumbling, but when he gets himself new clothes he does not choose the outfit of a black slave" (*Svenska Amerikanaren*, August 27, 1891). In other words, a Swede may be allowed to be bumbling and inept, but not to be pushy, frivolous, or a flashy dresser. It is understood that, of the undesirable characteristics, there is a spectrum from unacceptable to endearing.[19]

This is probably the universal reaction of a minority ethnic group seeing one of its members portrayed on stage. Since recognition, or being lifelike, is the foremost criterion of excellence, one is quick to point out "mistakes," but one is also delighted when the portrayal is "faithful," i.e., when it matches one's

own image of the group. In the Swedish responses to Yon, there is some criticism but mostly pride that Yon is a Swede (as opposed to German, Yankee, English, Irish, etc.): "As far as view-

Advertisement for Yon Yonson, *from* Svenska Amerikanska Posten, *January 3, 1893* ers of Swedish descent are concerned, it must do their souls good to see the characteristic traits of their nation so strongly and well expressed . . . at the expense of all the representatives of other nations appearing in the piece" (*Svenska Tribunen*, September 3, 1891). Yon is profiled against not only "American" characters, but a whole gallery of ethnic "types," all sensitizing the Swedes in the audience and making them reflect on—or at least become aware of—their own ethnicity. Yon may even become predictive, like a horoscope: Once you are "reminded" of what are typically Swedish traits—all positive, of course— you begin to recognize or cultivate them in yourself.

But surely no one could have taken seriously the laughable characters of Yon Yonson and Olle i Skratthult? No one would have wanted to emulate these constructs of Swedishness. Not even the pretty *dalkulla* could have been adopted as a viable contemporary persona. No one would have wanted to look like Yon or Olle, with their awkward body language, mismatched antiquated clothes, cloth cap, blond or red wig, and silly or slow-witted expression. They represented a stage of development that was past. No one had looked anything like them for a long time, and certainly nobody would dream of wanting to look like them in the present. There was a comfortable distance between them and the audience, a distance made greater by laughter.

Although no one wanted to look like Olle i Skratthult or Yon Yonson, or behave like them, they were both manifestations of a Swedish essence, and one may well have wanted to share in that essence. They provided the Swedish American with a model on a deeper level, not in appearance but in qualities, morality, and human potential. Their similarity in general appearance obscured the fact that on that deeper level, in essence and function, they were quite different. Yon Yonson and Olle i Skratthult differed significantly with respect to their role in popular mainstream culture, function in performative context (genre), and function vis-à-vis the audience.

Space does not permit a detailed examination of these functional differences. With regard to mainstream culture, suffice it to say that Yon Yonson captured public awareness—mainstream and Swedish—in a far more pervasive, enduring way than Olle i Skratthult. Yon came on the scene earlier and remained active for decades; he toured nationally; he was born in the popular theatre, *the* mass medium of the day; and he eventually made the transition to film. His type permeated mainstream culture and remains viable to this day. In contrast, Olle i Skratthult appeared later; was largely restricted to work within the ethnic culture; and performed in the rapidly declining vaudeville format. Although there were instances when Olle i Skratthult performed for "the outer circle," he remained a Swedish commodity, and therefore declined also with the general decline of the Swedish language.

As for the two other functional differences, they are hinted at in the characters' respective appearance. A careful look at the two reveals subtle differences in body language and costume. Olle i Skratthult, like most *bondkomik* characters, is not a young man. His costume—though rural, old-fashioned, and ridiculous—fits him well or is on the big side (the scarf is comically exaggerated). His makeup includes a blacked-out front tooth, signifying being toothless, a sign of old age. He wears heavy boots, and his stance is solid. Yon is younger and nimbler; he never has blacked-out teeth, and he is often shown wearing shoes instead of boots. He wears a short jacket as compared with Olle's long coat, emphasizing leg mobility. His stance is always awkwardly pigeon-toed, i.e., his body language is more apologetic. His too-short pants and too-small jacket spell "still growing."

Yon is, in other words, a young, vital type who has life ahead of him. He represents the simplicity and innocence of youth in a Rousseauian sense. Olle is more mature, or ageless, and possesses a fund of accumulated peasant wisdom. He represents the simplicity and innocence of the "folk." While Olle i Skratt-

Advertisements for Ole Olson, *depicting Ole both as a recent arrival and as an established immigrant, from* Svenska Folkets Tidning, *November 12, 1890, and* Svenska Amerikanska Posten, *November 18, 1890*

hult was the unchanging stage persona of one man, Yon Yonson—once launched by Gus Heege—was played by a succession of actors of various personalities. In other words, the character evolved over time and there was a proliferation of "Yons." The features that remained constant in the various Yon portrayals— pigeon-toed stance, too-small clothes—are thus doubly significant as markers of Yon's essence. They signify that he is "a growing boy," edging his way into the world. Yon Yonson is a man at an expansive time and place in his life. And— most important of all—he changes in the course of the play, from Swedish green- horn yokel to American urbanite. This fact is easily overlooked when studying pictures of Yon, since they almost always show the Swedish greenhorn yokel, i.e., the stage in his development with the greatest exotic and comic appeal. On the other hand, "Ole Olson," Heege's first Scandinavian greenhorn creation, is depicted both as immigrant yokel and "dapper dog."[20]

The greatest difference between Olle and Yon lies in the operating myth that each character taps into. These myths are fundamentally linked to the dif- ference in the characters' capacity for change. Whereas Yon Yonson grows and is transformed before our eyes from a greenhorn to an acceptable member of the dominant culture, Olle i Skratthult is fixed and unchanging. Yon's trans- formation requires and shapes a full-length play, Olle appears—as do all *bond- komik* characters—only in songs or skits, monologues, frozen situations with a quick payoff, or possibly cameo appearances—as when Olle i Skratthult played Löpar-Nisse in *Värmlänningarna*. Olle is never called upon or allowed by his genre or performance formats to adapt or change; at the most, he is allowed to respond to modern times with predictable puzzlement and dismay. The point of the play *Yon Yonson* is that the Swedish immigrant is adaptable, ingenious, and capable of change. Compared with greenhorns of other nationalities, the scenario for the Scandinavian greenhorn tends to stress his resilience and, if de- veloped over time, eventual triumph and assimilation. The point of Olle i Skratthult lies in his permanency.[21]

Yon's pre-plot history is unimportant, we do not "see" Sweden in him: he speaks no specific dialect, has no home province, and is in a sense "rootless." In- stead, he reflects the open horizons of the United States, traveling as a migrant worker with casual ease from state to state ("My name is Yon Yonson, I come from Wisconsin . . ."). Since he evokes no images of Sweden, he generates no nostalgia for the old country. Olle, on the other hand, *is* the old country seen through a specific Värmland character (lifted across the Atlantic for our ben- efit). His power to generate nostalgia increases over time, as long as such nos- talgia is satisfying a need in his audiences. And whereas both Yon and Olle evoke stages that the audience has indisputably left behind—Yon the immi- grant's greenhorn stage, Olle the Swede's pre-urban existence—Olle's "yokel- dom" exerts a powerful attraction by its permanence and roots in the past, whereas Yon's greenhorn stage has no sentimental value. Yon, on the other hand, has a post-plot history, i.e., a future. Olle looks backward; Yon looks forward.

The operating myth in Yon Yonson (and Ole Olson) is the promise of progress, transformation by one's own powers (only possible in America), and material success, all neatly signified by Yon's changed costume in the last act. The operating myth in Olle i Skratthult's dialect material is that Swedes (in America) are linked back to an essential common goodness, simplicity, and naturalness, which gives them a sense of identity and values enduring even into the second and third generation.

With regard to the difference in the way the two characters function for their Swedish American audiences, one can say that Yon equips for change while Olle serves a conservative function. Yon and Olle both exorcise ghosts by laughter, but the response to Yon is more ambivalent, a mixture of pride and shame. Olle makes his Swedish audiences more Swedish, strengthens them in their stand against the dominant culture. Yon aligns his Swedish audiences with mainstream values and helps assimilation, but also promotes ethnicization—the deliberate reclaiming of a no-longer-taken-for-granted identity—lifting out Swedishness for perception by contrasting it with other ethnicities as well as with the mainstream. Olle evokes nostalgia, looks back to a time of now-lost innocence, reflects Sweden and local rootedness (the farm, the parish, and the province). Yon evokes no specific nostalgia in Swedish Americans apart from what they may share with a mainstream audience generally yearning for "the good old days."

The different formats (full-length play versus comic monologues) dictate that Yon is changing—moving toward a future great with things to come—while Olle is always the same. A play is a natural medium in which to create a character that undergoes a change, while a character in, for example, a cartoon is caught in a fixed moment of maximum awkwardness. Heege's major point in both *Ole Olson* and *Yon Yonson* is the transformation of the main character from a greenhorn to an American hero, demonstrated by his change of costume. Olle does not change, and therein lies his attraction. He is secure, permanent, and safe. Yon embraces the future, while Olle resists it.

While the operative myth personified in Yon is progress, the operative myth in Olle is enduring goodness. One may laugh at Olle and distance oneself, but there is great emotional accord between him and his audiences, growing stronger as long as the audience feels a need to nurture its Swedishness in the face of the mainstream culture. The tenderness generated by the Olle character may also have something to do with the perception—wrong though it may be—that Olle is a simple, non-commercial creation in a low-tech venue, while Yon appears in a high-tech spectacle in a commercial venue, supported by a group of unmistakably professional American actors. Since the 1890s, Yon Yonson has had enormous impact on Swedes in America, not just because the timing of his introduction was right and he was disseminated by a nationwide touring apparatus, but also because he is a sympathetic character, young, vital, and almost romantic (he does get the girl). He undergoes change, looks to the future, and allows for pride in Swedishness as well as pride in Americanization. He functions for Americans, Swedish Americans, and recent immigrants.

It is clear that both Yon Yonson and Olle i Skratthult—as well as other Swedish types seen on stage—had an impact on the immigrants' self-image and their development of an ethnic identity, as well as their incorporation into American life. The complex nature of this impact is outside the scope of this study. It should be pointed out, however, that the hitherto largely unexplored and difficult-to-quantify interchange between Swedish-created and American-created Swedish types nevertheless helped shape the types on both sides in a complex process of mutual reinforcement. When this "bleed-through" began, how it flowed, and at what time—all this deserves exploration. Because of the local ties to both Yon and Olle, the Twin Cities area is particularly promising for an investigation of this phenomenon.

In conclusion, many aspects of Swedish theatre in the Twin Cities remain and deserve to be explored. With regard to a developing ethnic identity, theatre contributed significantly to audience "Swedishness," though in different ways and to a varying degree at different times, since it was always vulnerable to attacks from religious factions, lack of leadership, competition from popular mainstream entertainment and, eventually, film. It consistently promoted Swedishness through the use of the Swedish language, many times augmented by repertoire requiring specifically Swedish settings and characters. Ironically, the best known stage-Swedes in the Twin Cities were Yon Yonson and Olle i Skratthult, neither of them a character in a Swedish play, and, of the two, the American-created Yon Yonson eventually had the most lasting impact, "performing ethnicity" for Swedes, Swedish Americans, and Americans alike.

* * * *

NOTES

1. There is no work about theatre in Swedish America comparable to Henriette C. Koren Naeseth's major inventory, *The Swedish Theatre of Chicago 1868–1950* (Rock Island, Ill.: Augustana Historical Society, 1951). Lesser and more recent overviews are Anne-Charlotte Harvey, "Swedish-American Theatre," in *Ethnic Theatre in the United States*, ed. Maxine S.

Seller (Westport, Conn.: Greenwood Press, 1983); and Lars Furuland, "From *Vermländin-garne* to *Slavarna på Molokstorp*: Swedish-American Ethnic Theater in Chicago," in *Swedish-American Life in Chicago: Cultural and Urban Aspects of an Immigrant People 1850–1930*, Philip J. Anderson and Dag Blanck, eds. (Urbana and Chicago: Univ. of Ill. Press, 1992). A nationwide inventory along Naeseth's lines is long overdue, but would require a massive coordinated effort. This study of theatre in the Twin Cities draws on brief published references in classic Swedish American sources, such Ernst Skarstedt, *Svensk-Amerikanska folket i helg och söcken* (Stockholm: Björck & Börjesson, 1917), and *Våra pennfäktare* (San Francisco: Ernst Skarstedt, 1897); Johan Person, *Svensk-Amerikanska studier* (Rock Island, Ill.: Augustana Book Concern, 1912); and Alfred Söderström, *Minneapolis minnen. Kulturhistorisk axplockning från qvarnstaden vid Mississippi* (Minneapolis: [published by the author, 1899]); but also Swedish observations like Hjalmar Cassel, *Bland svenskar och yankees* (Stockholm: Albert Bonniers, 1894); and Carl Sundbeck, *Svensk-Amerikanerna* (Stockholm: P. C. Askerbergs Bokförlag, 1904). Primary sources include interviews with Olga Lindgren Nilsen of St. Paul, her collection of theatre memorabilia, materials collected by the Minneapolis-based Olle i Skratthult Project in the 1970s, and—above all—the Swedish American press. I am greatly indebted to the Swedish Emigrant Institute, Växjö, for the two research grants enabling me to access its microfilm collection of Swedish American newspapers.

2. There is a fine distinction between "ethnic" and "Swedish" cultural expression in an American context. When does the immigrant native expression cease to be merely Swedish and become ethnic? It has to do with the degree of the group's self-awareness and the deliberateness with which it projects its self-image. But since ethnicity is situational and contextual, the difference between "ethnic" and "Swedish" does not exist to an outsider; to that person whatever the Swedes do is all "ethnic." My position is that, however unaware the group is of an outside, American label, the expression is *de facto* ethnic merely by being situated in a non-Swedish context. Swedish theatre in America is always ethnic—only more or less so. Seller, ed., *Ethnic Theatre*, gives a broad overview of the various functions of ethnic theatre.

3. Insofar as they had any theatre, rural areas shared in the urban areas' theatre events through a touring network. Once, perhaps twice, a year, a Swedish show would come to town. Though the touring shows were produced and mounted in urban centers, they gradually lost their urban audiences when the latter became too sophisticated for the conservative fare preferred in the country.

4. The papers read for this study include: *Nya Verlden* (Minneapolis), *Westerlandet* (Stillwater), *Medborgaren* (Lindstrom), *Vårt hem* (Minneapolis), *Svenska Folkets Tidning* (Minneapolis), *Svenska Amerikanska Posten* (Minneapolis), *Monitören* (St. Paul). The major papers, *Svenska Folkets Tidning* (SFT) and *Svenska Amerikanska Posten* (SAP), included columns with St. Paul news.

5. The Grand in St. Paul and the Bijou in Minneapolis were both owned by the powerful New York–based Jacob Litt, owner and lessee of over twenty theatres across the country. He personally supervised his local managers and frequently toured the Midwest in the 1890s. For an account of commercial theatre management practices around the turn of the century, see Paul S. Newman, "Careers in Contrast: The Managerial Practices of L. N. Scott and Theo Hays and Their Influence on Twin Cities Entertainment, 1890–1929" (Ph.D. diss., Univ. of Minn., 1991).

6. In the 1880s, when Minneapolis was a smaller, backward town compared to metropolitan Chicago, the Swedish actors in Chicago enjoyed visiting the Twin Cities and sharing their theatrical riches with them. The Twin Cities cheerfully played host (Ernst Lindblom, *Svenska teaterminnen från Chicago* [Stockholm: Gullbergs, 1916], 112–15).

7. For information about Olle i Skratthult, see my "Swedish-American Theatre" in Seller, ed., *Ethnic Theatre*, 491–524, and *Olle i Skratthult's Greatest Hits* (St. Paul: Great American

History Theatre, 1992). For a list of other treatments of Olle i Skratthult, including articles by Maury Bernstein, see my Bibliography in Seller, 520–24.

8. During the 1887–88 season, the Nordiska Amatörsällskapet (Nordic Amateurs) performed both the Swedish *Järnbäraren* (The Iron Carrier) and the Danish *Gjenboerne* (The Next-door Neighbors), (*SFT*, Nov. 16, 1887; Mar. 28, 1888). The Svenska Dramatiska Sällskapet from Chicago visited the Twin Cities in the spring of 1888 with three performances: *Värmlänningarna* on Apr. 26 at Turner Hall in St. Paul and Apr. 27 at People's Theatre in Minneapolis; and *Anderson, Petterson och Lundström* on Apr. 29 at Harmonia Hall in Minneapolis. All performances were followed by *bal*, and the tickets were fifty cents. All three events were favorably reviewed in the local press (*SFT*, May 2, 1888); the two artists from Sweden were Carl and Anna Pfeil; the company was Svenska Dramatiska Sällskapet, on tour Apr.–May 1888 (Naeseth, *Swedish Theatre of Chicago*, 71f.). *Bland svenskar och yankees* (Stockholm: Albert Bonniers, 1894), 61f.—All translations mine, unless otherwise noted.

9. The lack of advertisements or reviews may not necessarily mean a lack of performances. Restricted advertising budgets, change in editorial policies and newspaper ownership may have precluded theatre notices in any one season.

10. Ernst Lindblom, *Mina teateraftnar* (Stockholm: C. L. Gullbergs förlag, 1917), 38.

11. The premiere of *Yon Yonson* in the fall of 1890 (date unknown) at Norrmanna Hall may have been an "audition" for Litt, who arranged the play's subsequent tour, which opened officially in Utica, New York, on Dec. 27, 1890. The play went on to have 111 performances across the country before opening in New York City on Dec. 28, 1891. I am greatly indebted to Douglas McDermott for the touring schedules and partial cast lists of Heege's two plays *Ole Olson* and *Yon Yonson* between 1889 and 1895. Regular American offerings at the Bijou and Grand merited a small information item in the Swedish papers, whereas *Yon Yonson* was given columns of narrative hype, illustrations from the show, and wide display ads (local press ads for the Bijou Theatre in Minneapolis, Theo Hays Collection, MHS). For a more detailed discussion of *Yon Yonson*, see my "Holy Yumpin' Yiminy: Scandinavian Immigrant Stereotypes in the Early Twentieth Century American Musical," *Approaches to the American Musical*, Robert Lawson-Peebles, ed. (Exeter: Univ. of Exeter Press, 1996), 55–71; and my unpublished paper, " 'My name is Yon Yonson, I come from Wisconsin . . .': Swedish Immigrant Types on the American Stage and Their Function in Assimilation/Ethnicization," Immigration and Performing Arts Conference, Univ. of Minn., Mar. 1996.

12. *Valkyrian* 5:455.

13. For a description and analysis of Hanson's works, see my "The First Swede in Worcester," *Swedish-American Historical Quarterly* 46 (1995): 74–92. Rosengren chose a name for his peasant persona that is very close to that of the father of *bondkomik*, the beloved storyteller Karl Peter Rosén, "Jödde i Göljaryd" (1855–1900), whose folk stories and songs dominated popular culture in Sweden in the 1890s until his untimely death in 1900. The most graphic example is probably Olle's expurgation of "Flickan på Bellmansro" (The Girl at Bellmansro), in which the verse about the illegitimate child is cut and the line "och under tiden har han blitt far" (and meanwhile he has become a father) is changed to "och under tiden har han blitt kvar" (and meanwhile he has remained).

14. Cassel, *Bland svenskar och yankees*, 60.

15. Maria Sonander-Rice Collection, Minneapolis. See Harvey, "Swedish-American Theatre," in Seller, ed., *Ethnic Theatre*, 520.

16. Märta Ramsten, Svenskt Visarkiv (Swedish Archive for Folk Song and Folk Music Research), interviewed in *Smålänningen*, Oct. 10, 1981; Sten Bockman, *Norra Skåne*, July 26, 1996; Furuland, "From *Vermländingarne* to *Slavarna på Molokstorp*," 135, 140.

17. Plays by local writers were more frequent in the bohemian circles of turn-of-the-century Chicago than in the Twin Cities. The best-known extant play set in the Twin Cities is Otto E. Anderson's *Smålänningarna* (Minneapolis: Otto E. Anderson, 1919), written to honor Swedish Americans serving under the American flag in World War I, and to boost

the pride of Swedish Americans generally. This play was, however, not commissioned for performance and no production of the play has been documented.

18. For the first five seasons, 1890–95, *Yon Yonson* came through the Twin Cities each season. After that, it is unclear whether it appeared each season, but it is documented as late as 1905. Also Heege's first Swedish dialect play, *Ole Olson,* had its "out-of-town tryout" in the area (in Stillwater on Mar. 27, 1889), and went on to include the Twin Cities on its national tours.

19. The "outfit of a black slave" probably consisted of the boldly checkered pants worn by comic black characters in mainstream American theatre. The choice may have been dictated by limited costume budget, Heege's lack of Swedish sensibility, or a desire for something looking very "American."

20. There were also *Ole Olson* and *Yon Yonson* spin-offs, Swedish-dialect plays by Heege and other authors, featuring Yon-type characters. Landis Magnuson, the authority on the so-called Ole plays, has graciously shared his work with me ("Swedish-American Dialect Plays: Bringing Laughter to the Hinterlands," unpublished paper); *Ole Olson* predated *Yon Yonson* by eighteen months, toured widely, and gave rise to numerous spin-offs, but the title character never quite achieved Yon Yonson's emblematic function, possibly because he was conceived as a Scandinavian type, then changed to Swedish. There is no romantic conclusion to Ole's story, and his appearance, whether as yokel or "dapper dog," is comical. In other words, no comic potential was lost by showing him as he looked after his transformation (*SAP*, Nov. 18, 1890, and *Westra Posten* [Seattle], Apr. 15, 1892).

21. Some aspects of the greenhorn appear to be culture-specific: the Swedish greenhorn is in a "can do" mode, whereas other cultures stress the greenhorn as misfit, as, e.g., in the Yiddish ballad "Die Grine Kuzine."

Dania Hall: At the Center of a
Scandinavian American Community

DAVID MARKLE

During the mid-1880s, members of the Society Dania, a benevolent organization in Minneapolis dedicated to helping young Danes coming to America, began to plan for a meeting place and cultural center. They founded the Dania
Hall Building Association and commissioned Norwegian architect Carl Struck.
Louis Meldal, one-time president of the Society Dania, sold land located at
Cedar Avenue and Fifth Street to the association for $11,000, and a deed was
filed May 4, 1886, which included a prohibition of alcoholic beverage on the
premises (soon countermanded). The cornerstone of Dania Hall was laid a
month later, on the thirty-seventh anniversary of Danish independence, and
the festivities included a march down Cedar Avenue, then Washington Avenue
to the Union Depot and back again. There were many prominent speakers, including Lars M. Rand, who referred to "the social relations between Swedes
and Danes in Minneapolis . . . so interwoven with one another that nature itself feels aggrieved when we fail to work hand in hand." Rand went on to say
that Dania's cornerstone was "the foundation of a building within whose walls
the spirit of intelligence, unity, friendship and brotherly love will be taught . . .
not only among Danish citizens of Minneapolis, but the Norwegians and the
Swedes as well." Happily, Rand's words proved true. The completed building
was dedicated in another elaborate ceremony on November 10, 1886, at which
Rand was again a featured speaker. Next day, the *Minneapolis Tribune* carried
the following item:

> On the fifth day of June last, was laid with due ceremony the cornerstone of
> Dania Hall, which is by all odds the finest structure in that portion of the
> city. Last evening Dania Hall stood complete and over 300 Danes were pre-
> sent to witness its dedication.[1]

The large multi-purpose hall comprising the third and fourth floors was an open room 44 feet wide, 65 feet long, and 23 feet high, with a horseshoe-shaped balcony and a proscenium stage. The balcony alone seated 200, and another 600 could be accommodated on the theatre's main floor by setting up chairs. Across the stage, the curtain read *Ej Blot Til Lyst* (not for fun only), just like the curtain at the Royal Theatre in Copenhagen. The second floor initially housed six offices, a billiard room, a library, a small hall with a tiny stage or lecture platform, and the Society Dania fraternal rooms. There was space for two stores on the street level, and the basement housed additional offices, a kitchen, a dining hall, and J. M. Jackson's barbershop. Dania Hall's main entrance was on Fifth Street; patrons would enter through wrought iron gates with large, stylish gas torches to the left and right, where a wide wooden staircase led to the upper floors.[2]

In 1896, Society Dania bought the property from the Building Association for $23,300, the amount of the remaining debt. The original cost of the building and land together totaled $35,000, a substantial amount at a time when immigrants could book passage to America for less than $20. In his 1899 book *Minneapolis minnen* (Minneapolis Remembrances), the Swedish American journalist Alfred Söderström wrote:

> Among associations here, Dania enjoys a great reputation, and although the Danes are only a small segment of the Scandinavian population in Minneapolis, through harmony and unity they were the first to build themselves a monument for which they have reason to feel proud.[3]

Differing Attitudes about the Neighborhood

During its first few decades, Dania Hall served Scandinavian Americans in Minneapolis as a gatherer and radiator of positive attitudes throughout the Cedar-Riverside neighborhood and beyond. Although it catered to the residents of many areas, Dania Hall was inevitably associated with its immediate neighborhood and was, therefore, strongly affected by external attitudes about this Scandinavian enclave.

The immigrant group that dominated Cedar-Riverside at first was Norwegian, later outnumbered by waves of immigrant Swedes whose percentage peaked around 1920 when earlier Swedish immigrants retiring from farms may have helped swell the total. Cultured individuals as well as common folk came, and the generally working-class neighborhood quickly developed a down-to-earth and very lively character.[4]

Not everyone approved, however. In his novel *Længselens Baat* (The Boat
of Longing), Norwegian American novelist Ole Rølvaag describes the emotional vicissitudes of young immigrant Nils, for whom the downtown store
windows on Nicollet Avenue display unattainable dreams. Nils is earnest, hard
working, and often troubled by what he sees happening around him:

> Nils was doing the janitor work in eight Cedar Avenue business places. Four
> were saloons, in which he swept and washed floors. The others were stores. . . .
> And he rated himself prosperous. He was now earning nine dollars a week,
> and the work wasn't hard, either. . . except that it kept him up late nights.
> The stores he always did early in the morning, and was then through with
> them for the day. The saloons were worse, for they required two cleanings
> daily. . . . It was most disagreeable on days when he had to wash the places . . .
> a saloon might become revoltingly filthy after a ribald Saturday night. Nils
> couldn't understand how people could make such beasts of themselves; they
> scarcely resembled human beings any longer—no, not even animals. And
> they were Norwegians, too, many of them.

The lonely Nils finds some consolation by expressing his introspective longing
musically with his violin.[5]
   In 1884, Minneapolis mayor George Pillsbury was able to gain approval for
the liquor patrol limits with the help of many Scandinavian allies who may have
harbored aversions akin to Nils's. The theory behind liquor patrol limits was
geographically to segregate liquor establishments, thus keeping alcohol out of
most residential areas and making it easier for the police to patrol the saloons.
Downtown Minneapolis would continue to have liquor; residents of Germanic
northeast Minneapolis also insisted on it. According to Jim Hathaway, in
Cedar-Riverside's case:

> This district had the highest percentage of foreign-born in the city. Many
> Scandinavians lived here, but the area's lively character [generated over-
> whelming] anti-liquor sentiment. Curiously, many Scandinavians were hard
> drinkers at the time of their arrival in their adopted country, pure alcohol
> having been a common beverage with them. But after residence in the U.S.
> many tended toward abstinence.

It should be noted, however, that although the Sixth Ward was known for its
rooming houses and low-cost hotels, in 1885 it contained 500 more houses than
any other ward in Minneapolis. At first the patrol limits seemed to have solved
some problems, but by 1902 a "two-mile stretch of Washington Avenue, had 101
of the city's 360 saloons," and Cedar-Riverside was saturated.[6]

Six years after the measure took effect, the old Sixth Ward—which was then essentially Cedar-Riverside—elected the colorful Norwegian American politician Lars M. Rand as alderman. Rand established a long-standing record by holding a seat on the City Council for twenty years, from 1890 to 1910. An old-fashioned ward boss and skilled parliamentarian, he was thoroughly disliked by the foes of liquor for being a friend of the saloonkeepers. He was also known, however, as a warrior against the power elite and as a politician who consistently advocated the majority interest (which in his ward apparently meant pro-saloon). It seems that the saloons coexisted quite well with the frequent events at Dania Hall, the Southern Theater, and other dance halls. Longtime Seven Corners druggist Hugo Peterson estimated that, in the old days, Saturday night crowds seeking entertainment in the area's halls would total 10,000 to 12,000 persons.[7]

Of course, not everyone joined in the fun. Some, like the frugal and hardworking memoirist Evelina Månsson, carefully avoided frivolity, not to mention alcohol:

> The dances, masquerade balls and the like that were very often arranged by the Swedish-American young people at one of their "halls," such as Swedish Brothers, Dania, Norrmanna and others, I never attended, with the exception of a single time at Norrmanna hall. I thought that these entertainments were altogether empty and superficial—left no substance. And not just that they were empty pleasures, they also became expensive through expenditures on clothing—because everyone naturally sought to outshine the others—and so in time, through disturbed rest, undermined health. Nor did I have any further use either for such things as theatre, movies, or circuses— I viewed two theatrical presentations in six years.

Månsson enjoyed the music of the Swedish American churches, and it may be that she attended services at St. Ansgar's Protestant Episcopal Congregation, a very traditional church then located on Fifth Street and Nineteenth Avenue, just a few doors east and across the street from Dania Hall's main entrance.[8]

How does one explain such contrasting attitudes and lifestyles? St. Ansgar's had been established in 1893, during the tenure of Alderman Rand, and was located less than a block from lively Cedar Avenue. Although St. Ansgar's was probably not a bastion of pietistic religiosity, the pastor was certainly no Gösta Berling. One is led to the conclusion that the neighborhood must have enjoyed an atmosphere of general tolerance; it readily accommodated smaller ethnic immigrant groups who differed greatly from Scandinavians, as well as various faiths.[9]

Augsburg Seminary (now Augsburg College), which came to Cedar-Riverside in 1872, survived and grew at its location just three blocks east of Cedar Avenue—although for many years its prevailing philosophy of abstinence in a Norwegian-Lutheran pietistic framework was paralleled by attitudes of "isolationism" and "withdrawal tendencies," and an "anti-urban orientation." In fact, from 1921 to 1946, Augsburg College retained suburban property for a potential move. Thus the histories of Augsburg and the neighborhood ran largely on separate tracks until recent times.[10]

Trinity Lutheran Congregation, the church most closely associated with Augsburg and situated nearby at Twentieth Avenue South and Ninth Street, did not seek invisibility; in fact one of its early pastors, M. Falk Gjertsen, was one of the best-known Scandinavians in Minneapolis. Gjertsen and other Trinity pastors inveighed against drink, but the congregation's considerable involvement with global missions, the service of Gjertsen and another of its early pastors on the public school board, and the church's extra appropriation of money to aid the destitute during the restricted budget times of the Great Depression all suggest an attitude of active benevolence.[11]

Located more strategically on Cedar Avenue and Seventh Street among the saloons was the unmistakably helpful presence of that tireless provider of comfort and unselfish promoter of good will, the Salvation Army. Scandinavians felt particularly welcome there, where the languages of the old country were understood. The No. 4 Corps (also known as the Temple Corps) began its work in the 1880s or 1890s near Seven Corners. In 1923, No. 4 built a substantial temple at 614 Cedar Avenue. Only the No. 3 Corps in Brooklyn, New York, preceded No. 4 in ministering especially to Scandinavian Americans.[12]

For a brief time, Evelina Månsson lived one block up the street at Sixth and Cedar, and it is not surprising she did not remain long in the Cedar-Riverside neighborhood. Many others who stayed and immersed themselves in the life of the community have remembered the experience with pleasure. In a 1973 article, Patricia Hampl relays fond memories from Violet Olson: "Oh, it was quite well known: 'Let's go to Cedar and have some fun.' Cedar Avenue was jumping!" And from Chester Anderson:

> We had everything right here. There was dance halls galore; there was pool rooms galore; and, of course, you had the beer joints galore. It was a nice place to live. Everybody was a working class of people. We didn't have anything.

Hampl suggests that "There was a magical quality, a timelessness about the Cedar Avenue of the saloons and dance halls then. 'Boy! Would that time ever go fast,' Chester Anderson said. . . . 'Pretty near 7 A.M. and you'd have to be to work! Olle, grab the overalls! Where did the night go?'"[13]

Growing Up in Cedar-Riverside

The neighborhood was much more than nightly entertainment; it was a place of family life, work, and growing up. Incomes tended to be low, which also colored attitudes about the neighborhood. Lib Pierotti's recollections of childhood years from 1903 to 1915 include some of the Scandinavian aspects of the neighborhood as seen by a member of the small Italian American contingent, but more often he describes things economic: for example, people waiting until Christmas eve to buy trees at bargain prices and then waiting until 9:00 P.M., when Holtzermann's store cut toy prices in half, to buy toys for their children.[14]

Pierotti remembers children becoming "'temporary' Presbyterians" so they could get a bag of Christmas candy at Riverside Chapel on Twentieth and Riverside, and how "The good old 'Pill House'" (Pillsbury Settlement House) gave holiday parties for poor children. For many children of poor parents, "one of the biggest Christmas events of the times was the annual Elks Lodge Christmas Party. The B. P. O. E. (we called them Best People on Earth)." It is evident how important the fraternal organizations and spirit of mutuality must have been for the neighborhood's many Scandinavians.

That spirit of mutuality was often seen in everyday play and entertainment, as well. Lorayne Andersen Bellows remembers attending events as a girl at Dania Hall with her parents. Her Danish-born father, Nels Andersen, "had a good voice and he sang at dances there, not from the stage but from the dance floor while people danced, and he sang in Danish, Swedish or Norwegian."[15]

The Pillsbury Settlement House on Fourth Street and Sixteenth Avenue was a provider of much-needed social services; in 1933 the attendance at the House's facilities and classes nearly reached 200,000, and there were twelve resident workers. Ed Currie, who was elected head resident in 1932 and later became director, was especially helpful. As one "alumnus" put it: "You have to understand, in those days we were all part of minority groups and we were poor. We had to be tough to survive. But thanks to the Pill House and Ed Currie, we had discipline and inspiration."[16]

Margaret Ryman Cartwright remembers being put in a baby carriage by her mother who then left her at Pill House all day "because she had to work." A few years later, the young Margaret often raced the horse-drawn fire engine when it left the fire barn on Fourth Street and Fifteenth Avenue, near her girlhood home. Was it a good place to grow up? "Oh yeah, there was never a dull moment. I had my share of bruises. . . . I was the one running from building to building. Any excitement, I wanted to know where it was and who it was." Cedar-Riverside was an egalitarian place to live: "It was the biggest city of Swedes! Nobody was any better than anybody else."[17]

The neighborhood also enjoyed some of the charms of a small town with its own retail district. In a 1972 interview, Solvig Hansen said this was the place: "I didn't live in the area, but I came down here every Saturday night. There were all kinds of stores and coffee shops." Similarly, Ida Hansen remembered growing up on the river flats (Bohemian Flats) and coming "upstairs" to the fine shops of the neighborhood: "It was a lovely place to be a child." There were some impressive careers as well. Orville Freeman, later to become governor and United States Secretary of Agriculture, was an alumnus of the Pill House.[18]

Early Activities in Dania Hall

Throughout much of Dania Hall's first hundred years, its spaces were used for many purposes. Larger rooms were rented out for parties, wedding receptions, meetings, and dances. During Dania Hall's early decades, the Cedar-Riverside neighborhood contained a rich mixture of ethnic groups including Slovaks, Germans, and Rumanian Jews (among others). All these groups used the building, but Dania Hall was especially popular with the many Scandinavians who were long predominant in the area and who understandably regarded Dania as a cultural center.

Being a physical landmark as well as a Scandinavian community center, Dania Hall served as a marshalling point for large outdoor gatherings. Colonel Hans Mattson wrote:

> In the Fall of 1887, residents of Minneapolis were honored with a visit by a great number of Swedish, Norwegian and Danish officers, non-commissioned officers and soldiers. They arrived at Minneapolis by special train from Chicago and were met at Union Depot by a crowd of people estimated at 10,000. The Swedish Guard, Normanna infantry and Society Dania were arrayed in front of the station. The guests were taken in hand by the festival committee and led in procession through the illuminated streets packed with eager spectators, to Dania Hall where they ate a splendid supper to background music by Svea and Normanna music choirs.

Mattson, elected the previous year as Minnesota Secretary of State, was that festival's spokesperson.[19]

Similarly, ten years later on the afternoon of May 17, Scandinavian groups from the south side of Minneapolis gathered at Dania Hall to parade downtown to Third Street and Nicollet Avenue, where they met groups from the north side. Together they paraded to Loring Park, where a crowd of 20,000 to 25,000 witnessed the unveiling of Jakob Fjelde's statue of the beloved Norwegian violinist Ole Bull.[20]

Throughout each year within Dania Hall there were home talent plays, concerts, balls, lectures, and other programs. Society Dania held Thanksgiving turkey raffles and annual November festivals featuring roast goose, and for Christmas set up a huge tree decorated with Danish and American flags. A rare surviving document from September 1889 lists the details of four Society Dania evening programs, which featured musical numbers and speeches— including a talk by Rev. Kristofer Janson and music by Ringwall and Thule's orchestra—followed by a dance. The participation of the Norwegian Janson and the Swedish American musician Oscar Ringwall exemplify the routinely pan-Scandinavian character of activities in Dania Hall.[21]

Dania Hall in 1906. Four stories in height with a distinctive corner tower, the building's architecture exhibited characteristics of High Victorian Eclecticism combined with Gothic overtones.

The stage of the extraordinary multipurpose hall was the scene of many musical and dramatic entertainments, such as a 1915 production by the Svenska Teatersällskapet (Swedish Theatre Society) of Strindberg's *Fadren* (The Father) under the direction of Ragnar Johansson "from Stockholm." It was the first presentation of Strindberg in Minneapolis, and apparently it gave rise to a new dramatic club, *Strindbergarna* (The Strindbergians), who produced the play again the following year at Dania Hall with a similar cast under Johansson's direction.[22]

Ungdoms Förening af 1905 (Young People's Association of 1905, named after the year of its founding) presented one or two Danish plays every year in Dania Hall to capacity audiences until the 1930s. An early program survives from a production of Björnsterne Björnson's comedy *De Nygifta* (The Newlyweds) by an unnamed or *ad hoc* group on Dania Hall's stage, an event concluded by a dance. Another early document announces a "GREAT CONTEST PLAY" between the Swedish theatrical society Norden presenting the one-act comedy *Hans Tredje Hustru* (His Third Wife) and the Norwegian amusement club Tryg presenting the one-act vaudeville *Kusine Lotte* (Cousin Lotte). The listing goes on to name the contest's judges, who are, apparently, a Swede and a Norwegian (Mr. Hjalmar Nilsson and G. Biornstad), and to announce the evening's customary conclusion—a dance, this time involving Jacobson's Orchestra.[23]

The young Norwegian writer Knut Hamsun, who later became famous and won the Nobel Prize, lived in Minneapolis for a time during the late 1880s and caused quite a stir in the little Scandinavian intellectual enclave on Cedar Avenue. He had been brought to Minneapolis by the prominent liberal pastor and writer, Kristofer Janson, who encouraged Hamsun's literary efforts. According to journalist and local historian Carl G. O. Hansen:

> I doubt if there among the Norwegians in Minneapolis ever were two more distinctive individuals, mentally as well as physically, than Kristofer Janson and Knut Hamsun. As I am writing these lines I see before me with the eye that penetrates into the distant past, Knut Hamsun strutting down Cedar avenue—figure erect, more than six feet tall, well proportioned, fine, chiseled features, smooth-faced, dressed in a tight-fitting jacket (*Nansen-jakke*)—and near-sighted, so much so that the book or newspaper which he invariably had with him had to be held close up to his eyes.[24]

Hamsun enjoyed spending time across the street from Dania Hall chatting in the offices of *Felt Raabet* (Battle Cry,) a liberal temperance paper. *Felt Raabet* announced a series of eleven lectures by Hamsun on modern movements in literature exemplified by Balzac, Flaubert, Zola, Björnson, Ibsen, Lie, Kielland, Kristofer Janson, Strindberg, and others. After the first lecture, the location was changed to Dania's little hall (on the second floor). Hamsun's best re-viewer for these was the local but highly cultured Swedish American journal-ist, Victor Nilsson. Hamsun's farewell appearance on March 28, 1888, was in Dania's large hall: "Thoughts on Esthetics—Life in Minneapolis," a rather deprecatory criticism foreshadowing his book, *Fra det moderne Amerikas Aand-sliv* (The Cultural Life of Modern America.) Hamsun's friend Janson, who had given introductory remarks before the talk, felt compelled to respond soon af-ter with his own lecture on "Life in Minneapolis." Nilsson reviewed Janson's presentation, reporting that Janson "gave great recognition to Mr. Hamsun's talk, but showed how for the most part it held up too great a yardstick against our young city." Nevertheless, the following year (after returning to Norway), Hamsun sought to get his new book reviewed in America, so he wrote to his val-ued Minneapolis critic, Victor Nilsson. Hamsun also wanted Nilsson to persuade the well-known writer, Gustaf af Geijerstam, to review the book in Sweden.[25]

Intellectual activities were a continuing element of the programs in Dania Hall. For example, Alfred Söderström's 1899 account notes that the literary as-sociation *Fram* (Forward), a group with seventy-five members, held weekly meetings there. It was not by facilitating high culture, however, that Dania Hall took a unique place in history, but rather by nurturing a special kind of popu-lar entertainment.[26]

Interior of Dania Hall's large hall, 1969.
At that time the original large gas chandelier was still in place.

At the turn of the century, Dania's large hall became the birthplace of Scandinavian-language vaudeville, a New World form of entertainment in the languages of the old country—Swedish, Norwegian, and Danish. Such an evening's enjoyment might consist of a theatrical production, probably light-hearted or farcical, and then musical entertainment and comedy, followed by a dance. Dania's large hall, with its moveable seating and level wooden main floor, had been purposely designed to accommodate dances and large social functions. Many Minneapolis-based Dania Hall entertainers became national pioneers of America's ethnic recording industry. The Danielson Brothers Orchestra, Thorstein Skarning, Ted Johnson, and others were national recording artists for widely distributed labels such as Columbia and Victor.[27]

The best-known group was that of Hjalmar Peterson, better known as "Olle i Skratthult" (Olle from Laughtersville). Olle became quite famous as a musician and comedian, although for many years on national tours his group also performed plays. Olle's touring company contained as many as twenty performers including his first wife, Olga Lindgren-Peterson, who was one of the stars. According to Anne-Charlotte Harvey:

> Wherever the Olle i Skratthult Company went, it was welcomed, loved and remembered. Newspaper clippings from small country towns as well as Chicago and New York attest to the extraordinary popularity of the company and, particularly, of Olle himself. One apocryphal anecdote tells of a man in Lindstrom, Minnesota, who actually died laughing at Olle i Skratthult.[28]

In 1915 Olle recorded *Nikolina*, one of America's most popular songs in a Scandinavian language, and became Cedar Avenue's hero. Swedish television has done two prime-time documentaries on the life and coast-to-coast career of Olle i Skratthult, and a museum now honors him in the city of his birth, Munkfors, Sweden. The Ellis Island Museum in New York City also has his likeness on permanent display.

The Later Years

Scandinavian vaudeville waned after the Depression and so did Society Dania activities. Meanwhile, the Scandinavian presence in Cedar-Riverside gradually diminished. In 1963, the Society sold its building to pharmacist Phil Richter for only $35,000. Since 1948 Richter had been operating on the first floor where there had been a drugstore since about 1910. He had acquired the business from Seiver Moe who had also operated a hardware store in the smaller commercial space in Dania's southeast corner.[29]

Caretakers had long lived in the building. In the 1920s, Anna Olson, wife of

DET GAMLA ODÖDLIGA

VÄRMLÄNDINGARNA

TAL-, SÅNG- OCH DANSSPEL I SEX ATKTER
af
FREDRIK AUGUST DAHLGREN
UPPFÖRES

Söndagen den 17 januari
Kl. 8:15 e. m.
Å

DANIA HALL CEDAR AVE. OCH 5TH ST.

Ett 30-tal personer komma att merverka, däribland:

MARIA SONANDER	HARALD HEIBERG	CARL SKOOG
EDWARD VERNON	AUGUSTA LINDE	JOHN LIND
KLARA LARSON	ANNA LINDQUIST	WM. BENSON
GOTTFRID NORD	FRITZ YOUNG	GUSTAF LARSON

Med många flera

RESERVERADE BILJETTER TIL 50c OCH 35c
I förköp hos Apotekare J. O Peterson, 1501 Wash. Ave. So.

Program for a performance of Värmländingarna *at Dania Hall*

the caretaker, caught pigeons from upper story overhangs and roasted them. During Richter's ownership, there were still Danish American caretakers who lived in a small apartment in the front part of the building's second floor. For many years the adjacent Holtzermann's Department Store had used Dania's basement for storage (front half) and as a display area (back half) with access via the Holtzermann building.[30]

When I came to the neighborhood to live in 1962—I had first gotten a look at it in 1959—there were still remnants of the historic community, greatly diluted by the growing number of students and other young people. The University of Minnesota had not spread across the Mississippi River to establish a West Bank campus in the neighborhood. Freeways, which catered to a sprawling suburbia, had not yet begun to split or isolate Minneapolis neighborhoods and hamper traffic circulation on city streets. The liquor patrol limits were still in effect, and the Salvation Army band still played outdoors on Sunday at the Cedar Avenue mission.[31]

A trace of old Scandinavian flavor still lingered in Cedar establishments. At Ellison's on Cedar Avenue—where raw lingon, anchovies, and pickled herring were sold from large barrels during the holiday season—the expert butchers greeted and thanked customers in Swedish. Brodahl's Restaurant served *lutefisk* every day; the option was drawn butter or cream gravy. Moberg's grocery store seemingly had hundreds of varieties of canned sardines, herring, and other specialty items. Ray's Lunch would soon offer yellow pea soup once a week. On Seven Corners (Washington and Cedar Avenues), the Samuelson sisters sold *Svenska Dagbladet* and other Scandinavian newspapers as well as ice cream treats and tobacco. Next door, J. O. Peterson Drug was still run by J. O.'s son, Hugo. Immediately

Popular Swedish immigrant actress and singer Maria Sonander Rice, who appeared at Dania Hall many times, in a costume of Värmland province

across Fifth Street from Dania Hall, the Five Corners Saloon interior was more brightly lit in the evening than during the day; the jukebox still contained *Nikolina* and *Johan på Snippen*. And Dania Hall was functional, although its large hall was little used.

My southern Minnesota parents were not pleased that I had located to Cedar-Riverside. For them, the neighborhood had a bad reputation. They were not aware of the significant difference, both geographic and social, between a notorious establishment such as the Persian Palms nightclub on Washington Avenue, on the one hand, and Cedar-Riverside establishments, on the other.[32]

It is especially notable that Minneapolis city directories for 1963–64 listed at least twenty-two liquor establishments on the nine blocks of Cedar Avenue north of Franklin Avenue, but comparative crime statistics published from time to time in the Minneapolis newspapers indicated that Cedar-Riverside was then one of the safest neighborhoods. Though changed from the old days it remained one of the liveliest districts of Minneapolis, and it also continued to be a real neighborhood where people quite different from one another got acquainted. There was a rare degree of tolerance that seemed to be an old tradition: "Nobody was any better than anybody else."

During the 1960s, Cedar Riverside Associates (CRA) had begun acquiring land for a sweeping urban renewal project, which essentially promised to pave over most of the neighborhood from the recently constructed interstate highways 35W and 94 to the Mississippi River and replace most of the old buildings with new, predominantly high-rise structures. CRA's acquisition of existing housing accelerated the change from what was left of a working-class Scandinavian neighborhood to one of (a 1960s university-oriented) counter-culture: hippies, war protesters, "pot" smokers, "acid heads," and dropouts, in addition to ordinary students. The neighborhood earned a new label; suburban families were seen rolling up their car windows and locking their doors as they drove past Dania Hall where a bare-footed, brain-damaged but harmless "speed freak" often perched like a bird on the peak of the waste receptacle, and where others of aberrant appearance—for example, a young woman wearing nothing but a bib overall—might come into view.[33]

Dania Hall's large hall was the scene of dances and séance-like gatherings at the time. Local rock groups such as The Litter, Jokers Wild, T. C. Atlantic, and the Paisleys, sometimes accompanied by psychedelic light shows, drew sizeable crowds. Dances had been held there for many years without a permit, but owner Phil Richter decided to apply for a dance hall permit when one group wanted to advertise its events. After repairing some minor cracked plaster as required by the inspector, Richter got the permit. Alderman Jens Christensen, however, claimed he had seen fire hazards and requested further inspections. Richter accused Christensen of applying pressure to help CRA acquire the building. Following the testimony of a City "secret agent" in the summer of 1968, the five member City Council Licenses Committee voted to deny the permit. Ironically, those voting to deny were Scandinavian Americans. Unfortunately for the large hall, the action led to the prevention of practically any public activity there without substantial and expensive improvements, such as the addition of an elevator. Later that year, CRA acquired Dania Hall and knocked a hole in the wall between the large hall and the Holtzermann building in the hope that a way could be provided to deal with the building's fire code problem, but this proved unworkable.[34]

CRA completed the first phase of its "new town-in-town" redevelopment in 1972 with the Cedar Square West complex, 1,300 units of housing on 8.9 acres of land across Cedar Avenue from Dania Hall. The other residents still had what amounted to a "small town in town," and they wished to continue their relaxed, unconventional lifestyle with its 1950s economic framework. The rebelliousness of young residents and their antagonism toward redevelopment and rent increases provided the appearance of mass action and solidarity, which a small group of self-styled radical activists used to gain power in the neighborhood's urban renewal process.

By the 1970s, the University had acquired and cleared a substantial area for its West Bank campus. Except for institutional land, almost the entire neighborhood had been designated a tax increment district to finance redevelopment. The tax increment district would capture property tax on increased value—such as the new buildings of Cedar Square West—at a loss to the county, to city essential services, and especially to the school district. The activists then stopped CRA with an environmental lawsuit and took control of the officially recognized neighborhood citizen participation group. Their handling of neighborhood dissent was expert and sometimes brutal, a new political bossism that was a far cry from the neighborhood's traditional tolerance and good will, or the conviction that "Nobody was any better than anybody else."[35]

Meanwhile, the Snoose Boulevard Festival, an annual occurrence from 1972 to 1976, was a major Cedar-Riverside event that eventually attracted national and international attention. Organized by Maury Bernstein, it was primarily a celebration of the popular Scandinavian musical heritage of Cedar-Riverside, and Dania Hall served as a physical centerpiece, a sort of "architectural mascot," according to Bernstein. The Festival drew as many as an estimated 100,000 attendees for a two-and-a-half day period. One Minneapolitan reports a typical Festival encounter with an elderly gentleman who exclaimed, "Yumpin yimminy, look at all the people; it's yust like the old days!"[36]

But once again, not everyone joined in the fun. Criticism amounting to opposition came from persons associated with the American Swedish Institute, particularly from the former director who objected to making a festival out of what he termed "the seamy side" of immigrant history. The criticism received press coverage in both Minnesota and Sweden and did not signify a personal eccentricity; rather, it expressed widely held attitudes about the neighborhood, the immigrant drive for respectability, and the wish to forget the days when Scandinavians were a poor, repressed, unassimilated group. These were also important reasons for Dania Hall's neglect and disuse—Dania Hall's guilt by association.[37]

The Struggle to Redevelop

In 1975, through efforts of the Danish American Fellowship and the Minnesota Historical Society, Dania Hall was placed on the National Registry of Historic Places. Beginning in 1976, and continuing for more than ten years, the official neighborhood group's annual projection for the use of tax increment money included $1.1 million for renovation of Dania Hall. Although the group took no action, in 1977 it did sponsor a study and public forum on Dania Hall. During the period of 1975 to 1989, the tax increment district captured more than $34 million, almost all of which was spent on administrative costs and expensive rehabilitation of low-income housing for the activists and others acceptable to them. None of the money was spent to renovate Dania Hall.[38]

In 1986, Dania Hall was acquired by the Minneapolis Community Development Agency (MCDA). The first and second floors remained in use until 1991, when the building nearly succumbed to a fire, which some believed to have been the work of young arsonists. The roof sustained heavy damage, and there was also damage to the large hall, particularly to the ceiling. MCDA subsequently installed a very solid roof that closely followed the original lines, and, according to an MCDA spokesperson, at least one example of an interior architectural element had been saved.[39]

Many stage-oriented groups looked at Dania Hall and were charmed by the building and interior but found the stage space and ancillary facilities inadequate for full-time theatre; after all, the large hall was indeed a multi-purpose hall, not a theater. An exception was the Hosmer Brown group involved with the Lyndale Theatre Garage. This group had obtained temporary exclusive development rights to Dania Hall in 1989 and incorporated as Dania Building Conservation Corporation. The Browns went so far as to commission a professional study of the building, but they gave up rights in 1992.

During this period of disuse, there was an ongoing threat to the historically listed interior of the large hall because of the agendas of some developers and the prevailing "skin-deep" philosophy of historic preservation that only values facades. In 1993, two developers advanced plans, one including auditorium renovation and another—by the West Bank CDC (WBCDC)—that proposed "mothballing" the auditorium for a use to be decided later. The WBCDC proposal was worrisome because the developer had originally proposed converting the upper stories into housing; WBCDC obtained temporary exclusive development rights from MCDA but, fortunately for the auditorium, was unable to secure funds.[40]

In 1995 Glen Olsen obtained rights with a sensitively conceived renovation proposal, and he gave Dania Hall a second chance for a predominantly Scandinavian function. Olsen, a construction expert active in Danish American activities, had been one of those most responsible—the other being State Historical Architect Charles Nelson—for the securing of Dania Hall's preservation listing. He engaged in extended discussions with various Scandinavian organizations and did arouse some interest in using a renovated Dania, but the groups were unwilling to make significant financial commitments to the redevelopment. Feeling rather discouraged, Olsen was reluctant to continue to exclude other developers under such circumstances, although he stated his continued interest.

Very soon in the summer of 1996, another developer obtained the rights for the purpose of turning Dania into housing. Steve Schwanke repeatedly vowed near-readiness to begin redevelopment, but he and his partner, Harold Truesdale, seemed unable to obtain significant funding and tenant commitment. Nevertheless, they requested and obtained renewals of rights, ultimately holding on to them longer than any other developer. Most crucial of the renewals depended on approval at a neighborhood meeting on July 16, 1997, which was attended by fewer than twenty individuals, despite extensive door-to-door distribution of notices by preservationists. All but four voted to continue the rights and effectively authorize the destruction of Dania's auditorium. One of those in the majority was a Scandinavian American emeritus professor who had been active on the board of the Nordic Center at Augsburg College.[41]

Much of the problem these developers encountered, as had others, no doubt was the progressive deterioration of conditions on Cedar Avenue, particularly from Third Street south to Eighth Street. Individuals who returned after being elsewhere for a number of years expressed shock at the obvious decline in both the appearance of the street and the reduced level of business activity. The University of Minnesota had largely turned its back on its neighborhoods and had neglected student-housing needs while sponsoring eateries and other businesses on the campus itself. The new Carlson School of Management building effectively walled off the campus from the Cedar-Riverside area. The neighborhood activists had partially isolated their home-turf east of the Cedar Avenue business district by creating physical barriers, while at the same time

they were often inclined to make vehement demands for restrictions on business activity, especially regarding hours of operation and the availability of
liquor. Their leasehold co-op housing had long been essentially off limits to
full-time students because of the requirements of the governmental housing
subsidies that had been part of the redevelopment financial packages. Across
the street from Dania, the large high-rise Riverside Plaza apartment complex
(formerly Cedar Square West) contained fewer and fewer students as it housed
more and more immigrants. In short, neighborhood businesses depended on
customers from outside the neighborhood, but such visitors might be repelled
by the run-down appearance of many facades and the limited amount of on-
street parking, or they might harbor an aversion toward the many individuals
of color to be seen in the vicinity.

For Schwanke and Truesdale, their hope was a novel source of funds, the
city's Neighborhood Revitalization Program (NRP). It was modeled after the
Cedar-Riverside example, which is ironic given the decline of Cedar Avenue.
It is also ironic that Cedar-Riverside was the last neighborhood to participate
in NRP, although there was not much to prevent it except the resistance of a
small but influential neighborhood cadre. Under pressure from businesses, however, the city council member representing most of Cedar-Riverside's precincts
insisted that the neighborhood should begin its NRP and warned that the city
would not provide funds to redevelop Dania Hall from any other source. Meanwhile, the city continued eagerly to spend large amounts of non-NRP money on
numerous downtown projects such as theater renovations, including moving
the Shubert in 1999 at a cost of five million dollars for transportation, setting a
world record for the heaviest building ever moved. In comparison, the total
projected renovation cost for Dania Hall was 2.7 million dollars.[42]

On March 30, 1998, the MCDA Operating Committee approved another extension for the developers, who continued to say that they intended to put
housing into Dania Hall. During the following months, the NRP money ship
began moving into harbor. At a relatively well-attended neighborhood meeting on July 28, substantial support finally emerged for the renovation of the Dania auditorium. At that point, it also became clear that Gar Hargens, a Danish
American architect with excellent preservation experience, would work on the
project. From then on, enthusiasm for genuine renovation grew, even when
more money was required. In early August, a study was released that had been
completed earlier in the year by the Carlson Volunteer Consultants at the University of Minnesota; it indicated the likely viability of "restoring Dania Hall . . .
to its original intent as a hall for rent," based on two market surveys. The study
very likely also had some influence through an earlier release to the expert panel

convened by the Minnesota Historical Society and the MCDA. The panel's own interesting report can essentially be characterized by an off-the-cuff remark by panelist Charles Nelson: "Sometimes original use is best use." Congressman Martin Sabo, long aware of the significance of Dania Hall, obtained an unexpected additional $300,000 in federal money for the renovation. New immigrants, particularly the numerous Vietnamese and Somalis in Riverside Plaza, looked forward to using the auditorium.[43]

But who would use the street-level main floor of Dania? This was a problem that received only questionable solutions. In hindsight, the best time to fix Dania Hall must have been the period from 1977 to 1990 when it was still physically intact, when costs were low and money was available. A renovated Dania Hall would have buoyed the area and probably would have helped to prevent much of the surrounding deterioration. Now that residents were finally allowed to focus their attention on this important building, they became excited, but the building's environment remained troublesome. Cedar Cultural Center, across the street, drew large crowds for its musical events, but afterwards they did not linger in the neighborhood. In February 2000, Schwanke and Truesdale had still not satisfied all requirements, and the development agreement remained unexecuted. The prospective first-floor tenant—a jazz club—pulled out. At one meeting, some residents wanted to require the club to close at 11:00 P.M., unreasonable for attractions of that nature.[44]

Nevertheless, work proceeded on a provisional basis by MCDA using NRP money. Contractor Gerry Flannery was very fond of the project and later observed that "his employees enjoyed it because the community supported it so strongly, and people walking by during working hours would flash a thumbs-up sign or shout out words of encouragement." Architect Gar Hargens said, "People would stop you on the street and were so excited about it. . . . Dania was like a boy-scout camp. It seemed like everyone had memories of it." Close to a million dollars had been spent, and a great portion of the renovation had been accomplished, including the construction of an elevator shaft at the rear of the building. A sprinkler system was scheduled for installation in a week or two.[45]

Early in the morning of February 28, 2000, a number of individuals who happened to be within hearing distance of Dania Hall noticed what sounded like two series of gunshots, but there was no gunplay. Not long after 1:00 A.M., the lower levels of Dania were ablaze, and within twenty minutes, while sirens of fire engines approached, it already appeared as though the building would be a total loss. For anyone who loved Dania Hall, it was truly a hellish scene. The blaze very quickly became an intensely hot four-alarm fire, and the firefighters concentrated on saving the rest of the block. At their height, the flames

extended perhaps three or more stories higher than the building, and an automobile parked in front partially melted. Walls collapsed, and by 3:00 A.M. most
of Dania Hall was gone.[46]

Consider, for a moment, the fate of the seven wonders of the ancient world:
how important is the one that remains, especially for Egypt. And then consider
how one must search long and hard for any reminder that Cedar-Riverside was
once a Scandinavian neighborhood. Dania Hall was so much more than bricks
and mortar. At a March 2 memorial meeting at the Cedar Cultural Center, several hundred individuals, including some of the neighborhood's recent immigrants, shared their memories. After the meeting was well underway, we heard
a 1975 recording of *Hälsa dem därhemma* ("Greet Those at Home") sung very
beautifully at the age of 79 by Olga Lindgren-Nilsen (formerly Lindgren-
Peterson), who was Olle i Skratthult's first wife. After further exchanges
of friendly thoughts and memories, the meeting closed to the strains of another
recording by the same artist. This time it was a wistful American melody with
Swedish words, *Barndomshemmet* ("The Childhood Home"), saying that
though the years have passed, the childhood home is not forgotten.

And now, Dania Hall exists only in memory and imagination as a monu-
ment to the richness of Scandinavian immigrant life in America.[47]

✳ ✳ ✳

NOTES

The author wishes to thank Maury Bernstein, without whom this paper would never have
been written, and Marianne Tiblin and Lance Brockman, who generously supplied materials from their own files. Many others helped who are too numerous to list, but a few of
their names appear below in the notes.
1. "Dania Hall Cornerstone," *Minneapolis Tribune*, June 6, 1886, p. 5. The article provides
a synopsis of Rand's speech, not an exact text.
2. "Dania Hall Dedication," *Minneapolis Tribune*, Nov. 11, 1886, p. 4; Judith Anderson,
Dania Hall (Minneapolis: Cedar Riverside Project Area Committee, 1977), 4.
3. Alfred Söderström, *Minneapolis minnen. Kulturhistorisk axplockning från qvarnstaden
vid Mississippi* (Minneapolis: published by author, 1899), 292, 293, trans. mine.
4. Byron Nordstrom, "The Sixth Ward: A Minneapolis Swede Town in 1905," in *Perspectives on Swedish Immigration: Proceedings of the International Conference on the Swedish
Heritage in the Upper Midwest, April 1–3, 1976, University of Minnesota, Duluth*, Nils Hasselmo, ed. (Chicago: Swedish Pioneer Historical Society and the Univ. of Minn., Duluth,
1978), 163.
5. O. E. Rølvaag, *The Boat of Longing*, Nora O. Solum, trans. (New York: Harper & Brothers, 1933), 97.
6. Jim Hathaway, "The Liquor Patrol Limits of Minneapolis," *Hennepin County History*
44 (1985): 5, 6; Byron Nordstrom, "Ethnicity and Community in the Sixth Ward of Min-

neapolis in 1910," in *Scandinavians and Other Immigrants in Urban America: The Proceedings of a Research Conference,* Odd S. Lovoll, ed. (Northfield, Minn.: St. Olaf College Press, 1985), 41; Dan Armitage and the West Bank Historical Collective, "The Curling Waters: A West Bank History," *Minnesota Daily,* Sept. 27, 1973, Complement p. 17. Armitage provides an interesting, readable report, but it is undocumented and contains some errors.

7. It is interesting that Söderström, usually so ready to include Norwegians and Danes, does not mention Lars M. Rand in *Minneapolis minnen,* which was published during Rand's long tenure on the City Council. Possible reasons: Rand was a friend of liquor; Söderström was not. Rand was a Democrat; Söderström a Republican. Söderström, *Minneapolis minnen,* 86f., 134; Carl H. Chrislock, "Profile of a Ward Boss: The Political Career of Lars M. Rand," in *Scandinavians and Other Immigrants in Urban America,* 93–110; Armitage, "Curling Waters," 22. "Seven Corners" was (and is) the name commonly given the area around the intersection of Cedar Avenue and Washington Avenue; sometimes it was also used broadly in reference to the entire area of shops and public establishments in what is now the Cedar-Riverside neighborhood.

8. Evelina Månsson, *Amerika minnen. Upplevelser och iaktagelser från en 6-årig vistelse i U.S.A.* (Hvetlanda: Svenska Allmogeförlaget, 1930), 54, trans. mine.

9. Söderström, *Minneapolis minnen,* 237. At the beginning of Selma Lagerlöf's novel *Gösta Berlings saga,* the above named priest and carouser loses his job.

10. Carl Chrislock, *From Fjord to Freeway* (Minneapolis: Augsburg College, 1969), 129, 149f.

11. Carl G. O. Hansen, *My Minneapolis* (Minneapolis: published by author, 1956), 182f.; Chrislock, "Profile of a Ward Boss," 98f.; Rev. Paul Rogers, oral communication to author, Apr. 28, 1997. Trinity's church building was taken in 1966 for I-94 freeway construction, but church meetings have continued at other locations. I observed that Trinity's neighborhood involvement during the 1970s and 1980s was primarily to cooperate with the activists and promote its remaining real estate interest as owner of a small city block in Cedar-Riverside, which contained dilapidated housing. Trinity's faith was rewarded when the block was redeveloped in 1991 by a developer favored by the city and the activists, using publicly facilitated financing.

12. Col. Stig Franzén, and Maj. Robert Johnson, 1997 telephone communications to author. Col. Franzén was present at the conversion of Olle i Skratthult into the Salvation Army fold. Also, see K. A. Walden, ed., *Genom 45 år. Återblick över Frälsningsarmens skandinaviska arbeta i Amerika, 1887–1933* ([New York?]: The Salvation Army, [1933?], 10f., 104.

13. Patricia Hampl, "Travels on the boat of longing: the snoose boulevard festival," *Preview* (Collegeville, Minn.: Minnesota Educational Radio, Inc., 1973), 6f.

14. Lib [Livio] Pierotti, "The Holidays in Seven Corners," *Many Corners* 2 (Nov.–Dec. 1974): 6.

15. Lorayne Bellows, telephone conversation with author, Nov. 11, 1993.

16. B. C. Rossmann, "The 'Pill House,'" *Many Corners* 2 (June 1974): 9.

17. Margaret Ryman Cartwright, interviewed by author Mar. 14, 1997, and Apr. 26, 1997. According to the Minneapolis Fire Department, the Cedar-Riverside firehouse used horses until 1922.

18. Solvig Hansen, quoted by Doug Stone in "In the Open," *Minneapolis Tribune,* Apr. 10, 1972, p. 1B; Ida Hanson, quoted by Peter Vaughn in "Those Were the Days: Snoose Boulevard will live again," *Minneapolis Star,* Apr. 6, 1972, p. 1C; Lib [Livio] Pierotti, "When it was Seven Corners/ Remembering Ed Currie," *Many Corners* 3 (Apr. 1973): 18.

19. Hans Mattson, *Minnen af Ofverste H. Mattson* (Lund: C. W. R. K. Gleerups förlag, 1892), 336, trans. mine.

20. Söderström, *Minneapolis minnen,* 341–45.

21. Caroline Olsen, "Dania Hall, 100 years old in 1986," broadside, Aug. 1986; "Society Dania's Fair Program," Sept. 26–29, 1889, collected by Lance Brockman.

22. Program for *Fadren* (Feb. 26, 1915), Maria Sonander Rice and William Rodman Rice Papers, MHS. The file also contains a newsprint clipping of an unidentified review of this production; Program for *Fadren* (Jan. 23, 1916), collected by the Olle i Skratthult Project, courtesy of Maury Bernstein.

23. Olsen, "Dania Hall," and Clinton M. Hyde, "Danish-American Theatre," in *Ethnic Theatre in the United States*, Maxine Schwartz Seller, ed. (Westport, Conn.: Greenwood Press, 1983), 103; Program for *De Nygifta* (Sun., Feb. 2, no year), Maria Sonander Rice Papers, MHS; "Great Contest Play," handbill for event on Sunday, Feb. 4th, no year, collected by Lance Brockman.

24. Hansen, *My Minneapolis*, 105.

25. Harald Naess, *Knut Hamsun og Amerika* (Oslo: Gyldendal Norsk Forlag, 1969), 78–81, 84f., trans. mine; Knut Hamsun, *The Cultural Life of Modern America*, Barbara Gordon Morgridge, ed. and trans. (Cambridge: Harvard Univ. Press, 1969), xxi.

26. Söderström, *Minneapolis minnen*, 293.

27. Photographs and information collected by the Olle i Skratthult Project, communicated by Maury Bernstein.

28. Anne-Charlotte Harvey, "Swedish-American Theatre," in Setter, ed., *Ethnic Theatre*, 508.

29. Anderson, *Dania Hall*, 4f.

30. Ibid; Olsen, "Dania Hall."

31. The patrol limits were abolished in 1974. Some of the Cedar-Riverside liquor licenses were acquired by CRA, often at considerable expense, in order to retire them or have them moved elsewhere.

32. David Rosheim, *The Other Minneapolis, or the Rise and Fall of the Gateway, the old Minneapolis Skid Row* (Maquoketa, Iowa: Andromeda Press, 1978). The Persian Palms was part of an eastward-extending tentacle of the old Minneapolis tenderloin centered in the Gateway district around the intersection of Washington and Hennepin Avenues. Evidently Ray's Lunch relocated to 422 Cedar in 1963 after displacement from 115 Nicollet because of Gateway demolition.

33. Judith A. Martin, *Recycling the Central City: The Development of a New Town-in-Town* (Minneapolis: Center for Urban and Regional Affairs, Univ. of Minn., 1978). Martin's account of the Cedar Square West experiment is first rate. Also see Jennifer Vogel, "Faulty Towers," *City Pages* 13 (Sept. 4, 1991): 8–15, for later history, especially the transition to Riverside Plaza and new ownership. When Vogel's article appeared, representatives of the new developers, the official city-recognized neighborhood group, and the city (here, Minneapolis Community Development Agency) jointly attempted to pressure the Minneapolis-based weekly journal into making a major retraction, but *City Pages* responded by correcting errors which were few and very minor.

34. "Dania Hall Dances Are 'Happenings'," *Minneapolis Star*, Feb. 8, 1968; Armitage, "Curling Waters," 24. During the late 1960s and early 1970s, Loyce Houlton's Minnesota Dance Theatre used the large hall for practice and rehearsal, but not for events. The present author interviewed guest choreographer David Lichine there in 1970. Probably the last event in the large hall took place in Apr. 1970, with a one-time authorization after special inspection by the fire department and other authorities. According to Glen Hanson, members of the Jokers Wild band registered surprise on looking out over the "abnormal" crowd that had arrived. The hall had been hired for an event for students following a Robert Rauschenberg opening at Dayton's Gallery 12. Apparently Rauschenberg enjoyed the party. Glen Hanson, 1997 communication to author, clarified by Felice Wender (former director of Gallery 12); Bernie Shellum, "Building Owner: Alderman Uses Sales Pressure," *Minneapolis Tribune*, Jan. 12, 1968; "Testimony of City 'Secret Agent' Opposes Dania Dance Hall Permit," *Minneapolis Tribune*, June 27, 1968. Also see "200 Youths Protest Dania Hall Closing," *Minneapolis Tribune*, July 4, 1968; CRA communication to author, 1993.

35. Under tax laws still in effect, the State of Minnesota automatically makes up the school district's loss by formula, so that the loss is borne by the entire state's education fund. Tax increment financing is a form of taxation without representation for those who do not vote within the local jurisdiction that creates the tax increment district; Randy Stoecker, *Defending Community: The Struggle for Alternative Redevelopment in Cedar-Riverside* (Philadelphia: Temple Univ. Press, 1994). Stoecker's book is post-modernist urban sociology. As a student, Stoecker lived in the neighborhood and is a friend of the activists. The relatively small part of his account that purports to be historical material is biased and riddled with omissions, but the book does verify the activists' view of themselves as Marxist-Leninists. Others have criticized the activists as hypocrites who helped destroy a community and enabled one politically favored private developer to become rich at public expense in order to serve their own interests. City officials have consistently supported the activists and continue to cite this period of Cedar-Riverside history as a model for other neighborhoods. Regarding the favored developer, see Vogel, "Faulty Towers," as well as Mike Kaszuba, "Risk-taking developers land many city projects, but some cry favoritism," *Star Tribune*, June 18, 1990, p. A1; and Allen Short, Patricia Lopez-Baden, Dennis J. McGrath, "Money, politics play key roles in development: MCDA staff preferred another firm, but high-priced bidder got lucrative townhouse job," *Star Tribune*, Mar. 24, 1994, p. A1; Some racial discrimination did exist, however, in relations with black neighborhood residents. See Armitage, "Curling Waters," 23. Swedes are not necessarily free of prejudicial views; see Månsson, *Amerika minnen*, 75f., 89. The activists institutionalized their discrimination by departing from the principle of one person—one vote in neighborhood elections and giving their area three times more representatives per resident than the high-rise area that contained most of the residents, namely those who were increasingly—later overwhelmingly—people of color, disabled, or elderly. In defense of his friends, Stoecker strains to rationalize: "And the radical ideology of participation was maintained most strongly by leaders. The ability of leaders to organize the neighborhood vote and persuade City Hall to abide by drastically reduced representation of Cedar Square West residents illustrates the strength of the commitment to participatory democracy even in a representative democratic structure." Stoecker, *Defending Community*, 154.

36. Hans-Ingvar Johnsson, "Svenskarnas vilda Snusfestival hit i TV i höst," *Dagens Nyheter*, Apr. 39, 1973, p. 12. Popular turn-of-the-century Swedish American periodicals such as *Svenska Amerikanska Posten* help document the association of "snoose" with a Swedish American street; the popularity of *snuset* is clear from the number and variety of advertisements, which are often quite amusing from a present point of view; Maury Bernstein, communications to author, 1993. Unfortunately, the Salvation Army's property at 614 Cedar Avenue was taken by the city and demolished (where it remains a vacant area of the Public Housing campus), but the Temple Corps returned to participate in the Festival. Some of the Festival attendees came specifically because of the Salvation Army; Chester Milosovich, oral communication to author, Mar. 1997.

37. Irv Letofsky, "Some Swedes disapprove of Snoose festival," *Minneapolis Tribune*, May 23, 1974, p. A1; and Hans-Ingvar Johnsson, "'Snusfestival' i USA. Fejd ger krydda åt årets upplaga," *Dagens Nyheter*, May 26, 1974.

38. A study of 1989 government documents and related sources concerning the "Parcel B" project (primarily a rehabilitation of single bedroom and efficiency units) indicates that total input costs per unit were $170,591, mostly public costs. Developer investment was less than $16 per unit; Hennepin County tax records and records of the Minneapolis Community Development Agency.

39. Mark Brunswick, "Fire strikes historic West Bank building: Dania Hall was center for early immigrants, '60s hippies," *Star Tribune*, July 19, 1981, p. 1A, 2B.

40. According to Glen Olsen, however, the placement of the new steel girders would have prevented duplication of the original auditorium ceiling.

41. Proposal of Lappin & Associates.

42. Steve Schwanke held the rights, first using the name RLK Associates, and later Heritage Venture, but ultimately the developer entity was Dania Hall Group, with Schwanke and Harold Truesdale as general partners. The president of Riverside Bank had gotten Schwanke interested and had arranged an operating loan of some $50,000. NRP, ostensibly an exercise in quasi-Jeffersonian grassroots democracy, receives its money from a project fund created by the renewal and pooling of some tax increment districts, whose original life was about to expire. One of the renewed districts is Cedar-Riverside; the "influential" individuals are, namely, Tim Mungavan and his associates. Mungavan had apparently become the most influential person concerning the official neighborhood organizations and their connections with city government. Procedural questions were raised futilely about this arrangement and the lack of participatory democracy with regard to NRP money and neighborhood development projects. See Kirk Hill, "'Neighborhood' Serves as a Politically Convenient Fiction," *Star Tribune*, Jan. 30, 1999, p. 23; Joseph Hart, "Sold Down the River," *City Pages*, Jan. 7, 1998, p. 10. At neighborhood meetings, Campbell strongly advocated committing approximately half of Cedar-Riverside's NRP funds to the Dania Hall renovation, prior to the neighborhood commencing NRP itself, and she stated that no evaluation of alternative developers would be allowed, even though the NRP funds were not previously available.

43. Peter Ritter, "Theater of the Absurd," *City Pages*, Feb. 23, 2000, p. 8. The Shubert's nonprofit developer, Artspace, must raise some $22.5 million in order to renovate the building. The 2000 legislative session did not fulfill Artspace's hope for state bonds. If Artspace fund-raising is unsuccessful, the city must either tear down the Shubert or else use other resources; Tim Mungavan, "Dania Hall: Great Ideas for a Great Building," *Seward Profile*, Feb. 1998, p. 8. At this point, Mungavan still publicly supported the possibility of housing in Dania; David Markle, "Dania Hall and Cedar-Riverside's NRP—Another Viewpoint," *Seward Profile*, Mar. 1998, p. 6; also Markle, "Another View on Dania Hall," *Seward Profile*, Sept. 1998, p. 4. The present author was among those criticizing the process as well as the developer's plans. See also David Markle to NRP Policy Board, Aug. 20, 1998. Aside from Dania, the Cedar-Riverside NRP "First Step" plan continued the pattern of exploiting an undercount of residents of Riverside Plaza. Despite the resulting misallocation of money and resources, an influential leader of the Vietnamese residents publicly supported the undercount, possibly because of fear of the U.S. Immigration and Naturalization Service or because of concern about overcrowding, and he has indicated that he also resists a full count in the 2000 census. A plan was aired and approved in outline. It guaranteed significant low-cost access to the auditorium by groups based in Cedar-Riverside, including immigrants. It was also quite restrictive to the developer and gave considerable authority to a "community technical committee" composed of Mungavan, a Mungavan ally, and Peter Goelzer (all of whom had been strong advocates of housing in Dania), plus a representative of MCDA and an official of the local bank. For a final version, see "NRP Early Access Funding Agreement (Cedar Riverside: Rehabilitation of Dania Hall)," Minneapolis Community Development Agency, Aug. 19, 1999. As of Mar. 2000, MCDA provided the unexecuted development agreements only on the submission of a Minnesota Data Practices request; Kungshien Chu, Cory Kopp, Kim Lothrop, Travis Sell, Ines Sira, and Clay Webb, "The Restoration of Dania Hall," Carlson Volunteer Consultants, Carlson School of Management, Univ. of Minn., 1998; "Dania Hall Reuse Study," Minnesota Consultation Team and Thomas R. Zahn & Associates, for the Minneapolis Community Development Agency and the MHS, Summer 1998. Jim Sutherland, MCDA's commercial development manager for the neighborhood, also seemed sympathetic to genuine renovation.

44. Linda Mack, "Another Chance for Dania Hall," *Star Tribune*, Aug. 28, 1999, p. B1; "For the Love of Music: 10 Years of the Cedar Cultural Centre," *Twin Cities Review*, Jan. 21, 1999, p. 8. The development agreement underwent repeated redrafting, apparently at the behest of Campbell and Mungavan.

45. Mark Connor, "Cedar Riverside Sees Controversy, Hardship: Dania Hall Leveled in Fire," *Southside Pride*, Mar. 2000, p. 1; Gar Hargens, quoted by Bert Berlow and Todd Cota in "Fire: Dania, Dreams Go Up in Smoke," *Seward Profile*, Mar. 2000, p. 9; Jonathan Kaminsky, "Haste Laid Waste," *City Pages*, Mar. 22, 2000, p. 8.

46. David Hawley, "Historic Dania Hall Is Lost to Raging Flames," *Saint Paul Pioneer Press*, Feb. 29, 2000, p. 1A; Chuck Haga, "Fire Destroys Immigrants' Haven," *Star Tribune*, Feb. 29, 2000, p. A1; Jim Adams, "Tossed Cigarette May Have Lit Fire That Destroyed Dania Hall," *Star Tribune*, Mar. 9, 2000, p. B1; Burt Berlow, "Dania Hall Saga Continues Even After Blaze," *Seward Profile*, Apr. 2000, p. 11. Few observers familiar with the building, the circumstances, the alleged suspect itinerant, or the difficulty of starting a wood fire with a cigarette butt believe the cause to be a tossed cigarette. Adams and Burlow reported that on the morning of the fire, WBCDC director Mungavan found a substantial piece of charred wood on his front porch more than a half-mile distant from Dania Hall. Apparently no one else reported such an occurrence. Adams's Mar. 1 article relayed interesting suspicions on the part of city council member Joan Campbell. The article also quoted Mungavan as saying: "Who knows what it [the charred wood] means, but if someone wanted to deliver a message that it was an intentional fire, I would have been the right person to deliver it to, because of everyone in the neighborhood, I am the person . . . identified with Dania Hall." Unfortunately the arson investigation lacked propulsion from any substantial insurance loss (see Kaminsky, previous note).

47. These are as yet unpublished recordings furnished for the occasion by Maury Bernstein.

Forskaren:
A Swedish Radical Voice in Minneapolis, 1894–1924

MICHAEL BROOK

Forskaren had a short history in Rockford, Illinois, before moving to Minneapolis. Edward Fjellander (a printer) and Frithiof Malmquist (a carpenter on his way to becoming a journalist and poet) founded the little weekly in 1893. No copies from its Rockford period survive, but the consensus is that it was, as it remained, "an organ of socialism and free thought." *Forskaren* also seems to have indulged in unwise criticism of some Rockford worthies, however, with the result that Fjellander and Malmquist got into trouble with the law and found it best to leave town.[1]

Once arrived in Minneapolis, Fjellander and Malmquist (as assistant editor) continued to run the paper, and a significant Minneapolis figure entered the scene as general manager. Edward (originally Carl Edward) Grunlund managed the paper until it ceased publication in 1924. Malmquist left in 1896, and Fjellander in the following year, both for Chicago. Malmquist became a leading figure in the Chicago Swedish press (managing editor of *Svenska Amerikanaren* upon his death in 1939) and in the Independent Order of Vikings. Fjellander's life is more obscure, but he is known to have edited *Idealisten*, a liberal monthly sympathetic to phrenology, from 1905 to 1906, and to have been co-editor of a temperance monthly, *Fältvakten* (The Field Guard) in 1914.[2]

Fjellander was succeeded as editor of *Forskaren* by Charles (originally Karl) Borglund in 1897 or 1898, the names Grunlund and Borglund appearing together on the masthead on November 1, 1901, as "editors and publishers." At this point *Forskaren* was being published in tabloid size (having been a broadsheet from 1894 to 1897), and tabloid publication continued through 1904, after which the paper appeared in magazine format to the end. The Royal Library in Stockholm accurately describes it as a newspaper for the years 1894–1904 and as a periodical from 1905 to 1924.[3]

Borglund and Grunlund established the character of the magazine, which continued with little change, perhaps too little change, after Borglund's death in 1911 until it ceased publication in 1924. While he lived, Borglund seems to have been the creative partner. Grunlund, the business manager, kept the magazine going in the spirit of Borglund as long as he could. Direct evidence is lacking, but it seems likely that he continued to issue *Forskaren* partly as a tribute to Borglund's memory.

Forskaren's "program" was printed from time to time in the magazine and in the pamphlets issued by Forskaren Publishing Company. Its message was that *Forskaren* would seek the truth in every sphere, but concentrate its attention on "injustice in the social sphere and delusions in the sphere of religion." Although the program does not specifically say that religion and capitalism support one another and that a just society cannot be built on foundations of "superstition," that message comes through when one examines the text of the paper. It derives from the now half-forgotten Swedish social prophet Viktor Lennstrand and his doctrine of "utilism." In 1910 *Forskaren* published three articles by Lennstrand, two pieces about him having appeared in 1905, on the tenth anniversary of his death, but this is probably related to Borglund's stated intention to collect and edit Lennstrand's writings, an achievement that his declining health and eventual death made impossible. Articles by Lennstrand appeared from time to time after Borglund's death, but no book was ever published, although two pamphlets had been issued in the late 1890s.[4]

Grunlund was born in Berga, Kronobergs län, in 1864, became a printer in Sweden, and emigrated to the United States and Minneapolis in 1896. He soon became his brother John's partner in Grunlund Brothers, but relinquished his share of the business. There is no direct evidence, but he likely printed *Forskaren* from the beginning. After the death of the magazine, Grunlund struggled on as a job printer for another ten years at the same address as *Forskaren*. He died in poverty in 1940, aged seventy. Among his personal property was a "stock of old newspapers and magazines which has no value except as waste paper." So wrote the appraiser of his estate, who valued the papers at five dollars. The administrator, Edward's brother John, disposed of them "at a greater than appraised value." Presumably they no longer exist, and the composition of the collection is unknown. Grunlund is not known to have been a member of a political party or trade union; his standing as an employer presumably made him ineligible for union membership. As a young man he was treasurer of Framtidens Hopp (Hope of the Future), a Minneapolis lodge of the Verdandi Order, a temperance group still in existence in Sweden, then and now allied with the Social Democratic Party, although its American members leaned towards the Industrial Workers of the World (IWW), irreligion, and war-resistance.[5]

Borglund, apparently a child of poverty in Sweden, was born at Ervalla (in Västmanlands or Örebro län), left school at eleven, and worked as an agricultural laborer until his emigration to the United States in 1889, which was followed by four years as a laborer in sawmills, lumber camps, and iron mines in the Upper Midwest until about 1893, when he came to Minneapolis. Here he set seriously about self-improvement, which he had begun by joining the International Order of Good Templars (IOGT) in 1890, spending the next four years as student and teacher at Wraaman's Academy. According to Grunlund, his friend studied Latin, mathematics, science, and philosophy; taught English, Latin, and mathematics; and was at this time much interested in theosophy. He met Grunlund in 1897 and at once began to work part-time on *Forskaren*, keeping his teaching job at Wraaman's. After the end of the school year, he went to work full-time at *Forskaren*, taking over the editorship and becoming Grunlund's business partner.[6]

Having no trade or profession, and fearing poverty in old age, Borglund decided to qualify as a physician, entering Hamline Medical School in St. Paul in 1905, transferring to the University of Minnesota in 1908 for a year, and graduating from Marquette University Medical School (Milwaukee) in 1909. During this period of schooling, Grunlund persuaded him to do much less writing for *Forskaren*, but his health, undermined by the hardships of his youth and the strain of editorial work and study, was broken, and he died in 1911, leaving Grunlund to take over the editorial chair. Borglund was buried in Lakewood Cemetery, Minneapolis. *Forskaren* ran a campaign to raise money to erect a bauta stone, similar to that put up in Gävle to commemorate Viktor Lennstrand. Six hundred and forty-eight dollars was collected, and the stone was inaugurated in 1917. Grunlund was eventually buried in the same grave lot.[7]

In its magazine period, and under Borglund's editorship, each issue of *Forskaren*, by this time a monthly, contained sixty to eighty pages of text, three-quarters of this being devoted to articles, the remainder to more or less regular features. The half-dozen articles were on science, religion, medicine, politics (although not often current affairs), were sometimes in the form of biographical sketches, and were often translated from German or English, or were reprints from periodicals or newspapers published in Sweden. Some were published in a number of parts; thus, Georg Bang's treatment of "Marxism" (translated from the original Danish) appeared in ten parts during 1907. Each number contained a lengthy piece (up to twelve pages) signed by Borglund and forming what at present might be called a "column," often dealing with matters of current interest. By 1922, each issue consisted of only sixteen pages, although no months were missed, as had occasionally happened in what were, generally speaking, better days.

The main content of *Forskaren* was educational in a fairly ponderous way, and not closely related to current politics (except for Borglund's columns), but the various features at the back of the magazine were livelier. These features consisted of short book notices (of books in either Swedish or English) and news items from Sweden (not unlike those published in any Swedish American newspaper, but reflecting *Forskaren's* interests and values). More significant were "Spegelbilder från 'ordets förkunnares' lif och läror" (Reflections From the Life and Teachings of "Preachers of the Word"), exposing crimes and misdoings of ministers of religion and reported cases of religious mania; "Från slagfältet" (From the Battlefield), reporting the social battlefield in the United States and abroad; and "Från papperskorgen" (From the Waste Paper Basket), consisting of letters from *Forskaren's* subscribers related either to the magazine itself or to the circumstances of the letter-writers. The correspondents' addresses were usually given (although sometimes incompletely), making these letters rather valuable.

A more detailed analysis of these letters, based upon a count of those published in the years 1911–14, is reported below. Where a home address was given, the totals for states and Canadian provinces could be computed (omitting states and provinces represented by fewer than ten letters):

Minnesota	89
Washington	32
California	27
Illinois	17
Michigan	17
Wisconsin	16
Pennsylvania	14
Massachusetts	13
Oregon	13
Utah	10
British Columbia	12
Saskatchewan	11

The great lead of Minnesota is perhaps not surprising. What may surprise is the distribution: for every correspondent in Minneapolis, St. Paul, or Duluth, there were three in small settlements such as Elm Park, Little Falls, Curran, or Badger. The Illinois correspondents were almost all from Chicago and other urban centers, while those of Michigan were mostly from small cities of the type of Escanaba, Ishpeming, Ironwood, and Negaunee.

When *Forskaren* moved to Minneapolis in 1894 it announced that it was being printed in 10,000 copies. The claim is difficult to accept, especially since

Forskaren

Ögat är kroppens ljus, förnuftet själens, forskeu därför och frambringen i dagen det godt är.

ÅRG. IX. No. 12. LÖP. No. 361.   MINNEAPOLIS, MINN., 15 NOVEMBER 1901   LÖSNUMMER 10 CENTS.

FORSKAREN.
—(THE INVESTIGATOR.)—
Published Semimonthly by
FORSKAREN PUBLISHING CO.,
at 1119 Washington Avenue South, Minneapolis, Minn.

—Subscription price $1.50 per year.—

Entered at the Minneapolis Post Office as Second-Class Matter.

CHARL''S BORGLUND } Redaktion och utgifvare.
EDWARD GRÖNLUND }

☞ Alla försändelser till FORSKAREN adresseras:
FORSKAREN PUB. CO.,
STA. B,   MINNEAPOLIS, - - - - MINN.

☞ Pänningar sändas bäst genom moneyorder, expressorder eller i registreradt bref. 1- och 2 cents frimärken mottagas ock, då beloppet understiger en dollar.

PRENUMERATIONSAFGIFTEN MÅSTE ERLÄGGAS I FÖRSKOTT.

☞ *Forskarens läsare finna icke tidningen uppfyld med humbugsannonser af något slag, icke häller detaljer Forskaren på något sätt i de olika kapitalistpartiernas politik och har följaktligen icke — likt andra tidningar — någon inkomst vid valkampanjerna. Således häller ha vi, tidningens utgifvare, något kapital att för foga öfver.* ☞ *Häraf må det vara lätt begripligt, att Forskarens enda inkomstkälla är prenumerationsafgifterna, ty med dessa skola vi bestrida omkostnaderna.*

ADRESSER ÖNSKAS.

☞ *Alla Forskarens vänner och läsare uppmanas på det vänligaste att till oss insända namn och adress på bekanta och vänner, och vi vilja sända dem profnummer af Forskaren. I första rummet önskas adresser till frisinnade landsmän, och hvar och en nog känner några sådana. så kan man, genom att sända oss adresser till dessa, vara oss behjälplig i spridandet af de idéer, hvilka Forskaren förfäktar, ty därigenom vinnes nya prenumeranter.*

OBSERVERA!

☞ *En del af Forskarens vänner skänka bort tidningen för kort tid åt någon vän eller bekant för att på så sätt göra den känd och väcka intresse för densamma. Därför, om Forskaren kommer Eder tillhanda, utan att Ni själf gjort någon anhållan därom, så frukta icke för att taga emot tidningen, ty om Ni ser efter på den röda adresslappen finner Ni, att afgiften är erlagd t förskott för viss tid.* ☞ *Har Ni dock på det vänligaste om bedd att, då den tid, för hvilken prenumerationsafgiften är erlagd, är tilländalupen, Ni ville godhetsfullt underrätta oss om Ni fortfarande önskar läsa Forskaren, och om så är händelsen — hvilket vi tro skall bli fallen af några månaders nog studerande af innehållet —, med Ni själf insända afgiften, som måste erläggas i förskott.*

PROFNUMMER.

☞ *Vi önska få Forskaren händ å alla platser i landet, där våra landsmän bygga och bo. Vi äro förvissade om, att det finnes tusentals svenskar i Amerika, som skola förstå värdet af en tidning som denna och skola hälsa Forskaren välkommen, det gäller blott för tidningen att leta sig väg till dessa landsmän, och vänskapen följer bekantskapen. Vi sända där för proftr : till alla, hvars adresser vi kunna erhålla, och nu detta förklara orsaken till, att ett exemplar af detta nummer möjligen blir sändt åt någon, som själf icke begärt detsamma. Till den eller detsamma vilja vi säga : Forskaren kommer till Eder med en vänlig anhållan att blifva noga granskad från första till sista bladet. Då Ni tagit del af innehållet, så fäll Edert omdöme om detsamma. Blir detta omdöme till tidningens fördel, låt oss då säga Er, att Forskaren mer än väl behöfver Edert understöd, och det kan Ni bäst gifva genom att genast — och innan Ni glömmer bort det blir förloras tidningen och därmed afven adressen — insända Er prenumeration, samt förmå Edra vänner och grannar att göra sammaledes.*

KARL MARX.

Karl Marx föddes i Trier, Tyskland, den 5 maj 1818. Fadern var en sedermera döpt judisk advokat. I föräldrarnes hus voro snille och världsmannabildning hemmastadda. Familjens älsklingsskriftställare voro Rousseau och Shakespeare, och den sistnämnde var ständigt Marx' älsklingspoet. Marx studerade i Bonn och Berlin, i början juridik, men sedermera företrädesvis filosofi. Han blef en ifrig lärjunge af Hegel och ämnade just söka filosofisk docentur i Bonn, när hans dåvarande intime vän Bruno Bauer bortrycktes från universitetet af den reaktionära våg, som just då åter flödade öfver de preussiska universiteten. Denna händelse bestämde Marx att lämna akademien (1842), och det som i sådana fall af förfelad lefnadsuppgift plägar ske inträffade. Marx blef journalist. Kort därefter vardt han hufvudredaktör för "Rheinische zeitung" i Köln. År 1843 gifte han sig med Jenny von Westphalen, dotter till den preussiske ministern baron Edgar von Westphalen, och hvars föräldrar den Marxska familjen länge umgåtts. Året därpå blef emellertid tidningen på grund af revolutionära tendenser indragen, och Marx blef af den preussiska polisen drifven ur landet. Han flyttade då till Paris, där han, tillsammans med A. Ruge, utgaf "Deutsch-französische jahrbucher". Men redan följande året blef han, som man antager på anmodan från Preussen, af Guizots ministär utvisad ur Frankrike. Han begaf sig då till Bruxelles, hvarest han fortsatte sina ekonomiska studier samt författade, utom smärre arbeten, sin "Misère de la philosophie" (1847), en blodig kritik af Proudhons "Philosophie de la misère", samt—i förening med sin vän Friedrich Engels — en utförlig kritik af den nyaste tyska filosofin, hvari han lösgjort sig från Hegels skola. I förening med Engels bildade han "den tyska arbetarebildningsföreningen" och utfärdade det berömda "kommunistiska manifest",

som år 1847 framlades som program för "de rättrådiges förbund" i Bruxelles, hvilket antog det och därigenom ombildades till "kommunisternas förbund". Detta manifest, hvilket sedermera utgifvits i otaliga upplagor på de flästa kulturspråk, slutar med de bekanta orden: "Proletärer i alla länder, förenen eder! I hafven ingenting annat än edra kedjor att förlora, men en värld att vinna."

År 1848 utbröto de revolutionära rörelserna i Tyskland, och Marx begaf sig dit, efter att ha blifvit utvisad från Bruxelles. Tillsammans med sina vänner Engels, Wolff och poeten Freiligrath grundade han i Köln "Neue rheinische zeitung", hvilken tidning på ett förtjänstfullt och frimodigt sätt förfäktade arbetarnes sak gent emot såväl reaktionen som den tyska demokratin. Efter ett års tillvaro blef emellertid tidningen indragen och grundarne utvisade. Marx reste då till Paris, men förvisades inom kort äfven därifrån och flyttade så till London, där han sedan förblef bosatt till sin död, den 14 mars 1883.

I London utvecklade Marx en liflig värksamhet dels såsom skriftställare, dels såsom socialistisk agitator och partiledare. År 1864 bildades "den internationela arbetareförbundet" (den s. k. "Internationalen"), i hvilket Marx under flera år var den ledande själen. Sitt lefvebröd fick han hufvudsakligen genom publicistisk värksamhet. En lång tid skref han korrespondenser för New York Tribune samt lämnade bidrag till andra amerikanska tidningar och tidskrifter. Därjämte utgaf han en del arbeten, t. ex. "Enthüllungen über den communistenproces in Köln", "Der 18 Brumaire des Louis Bonaparte", "Herr Carl Vogt" samt, efter fleråriga förstudier, "Zur kritik der politischen oekonomie" (1859), af hvilket "Das kapital" är en fortsättning. Detta arbete ("Das kapital") har blifvit kalladt socialisternas bibel, och det är väl förtjänt af det namnet. Det är det mäst tankedigra och grundliga ekonomiska arbete, som någonsin skrifvits, hvilket t. o. m. Marx' ärlige motståndare erkänt. Visserligen är det icke värdslärt, men det är icke därför, att Marx ej kunde skrifva väl, utan därför att Marx intränger så djupt i tankens labyrinter, att det är svårt att följa honom. De i detsamma uttalade idéerna ha varit fruktbärande i nästan alla länder, och den dag skall komma, då alla jordens folk skola med tacksamhet och beundran se upp till den man, som uträttat så mycket för de trälande massornas frigörelse.

FORSKAREN utkommer den 1 och 15 i hvar månad.

PRENUMERATIONSPRIS:
$1.50 för helt år, 80c. för half år och 45c. för 3 mån.
Till Sverge $1.75 per år.

☞ Från flera håll ha vi erhållit uppmaningar att förklara de främmande ord, som förekomma i tidningen. Det enda sätt, hvarpå vi kunna göra detta, är genom införandet af en ordlista, och vi ha gjort början i detta nummer. Nämda lista återfinnes på 12:te sidan.

Grunlund stated a year later that it had fewer than 600 subscribers (although copies were sold on newsstands, the magazine mostly went to postal subscribers). *N. W. Ayer & Son's American Newspaper Annual* reports a circulation of 3,000 in 1905 and 2,500 in the years 1914–20, falling away to just over a thousand in the paper's final years. As with Swedish American papers generally, unpaid subscriptions were always a problem; a fourteenth-anniversary editorial in 1907 asked, "How many of *Forskaren's* readers suspect, do you think, that during the past fourteen years we lost more than $5000 (say *five thousand dollars*) in [unpaid] subscriptions?" The annual subscription was $1.50, so more than 1,500 subscriptions (a yearly average of more than a hundred) were lost.

Forskaren was published in Minneapolis and had probably a quarter of its circulation in that city. How much attention did it give to local matters? Most of the local coverage consists of announcements and reports of meetings and social gatherings organized by the local branch of Frihetsförbundet (the Scandinavian Liberty League), a free-thought group whose chairman was Edward Grunlund and which held a Sunday school for the children of members of the IOGT and Verdandi Order temperance groups, and (much less often) socialist organizations and religious bodies such as the First Scandinavian Unitarian Church and the Yggdrasil Theosophical Society, both of Minneapolis.

Forskaren usually made a few comments on presidential elections. In 1908 it was enthusiastic for Debs and the Socialist Party and sympathetic to the much similar Socialist Labor Party. In 1912, when all the comments on the campaign appeared in "Thoughts and Reflections," which after Borglund's death was written by Grunlund, the Democrats and Bull Moose Republicans were attacked with equal vigor. The Socialist Party ran Allan L. Benson for president in 1916, and *Forskaren* published two articles or speeches by him (both translated by Ernest A. Spongberg), together with a translation of the party's national platform. In 1920 very little was said, but Grunlund's move to the left produced some interesting comments in 1924: he thought that the Farmer Labor convention in St. Paul had made the mistake of being frightened by the Communist Party, which would give the victory to the Republicans or the Democrats (he did not mention the Socialist Party), and that the La Follette campaign would simply repeat the Populist campaign of 1896, which was now inadequate.[8]

There are, as far as it known, no surviving business records of *Forskaren*. Almost everything must be gleaned from the columns of the magazine itself. Walfrid Engdahl, however, told me something of its workings in conversations and interviews in the early 1970s, and I will draw on these in what follows. His information must be taken to refer to the period from 1913 to 1918, when he was actively involved in the running of the paper. Borglund did translations from English on controversial topics and current affairs. Translations from English were also made by Karl J. Ellington and by Ernest A. Spongberg (Ernst A. Späng-berg). Engdahl, who held the full-time paid position of assistant editor from 1913–15 and was part-time unpaid assistant editor from 1915–1918, did no trans-lations. One typesetter had to be paid regularly, while Grunlund and (until his death in 1911) Borglund lived by job-printing, producing a few small magazines and printing for the IOGT. They printed in Swedish and Norwegian and occa-sionally in English. Articles by people not on the editorial staff were paid for individually. Engdahl emphasized that material originally in other languages (notably German) and published in Sweden was reprinted by permission of the Swedish publishers, but without payment. Newspapers and periodicals published in Sweden were received by exchange (e.g., *Brand* and *Socialdemo-kraten*) or by payment. David Holmgren must have done some regular work for *Forskaren*, perhaps excerpting, and, while not paid, was allowed to take the Swedish papers home. During Engdahl's time at *Forskaren*, he edited four of the regular features ("Reflections," "From the Battle Field," "Free Words, Free Thoughts," consisting of readers' letters on subjects of general interest, and a roundup of Minneapolis news).[9]

Walfrid Engdahl (1890–1979) was a carpenter, born at Ellenö på Dal, near Vänersborg, on March 5, 1890. Before emigrating to the United States he was a member of the famous Stockholms Norra, a syndicalist young people's club. After spending some time in the Pacific Northwest, on both sides of the inter-national border, he must have come to Minneapolis by 1913, when he took up his full-time position at *Forskaren*. He was a member of the IWW, taking part in some of its free speech fights and in 1919 being secretary of the "East of the Rockies" sub-committee of its Bail and Defense Committee. Besides being a working carpenter in Minneapolis, he was business agent for the carpenters' union there c. 1927–c. 1933, and while under Floyd B. Olson's Farmer Labor ad-ministration during the 1930s he was assistant purchasing agent for the State Highway Department and purchasing agent for the State Board of Control. From about 1948 to 1955, he was in charge of the construction and maintenance of public welfare buildings of Minneapolis. He was also active in the Farmer Labor Party, and during the 1950s served as secretary of Local No. 7 of the United Brotherhood of Carpenters and Joiners of America, also writing a regular col-umn for the *Minneapolis Labor Review*.[10]

Karl Johan Ellington (1863–1943) was one of Swedish America's true origi-nals. Most of his adult life was spent in Sweden and the United States in alter-nating ten-year periods, although his final twenty years were lived in the Pacific Northwest (mainly, it appears, at Port Angeles or Mount Vernon, Washington). During his first period in America, Ellington worked in an organ factory in Mo-line, Illinois, and also became associated in 1891–92 with the Minneapolis socialist paper *Gnistan* (The Spark), edited and published by Axel Lundeberg, contributing two articles and forming a support club in Moline in 1891. After his return to Sweden in 1893, he contributed to socialist newspapers and edited the biweekly periodical *Fria Tankar* (Free Thoughts) during 1897–98, in which he appealed to "my friends in America" for support. During this time he also wrote the pamphlet *Hvilka böra vara socialister?* (Who should be socialists?), published in Stockholm in 1902, with a second edition appearing in Jönköping in 1907.

Ellington's second American decade (c. 1903–c. 1913) included unemployment in Chicago, work in an engineering workshop in Moline, and a move to San Francisco and then Seattle and Port Angeles, Washington, where he worked as a piano and organ tuner. These activities had been preceded by a spell of some months working in the *Forskaren* office, where he translated Thomas Paine's *Age of Reason* into Swedish (*Förnuftets tidehvarf*, 1903, reprinted 1904 and 1906; also reprinted in Stockholm in 1906 by Frihetsförbundets förlag). In later years he translated Robert Ingersoll's *Thanksgiving Sermon* for *Forskaren* (*Tacksägelse-predikan*, 1909). It is possible that he edited *Forskaren* on his own for a few months, to enable Borglund and Grunlund to take some time off, and he had about twenty articles published in the paper between 1905 and 1912, including *I proletärhelvetet* (In the Proletarian Hell), part of which appeared in English in H. Arnold Barton's *Letters from the Promised Land: Swedes in America, 1840–1914* (1975). The last ten-year spell in Sweden seems to have been largely devoted to propaganda for building in rammed earth; Ellington published privately a book on the subject, *Billiga bostäder av pressad jord (pisé de terre)* (Stockholm, [1920]), which is said to have been translated into Danish, Finnish, and Norwegian, and was certainly translated into English. A house was built on "Ellington's system" in Kävlinge, Skåne, probably in the 1920s, and was observed to be standing and in good condition in the mid-1970s.[11]

David Holmgren (1846–1916) has already been mentioned. He was an ordained minister of the Church of Sweden, being pastor of Varnhem in the diocese of Skara from 1879 to 1902, when he was removed from his office. He was then involved in a long lawsuit over his activities as administrator of a church trust in Varnhem, where he had made decisions in an irregular manner, and was finally condemned to a term of imprisonment, which he avoided by fleeing to America in 1906. His position as a fugitive does not seem to have been held against him in Swedish America. Although he had sat in the Riksdag as a member of the Liberal Party (*Liberala samlingspartiet*), he was employed in this country by the Socialist Party as a travelling speaker, entrusted with the work of spreading the socialist gospel among the Swedes of Minnesota. In Minnesota he ministered to two small congregations, a group of Swedish Unitarians at

Dalbo, Minnesota (Isanti County), and, from 1912 until his death, the newly
founded First Scandinavian Unitarian Church of Minneapolis. Holmgren visited Borglund and Grunlund in 1908, impressing them so favorably by his moral
stature and intellectual openness that, despite their religious differences with
him, they invited him to contribute to *Forskaren*. Some autobiographical notes
were followed by two multipart series, *Vill du bliva frälst?* (Do You Want to be
Saved?) and *Vad är frihet?* (What is Freedom?). When Holmgren became minister of the Scandinavian Unitarian Church in Minneapolis in 1914, *Forskaren*
wrote "[Holmgren] fills the place of 'clergyman' in a Swedish Unitarian congregation organized by him, and that he should at the same time be a contrib-
utor to *Forskaren* is not appropriate." Certainly there are no more articles by
him, but good relations seem to have been maintained, and his obituary was
written by Ernest A. Spongberg (1881–1938), a new figure in the columns of the
magazine.

   A Swedish literary historian has described Spongberg as "a legendary figure"
and has placed him among the Young Socialists (i.e., syndicalists) who contributed short stories to the Swedish Social-Democratic press. He also wrote
for the anarchist paper *Brand* (Fire) as well as traveling widely in Europe and
the U.S. as correspondent for *Socialdemokraten* and *Göteborgs Aftonblad*. He
settled in America in 1906 and, after newspaper work in Seattle and various
jobs in Minneapolis (including editorial and advertising assignments on *Svenska Folkets Tidning* and selling work outside newspapers), joined *Forskaren* in a
part-time capacity, after Engdahl left the paper (presumably in 1918) and worked
into the nineteen-twenties. Engdahl remembered him as a Social Democrat,
interested in the co-operative movement. From 1920 his job at *Forskaren* must
have been very part-time indeed, for he joined the staff of the Swedish consulate in Minneapolis. He seems to have joined the establishment even before
then, for in 1915 or 1916 he published *Sweden up to Date* (on "Swedish progress,
industrial upswing, maritime development, social improvements, etc."). Other
works by him include *What's What in the War?*, a pro-German pamphlet, and
a life of Jenny Lind. An early contribution to *Forskaren*, reprinted from *Svenska Folkets Tidning*, was "London nattetid" (London at Night), no doubt origi-
nating during the author's time as a correspondent for *Socialdemokraten* and
anticipating Ivar Lo-Johansson's social reportage of the 1920s.[12]

   One additional member of the *Forskaren* circle requires attention. Knut (or
Knud) Martin Olsen Teigen (1854–1916) was unusual among *Forskaren*'s contributors in that he was Norwegian and American-born (in Koshkonong, Wisconsin) and in that he was publicly *opposed* to the temperance movement. As
a young man, he had what appears to have been a successful medical career in
North Dakota, where he wrote many articles for the Populist Norwegian news-

paper *Normanden*, published in Grand Forks from 1887, but he was disappointed by the failure of his political ambitions in that state and came to Minneapolis in 1894, devoting himself in the latter part of his medical career to the study of nervous and mental disease. After coming to Minneapolis, he published verse and fiction in Norwegian, his work being highly regarded by Waldemar Ager, the Eau Claire editor and cultural leader, who described him as "the most gifted Norwegian-American writer (*digtere*)," yet one destroyed by his rootlessness.

Forskaren published a number of articles (all in Norwegian) by Teigen, notably a series of five in 1909 on Norwegian American culture. A recent article on New Norwegian in America has paid some attention to his work in this language. In 1909, Teigen began publication of an English-language periodical, *The American Buffet*, short-lived and devoted to ridicule of the temperance movement. In September 1913, *Forskaren* printed a short note to the effect that Teigen was bedridden and in poverty, his destroyed health being the result of an accident in Minneapolis two years earlier. The information had been conveyed by his (second) wife, Aman-Roos, apparently a member of the aristocratic Roos family and hence a relative of Herman Roos (1821–80), the liberal and anticlerical editor of *Svenska Amerikanaren*. The note ended with an appeal for financial help for the Teigens. Their situation did not improve, however, and on July 4, 1916 (by mutual agreement), K. M. Teigen killed his wife and then himself.[13]

Why did the paper, which was started in Rockford, come to Minneapolis? Life in Rockford may have been uncomfortable, but Chicago, which both Fjellander and Malmquist knew, had a larger number of Swedish-born (49,000 in 1890) than Minneapolis (nearly 20,000 in 1890) and St. Paul (nearly 12,000 in that year) put together. Perhaps the newer urban centers were seen as more promising or more attractive because of their newness; perhaps (there is no evidence) Fjellander and Malmquist knew Grunlund and had been in negotiations with him.

Who read *Forskaren?* In regard to its Minnesota readers, it seems that the paper did not appeal to city industrial workers as much as to rural residents— the kind of rural radical or village atheist who had supported the free-thought paper *Upplysningens Tidehvarf*, published in Hutchinson, Glencoe, and Grove City, Minnesota, twenty years before.[14]

Lastly, what was the nature of *Forskaren?* The inseparability of its socialism from its free thought has been shown, which may account for the tenacity of its small body of readers but may also have repelled a potential readership of a less dogmatic frame of mind. Its position may also have been weakened by its non-party socialist position. In 1908, Borglund, presumably in an answer to a correspondent, wrote: "We are not at home or interested in party questions," and this attitude was maintained to the end.

208   MICHAEL BROOK

* * * *

NOTES

1. Frithiof Malmquist, "När man startar utan kapital," in Alfred Söderström, *Blixtar på tidnings-horisonten* (Warroad, Minn.: n.p., 1910), 160f.; Söderström, *Minneapolis minnen. Kulturhistorisk axplockning från qvarnstaden vid Mississippi* (Minneapolis: published by the author, 1899]), 185f.; J. Oscar Backlund, *A Century of the Swedish American Press* (Chicago: Swedish American Newspaper Company, 1952), 91; Dirk Hoerder, ed., *The Immigrant Labor Press in North America, 1840's–1970's: An Annotated Bibliography,* 3 vols. (New York: Greenwood Press, 1987), 1:154f.

2. Ernst Skarstedt, *Pennfäktare. Svensk-amerikanska författare och tidningsmän* (Stockholm: Åhlen & Åkerlunds förlag, A. Bonnier, 1930), 59f. (Fjellander); *Svenska Amerikanaren Tribunen,* Mar. 23, 1939, p. [1] (Malmquist).

3. Edward Grunlund, "Karl Erik Borglund," *Forskaren* 19 (1911): [291]–308, esp. 298ff.

4. *Forskaren* 13 (1905): 206, and 24 (1916): Supp., [40]; [Anon.], *Kampen för tillvaron och socialismen,* andra uppl. (Minneapolis: Forskaren, 1905), outside back cover (all *Forskaren's* program); Herbert Tingsten, *Den svenska socialdemokratins idéutveckling,* 2 vols. (Stockholm: Bokförlaget Aldus/Bonniers, 1941, 1967), 2:254f.; Lennstrand, *Forskaren* 13 (1905): [623]–629; Charles Borglund, "En förklaring och en ursäkt," *Forskaren* 18 (1910): 124; Lennstrand and Per Nymansson, *Tänk själf* (n.p., c. 1897); Lennstrand, *De fyra evangelierna, dess uppkomst och historiska värde* (Minneapolis: n.p., 1899).

5. Algot C. Strand, *A History of the Swedish Americans of Minnesota,* 3 vols. (Chicago: Lewis Publishing Co., 1910) 3:1087; Skarstedt, *Pennfäktare,* 66; Minneapolis city directories, 1891–1901, 1924–34; probate file no. 55848 (Carl Edward Grunlund), Probate Court, Hennepin County, Minneapolis; *Arbetaren,* New York, July 25, 1907, p. 4 (name given as Grönlund).

6. Grunlund, "Karl Erik Borglund," [292]–300.

7. Grunlund, "Karl Erik Borglund," 300–303; Skarstedt, *Pennfäktare,* 37; Paul W. Anderson, Executive Vice President, Lakewood Cemetery Association, Minneapolis, to author, Oct. 2, 1972 (in author's possession).

8. *Forskaren* 16 (1908): Supp., 197; 20 (1912): 243, 287f., 325ff.; 24 (1916): [269]–274, [293]–296, Supp., 112–16; 32 (1924): 70, 83f.

9. Interviews of and conversations with Walfred Engdahl, Oct. 15, 1968; Feb. 1970; Apr. 4 and May 27, 1972, all in author's possession. Engdahl, "Lokalt," *Forskaren,* Jan.–Apr., July 1913.

10. "Dalslänning i USA var Joe Hills kampanjbroder," *Svenska Amerikanaren Tribunen,* Nov. 8, 1972, clipping in untitled scrapbook, Box 2, Bengston (Fredrickson) Papers, Swedish American Archives of Greater Chicago, North Park Univ., Chicago, Ill.; *One Big Union Monthly,* Nov. 1919, p. [5]; Frank Engdahl to author, Minneapolis, July 31, 1989 (in author's possession).

11. [Carl Mattson], "Till Karl J. Ellingtons minne," *Svenska Posten,* Seattle, Feb. 18, 1943, p. 3; Skarstedt, *Pennfäktare,* 52f.; Ellington, "I proletärhelvetet," *Forskaren* 13 (1905): [89]–109; Hoerder, ed., *Immigrant Labor Press,* 3:157; Berhnard Lundgren, *Sveriges periodiska litteratur, 1645–1899. bibliografi,* 3 vols. (1895–1902), pt. 3, no. 1656; Olle Josephson and Marie Hedström, *"Akta er för socialdemokraterna!" Den tidiga arbetarrörelsens agitationsbroschyrer* ([Stockholm:] Arbetarns Kulturhistoriska Sällskap/Arbetarrörelsens arkiv och bibliotek, 1995), p. 217; Sture W. Lantz, *I kamp för en identitet. En krönika om människors villkor i omvandlings-bygd* ([Stockholm:] Arbetarnas Kulturhistoriska Sällskap, 1976), 138.

12. Axel Uhlén, *Arbetardiktningens pionjärperiod. 1885–1909* (Johanneshov: Bokförlaget Vanadis, 1964), 215, 152, 222; *Bläckfisken,* utgiven av Svenska journalistförbundet [its *årsbok,* 1920/21], 247; Minneapolis city directories, 1907–11, 1913; Walfred Engdahl interview, Apr. 4, 1972; *Forskaren* 24 (1916): Supp., [13], advertisement for *Sweden up to Date*; Spongberg, *What's What in the War?* (Des Moines, Iowa: n.p., [1917]; *The Life of Jenny Lind,* Oct. 6, 1820–Nov. 2, 1887 (Minneapolis: 1920); "London nattetid," *Forskaren* 15 (1907): [295]–298.

13. Untitled biographical essay on Teigen, possibly by Ludvig Hektoen, Box 5, Knut Gjerset Papers, Norwegian American Historical Association, St. Olaf College, Northfield, Minn. (another copy in Hektoen Papers, NAHA); J.B. Wist, "Pressen efter borgerkrigen," in Wist, ed., *Norsk-Amerikanernes festskrift* (Decorah, Iowa: Symra Company, 1914), 133–38; *Minneapolis Daglig Tidende*, July 6, 1914, p. 4, obituary; Waldemar Ager, "Norsk-amerikansk skjøn literatur," in Wist, ed., *Norsk-amerikanernes festskrift*, 297f.; Teigen, "Usonas vikinges-tamme," *Forskaren* 17 (1909): [100]–104, [134]–141, [170]–174, [244]–250, [337]–342; Arne Sunde, "A Minority within a Minority: The Promotion of Nynorsk in the United States, 1900–1920," *Norwegian American Studies* 34 (1995): 189; "Dr. K.M. Teigen – sjuk och i ekonomisk betryck," *Forskaren* 21 (1913): Supp., 159; Söderström, *Minneapolis minnen*, 448; Ulf Beijbom, *Utvandrarna och Svensk-Amerika* (Stockholm: LTs förlag, 1986), 180; *Svenskamerikanskt. Människor och förhållanden i Svensk-Amerika* (Växjö: Emigrantinstitutets Vänner, 1990), 92ff.

14. Helge Nelson, *The Swedes and the Swedish Settlements in North America*, 2 vols. (Lund: Gleerup, &c., 1943), 1:143, 203f. A file of *Upplysningens Tidehvarf* exists at the Royal Library, Stockholm, and has been microfilmed for the MHS. *Forskaren* 16 (1908): Supp., 102.

Svenska Amerikanska Posten:
An Immigrant Newspaper with American Accents

ULF JONAS BJÖRK

As more than a million Swedes made their way across the Atlantic to America between 1846 and 1930, a press of some 225 Swedish-language newspapers sprang up to help them adjust to American society and preserve a sense of their own origins. One of the most successful of these newspapers is the subject of this essay: *Svenska Amerikanska Posten*, published in Minneapolis from 1885 to 1940.[1]

Despite the paper's indisputably large circulation, the treatment of *Posten* in Swedish American historiography has been curiously dismissive. The attitude toward the paper is most evident with Fritiof Ander, the premier historian of the Swedish immigrant press, who claims that the Minneapolis weekly did not have "any significant influence" on its readers. To explain why Ander saw *Posten* that way and to provide an assessment of what the Minneapolis weekly did achieve, this study looks at individual histories of the paper, both early and recent, and, above all, examines *Posten*'s own pages to see how it defined its accomplishments.[2]

Svenska Amerikanska Posten was launched midway through the decade that saw the largest-ever influx of immigrants from Sweden to the United States. Between 1881 and 1890, an average of 32,428 Swedes left their homeland for America every year, and by the end of the decade the Swedish-born population of the United States had more than doubled, rising from 194,000 to 478,000.[3]

Nourished by that influx, the Swedish-language newspaper press grew in spectacular fashion, from sixteen weekly newspapers in 1880 to forty-one ten years later. Minnesota, home to 21 percent of the Swedish-born in America in 1890, was a particularly fertile ground for Swedish-language journalism. When *Posten* made its debut in March 1885, it faced competition from three established weeklies and a struggling daily.[4]

Consisting of four pages and dedicated to the cause of temperance, the new member of the Swedish American press was unprepossessing in appearance and a typical Swedish-language weekly in content. The first page was reserved for general news about America and Minneapolis, the second for editorials and a serialized novel, the third for news from Sweden, and the fourth for items about the Swedes of Minneapolis and St. Paul, as well as general news from those two cities. Some thirty advertisements were also part of the content, many for Swedish businesses and professionals.[5]

The editor of the paper was N. P. Lind, a Swedish-born immigrant with a background as a theology student, and his contribution would prove nearly disastrous for the paper. According to one account, Lind regarded opponents as "mortal enemies" and "flayed" them in the columns of his paper, and another history of *Posten* characterized the editor's writings as "erratic and intolerant." To a latter-day reader, Lind's editorials do not seem more vitriolic than those of other Swedish American newspapers of the 1880s, an era when partisanship and personal attacks were commonplace, but a few of his pieces must have gone too far, because some of the editor's targets initiated costly libel suits against *Svenska Amerikanska Posten.*[6]

The thankless task of dealing with the expenses associated with legal proceedings on top of the usual financial challenges of a newly launched newspaper fell to the paper's business manager, and the two men who held that position during *Posten*'s first two years both proved unequal to the task. It took the appearance of the paper's third manager, Swan J. Turnblad, to turn *Posten*'s fortunes around.[7]

One reason the man who assumed control of the paper's management in 1886 succeeded was that he had experience in the newspaper business, having worked for several years as a typesetter. While that experience undoubtedly was valuable, one of the earliest biographies of Swan Turnblad probed even further into his subject's life, noting that Swan Johan was only eight years of age when he, his parents, and siblings left Sweden for the United States. Consequently, he had obtained all his education and work experience in the new country, and that had made him "more American than Swedish, i.e., bolder and more energetic in his way of doing business, calmer and more calculating," traits that had paved the way for the publisher's "great success as a businessman." Another observer also considered Turnblad's knowledge of the business environment of the new country a major reason for his accomplishments; by "staying ahead and adopting altogether American business methods," *Posten*'s publisher had made his paper popular among readers.[8]

Whatever the explanation, Turnblad showed considerably more initiative as *Posten*'s manager than his two predecessors had. He first turned his attention to putting the paper on sound financial footing. The solicitation of advertising became more methodical, which meant signing contracts with local and national agencies that bought space in *Posten's* columns for advertisers. To make the paper attractive to these advertisers, it was necessary to offer them a large number of readers, so a more effective means of recruiting subscribers was essential. To that end, Turnblad supplemented the subscription agents in specific locations that *Posten* had used since its earliest issues with solicitors who traveled from place to place.[9]

Next, in sharp contrast to his predecessors, the new manager exerted his influence on the paper's content. Prohibition and temperance pervaded *Posten's* columns during its first couple of years; now, they receded in prominence. The paper's prohibitionist "proclivities" had been an impediment when it came to "building up" the paper, Turnblad later claimed. To achieve the large circulation that he envisioned, the paper would have to be transformed from a partisan advocate to a general-interest publication.[10]

That was not a sudden transition. Editorial statements about the paper's purpose show that prohibition appeared to be the main reason for *Posten's* existence between 1885 and 1889. As the 1890s began, however, the paper started presenting itself in a different way to its readers:

> All the issues of the day will be dealt with from an impartial point of view, and we will have an opportunity to deal with the cause of temperance in a better manner than was the case before. Only the latest and best news will be reported. The Sweden department will be given particular attention. Our serialized novels will if possible be even more thrilling and instructive than before. And poems, sketches and short stories will not be forgotten.[11]

Shaping *Posten's* content meant asserting control over its editor. Some accounts claim that Turnblad dismissed Lind, but the editor did, in fact, stay on for two years under the new manager before leaving of his own volition in 1888. Still, there is no denying that the influence of Lind and subsequent editors diminished; during the last few months of Lind's tenure, his name was no longer listed in the paper, and his successor was not introduced at all. Not until Turnblad's brother Magnus assumed the editorship, in 1890, was the editor's name once again a regular part of the masthead. Further evidence of Swan Turnblad's control was an announcement in 1889 that he now was the largest shareholder in the company publishing *Posten*. Having achieved that position, Turnblad was free to shape *Svenska Amerikanska Posten* the way he wanted, and the first half of the 1890s became a crucial period in the paper's history.[12]

Turnblad early on showed an almost obsessive concern with circulation, size, and appearance, a concern that seemed influenced by American rather than

Swedish American newspaper publishing. From the first issues published under his management, readers were frequently treated to boastful claims about *Posten*'s ever-soaring circulation. Six months after Turnblad's coming aboard as manager, circulation supposedly stood at 5,000, a figure that was said to have doubled a year after that. Within three years, *Posten* claimed that it again had doubled, reaching 20,000, a fourfold increase in three years.[13]

The claims were habitually exaggerated. In connection with a 1908 lawsuit, Turnblad had to admit that his early statements of high circulations had amounted to "bluffing & boosting" because it had been the practice to exaggerate circulation between 1886 and 1897. Thus, an 1887 claim of 5,000 was 3,000 copies too high, while boasts in 1890 of a readership of 20,000 exaggerated the real numbers by 15,000. Only in 1897 were claims and real figures about the same. Even with the claims scaled down, however, *Posten*'s achievement in the area of circulation was impressive. The paper was gaining readers steadily.[14]

Equal to circulation as a measure of *Posten*'s success was the growing number of pages. Barely a year after becoming manager, Turnblad doubled *Posten*'s pages from four to eight, and four years later he added another four. *Svenska Amerikanska Posten* also told its readers, over and over, that appearance mattered, and changes in typography and layout were always conveyed to readers with a great deal of fanfare. The enthusiasm for the way the paper looked was matched by an enthusiasm for how and where *Posten* was produced. Readers were told on numerous occasions that Turnblad's paper was the first Swedish American paper to use both rotary presses and stereotyping (in 1889) and Linotype machines (in 1894). The infatuation with equipment and facilities is most evident in an 1896 history of *Posten* that says nothing about the journalists who edited the paper, but instead goes into great detail about improvements in production technology and about *Posten*'s ever-grander offices.[15]

The great attention paid to size and appearance was not allowed to overshadow content altogether, but that part of newspaper publishing did not seem to matter most to Turnblad in the early years, and it was not until 1891 that he began paying increasing attention to the editorial content of *Svenska Amerikanska Posten*—particularly news. In 1893, an editorial assured readers that *Posten* had "at its disposal a large staff of correspondents domestically and abroad" and that the news would be covered in an "alert and trustworthy" fashion: "what happens in other localities in the United States and abroad we are able to report rapidly and completely through extensive telegraphic and postal correspondence."[16]

The following year, Turnblad's attention to *Posten*'s content started going beyond the news pages. An editorial announcement promised innovations in the form of a department for women, a column where readers' questions would be answered, and pages for farmers, workingmen, temperance, and reform. To-gether with a guaranty of the continued presence of "editorials on the burning issues of the day, three thrilling serialized novels, printed in book format, en-tertaining and useful reading for young and old, etc.," the introduction of these new departments indicated that Swan Turnblad had arrived at a decision about what his paper was to contain. Although the titles and the space given to the individual sections would vary, they would remain part of *Svenska Amerikan-ska Posten* until the paper's last issue in 1940.[17]

Judged in terms of readership, Swan Turnblad's transformation of *Svenska Amerikanska Posten* had been a huge success a mere ten years after his arrival at the paper, resulting in a circulation of 20,000. Never shy about its accom-plishments, *Posten* in 1894 declared itself the "largest" and "most widespread" Swedish weekly in America, and Chicago journalist C. F. Peterson concurred when he evaluated Turnblad's success a few years later, judging it to be "with-out parallel" in the Swedish American press. In 1904, *Posten* passed the 50,000 circulation mark, according to the figures reported to newspaper directories, and for the next few years it was, at least in the directories, the largest Swedish weekly in the United States.[18]

Each issue of this giant in the Swedish American press was produced by a complex business organization, as an illustration in the 1902 Christmas issue showed. The staff members of *Svenska Amerikanska Posten* were presented as ornaments on a Christmas tree, with the publisher himself in the center. Turn-blad was surrounded by the four editors of *Posten's* staff, the correspondent writing from Sweden, the paper's advertising solicitor, its cartoonist, and the employee in charge of subscription premiums. At the top of the tree were the six female clerks who, under a male supervisor, handled bookkeeping and sub-scription lists. At the bottom, finally, were the paper's four traveling subscrip-tion agents and its seven typesetters.[19]

A typical *Posten* issue ran twenty pages in the early 1900s, with the front page reserved for major stories and the latest news, often accompanied by pho-tographs. In the subsequent pages, standing departments related news from the United States Congress and the Minnesota legislature, Swedish America, Min-nesota, Minneapolis, and St. Paul. Two pages offered news and a weekly review from Sweden, and items from the rest of Scandinavia had their own column. One page was reserved for "the farm, the barn, the garden" and for the women's department, which had the heading of "Woman and the Home" and dealt with topics such as "the kitchen," "pastimes," and fashion. Letters from readers were presented on a page called "The Voice of the People;" those letters that asked for advice were answered in one column if the inquiry was of a general nature and in another if it dealt with legal matters. Reading designed to entertain com-

For a time the largest Swedish weekly published in the United States,
Svenska Amerikanska Posten *towered over its competition,*
as illustrated by this front-page cartoon, April 23, 1901

A new home for the paper: the Posten
building, 500 Seventh Street South, Min-
neapolis, 1915. This photo appeared on the
front page, advertising the newspaper's
prosperity.

Page from Svenska Amerikanska
Posten, *July 1903*

manded a major share of each issue. Several of the editors contributed humorous columns, which were surrounded by jokes, poems, and short stories. No fewer than three serialized novels were also offered to readers each week.[20]

In many ways, the content followed the formula developed by Turnblad in the mid-1890s, but some experimentation continued. In April 1901, *Posten* became one of the first Swedish-language papers to run a regular cartoon, an innovation that was greeted with a "storm of protest from the Swedish-American press in general," according to one observer. Undaunted by the hostile reception, Turnblad forged ahead with his next innovation, a color comic strip, which began in March 1902 and lasted until August. Comics in Swedish reappeared in 1908 and were touted as an important part of *Posten's* content until they were removed in 1911 to make room for something "more useful," an additional farm page.[21]

As controversial as the introduction of comic strips and cartoons was *Svenska Amerikanska Posten's* attitude toward the use of English. In the fall of 1902, Turnblad announced that his paper would have an English-language supplement called the *Posten Junior*. It was intended for the immigrants' children, who did not have "the opportunity to acquire the Swedish language to an extent sufficient enough to read a newspaper in this language," and would contain stories, jokes, and other entertainment. Claiming that reader reactions to the *Posten Junior* had been nothing but favorable, *Svenska Amerikanska Posten* soon began publishing one or two editorials in English per issue, a decision that drew criticism from other Swedish American papers, in which the use of English was next to non-existent.[22]

The introduction of material in English appeared to be one of Turnblad's experiments, which, like the comic strips, were removed if they did not meet with reader approval. Apparently they did not, for the editorials were discontinued in early 1904, while the *Posten Junior* finally disappeared in the fall of 1905. Attempting once again to appeal to young, native-born Swedish Americans, Turnblad began running untranslated American comic strips in 1907, an experiment that lasted until 1910, when reader sentiment made it clear that it favored having "the newspaper exclusively Swedish in content." After that, English disappeared from the pages of *Svenska Amerikanska Posten*, with the exception of a few editorials during World War I, prompted by a need to defend foreign-language newspapers in a hostile American environment.[23]

As noted above, *Posten* entered the twentieth century with four editors on its staff beside Turnblad, making it one of the largest in the Swedish American press. The 1900–10 decade was to be one of change for the paper's editorial staff, however, with frequent turnovers in personnel. What signaled the beginning of that change was Magnus Turnblad's departure in 1902, after twelve years as editor-in-chief, and the passing of the old guard was completed when Herman Stockenström, Magnus's co-editor since the mid-1890s, died after only a few months as the new editor-in-chief.[24]

This turbulent era in the history of the *Posten's* staff is a good starting point for a brief discussion of Turnblad as an employer. In the thirty years between 1886 and 1915, *Posten* had twenty-five different editors on its staff. Restlessness was a common trait among Swedish American journalists, resulting in careers on many different newspaper staffs. Still, Johan Person, a *Posten* editor from 1912 to 1913, claimed that it was well known among his colleagues that Turnblad was "a hard employer who cannot keep his editors for long."[25]

Person had joined the paper's staff with low expectations, commenting beforehand that the salary was "dismal for such a large paper and for the amount of routine work required—not to mention the factory-like supervision as to working hours," and he proved right in his misgivings about the hours and amount of work. Discipline was "very strict," and the working day started at 8 A.M. and ended at 5 or 6 P.M. The door to the editorial offices was padlocked and opened only for one hour of lunch. Vacation time was unheard of, and Person's workload kept him "constantly occupied."[26]

The account of Nils F. Brown, on the staff between 1910 and 1913, echoes Person's in several respects. He, too, noted the long working hours and the nonexistent vacations, and Brown also found supervision strict, with the publisher "stealing into the editorial office" several times a day "to spy on" his employees and make sure they were working. Salaries were "the lowest possible," according to Brown, ranging from $12 to $15 a week in the early 1910s.[27]

Whether Turnblad stood out as a difficult employer is debatable, however. Person's career before and after *Posten* indicates that working hours were as long and as strictly enforced at *Svenska Kuriren* in Chicago and that the workload was as heavy on *Vestkusten* in San Francisco. As to salaries, remarks made by author and journalist Ernst Skarstedt in private letters suggest that $15 a week was an average salary for the majority of the editors in the Swedish-language press.[28]

In 1915, *Svenska Amerikanska Posten* and its staff moved into a building of its own after years of renting space from other businesses. The move was a symbol of the paper's prosperity, evidenced by a circulation of 56,000, the largest in the paper's history. The success of *Posten* was a reflection of the state of the Swedish-language press as a whole, which reached its peak both in number of papers (around fifty) and aggregate circulation (about a half-million) in the early 1910s.[29]

Unfortunately, three major events were soon to shrink the Swedish American newspaper press from fifty publications to twenty and cut circulation from half a million to less than 150,000 during the last twenty-five years of *Posten*'s life. The decline began with the war years, which produced growing anti-immigrant sentiments and soaring production costs. After the war, *Svenska Amerikanska Posten* claimed that newsprint costs had risen threefold, and postage rates and salaries had also gone up. While costs had risen, revenues had dropped, because advertisers had been scared off by propaganda against the foreign-language press.[30]

Further evidence of official and public hostility toward foreign-language newspapers was that *Posten*, like several other Swedish American papers, had been cited with disapproval by a congressional committee for publishing peace appeals before the United States entered the war and that the paper considered it necessary to publish editorials (in both English and Swedish) that defended the immigrant press and pointed to its achievements in assimilating its readers.[31]

It is possible that the difficulties of the war years and the resulting drop in circulation convinced Swan Turnblad that it was time to step down as publisher, and in October 1920 he sold *Svenska Amerikanska Posten*. It became evident very early, however, that Magnus Martinson, the new publisher, lacked Turnblad's business acumen, and that proved to be a sorely needed skill in the 1920s, the decade that witnessed the end of unrestricted immigration, the second event to affect the Swedish American press profoundly.[32]

Competition between the largest Swedish American papers sharpened in this climate of a shrinking overall readership, and *Svenska Amerikanska Posten* was hurt by the intensified efforts of its Chicago rivals *Svenska Tribunen-Nyheter* and *Svenska Amerikanaren* to recruit subscribers, not only in their home city but all across Swedish America, including Minnesota. A sign of *Posten*'s difficulties is that the paper did not report any circulation to newspaper directories between 1924 and 1927; when an estimate finally appeared in the 1928 *Ayer's* annual, it showed a drop of 25 percent compared with six years earlier. Assessing the paper's situation in 1927, when Martinson had driven it close to bankruptcy, one observer claimed that *Posten* had seen "its glory days a long time ago."[33]

After Martinson was forced to step down as publisher by the paper's creditors, a new board of directors was appointed, and it asked Turnblad to return as manager-publisher of *Posten*. Within a short time, he once again became its *de facto* owner; ownership of the paper changed once again in 1929, when Turnblad included his paper and its production plant in a large-scale donation made by him and his family to create the Minneapolis-based American Institute for Swedish Art, Literature, and Science. Swan Turnblad continued to lead the newspaper enterprise until his death in 1933, however.[34]

Still, even a man with Turnblad's business sense found it difficult to run a Swedish-language newspaper successfully during the Depression. It was the last major event in *Posten's* lifetime to deal a blow to the Swedish immigrant press, because a readership already reduced by the end of mass immigration now had difficulty paying for its papers. Seven years after Turnblad's death, his daughter Lillian sold *Svenska Amerikanska Posten* to the only large paper left in Chicago, *Svenska Amerikanaren-Tribunen.*[35]

Judged by the conventional standards of newspaper achievement, *Svenska Amerikanska Posten* was clearly a success. Its circulation placed it among the three largest newspapers during the peak years of the Swedish-language press in America, and the paper made its publisher a prosperous man. In light of those facts, how can the dismissive attitude of historians such as Ander be explained, and how shall we evaluate Swan J. Turnblad's contribution?

The answer to these questions lies in recognizing that Turnblad did not fit the standard definition of a great journalist, something that is evident when his contemporaries tried to define his achievements. In unusually vague language, Ernst Skarstedt claimed that Turnblad with *Posten* had achieved "a tangible expression of his personal opinion of what a paper should be" and pointed to *Posten's* publisher raising his paper's circulation from 1,400 copies in 1886 to more than 40,000 at the turn of the century. Somewhat more concretely, C. F. Peterson stressed how "well-liked" the paper was by its readers, and historian A. E. Strand cited the satisfaction and huge patronage of advertisers as the main sign of the paper's success.[36]

All these accomplishments lay in the realm of business, and that was not where Ander looked for newspaper greatness. Following an older and abandoned American tradition, as well as a Swedish one persisting at the time, he saw journalistic success as the editorial leadership a newspaper provided. That was a standard that stressed the editorial page at the expense of other parts of the newspaper and identified papers with prominent editors, such as *Hemlandet's* Johan Enander.

Turnblad, who seldom wrote for his paper, could lay no claim to such leadership, and he did not seem to covet it, for that matter. Although the paper's editorial positions were the subject of occasional self-praise, they were only one among many good qualities pointed out to readers, and less and less was said about them as time progressed. Politics, the traditional focus of editorial pages, provides the best illustration of Turnblad's attitude. In a press that was overwhelmingly Republican in party affiliation, *Posten* had made waves in the early 1890s by throwing its support to the Democrats. Turnblad appeared to view the change partly as a business move, however, explaining that the earlier prohibitionist stance had made it difficult to attract advertising.[37]

Nor could *Posten* be called a Democratic stalwart; only a few years after the switch in allegiance, the paper declared that it was "independent" and did not "hang like a flapping paper kite on the coattails of any political party." Instead, in what was perhaps an unintentionally revealing comment, *Posten* declared in 1896 that it measured the correctness of its political leanings by whether "the great general public... could approve of it." Where other Swedish American papers sought to lead the immigrants, Turnblad's weekly strove for approval by its readership.[38]

A move away from affiliation with political parties and a declining tendency to let politics define the readership were two increasingly evident characteristics of American newspapers in the latter half of the nineteenth century, and it was this tradition that Turnblad appeared to identify himself with, not the Swedish American one championed by Ander. In 1908, for instance, *Posten* told its readers that "*Svenska Amerikanska Posten* has always... wanted to keep up with the large American papers." Nils F. Brown disdainfully compared *Posten's* publisher to William Randolph Hearst, and if Brown's scorn is removed from the comparison, it is not an inappropriate one. Like Hearst and other publishers of the late nineteenth century, Turnblad was concerned with circulation, popularity, and content innovations. It does not seem like a coincidence that when rival Swedish American papers in 1901 accused *Svenska Amerikanska Posten* of being a "yellow journal," a term that had first been applied to Hearst's newspaper in New York, the paper proudly accepted the label.[39]

* * * *

NOTES

1. Ulf Beijbom, "The Swedish Press," in Sally M. Miller, ed., *The Ethnic Press in the United States: A Historical Analysis and Handbook* (New York: Greenwood Press, 1987), 384.

2. Fritiof Ander, "The Swedish-American Press in the Election of 1912," *Swedish Pioneer Historical Quarterly* (herafter *SPHQ*) 14 (1963): 123f.

3. Hans Norman and Harald Runblom, *Amerikaemigrationen i källornas belysning* (Uddevalla: Cikada, 1980), 221f.

4. Alfred Söderström, *Blixtar på tidnings-horisonten* (Warroad, Minn.: n.p., 1910), 27f.; Helge Nelson, *The Swedes and the Swedish Settlements of North America*, 2 vols. (New York: Albert Bonnier, 1943), 2:6; O. Fritiof Ander, *Swedish-American Political Newspapers* (Uppsala: Almqvist & Wicksells Boktryckeri AB, 1936).

5. *Svenska Amerikanska Posten* (hereafter *SAP*), Mar. 24, 1885, p. 2.

6. Alfred Söderström. *Minneapolis minnen. Kulturhistorisk axplockning från qvarnstaden vid Mississippi* (Minneapolis: published by the author, 1899), 172; A. E. Strand, ed., *A History of the Swedish-Americans in Minnesota*, 3 vols. (Chicago: The Lewis Publishing Company, 1910), 1:302f. On Lind's background, see Ernst Skarstedt, *Pennfäktare. Svensk-amerikanska*

författare och tidningsmän (Stockholm: Åhlén & Åkerlunds förlag, 1930), 105; for an example of personal attacks, see "Se upp med Posten!" *SAP*, May 19, 1885, p. 2.

7. *SAP*, Nov. 3, 1886, p. 4; Lawrence Hammerstrom, "The Swedish American Publishing Company Stockholders' Lawsuit Against Swan J. Turnblad," *Swedish American Historical Quarterly* (hereafter, *SAHQ*) 35 (1984): 40; Strand, ed., *History*, 1: 303; Söderström, *Minneapolis minnen*, 181.

8. Söderström, *Minneapolis minnen*, 183; C. F. Peterson, *Sverige i Amerika. Kulturhistoriska och biografiska teckningar* (Chicago: The Royal Star Company, 1898), 123f.; *SAP*, Nov. 3, 1886, p. 4; "Svenska Amerikanska Postens Historia," *SAP*, Mar. 10, 1896, p. 1.

9. *SAP*, July 9, 1889, p. 4; Magnus Turnblad (hereafter MT) notebook, p. 11, 38 back of page (hereafter b), 30b, 31b, 33b, 36b, 38b; Magnus Turnblad Papers, *ASI*.

10. MT notebook, p. 45b.

11. *SAP*, Dec. 29, 1885, p. 1; Mar. 1, 1887, p. 2; Sept. 20, 1887, p. 4; Jan. 3, 1888, p. 1; Nov. 27, 1888, p. 1; Mar. 5, 1889, p. 1; "Anmälan för 1890," *SAP*, Dec. 24, 1889, p. 1.

12. Söderström, *Minneapolis minnen*, 181; Marie-Louise Sallnäs, "Emil Meurling and *Svenska Amerikanska Posten*," *SPHQ* 32 (1981): 43; *SAP*, Dec. 11, 1888, p. 4; "Anmälan för 1890," *SAP*, June 3, 1890, p. 4.

13. *SAP*, Mar. 1, 1887, p. 2; Jan. 3, 1888, p. 1; Dec. 23, 1890, p. 1; Dec. 24, 1888, p. 1; Feb. 19, 1889, p. 4; Dec. 24, 1889, p. 4; Feb. 11, 1890, p. 4; Apr. 1, 1890, p. 23; Oct. 13, 1891, p. 4; Dec. 20, 1892, p. 4; Jan. 2, 1894, p. 4; Feb. 27, 1894, p. 4; Jan 1, 1895, p. 4; Mar. 10, 1896, p. 1.

14. MT notebook, p. 52b, 12b, 46b, 22b, 11b, 13b, 26b; *SAP*, Mar. 1, 1887, p. 2; Feb. 19, 1889, p. 4; Dec. 24, 1889, p. 4; Dec. 23, 1890, p. 1; *Geo. P. Rowell and Co.'s American Newspaper Directory* 1897.

15. *SAP*, Sept. 20, 1887, p. 4; Dec. 24, 1890, p. 1, 4; Oct. 13, 1891, p. 4; Jan. 3, 1893, p. 4; Sept. 20, 1887; Dec. 8, 1890; "Svenska Amerikanska Postens Historia"; "Anmälan för 1890"; "En helsning till våra läsare," *SAP*, Feb. 27, 1894, p. 4.

16. "Anmälan," *SAP*, Dec. 12, 1893, p. 4.

17. "Tillkännagifvande," *SAP*, Feb. 6, 1894, p. 4.

18. *Rowell* newspaper directory, 1895, 1897; "Till våra läsare," *SAP*, Nov. 6, 1894, p. 4; Peterson, *Sverige i Amerika*, 123–24; *N. W. Ayer & Son's American Newspaper Annual and Directory*, 1891, 1901, 1906–16, 1918–23, 1925–41; *Rowell* directories, 1895, 1897, 1900, 1905.

19. *SAP*, Dec. 23, 1902, p. 12.

20. "Svenska Amerikanska Posten 1903," *SAP*, Dec. 23, 1902, p. 1.

21. *SAP*, Apr. 23, 1901, p. 1; Strand, ed., *Swedish Americans in Minnesota*, 1:303; "Fader Sven Återfunnen," *SAP*, Feb. 25, 1908, p. 1; "Till våra läsare," *SAP*, Feb. 8, 1911, p. 9. Although the two strips supposedly had the same protagonist, Fader Sven, the second one was apparently a translation of material from the *Chicago Tribune*.

22. "The *Posten Junior*," *SAP*, Nov. 25, 1902, p. 6; Dec. 16, 1902, p. 6; "*Posten Junior*," *SAP*, Nov. 4, 1902, p. 6.

23. "Än ett steg framåt," *SAP*, July 23, 1907, p. 9; "Till läsekretsen," *SAP*, Jan. 3, 1911.

24. "Tack för god vakt!" *SAP*, Sept. 2, 1902, p. 7. For the size of the editorial staffs of the Swedish American press, see Gustav Andreen, "Den nuvarande svensk-amerikanska pressen," *Prärieblomman* 1905, p. 167–79; *SAP*, Oct. 28, 1902, p. 1.

25. Person to Ernst Skarstedt, Aug. 19, 1911, Skarstedt Papers, Univ. of Wash.; Skarstedt, *Svensk-amerikanska folket i helg och söcken* (Stockholm: Björck & Börjesson, 1917), 167; Skarstedt, *Pennfäktare*; Söderström, *Minneapolis minnen*, 181.

26. Person to Skarstedt, July 12, 1912; Sept. 13, 1912; Person to Axel Lundegård, Apr. 23, 1913; Person to Skarstedt, May 2, 1912; Person to Skarstedt, Mar. 12, 1912, Skarstedt Papers, Univ. of Wash.

27. Nils F:son Brown autobiography, p. 7, typed manuscript, Univ. of Wash; Brown, "Ur svensk-amerikansk press-historia," *Canada-Tidningen*, Oct. 3, 1940, p. 3. Twenty years ear-

lier, Magnus Turnblad had been paid between $15 and $25 a week as editor-in-chief, while other editors were paid the same; MT notebook, p. 33b.

28. Skarstedt to Conrad Skarstedt, Jan. 3 and Apr. 20, 1915, Conrad Skarstedt Papers, Riksföreningen Sverigekontakt, Göteborg, Sweden; Karl Hellberg to Skarstedt, Nov. 20, 1927, Skarstedt Papers, Univ. of Wash; Ulf Jonas Björk, "'Nothing but a Hired Hand: Johan Person and the Swedish-American Press," *SAHQ* 42 (1991): 5–24.

29. Figures computed from *Ayer's* directories, 1905–40; "Svenska Amerikanska Posten's Nya Hem," *SAP*, Dec. 22, 1915, p. 1.

30. "Ett gif akt till våra läsare," *SAP*, Sept. 3, 1919, p. 6; "Till våra läsare," *SAP*, Aug. 14, 1918, p. 6.

31. "The Scandinavian Press," *SAP*, Oct. 3, 1917, p. 6; "Den utlandsspråkiga pressen," *SAP*, July 3, 1918, p. 6; "Brewing and Liquor Interests and German and Bolshevik Propaganda: Reports and Hearings of the Subcommittee on the Judiciary, United States Senate," *66th Congress, 1st Session, Senate Document No. 62* (Washington: Government Printing Office, 1919), 480, 570–75.

32. Sallnäs, "Emil Meurling," 50; "Svenska Amerikanska Posten i nya händer," *SAP*, Oct. 13, 1920, p. 8.

33. Linus Gustafson to Skarstedt, Oct. 15, 1927; Skarstedt Papers, Riksföreningen Sverigekontakt; Alexander Olsson to Skarstedt, Sept. 4, 1927, Skarstedt Papers, Univ. of Wash.

34. Sallnäs, "Emil Meurling," 51; "Swan J. Turnblad, tidningens mångårige utgivare, har avlidit," *SAP*, May 4, 1933, p. 1; Sept. 7, 1927, p. 6; Brown autobiography, p. 40f., 53; G. N. Swan to Oliver Linder, Apr. 30 and Aug. 26, 1927; Swan Papers, Swenson Swedish Immigration Research Center, Augustana College, Rock Island, Ill.; Hellberg to Skarstedt, Sept. 3, 1927, Skarstedt Papers, Univ. of Wash.

35. "Svenska Amerikanska Posten upphör," *SAP*, Sept. 11, 1940, p. 8; "Till våra läsare," *SAP*, June 21, 1933, p. 8; Sture Lindmark, *Swedish America, 1914–1932* (Uppsala: Läromedelsförlagen, 1971), 227–31.

36. Strand, ed., *History*, 1:302; Peterson, *Sverige i Amerika*, 124; Skarstedt, *Pennfäktare*, 193.

37. MT notebook, p. 45b; Ander, "Swedish-American Press," 123f.

38. "Om oss sjelfva," *SAP*, Dec. 29, 1896, p. 4; "Svenska Amerikanska Postens Historia."

39. "Den 'gula' tidningspressen," *SAP* Oct. 8, 1901, p. 6; "Fader Sven återfunnen."

Teaching Swedish in the Public Schools:
Cultural Persistence in Minneapolis

ANITA OLSON GUSTAFSON

From the time the first streams of immigrants left Sweden for America, Minnesota was an important destination for Swedish settlers. Not only did parts of Minnesota resemble Sweden, but, most importantly, the timing of the exodus coincided with the opening of fertile Minnesota farmland to white settlement. After 1880, when the largest surge of Swedes left for America, urban areas became important magnets of settlement for not only the Swedish immigrants, but for many European groups as well. Many of these Swedes found their way to Minneapolis-St. Paul. When Minnesota's Swedish-born population peaked in 1905 with slightly more than 126,000 people, the Twin Cities' Swedes numbered about 38,000, which represented the second-largest urban concentration of Swedes in America, after the much larger city of Chicago. Furthermore, John Rice has pointed out that "almost 7.5% of the Twin Cities' population was Swedish born, a proportion far larger than that of any other city of more than 100,000 people in the nation." It was in this context of ethnic dominance that Swedish leaders in Minneapolis cooperated with their Norwegian and Danish cousins and campaigned for Scandinavian languages to be added as elective subjects in the city's high schools. Their efforts paid off handsomely. School officials agreed in 1910 to add Swedish and Norwegian to the high school curriculum as optional courses of study in schools with enough student interest to sustain an adequate enrollment. The Minneapolis public high schools began offering Swedish in the fall of 1910 and continued to do so for over six decades. The persistence of Swedish instruction in the public schools resulted from the numerical strength of the Swedes compared to other ethnic groups, their ability to influence policy decisions in public education, and the desire to pass along linguistic traditions to postimmigrant generations.[1]

Swedish immigrants' attitudes toward their new land reflected a divided identity; they wanted to succeed in their newly adopted homeland, but they also hoped to preserve some of their Swedish culture and heritage. The campaign for Swedish in the public schools of Minneapolis offers a case study for how this hybrid Swedish American identity played itself out in a public arena. Swedish immigrants embraced the opportunity for their children to partake in a public school education, hoping that such schooling would provide them with skills necessary for success in America. Swedish parents, however, also wanted to ensure that the second generation would not completely lose sight of their own ethnic heritage, particularly a knowledge of the Swedish language. By offering Swedish language classes in the public high schools, these two conflicting agendas could be somewhat ameliorated. The success of such efforts, however, was completely dependent upon the strong Swedish and Scandinavian presence in the city of Minneapolis. This study will also offer a brief comparative glimpse at a similar effort to add Swedish to the public school curriculum of Chicago, a city with over twice as many Swedes as Minneapolis but where Swedes faced competition from other larger ethnic groups. In such a setting, Chicago's Swedes achieved short-term success by adding Swedish classes to the public high schools, but the effort could not be sustained, and it was dropped from the curriculum in less than a decade.

Scandinavians dominated the demographic composition of Minneapolis in 1910. Like many other urban areas in America, a large proportion of the city's population was decidedly ethnic. Nearly 29 percent of Minneapolis' population in 1910 was foreign-born; these immigrants and their children made up over 67 percent of the city's 301,408 inhabitants. Swedes made up the single largest ethnic group in Minneapolis, with 26,477 Swedish-born individuals and 26,278 children of Swedish immigrants, for a total count of 52,755 inhabitants of Swedish stock—over 17 percent of Minneapolis's total population. Norwegians ranked second among the city's ethnic groups in 1910, with 34,271 people of Norwegian stock, or 11.4 percent of the city's total population. Germans were the third largest group of foreigners in the city. The number of individuals of German stock (29,992) represented 10 percent of the city's inhabitants. The total number of Swedes, Norwegians, and Danes and their children living in Minneapolis in 1910 comprised over 30 percent of the city's entire population. (See Table 1.) By comparison, although Chicago held the largest urban concentration of Swedes in the United States in 1910 with 117,000 people of Swedish stock, Swedes ranked as the sixth-largest ethnic group in that city, behind the much larger German group, the Austrians, Irish, Italians, and Poles. Thus, despite the fact that Chicago's Swedes were larger in terms of actual numbers, the Swedes in Minneapolis dominated the ethnic composition of that city to a much greater degree.[2]

Table 1
The Scandinavian Population of Minneapolis, 1910

	Sweden	Norway	Denmark	Total Scandinavia
Number foreign stock	52,755	34,271	3,889	90,915
% of foreign stock	26.1	16.9	1.9	44.9
% of total city population	17.5	11.4	1.3	30.2
Number foreign born	26,477	16,401	2,030	44,908
% of city's foreign born	30.8	19.1	2.4	52.3
Both parents foreign	22,326	14,267	1,310	37,903
One parent foreign	3,952	3,603	549	8,104

	Other Groups		
	Germany	Canada	Ireland
Number foreign stock	29,992	13,696	13,595
% of foreign stock	14.8	6.8	6.7
% of total city population	10	4.5	4.5
Number foreign born	8,650	5,877	2,867
% of city's foreign born	10.1	6.8	3.3
Both parents foreign	14,798	2,423	7,180
One parent foreign	6,544	5,396	3,548

The most comprehensive study about Swedish in the nation's public schools is Esther Chilstrom Meixner's 1941 Ph.D. dissertation, "The Teaching of the Scandinavian Languages and Literature in the United States." According to Meixner, Minneapolis was the pioneer in offering Swedish languages classes in the public schools, paving the way for similar efforts in other locations. Her research indicated that South and East high schools in Minneapolis were the first public high schools in the nation to add Swedish to their curriculum in 1910, and other schools quickly followed. During the 1910–11 academic year, the school systems in Svea and Cokato, Minnesota, and Rockford, Illinois, approved Swedish instruction, and, by 1913, seven additional schools in Minnesota, Illinois, and Iowa had done so. National efforts at expanding Scandinavian instruction in the schools gained momentum after the Society for the Advancement of Scandinavian Studies was organized in 1911. Founded for the purpose of promoting and keeping Scandinavian culture alive in the United States and comprised mainly of professors of Scandinavian in colleges and universities throughout America, this group worked to promote language instruction in public secondary schools. These efforts at Scandinavian agitation met with success during the early part of the decade; by 1913, forty-five schools nationally offered Scandinavian instruction, with an enrollment of over 1,190.[3]

In the early years of the Minneapolis high schools, the curriculum concentrated upon the study of the classics, in order to prepare a student for university work or for a teaching career. The Board of Education first published an *Annual Report* in 1873, and these reports provide valuable information about curricular issues and the general academic approach of the city's schools. In the 1870s, Latin was emphasized throughout the curriculum, even before a student arrived at the high school. German was offered as an elective subject beginning in the first term of the tenth grade, and Greek was added as another alternative in the third term of the tenth grade. Both languages continued to be offered until the final term of a student's senior year. But these academic options reached only a minority of the city's student population, since the public high school itself was only beginning to gain credibility. O. V. Tousley, the superintendent of the Minneapolis public schools, argued vehemently for the importance of offering a free secondary education to the masses in the 1878 *Annual Report*. Not only were public grammar schools important for the future of the American republic, he argued, but public high schools would provide to all members of society the opportunity for advancement. Public high schools would be a training ground for future teachers—educating them beyond the level of the grammar schools in which they would teach. But even more importantly, public high schools would provide opportunities for advancement to the city's immigrants, allowing them a ticket out of the laboring class if they so desired.

"There is nothing more favorable to the character of the foreigner newly arrived on our shores," Tousley argued, "than this, that he is everywhere eager to avail himself of school privileges." Tousley hoped for the end of a caste society, in which immigrants filled the ranks of laborer and only the privileged could afford a high school education. Even so, most students left school after the ninth grade to go to work. In 1884, of the city's nearly 12,000 public school students, only 188, or 1.6 percent, were enrolled in high school, and, from 1878 to 1887, an average of only 17.1 students actually graduated from the city's public high schools each year. Although the public high schools offered the opportunity for educational and possibly social advancement, the economic realities faced by most students forced them into the job market by the time they were fifteen years old.[4]

As a response to these pressures, in 1887 the public high schools added a manual training department in order to offer a vocational education to high school students. The thirty places in this program filled immediately, and many more students could have been recruited if the schools could accommodate them. The 1887 *Annual Report* noted, "This course seems to attract and hold boys who would, at this stage of their work, drop out of school if such a course were not offered." From this point on, the public high schools attempted to balance the vocational needs of its urban population with the loftier prospect of advancement through a classical education. In the process, not only did the high school enrollment grow, the overall curriculum took steps toward a more practical and modern approach to education. What this meant in terms of foreign language instruction in the high schools was that French was added as an elective subject in 1887, the German language curriculum was revised and strengthened in 1890, and Greek instruction was dropped in 1898. In 1901, the president of the Board of Education, Thomas F. Quinby, M.D., argued for the addition of Spanish as an elective subject. His justification for Spanish classes centered upon the language's practicality. "From a purely commercial and utilitarian standpoint," he wrote in his report, "the advantages of a knowledge of this tongue must appeal forcibly to every citizen who has the commercial supremacy of his country at heart." His suggestions were not initially heeded, however, and Spanish was not added to the high school curriculum until 1915, well after the Swedish and Norwegian languages had been approved. Although a few disgruntled parents expressed their concern over a declining classical education in the high schools, the vast majority of students supported this change in policy by participating in the high school program to a much greater degree. By 1892, nearly 1,300 students attended the city's high schools; the number skyrocketed to nearly 2,500 by 1900; and enrollment increased even further in the early decades of the twentieth century.[5]

There were subtle ways that the Scandinavian influence found its way into the school system. For example, a manual training department was added in 1899 and given the name "sloyd," after the Swedish word *slöjd*, meaning handicraft. High school choral groups performed songs such as "Norse Lullaby" and "Song of the Vikings" at commencement exercises, and, in 1900, the featured essay read by graduate Lydia Seaberg focused upon "Some Customs of the Swedes." Graduation ceremonies for South High School were held at the Swedish Tabernacle in 1899 and many times thereafter. Dance troupes performed Swedish and Old English folk dances at the eighth grade graduation exercises in 1911. In numerous ways, Swedish ethnicity was woven into the fabric of everyday life in Minneapolis. Adding Swedish language courses to the high school curriculum seemed like a natural extension of this comfortable relationship between the arena of public education and the Swedes' desire to preserve their ethnic heritage.[6]

The first reference to Swedish language instruction in the public high schools in Minneapolis appeared in the Board of Education's minutes on March 29, 1910. The minutes stated that "a communication was read from the Elim Swedish Baptist Church, requesting that the Scandinavian languages be included in the high school course of study." The petition was the first one to appear before the Board of Education, but it represented a much larger effort among Scandinavians in Minneapolis to agitate for Swedish in the schools. The petition itself was preprinted, with a blank where the name of the petitioner was to be inserted. It read as follows:

> WHEREAS, The Scandinavian Languages may, according to the laws of the State of Minnesota, be introduced into the course of any High School at the discretion of the local board of education:
>
> WHEREAS, They are of great practical importance in a state where the Scandinavians form about one-half the population:
>
> WHEREAS, They alone render accessible numerous and varied scientific works and periodicals of great value, which have not been, and will not be, translated:
>
> WHEREAS, They possess extensive literatures of the highest excellence, of which the greater part will not be translated, and the most typical and artistic works cannot be adequately rendered in any other tongue:
>
> WHEREAS, They are now accepted for admission by the State University to the extent of two year-credits:
>
> THEREFORE, BE IT RESOLVED, That we _____ (The Elim Swedish Baptist Church, Minneapolis, Minnesota) earnestly request the Board of Education of Minneapolis to introduce the Scandinavian Languages as electives into the course of one or more High Schools of the City.

In this case, the petition was signed by V. E. Hedberg, pastor of the Elim church. The Board of Education referred the entire matter to its Committee on Text Books and Course of Study, effectively delaying any decision. It became clear to Swedish leaders that another tactic would need to be pursued in order to convince the board to take action.[7]

An entire delegation of Scandinavian leaders presented itself to the Board of Education at its next meeting on April 12, 1910, urging the board to address the Scandinavian language issue. The petition claimed that the group represented "about sixty Scandinavian organizations in Minneapolis with a united membership of approximately 30,000," and committee members earnestly requested that the Board of Education "introduce the Scandinavian Languages as electives into the course of the high schools of the city on the same terms as German and French." Another petition, similar to the one submitted by the Elim church, was also presented to the board by the members of the Brotherhood of the Bethany Presbyterian Church. It was the delegation's appearance, however, not merely the receipt of petitions from individual groups, that really impressed the board. In fact, the delegation of eight Scandinavians actually outnumbered the five members of the Board of Education present at the meeting. After the petition was read, board member Steele moved that the "Scandinavian languages be included in the high school course of study, and that the details be arranged by the superintendent and the principals of the several high schools." The motion carried unanimously.[8]

If Professor A. A. Stomberg's recollections are an accurate reflection of what took place that evening, the Board of Education was mighty impressed indeed. Stomberg, the Professor of Scandinavian at the University of Minnesota, served as secretary to the delegation. In a letter to Swedish community leaders in Chicago, Stomberg recounted the steps followed by the Minneapolis delegation, in the process offering strategic suggestions for the Chicagoans to follow in order to see Swedish adopted as a foreign language in that city's schools. He noted that it helped to have a Scandinavian, M. Falk Gjersten, on the Board of Education, but even if that had not been the case Stomberg believed that "in Minneapolis we would have carried the matter by the unanimous vote of the board." This impression was based upon his belief that the petition "came before the board with such backing, representing so many individuals and societies, that there was not a member of the board that would have cared to oppose the proposition." As to the reaction of the board members, Stomberg noted that they all were "extremely courteous and fair throughout and of course I believe that they gave us this fair treatment because they realized that our request was entirely fair." He humbly concluded, "members of the school board

told us afterwards that no matter had ever been laid before them in so dignified and convincing way as ours."[9]

Stomberg's letter also reveals a behind-the-scenes look at what took place
to mobilize the Swedish community in favor of the language issue. As a professor of Scandinavian, he certainly had his own special interest in having these
languages adopted by the public schools. Although he did not mention it directly, he undoubtedly realized that the Swedes had a better chance of having
their own language adopted if they cooperated with other Scandinavian groups.
This they did from the outset. Stomberg noted that he and the other leaders
committed to this issue started the movement by calling a mass meeting of
Scandinavians, which then "appointed a committee to inaugurate and conduct
a campaign." The committee immediately drew up the petition that was eventually presented to the board, then got in touch with as many Scandinavian organizations as possible. Over fifty-two churches and societies responded immediately by approving these petitions, having their officers sign them, and
sending them to Stomberg as secretary of the committee. Other organizations
continued to join the cause on a daily basis. The group then notified the president of the Board of Education and they agreed upon a date for their petitions
to be presented to the board, leaving nothing to chance. Stomberg revealed that
"Before going before the board we had selected speakers and each one had his
particular point to emphasize." And a little intra-Scandinavian rivalry did not
hurt the cause either. Stomberg reflected that when the campaign began, he
thought himself to be alone among the Swedes wanting their language to be
adopted in the schools, which he found to be very depressing. But it did not
take long before the Swedes showed "great enthusiasm and they did not by any
means lag behind our Norwegian friends."[10]

The Swedish press in Minneapolis duly noted the Board of Education's decision. *Svenska Amerikanska Posten*, published in Minneapolis, informed its
readers that Swedish, Norwegian, and Danish would be considered as elective
subjects in the city's high schools on the same level as French and German. The
newspaper also appealed to the Minneapolis Swedes' sense of pride as leaders
in Swedish America. Contradicting Meixner's report that the Minneapolis high
schools were actually the first to add Swedish to the public school curriculum,
the article noted that several locations in the eastern United States had already
begun to teach Swedish in the schools. It said, however: "Minneapolis is the
first city in the West that has taken this step, and examples will come to follow
in other places in the northwest." Elsewhere, people were simply waiting to see
the results of the agitation in Minneapolis before petitioning their own school
boards. Furthermore, the newspaper argued that efforts in the high schools
would also enhance the study of Scandinavian languages at the university level.

The article ended by commending the leadership committee for its "work to win a larger terrain for our forefathers' language out here."[11]

Coverage of the language issue by *Svenska Amerikanska Posten* thereafter shifted in tone from reporting the school board's decision to campaigning among Swedish Americans actually to take interest in the ramifications of that decision. The school board's action was not enough; now it was up to the Swedish students in the high schools to express an interest in taking Swedish courses. School board member M. Falk Gjersten wrote a letter published in *Svenska Amerikanska Posten* and addressed to parents with children in the city's high schools. The board's decision to offer Scandinavian languages, he noted, was "the largest recognition which our Nordic culture has won up to now." On May 20, 1910, a survey would be taken in all the city's high schools to determine how many students wanted to study a Scandinavian language the following year. This, Gjersten argued, would be a day of reckoning: "It shall then show how strong we [value] our mother tongue, and if we are a high-minded or an enslaved people. Should it contrary to all expectation show that merely a few want to learn our language and our literature, it would be a dishonor for the entire nation on both sides of the ocean." Therefore, he urged parents to convince their children to make the proper decision; namely, to express their intention to register for classes in their mother tongue. Meanwhile, Professor A. A. Stomberg used the press to urge pastors in Swedish American congregations to exhort parents and guardians of high schoolers to convince their children to register for Swedish classes. Swedish language study, he argued, would undoubtedly prove more beneficial to young Swedish Americans than the study of French or German. He declared that "no children of Swedish parents should neglect this opportunity to gain knowledge about their forefathers' language and culture."[12]

The efforts of Scandinavian leaders in Minneapolis paid off when 114 students expressed their interest in studying a Scandinavian language when they were polled on May 20. (See Table 2.) The school superintendent's report to the Board of Education indicated that sixty students registered their interest in Swedish and fifty-four in Norwegian. The strongest interest in Swedish was at South High School and at East High School, with twenty-four students registering at each school. *Svenska Amerikanska Posten* commented that the strong interest in Swedish at South High School was to be expected, because the area's population was heavily Swedish; the east-side results were a bit more surprising, however, because, it claimed, the area was not as Swedish-saturated. The superintendent of schools recommended that Swedish and Norwegian commence at both South and East high schools, and that Central High School, where only ten students had expressed an interest, also add Swedish. The Board of Education approved the addition of Swedish and Norwegian to the curriculum at East and South high schools, but it did not think ten students sufficient to offer Swedish classes at Central High School. On June 7, 1910, the Swedish press happily reported the decision of the Board of Education to its readers. Scandinavian leaders were undoubtedly relieved that their efforts had paid off—study of the Nordic languages would become part of the city high school's elective curriculum.[13]

Relief that Swedish classes would begin the following fall was tempered by the fact that relatively few students had registered for language classes. Students declaring their interest in Swedish at South, East, and Central high schools represented 2.7 percent, 2.2 percent, and .72 percent respectively of those schools' student population. *Svenska Amerikanska Posten* explained that only a quarter of the students in each school were polled; only those going into the first semester of their second and third year of high school were eligible to take elective foreign language classes. If the newspaper's one-quarter estimate was correct, the portion of students interested in Swedish was 10.62 percent of the eligible student population at South High School; 9.09 percent at East High School; and 2.89 percent at Central High School. (See Table 3.) Interest was sufficient to justify the addition of these elective courses to the high school curriculum, but it did not represent an overwhelming mandate by the Swedish American youth.[14]

The implementation of the new language courses went rather smoothly. Charles M. Jordan, superintendent of the public schools, noted in his annual report that the addition of Scandinavian language courses was the only major change in the high school curriculum in 1910. The main issues of concern centered on what textbooks to adopt and how to reimburse teachers for the expenses they incurred in obtaining curricular materials. Professor Stomberg noted that about sixty students total enrolled in Swedish at South and East high schools. Additional students enrolled the following semester and a small class

Table 2
Students Interested in Studying Swedish and Norwegian
in the Minneapolis Public Schools, 1910

Minneapolis High School	Total Students Enrolled	Number Interested in Swedish	% of Student Body Interested in Swedish	Number Interested in Norwegian	% of Student Body Interested in Norwegian
Central	1,382	10	0.72	5	0.36
East	1,055	24	2.20	16	1.52
North	963	1	0.10	2	2.08
South	904	24	2.70	30	3.32
West	1,147	1	0.09	1	0.09

was begun at Central High School, so the total number of students grew to approximately a hundred by the spring of 1911. Stomberg defended the academic integrity of these courses: "It was thought at first by a good many that these Scandinavian courses would afford a refuge for poor students, but that has certainly not become a fact. I think the classes in Scandinavian are looked upon as maintaining as high standards and the teachers have been extremely careful so that there should be no grounds for such suspicions."[15]

In 1912, The State Superintendent of Public Instruction for Minnesota, C. G. Schulz, lent his support to the Scandinavian language issue. He reported that "Scandinavian is gaining ground . . . Latin and Greek must inevitably give place in the public schools if the question is as to a choice between modern and dead languages. . . . The peoples of Scandinavia, Germany and other continental countries compose in great part the population of Minnesota. They have a natural pride in their ancestry and in the history and language of the fatherland." By 1913, 277 students in the Minneapolis high schools enrolled in Swedish classes. Overall, Scandinavian leaders in Minneapolis, representing the largest ethnic presence in the city, were able to wield substantial influence over the Board of Education. They adopted Swedish and Norwegian into the curriculum with no perceptible controversy. Scandinavian leaders convinced grassroots organizations to support them in their petition efforts, the issue was carefully laid out before the Board of Education, the board wholeheartedly agreed to offer Scandinavian languages in the high schools, and, once the superintendent identified the schools where interest was strongest, language classes were begun.[16]

Interest in Swedish continued to grow in subsequent years. In 1914, Superintendent Jordan reported that the "introduction of Swedish and Norwegian languages several years ago, seems to have met with general approval. The size of classes indicates that these subjects are popular in our schools." Esther

Table 3
Students Eligible to Take Swedish in the Minneapolis Public Schools

High School	Eligible Students*	% of Eligible Students Interested in Swedish
Central	346	2.89
East	264	9.09
North	241	0.41
South	226	10.62
West	287	0.34

*According to the estimate in *Svenska Amerikanska Posten* that one-fourth of the student body was eligible to enroll in elective language classes.

Chilstrom Meixner reported that 374 students enrolled in Swedish in the Minneapolis schools in 1916. A cost analysis of teaching high school subjects for the 1915–16 school year, found in the Board of Education Subject Files, shows that by 1916 Swedish had been added to the curriculum at four Minneapolis high schools—Central, North, East, and South high schools. Latin was the most popular foreign language studied, but German was close behind, by far the most popular modern foreign language in the schools. About half as many students studied French as German, both of which were offered in all the city's high schools. Swedish was the third most popular modern foreign language, with about 21 percent as many students as enrolled in German classes. Norwegian ranked after Swedish, and, finally, Spanish, a new subject offered only in two city high schools, ranked last.[17]

After this report was issued, the dynamics of World War I and the pressures for absolute Americanism impacted public education, particularly language study in the high schools. The Minneapolis Board of Education received bulletins from the Department of the Interior's Bureau of Education regarding its "America First Campaign." The immediate object of the campaign was to "induce the 3,000,000 non-English-speaking immigrants to attend night schools and learn the common language of America," but the pressure placed upon all immigrants to conform to an appropriate American way of life was obvious. State departments of education, women's groups, chambers of commerce, libraries, industries—all were encouraged to promote the study of English among the nation's foreign population. The Bureau of Naturalization of the U. S. Department of Labor wrote the Board of Education on October 27, 1916, proposing that a mass meeting be held in the city to the end that "the facilities of the public schools may be made known in the resident foreign communities and action taken to insure their larger attendance." Minneapolis officials obliged by calling such a meeting on February 1, 1917, at East High School. The meeting emphasized citizenship and public education; it opened with addresses by Mayor Thomas Van Lear and Director of the Evening Schools C. W. Jarvis; and it included speeches given in Swedish, German, and Polish. It closed with the singing of *America* by the audience.[18]

In such a volatile atmosphere, the most obvious foreign language to come under fire was German. In 1917, the superintendent of the Minneapolis public schools sent a box of fifty-six German books that were used in the schools to a well-respected local doctor and former president of the Board of Education, Thomas Quinby, asking him to examine the books for any potentially subversive content. On December 8, 1917, Quinby wrote back to Superintendent Jackson that he had read most of the books in their entirety; the majority, he claimed, were "written forty or more years ago, [and] contain nothing objectionable." But he did single out a few other books for suggested elimination. Any book that glorified the Kaiser, celebrated war, or was written by someone of questionable loyalty Quinby suggested be removed from the schools. One such book, *Anno 1870*, Quinby noted was written by a renegade Dane. "The book is a glorification of war," he wrote, "and the writer seems at times to be badly intoxicated with his own eloquence. 'Can it' would by my advice." Quinby further suggested that U.S. history and civics textbooks be translated into German to be used in German language classes. Jackson thanked Quinby for his suggestions and noted that the Board of Education would take his advice to heart. The superintendent's files also contain letters against teaching German in the schools and others calling into question the loyalty of some German instructors. Swedish was not immune to Americanization pressure, either. Maren Michelet, head of the Scandinavian Department at South High School and secretary of the Committee on Secondary Schools of the Society for the Advancement of Scandinavian Studies, noted that the Swedish language instruction was negatively impacted after the entry of the United States into World War I in 1917:

> During the war so much sentiment was aroused against the study of foreign languages (except French) that it is not strange that the study of the Scandinavian languages suffered thereby and made but little if any headway. Radical changes in the course of study in the Minneapolis high schools have curtailed the language study and thus diminished considerably the enrollment of the classes in Norwegian and Swedish. Still there have been sufficient numbers enrolled to justify the continuance of the work in both languages in all the high schools where the work had been introduced. I have no reports showing that either language has gained a new foothold, but this could hardly be expected.

The very fact that Swedish was not dropped from the curriculum was remarkable in and of itself.[19]

Although German continued to be part of the public school curriculum during and after World War I, its popularity among the students plunged. Departmental records of the Minneapolis public schools indicate that, in 1921, only thirty-nine students studied German in only one of the city's high schools, an estimated decline of 98 percent over prewar numbers. By comparison, that same year, 289 students were enrolled in Swedish classes in the high schools. Although these figures suggest that Swedish study declined by about 25 percent during the war, when compared to what happened to the German language in the schools, maintaining this size enrollment was quite an accomplishment. Over seven times as many students studied Swedish in the schools of Minneapolis as studied German, a complete switch from the prewar relative popularity of these two languages. The anti-German sentiment began to fade, however, and German language classes slowly regained their popularity. In 1925, 414 students studied German, which was once again offered in every high school, and, by 1934, that number jumped to 1,527. Comparatively, in 1925, 257 students took classes in Swedish, a slight drop from the number enrolled in 1921, and, by 1934, the number of students studying Swedish grew to 455. Enrollment in German classes had once again far surpassed the number of students in Swedish, but it is significant that interest in Swedish continued to be strong throughout the 1920s and the 1930s, when the Swedish language was losing its importance even within Swedish ethnic organizations.[20]

In fact, Swedish remained popular and available to high school students in Minneapolis for over thirty-five more years, due in large part to the successful career of Ruth Westerlund Peterson, who taught Swedish at South High School from 1928 to 1973. Student interest was sufficiently strong during these years to allow Peterson to teach a full load of Swedish classes each year. The vast majority of her students were the children or grandchildren of Swedish immigrants. It is difficult, however, to estimate student enrollment during these years. Esther Chilstrom Meixner estimated that, in 1940, 439 students studied Swedish in the public high schools of the city. A 1947 Program of Study for the public high schools indicated that Swedish continued to be a viable option for study, along with Latin, French, German, Spanish, and Norwegian. After 1949, the records of the Board of Education do not track student enrollment numbers, nor do they consistently report on the city's high school curriculum. The study of Swedish slightly declined in popularity during the 1950s and the early 1960s, but the fact that Swedish continued to be offered at South High School shows how persistent the Swedish ethnic identity remained in the city. Increasingly, students with a Swedish heritage had the opportunity to travel in Sweden, keeping alive an interest in the study of Swedish language and culture. It was not until after Peterson retired in 1973 that Swedish was dropped from the curriculum. By that time, the mostly third- and fourth-generation Swedish Americans lost interest in studying the Swedish language in the public schools,

and demographic changes in Minneapolis diminished the Swedish influence in the city.[21]

The Svithiod Club, South High School, from The Tiger *yearbook, 1921. The club contained some eighty members who participated in Swedish cultural activities, often with groups from area schools.*

The success of Swedish in the public schools of Minneapolis is particularly noteworthy in light of the fact that similar efforts in Chicago met with only short-term success. In 1911, one year after Swedish classes had begun in Minneapolis, leaders in Chicago's Swedish community contacted Professor Stomberg to seek his advice about how they could wage a similarly successful campaign in their city. They carefully followed Stomberg's suggestions by calling a community-wide meeting about the language issue and then initiating a petition effort among Swedish churches and organizations. These leaders brought their petition before the Chicago School Board in June 1911, but their reception by the board differed considerably from what had taken place in Minneapolis. Dr. Ella Flagg Young, superintendent of the Chicago public schools, decided to delay a decision about the introduction of Swedish in the schools until after an experiment with adding Polish as an elective subject in the high schools proved successful. The Swedes in Chicago did not appreciate her decision—it seemed to show preference for Poles over Swedes. Although there were over 20,000 more Poles than Swedes in the city, many Polish children attended parochial schools, so the Swedes in Chicago thought they should exert more influence over the school board's policy decisions. Finally, in January 1912, the school superintendent agreed to allow Swedish to begin in the schools the following fall, provided enough students enrolled in courses. What followed was a major campaign by Chicago's Swedish newspapers to drum up interest among the Swedish American youth for the language issue, a campaign that barely succeeded. Two classes of Swedish were begun at Lake View High School the fall of 1912, and, the following January, Englewood High School also added Swedish to its curriculum. Swedish remained as an elective subject in the public high schools of Chicago for less than a decade, from 1912 through 1917. With the outbreak of World War I, the Swedish language was dropped from Chicago's city high schools. Swedish leaders in Chicago succumbed to Americanization pressures evident during the war and ended their efforts to support the language issue. As merely the sixth-largest ethnic group in the city, and as a people who had been closely affiliated with the strong German presence in the city from their earliest settlement there, Swedes in Chicago did not want to emphasize their foreignness at a time when conformity ruled the day.[22]

By contrast, the remarkable longevity of Swedish classes in the Minneapolis schools reflected a less competitive ethnic environment than faced Chicago's Swedes, and, in such a setting, Swedes in Minneapolis continued to support Swedish in the public schools without raising concerns about their American loyalties. In fact, the continued success of Swedish instruction in the public schools of Minneapolis for over six decades testified not only to the fact that students wanted to study Swedish, but also that Swedish instruction was in itself noncontroversial. Thus Swedes in Minneapolis easily combined the divided-identity agenda: they fully participated in the public schools, allowing their children every opportunity for an American education, while at the same time preserving a corner of that public education for the transmission of their own ethnic culture through the teaching of the Swedish language in the high schools.

* * * *

NOTES

1. June Drenning Holmquist, ed., *They Chose Minnesota: A Survey of the State's Ethnic Groups* (St. Paul: MHS Press, 1981).
2. Statistics derived from *U.S. Bureau of the Census, Thirteenth Census of the United States, 1910,* vol. 2 Population (Washington, D.C.: U.S. Government Printing Office, 1913).
3. Esther Chilstrom Meixner, "The Teaching of the Scandinavian Languages and Literature in the United States" (unpublished Ph.D. diss., Univ. of Penn., 1941), 73f., 77; Meixner, 75, 77.
4. In 1878, the East and West divisions of the Minneapolis public schools united in order to form one single school district; *Annual Reports* (Minneapolis: Minneapolis Public School Records, 1878), 33; *Annual Report* (1884 and 1887).
5. *Annual Report* (1887), 70; *Annual Report* (1887, 1890, and 1898). A list of the high school *Course of Study* in 1914 does not include Spanish. A report on student recitations in the public high schools for the 1915–16 school year indicates that Spanish had been added in Central and West high schools, most likely that year; *Annual Report* (1900).
6. *Annual Report* (1899).
7. Meeting Files (Minneapolis: Minneapolis Public Schools Board of Education), Mar. 29, 1910.
8. Meeting Files, petition brought before the Board of Education on Apr. 12, 1910, signed by J. E. Granrud, Chairman; A. A. Stomberg, Secretary; J. G. Hultkrans; N. N. Ronning; L. Staunheim; Gist. Bothne; Mrs. T. W. Dahl; and Mrs. Frank Peterson; Meeting Files (Apr. 12, 1910).
9. A. A. Stomberg, Minneapolis, Minnesota, to Mr. Ernst W. Olson, Chicago, Ill., Mar. 9, 1911, Swedish Historical Society of America Collection, MHS.
10. Ibid.
11. *Svenska Amerikanska Posten,* Apr. 19, 1910, p. 8. Members of this committee were listed as follows: "Dr. J. G. Granrud; Professor A. A. Stomberg; Professor Bothne; Pastor N. Hansen in the Danish-Lutheran Immanuel Church; L. Stavnheim; Dr. Richard Burton, Chair of the English Department at the Univ. of Minn.; Editor N. N. Ronning; Professor David S. Swenson from the Univ. of Minn.; Mrs. T. H. Dahl; and Pastor J. G. Hultkrans from Bethlehem's Swedish Lutheran Church."
12. *Svenska Amerikanska Posten,* May 3, 1910, p. 20; *Svenska Amerikanska Posten,* May 10, 1910, p. 22.
13. Superintendent's Files (Minneapolis Public Schools: Charles M. Jordan's report of May 31, 1910). *Svenska Amerikanska Posten* published numbers that varied from these official tallies, claiming that fifty-six students indicated that they were interested in Swedish and fifty-eight wanted to study Norwegian; *Svenska Amerikanska Posten,* May 31, 1910, p. 8; Meeting Files, May 31 and June 7, 1910, p. 8.

14. Student Enrollments found in *Annual Reports* (1910); *Svenska Amerikanska Posten*, May 31, 1910, p. 8.

15. *Annual Report* (1910); Meeting Files (1910); Stomberg letter to Olson, Mar. 9, 1911.

16. As reported in Meixner, "Teaching of the Scandinavian Languages," 78.

17. *Annual Reports* (1912–14). Because of the interruption of the war years, another *Annual Report* was not issued until 1924, and the newer report format offered few details about curriculum and enrollment. Other Board of Education records, however, fill in some of the gaps created by this decline in the quantity and quality of the reports, but only sporadically; Meixner, "Teaching of the Scandinavian Languages," 80; Board of Education Subject Files, "Costs of Teaching High School Subjects Statistics," 1915/1916. These records indicate that student recitations per week in the foreign languages rank as follows: Latin—8,985; German—8,770; French—4,100; Swedish—1,870; Norse—1,495; and Spanish—620.

18. Subject Files, "Department of the Interior, Bureau of Education, Washington, America First Campaign, A Call to National Service"; Subject Files, General letter from the U.S. Department of Labor, Bureau of Naturalization, Washington, Oct. 27, 1916; Subject Files, "Program, Mass Meeting of Prospective Citizens Under the Auspices of the United States Bureau of Naturalization, Feb. 1, [1917]."

19. Subject Files, Thomas Quinby, M.D., to Mr. Jackson, Dec. 8, 1917; Subject Files, B. B. Jackson to Dr. Thomas Quinby, Jan. 10, 1918. One such letter was sent to Mr. Jackson on Sept. 20, 1917, and reads as follows: "Dear Sir, While you are looking up the standing of the teachers in our schools, I would suggest that you pay particular attention to Miss Minnie Koenig. Now there are 3 girls in the family and they are all pro German from the word go. Miss Minnie is a traitor if there ever was one. I don't know what she makes out to do. But I do know how she talks and feels at heart. They all are strong for Germany and always have been. So please look her up. Yours Truly, One who has heard her talk"; *Scandinavian Studies and Notes*, pedagogical Section, vol. 5, 1919: 246–48, as reported in Meixner, "Teaching of the Scandinavian Languages," 82.

20. I have estimated the 1916 enrollment in German classes to be 1,781. I arrived at these figures by using the number of students studying Swedish (374) and, knowing that Swedish recitations represented 21 percent of the number of German recitations each week, I have projected that the number of students studying German would be 79 percent higher than Swedish; Subject Files, "Minneapolis Public Schools Department of Administrative Research Report," May 17, 1935. The linguistic transition is noted in George M. Stephenson, *The Religious Aspects of Swedish Immigration* (Minneapolis: Univ. of Minn. Press, 1932), and Sture Lindmark, *Swedish America 1914–1932: Studies in Ethnicity with Emphasis on Illinois and Minnesota* (Uppsala: Studia Historica Upsaliensia, 1971).

21. Conversation with Ruth Westerlund Peterson, Mar. 1, 1997. Occasionally Peterson would teach a history course if necessary. "The Senior High Schools in Minneapolis," bulletins that answer questions which pupils often ask about the senior high schools, 1945–47; *The Minneapolis Public Schools: A Study by the League of Women Voters of Minneapolis*, Apr. 1967. Peterson thought instruction continued a year or two after her retirement, but it soon faded out. During her career, however, she never found the instruction of Swedish to be seriously threatened, and she always felt the strong support of Swedish ethnic organizations in Minneapolis. The last public high school in Minnesota to offer Swedish was in Lindstrom, where Helen Fosdick taught until 1988.

22. See Anita Olson Gustafson, "Ethnic Preservation and Americanization: The Issue of Swedish Language Instruction in Chicago's Public Schools," in Philip J. Anderson, Dag Blanck, and Peter Kivisto, eds., *Scandinavian Immigrants and Education in North America* (Chicago: Swedish-American Historical Society, 1995).

American Swedish Revisited

NILS & PATRICIA HASSELMO

Nils Hasselmo (NH): In this essay, I would like to try to link our past to our present and future. I will do that by linking some reflections on the history of the Swedish language in this country and this state to some of the issues confronting us today in Minnesota as significant numbers of Asian immigrants and refugees have settled here. It is important for us to understand the linguistic and cultural self-maintenance efforts of our own Scandinavian ancestors as we look to ways in which we can assist new generations with their linguistic and cultural self-maintenance efforts. Only by understanding those efforts, both historically and in the present, can we make sure that we continue the process of becoming Americans while respecting and drawing strength from many cultures.

In my case, my scholarly interest in the Swedish language in America has been combined with the real-life experience of becoming part of a Swedish American family and actually marrying a third-generation Swedish American, whose father as a minister was involved in the transition from Swedish to English.

Pat, can you tell a little bit about your own family background?

Patricia Hasselmo (PH): Nils and I are very pleased to share some reflections on the Swedish language in America. My own family, of course, lived through that transition. All of my grandparents came from Sweden. My father's parents homesteaded in Kansas and sent their children to Bethany College, where they had an opportunity both to maintain some contact with Swedish language and culture and to become prepared for life in American society. My father became a minister and served in Trinity Lutheran Church in Moline, Illinois, for forty-three years. His congregation was actually the first English-speaking congregation of the Augustana Synod in that city. Two of his brothers received Ph.D.s in history. One became dean of Gettysburg College in Pennsylvania, and the other became historian of the Gettysburg Battlefield in the same city. My mother's parents settled in Chicago, and she and her brothers received an education in various institutions, including Augustana College in Rock Island, Illinois.

NH: And one of Pat's cousins actually became the catcher for the Chicago Cubs! What better example is there of true Americanization?

PH: Now, Nils, we ought to get to the topic. Why did you decide to study the language of the Swedish immigrants?

NH: I discovered Swedish America in the attic of Denkman Library at Augustana in 1956. The library had large collections, reflecting the unwritten history of the Swedish language in America. Language contact tells us much about language, and about culture: How does the phonology, the morphology, the syntax work? What happens to the lexicon—the vocabulary? How are the languages used in different social settings? What happens over time? How does language change reflect culture change?

PH: What about the languages spoken in Minnesota today?

NH: Let me quote some recent data:

The 1990 U.S. Census:
Minnesota Household Language (persons five years and over) reports:

English only	3,811,700
Scandinavian	25,758

At least 10,000 persons may claim Swedish.

German	45,409
Spanish and Spanish Creole	42,363
French and French Creole	13,693

The Minnesota Refugee and Immigrant Assistance Division reports:

	1990 Census	1992 Estimate
Hmong	16,833	27,000
Other Laotian	6,381	7,000
Vietnamese	9,387	5,000
Cambodian	3,858	7,000

By comparison, let me quote some earlier U.S. Census figures concerning the Swedish American population (persons who are Swedish-born or have at least one Swedish-born parent) in Minnesota and the nation:

	Minnesota	% of Population	Nation
1890	164,676	12.57%	776,093
1910	268,018	12.92%	1,363,554
1930	270,773	10.56%	1,562,703
1960	156,788	4.59%	1,046,992

PH: I remember when we went to the Farmer's Market in St. Paul a few weeks ago. A sunny Saturday morning, there were lots of people, flowers, and vegetables. There were many Southeast Asians. You heard other languages around you. What were they?

NH: I think we heard Hmong, mostly: Hmong, the language of the mountain people in Vietnam and Laos who came here in large numbers after the Vietnam War. It is classified as a member of the Miao Jao language family—which may be an offshoot of the Sino-Tibetan languages. It is still a contested question. Maybe related to Japanese? This is just one hypothesis.

PH: Nils, this is not a class in linguistics! What we saw is the way it must have been seventy-five years or more ago at markets in St. Paul—when the Swedes came down from "Swede Hollow" and other places to sell and buy—only the language then was Swedish.

NH: Yes, history is repeating itself. I experience that in my work at the University. I meet ever-larger numbers of Asian American students. The new immigration is very much in evidence, as is broader participation by other minority groups. As we encounter Hmong linguistic and cultural self-maintenance efforts in Minnesota today, we see a repetition of Scandinavian linguistic and cultural self-maintenance efforts of a century ago. In 1883, a group of Norwegian and Swedish legislators were able to pass a law that required the University of Minnesota to teach Scandinavian, including Old Norse. I used to have a copy of that law in my desk—in case some dean or president would get the idea that Scandinavian languages could be eliminated from the curriculum! Now we are strengthening the study of the Asian and Asian American culture in the curriculum.

PH: Swedish America is not altogether gone. Last Sunday, we saw *Kristina i Duvemåla*, the new Swedish musical about Vilhelm Moberg's Karl Oskar and Kristina, in Swedish in Lindstrom, Minnesota. Many Swedish Americans had tears in their eyes when Kristina sang the song about the ship they met on the ocean, with the Swedish flag—sailing for *home*, for Sweden!

And the recent visit by the King and Queen of Sweden was a spectacular event. And the reenactment of the landing of the first immigrants in Taylor's Falls—this time accompanied by the Central Band of the Swedish Army! Isn't this Swedish America—still?

NH: Yes, it is certainly part of the fabric of contemporary American life. I even hear Swedish now and then, in the legislature, at the American Swedish Institute, from students who have studied in Sweden. Even the University of Minnesota mascot, the Gopher, used to whisper in Swedish to me a couple of years ago!

PH: It gets complicated, of course. Think about our own family now: German, French Canadian, Italian, Swedish. I love to hear our granddaughters Karen and Christina speaking their few words in Italian *and* Swedish and singing the songs we recorded for them.

NH: And it's time for German, French, and Swedish for Simone and little Nicholas, who was born last Saturday. What a delight for a linguist interested in bilingualism to have a multilingual family!

PH: Nils, enough about our family. We're supposed to revisit American Swedish.

NH: Yes, you're right—as usual. Here are a couple of additional comments on the contemporary situation.

The fact that the "language question" is not dead in the U.S. is shown by the debate about English as the official language. Actually, English has never been adopted as the official U.S. language. Why is that question being raised again? Obviously, it is because of the great influx of new immigrants, especially the large concentrations of Spanish speakers. I have no doubt that English will prevail, as it now has for two centuries in this country, further reinforced by its status as a world language. *The* world language.

But I'm concerned that we neglect the value of our linguistic diversity, our potential for communicating with a linguistically diverse world. I sometimes sense a new xenophobia behind the campaign for English as the official language. I think we must respond with intensified foreign language study—to meet other nations halfway—at least symbolically. I am concerned that we may be sliding the other way as far as popular sentiment is concerned.

PH: Nils, talk more about your first contacts with American Swedish. Go back to Chisago County in the 1960s, when you first began your work there—or to Worcester, Massachusetts, where you did fieldwork for your dissertation.

NH: I encountered Swedish as a language still used by older people in both of those places in the 1960s. I saw the last remnants of what for a century had been Swedish-speaking communities. I spoke to second- and third-generation Swedish Americans who still spoke Swedish fluently, with appropriate adaptations to the needs of a new speech situation, a new society.

PH: My father was the minister in the first English-speaking Swedish Lutheran Church in Moline, Illinois. I understand there was quite a struggle in the church over language.

NH: Yes, the debate on the "language question" became especially heated in the Swedish American churches. The language of their religious upbringing was for many so intimately intertwined with religion itself that it was very difficult for them to separate the two. The churches were also the most important of the Swedish American institutions, and the ones that were in the most direct sense a transplantation of an institution from the "Old Country." This was true especially in the case of the Augustana Synod and the Swedish Mission Covenant Church.

At the turn of the century, there were still very few signs of a language shift in the Augustana Synod. By 1907, only five of the 496 "missions" of the Synod used English. As late as 1921, 85 percent of the sermons in the Synod's churches were reportedly held in Swedish. In 1908, the English-oriented minority in the Synod formed an Association of English Churches to further their cause. But it was not until 1920 that the Illinois and Minnesota conferences started printing their minutes in English as well as in Swedish, and not until 1924 that the minutes from the synodical meeting were printed in English for the first time. Although no decision to adopt English as the language of the Synod was ever made, English must be considered its official language after the middle of the 1930s.

The change that took place during the 1920s is well illustrated by what happened to the Sunday school in Chisago Lake Lutheran Church in Center City, Minnesota. In 1920, there were seventeen Swedish and four English Sunday school classes in the church. By 1928, there were four Swedish and twenty-two English classes. The minutes from the annual meetings of the church show that

Costumed children's choir at Svenskarnas Dag *at Minnehaha Park, 1946*

as Swedish became threatened, special efforts were made to turn the church's "weekday (summer) school" into a Swedish *language* school. Apparently these efforts failed. By the end of the 1920s, very few children were learning the language of their ancestors.

PH: And didn't they teach Swedish in the public schools, too?

NH: The public schools were, of course, English-language schools. Many Swedish American children were confronted with the new language for the first time when they began first grade. Older people can still recall how—during the days preceding the beginning of school—their mothers tried to teach them such basic English phrases as "What's your name?" and "How old are you?" before sending them into an English-speaking world.

Minneapolis became a center for efforts to introduce the teaching of the Scandinavian languages in high school. Pressured by a petition signed by seventy-five local organizations, the city began its first Swedish high school course at South High School in 1910. By 1913, ten high schools in Minnesota, three in Illinois, and one in Iowa were teaching Swedish. Instruction in the Scandinavian languages in high school peaked in 1917, when more than sixty schools reported such instruction.

During World War I, foreign language instruction declined across the country, and in some twenty states legislation was introduced, severely hampering foreign language study. In 1925, only thirty-six high schools reported instruction in the Scandinavian languages. In recent years, high school instruction in Swedish has become extinct.

PH: I remember that you were so impressed with collections of Swedish American books, periodicals, and newspapers that you found in the Denkman Library at Augustana.

NH: Yes, it was a marvelous discovery—rediscovery, of course, since scholars like Fritiof Ander had already taken inventory of these materials and used them in their work. I am, by the way, enormously pleased that the Swenson Swedish Immigration History Center is now located in that library. The dust that covered the collections in 1956 has been effectively removed! It is a living collection for scholars.

Ander's bibliography from 1956, *The Cultural Heritage of the Swedish Immigrant*, was a very valuable source. It gave an overview of both literary works and periodicals. By 1870, fourteen periodicals had appeared. By 1910, the number was 130. Then a decline set in: 1910 (110), 1930 (49), 1940 (25), and 1950 (13).

The records of the Augustana Book Concern also show the great outpouring of publications. The peak was reached in the period 1906–10 with 151 titles in Swedish and total editions of 750,000. Again, a decline set in with the first World War, and in 1931–35 only eleven titles, 78,000 copies, were published.

Professor Ander's record of Swedish American *skönlitteratur*—fiction, essays, and poetry—is also impressive. In 1911–15, about fifty works appeared, and again a decline set in: 1921–25 (25), 1931–35 (9), and 1951–56 (1).

PH: Now you are throwing a lot of numbers at us! We get the picture: a very fast increase in Swedish-language publication, and education, during the last couple decades of the nineteenth century and the first fifteen years of this century, and then a rapid decline after World War I.

A major language *shift* by 1930?

NH: Yes, that's the picture.

PH: There were some who really thought that the language, the preservation of the language, was the key to preserving Swedish culture in this country.

NH: Yes, you're absolutely right. Let me tell you about the colorful Professor J. S. Carlson, my predecessor—many predecessors removed—who was a spirited advocate for that view.

He states it bluntly in one of his tracts from the early 1920s, years that were fateful for the immigrant languages: "The spirit of a people lives in its language." And if the spirit that is embodied in the language of a minority is a good one, the inevitable conclusion is, of course, that it is "wrong and a great sin to make this spirit homeless or, at least, inactive by forgetting or destroying the language which constitutes its home and tool."

Professor Carlson is very specific in his definition of the spirit that he attributes to the Swedish nation and finds embodied in the Swedish language. It is the spirit of freedom: "Sweden is the original home of freedom on earth, and America is the big, new home of freedom, and it was the Swedes who brought freedom from its original home to its new home. True popular freedom originated in Sweden." Other authors suggest a variety of qualities that are associated with the Swedish spirit. We find further emphasis on the spirit of freedom in lines concerning the Swedish language as one "never spoken by cowardly thralls" and the Swedes as a people "never trampled under heels." With a different meaning of the word "people," that of "the common people" rather than "the nation," some authors also put strong emphasis on the democratic aspect of the Swedish Spirit.

Från folket srungit har det språk,	The language you speak has sprung
du talar. . .	from the people . . .
[det] har ej födts i höga lärdomssalar,	[it] was not born in elevated halls
ej vunnit burskap uti kungaslott	of learning,
	[it] was not recognized in palaces
	of kings.

(Carl G. Norman, *Till svenska sång-mön i Amerika*)

In the last line, Swedish as the language of the common people is even put in
direct opposition to the foreign tongues at times spoken among the upper
classes in the old country.

The spirit is also strength and manliness, honesty and integrity, energy and
ambition—in short, most of the qualities required and admired on the American frontier. As suggested by Professor Carlson's statement concerning the old
and the new home of freedom, an effort was made to show that the spirit embodied in the Swedish language in every respect harmonized with the spirit of
true Americanism, even if it did not harmonize with what Professor Carlson
calls "the English-Irish Americanism," which was especially hateful because of
its aversion to the immigrant languages.

PH: Do you believe this too?

NH: Of course! Well, we are seeing here some reflections of self-assertion
by an immigrant group—not unknown today. It is common to claim attributes
that are highly valued by the group—and that are assumed to harmonize with
those of the new land.

PH: I've heard that Swedes are perhaps more prone to give up their own
traditions than others—to put it positively, that they are willing to accept what's
foreign—or new? Is there any truth to that?

NH: Some Swedish Americans certainly seem to have thought so. C. F. Peterson said that "no other foreigner becomes so thoroughly Americanized in
this linguistic respect as the Swede and the Norwegian." In some poems the
moral aspect of the problem figures very prominently. Giving up one's language and culture is an indication of moral inferiority. In Ernst Lindblom's
poem *Kontraster* (Contrasts), the problem is presented in the persons of two
Swedish girls who react very differently to the new environment. About the
first, "bad," girl it is said:

> The lisping Yankee language
> she shortly learned to speak,
> she got a raise in wages
> her Swedish she forgot.
>
> A spirit of pride had stolen
> into her Swedish soul,
> it slowly tried to quench
> the love of fatherland.
>
> She copied for that reason
> American women's ways.
> And in the end she suffered,
> The fate of being nothing.

The other, "good," girl stays faithful to her heritage and is ashamed "to let loose her bad English."

> The excellent young girl!
> I saw her later as guest
> visiting, not long ago,
> a patriotic Swedish fest.
>
> And sonorous her Swedish was,
> though not quite correct,
> She spoke it like so many,
> in honest dialect.

PH: What do you think?

NH: You're not going to let me get by with quotes?

Well, I don't believe in such generalizations. There are many factors that determine how change happens, and people's receptivity to it.

Let's face it: most immigrants left because they had a tough time! Like Kristina and Karl Oskar. The U. S. was in a sense really "the American Dream!" The dream of freedom, democracy, opportunity.

The attractiveness of American society has been great. It still is! And English has been, and remains, a necessary means to gaining full access to the opportunities of that society. The language shift was natural, and inevitable, given the nature of our society.

PH: My mother used to laugh herself into hysteria over Swedish American *mixat språk*.

NH: I know, I used to regale her with samples of my Swedish American materials. The Swedish Americans worried about what was happening to their language. And laughed about it.

One of the most popular linguistic subjects in the Swedish American literature is actually that of *mixat språk*, mixed language, one of H. L. Mencken's "Mongrelian languages." Even if English and Swedish may well "get along together," as Professor J. S. Carlson maintained, there arises a problem which Johan Person summarizes this way: "Two languages cannot exist side by side like English and Swedish in this country without one being influenced by the other." Skarstedt is one of a great number of Swedish American poets to poke fun at *mixat språk*.

Och derför mången hörs språken mixa	And therefore many a man he mixes,
och tala om hur han allt skall fixa . . .	and speaks a lot of the things he fixes . . .

But, he as well as most of his colleagues felt,

> that such a mixture sounds very bad.
> To turn the languages upside down,
> is rather ugly and bad a custom—
> and more than that.

An unknown author writes:

> What beauty and what poetry,
> in every language harmony.
> But language used by Svea's sons,
> that was once very sweet
> has changed in North America—
> these are its awful sounds!

And he goes on to fill the next few stanzas with the favorite idioms of *mixat språk:*

Man törnar kårnan, krossar strät,	One turns the corner, crosses streets,
man filar tajerd, kommer lät,	one feels tired, comes late,
gör business och blir chitad.	does business and is cheated.
Man huntar jabbar, kätcher work,	One hunts jobs, catches work,
man reser tjipt *till New-y-ork,*	one travels cheaply to New York,
av fränds *man bliver* tritad.	by friends one is treated.
Man mäkar baxar, fixar ting,	One makes boxes, fixes things,
man bliver member *i en* ring	one becomes a member in a ring
och stumbom afel lesig.	and sometimes awful lazy.
Man travlar rådar, tjänsar trän,	One travels roads, changes trains,
man spikar *engelskt mycket* plän,	one speaks English very plain,
blir hörtad *eller* kresig.	becomes hurt or crazy.

PH: Enough of that. I do wish my mother would have been here, though. She was proud of being Swedish—but she would laugh at all this *mixat språk.*

NH: It is important to point out that the "mixing" is a natural phenomenon. Modern English is a highly "mixed" language. So is modern Swedish. That's one way languages change, and remain functional, express a new culture. Such "mixing"—language change—is going on all around us among the new immigrants.

PH: There were some that thought that American Swedish would survive for the indefinite future?

NH: Yes. Some optimists thought that it would survive at least until the year 2000. It didn't happen.

PH: Now, how shall we wrap this up?

NH: The history of the Swedish language in America is an important aspect of the cultural history of immigration to America. It is important to the study of language contact and bilingualism, to issues linguistic, cultural—and political—which are rampant in our society, and in the world.

(This dialogue presentation was the keynote address at the conference "Swedish Life in the Twin Cities," Octrober 17, 1996, Minnesota History Center, St. Paul, Minnesota.)

Libraries, Immigrants, and Communities:
Perspectives on the Swedish Immigrant Experience
in the Twin Cities, 1889–1917

KERMIT B. WESTERBERG

As Swedish America celebrated the 150th anniversary of mass Swedish immigration to North America in 1996, it also observed several commemorations or
benchmarks in the history of the host society and that of the American public
library movement. That year marked the 120th anniversary of the founding of
the American Library Association [ALA] and its official publication, *Library
Journal* [*LJ*], both of which have stood in the frontlines of professional opinion
and advocacy on issues related to literacy, citizenship education, multiculturalism, community building, and general library services to ethnic minorities
and immigrants. These frontlines are extended today and, indeed, called very
much into question, when grassroots organizations such as "The English Only
Movement" and slogans such as "no tax dollars for multiculturalism" emerge as
very hard currency both in public and professional debate.[1]

The year 1996 also marked the 102nd anniversary of a seminal exchange of
ideas and opinions in the printed columns of *LJ* regarding the concept and value
of incorporating foreign-language literature in the holdings of American public libraries for the *express* use of new arrivals to these shores. Perhaps the first
librarian to go out on this "professional limb" was a Swedish-born bookseller-
turned-American-immigrant (with native roots in the university town of Uppsala), who became a distinguished public librarian and research bibliographer,
first in New York City and, later, in Chicago. His name was Axel Gustav Salomon
Josephson (1860–1944), and his viewpoints had an impact on public library-
community developments in the Twin Cities during the late 1800s and early
1900s.[2]

This essay is headlined as addressing "Libraries, Immigrants, and Communities." How are these defined in this context? Three basic elements come to mind in looking at the last two decades of the nineteenth century and the opening decades of the twentieth, several of which may be recognized as issues our American society continues to confront at its present *fin de siècle*. These may, with reference to the Twin Cities, be described as follows. First, the associative matrixes of ethnicity, education, and religion, which often translated into the formation of various types of lending libraries (secular literary societies, fraternal lodge and benevolent society libraries, as well as various church or parish libraries) among Swedes and other Scandinavians in the Twin Cities. Second, the physical configurations of immigrant settlements in various neighborhoods and wards of the Twin Cities as well as their shifts and transformations over time, which had an influence on public library planning and funding for extended community services. And third, the evolving dynamics of American public library ideologies, services, and leadership initiatives (both from native-born and immigrant-generation librarians) in addressing the issues of general literacy, access to multilanguage and cross-cultural resources, citizenship education, English-language instruction, and basic community-building among the Scandinavian population of the Twin Cities and the greater metropolitan area.[3]

This essay offers substantive perspectives on the *second and third elements* sketched above. In his classic study of the social history of the American public library movement, Sidney Ditzion surveyed the range of ideas, concepts, and philosophies that found expression in the foundation and growth of free public libraries. He explored the types of social conditions and concerns that had an impact on the library profession's sense of community outreach. One of the concerns that received serious attention from librarians during the late nineteenth century was the civic education of foreign-born populations in large urban centers and, in particular, the consequences of giving the ballot to the uninformed foreign-born voter. That the public library should function as a forum of enlightenment and education for immigrants with respect to American history and ideals was a commonly accepted objective. Differences of opinion arose, however, on the issue of supplying reading matter, especially fictional literature, in the mother tongues of immigrant populations. According to Ditzion, librarians parted company with the "superpatriots" on this issue, holding that if the library was to Americanize the foreign born it had to reach them by removing the barriers that, in the past, had made libraries unapproachable.[4]

The general role, intrinsic value, and proper selection of fictional literature for American public library patrons were issues that concerned librarians and public educators alike around the turn of the last century. There is evidence from the professional literature of the period that the mere stocking of popular, English-language fiction on public library shelves raised, for some, the specter of catering to mass reading tastes, thereby endangering the library's function as both a cultural and moral educator of its patrons. Other librarians recognized the practical need for supplying tax-paying patrons with popular fiction (e.g., dime novels and story weeklies), which at least brought them to the library, established a habit of reading, and, theoretically, paved the way for better or more enlightened reading. Doing so, however, did not mean that libraries should admit literature of a questionable nature or of a positively impure or immoral sort; this applied equally to original works in the English language and to works in foreign languages as well as their English translations. The tasks of evaluating and selecting the latter types of literature raised concerns of their own: who should do so for American public libraries, and what professional expertise did these persons have?[5]

In January 1894, a signed communication by Axel G. S. Josephson in that month's issue of *LJ* requested details from library professionals regarding the status, proportion, and use of "Scandinavian literature" in American libraries. He was particularly interested in knowing how this literature was classed and housed in respective libraries, how much of it was in demand by the resident Scandinavian-born population, and to which social classes (i.e., "laborers, ministers, or other educated people") most of the Scandinavian borrowers belonged. In July of that same year, Josephson reported, in a similar communication, that responses to his request had prompted him to develop a list of Swedish books "of value to American libraries, mostly books of standard authors, books on Swedish history—political, social, and literary—and religious works." He went on to explain that such a list seemed well motivated in light of the fact that the finding-lists of Swedish books in "some western libraries . . . represent the literature of a quarter a century ago, rather than of to-day." His own list would, with some "noted exceptions," contain works mostly produced during the previous twenty-five year period (prior to 1894), would be briefly annotated regarding the author or the work in question, and would not exceed 500 titles.[6]

Josephson's bibliography was, by his own words in the above-cited communication, definitely in the works by July 1894, and he promised updates on its progress. An unsigned *LJ* commentary in October of that year confirms the same with cited references from an unnamed article in the New York *Sun*. According to this newspaper source, the underlying reasons for Josephson's bibliography were "because there are about 100,000 Swedes in New York and Brooklyn, because Chicago has a greater Swedish population than any other city save Stockholm, and the joint cities of St. Paul and Minneapolis have nearly as many."

It was important, the article went on, that libraries with a large Swedish population provide readers with modern Swedish books, as at that time there were reportedly few libraries in which Scandinavian books could be obtained.[7]

After assessing the status of the Scandinavian literature departments at the Astor, Lenox, and other New York City libraries (with which Axel G. S. Josephson was intimately acquainted), the *LJ* commentary specified that the "Chicago Public Library has about 4,000 Swedish books, and there are perhaps as many in the public library of Minneapolis, while some other western cities have small collections. Few or none of these books, however, include those produced under the latest and most strenuous influence in Swedish literature." Moreover, "The great bulk of them were published before 1860, and there have been two periods of Swedish literature since then. The latter and more striking period of modern Swedish literature dates from about 1880, and of this new period the libraries of this country contain few or no books."[8]

In the same (October 1894) issue of *LJ*, an unsigned editorial piece took issue with Josephson's idealistic project, along the lines of what was called "library ethics." While there was no argument against scholarly-oriented collections of "the chief European languages . . . mainly designed as an aid to the study of those languages," there was grave concern expressed about the inclusion and circulation in public libraries of foreign-language literature in comparatively little-known tongues. This raised the issue "whether it is desirable . . . to keep up language divisions among a population which, by virtue of residence and assumption of citizenship at least, should be wholly American." The editorial thought it important to supply Swedish books to the public libraries mentioned in Josephson's article, but if the same idea were applied to *all* American cities, libraries would also be supplying such literature to "Germans, French, Italians, Hebrews, Hungarians, and Poles, not to mention Chinese." This was not conducive to good citizenship, the editorial warned, as it would mean a "polyglot public library issuing polyglot literature to the denizens of the various foreign 'colonies,' and serving as a most effective factor in maintaining those barriers of race and language which are the most difficult of all barriers to overcome and the most prejudicial to unity of sentiment and action."[9]

Josephson's reply to this editorial was polite, professional, but pointed. If the American public library wished to make good citizens of the foreign born, he said, it would do well to draw them under this influence by providing them with books in their own languages and about the country they had left behind. This would eventually provide them with the opportunity to become acquainted with the English language and to begin reading books about the customs and laws of their new country. Josephson stood aghast at the editorial's negativism on the matter, calling it "a ghost of the dead and buried know-nothingism that was hardly expected in the organ of such a progressive body as the American Library Association." He went on to comment: "Public libraries are used to provide readers of trash fiction with such stuff as they like, in the hope that this will by and by result in their reading literature. Is it more objectionable to keep a good selection of books in foreign languages, to draw to the library men and women, who surely, once having found their way to the library, will begin to read American books?"[10]

Was this just a tempest in a teacup? The answer is "no," especially when research is focused on the published library literature and its comprehensive attention to these issues, beginning in the mid-1890s and continuing through the first several decades of the twentieth century. Moreover, these issues had a direct bearing on public library developments among Scandinavians and other immigrant groups in the Twin Cities and outlying areas. Confirmation of this is found in the remarks made in 1898 by a leading representative of the Minneapolis Public Library, Gratia Alta Countryman. As Assistant Librarian (1892–1904) and Chief Librarian (1904–37), she played a central role in the development and extension of city and statewide library services to all classes of society. Quoting from her June 1898 article in *LJ*:

> For a number of years my views were similar to those expressed in an editorial of the *Library Journal* of October, 1894, which were in substance that the purchase of books in foreign languages should be minimized; that the library should not serve to perpetuate the barriers of race and language; that the library should be wholly American; and its influence tend wholly toward Americanizing the foreign-born. This seemed to me the true view until, happening over at the branch where [immigrants] were just receiving their new books, I saw them gathering around these treasures like flies around a molasses-jug. . . . My previous opinions were shaken, and the question naturally arose: 'Were they worse citizens because the city library supplied to them books in their own native language? Were they less good Americans because their adopted country and its institutions recognized their particular needs?' Nay, verily . . . rather their feeling would be one of gratitude and a sense of obligation that would bind them to the library and this country more than the national literature could possibly separate them.[11]

In this same article, Countryman related the details of a personal conversation she had with a Scandinavian immigrant patron at one of the Minneapolis branch libraries in a largely Scandinavian district. Explaining to him that she had never seen a Scandinavian *child* approach the several thousand volume collection of Scandinavian literature housed at that branch, she asked whether he did not want his own children to retain a knowledge of and a feeling for their

own native language. The immigrant replied that as his children were now living in the United States, he wanted them to learn and use English, to read English books, and to adopt American customs.

Countryman concluded from this that the presence and accessibility of foreign literature in the public library did not produce anything but American
loyalty and certainly did not perpetuate any barrier of race. On the contrary, a
"cosmopolitan library" equipped with foreign-language books could do more
for the cause of citizenship and loyalty than a library that sat idly by and did
nothing at all for the immigrant public. The availability of this literature would
not only be the magnet or "bait" that was capable of attracting the immigrant
to the public library but also the "ounce of prevention" needed to "stem the
tide of poverty, ignorance, insanity and criminality among great numbers of
American immigrants." Countryman emphasized in this connection that up to
1898 "the Minneapolis Public Library has never refused a request from any nationality, even if the finances allowed but a small outlay."[12]

So much for this running debate, or ongoing dialogue, among library professionals in their journal literature. How were these issues actually played out
in terms of specific services for the Scandinavian immigrant patrons of the
Twin Cities libraries? The Minneapolis Public Library (MPL) officially opened
its doors in December 1889. Of the two printed finding-lists or catalogs available to the public on the occasion, one (25 pp.) was specifically designed as a
guide to foreign-language holdings (German, French, Dano-Norwegian, Swedish, Italian, and Spanish-Portuguese), complete with classification numbers.
The other list (38 pp.) comprised English prose fiction and young people's books,
supplemented in February 1890 by a general finding-list (186 pp.) covering the
balance of the library, and, in November of that year, by a new edition of the
former (138 pp.), arranged by title and author. The Swedish literature section
of the first finding-list, covering sixty-three authors or main entries, totaled
more than 250 volumes in unspecified subject categories. Fictional titles were
largely represented by collected works of early and mid-nineteenth century
authors; the popular novel *genre* was limited to the period favorites, August
Blanche (thirteen volumes) and Emilie Flygare-Carlén (thirty-five volumes).[13]

On April 23, 1890, the second branch of the MPL was established at Franklin
and Seventeenth avenues, receiving the designation "South Side Branch, B." Its
first assistant-in-charge was the Norwegian Halvor Askeland, who retained that
post for nearly twenty years (1890–1909). Like the North Side Branch (opened
in February 1890), the Franklin Avenue Branch functioned as a delivery station
and reading room, supplying some fifty leading periodicals and several hundred volumes of miscellaneous literature for reference use. In other words, it
emerged at this stage as an ordinary community library, serving the basic needs

of residents on the city's south side. In time, however, it would serve a more fo-
cused purpose, as a result of the ethnic composition of city wards in the area.
Swedes and other Scandinavians were strongly represented in the 6th Ward
(Cedar-Riverside) during the 1890s and around the turn of the century, but
soon began to settle in the 11th Ward, including the eastern section of Franklin
Avenue, immediately to the south. In 1904, the MPL took the step of shelving all
Scandinavian books (about 6,000 at the time) and a dozen or more Scandina-
vian periodicals in the two large rooms of a Franklin Avenue storefront (then
on lease for an additional five years), which continued to serve as the South
Side Branch up to 1915.[14]

In November 1891, a third branch library ("C") was opened on University
Avenue on the city's east side. Chosen as its first assistant-in-charge was the
Swedish-born Victor Nilsson, who in a number of respects distinguished himself as an exponent of educational and cultural interests within the Swedish
American community. Aside from his early career as an assistant editor of a local Swedish-language newspaper and his long-standing contributions to
Swedish American music and drama circles, he authored two monographs that
won him some national renown. In 1899 Nilsson also became the first person to
obtain a doctoral degree from an American university (University of Minnesota)
with the Scandinavian languages, history, and literature as a major line of study,
and Old Norse as a specialty.[15]

It is his librarianship at the East Side Branch (1891–1903) and his knowledge
of the contemporary Swedish literary scene that command particular attention
here. On December 28, 1894, an article appeared under his name in the Minneapolis *Journal*, entitled "The Public Library: A Talk on its Swedish Collection." Nilsson's remarks came in direct response to an earlier article in the New
York *World*, reporting on Axel G. S. Josephson's campaign to incorporate a collection of modern Swedish literature in New York City libraries. According to
Nilsson, the newspaper article had reported that there were 4,000 Swedish
books in the MPL, but that most of them had been published before 1860, and
that there had been two periods of Swedish literature since then. Nilsson wished
to set the record straight for his readers on the Minneapolis side of the ledger.[16]

He related that a large installment of Swedish literature had been purchased by the MPL in the fall of 1890, "embracing what little of real value had
been published in Sweden before 1860 and 1880," together with a large and "most
complete collection of works of the new so called realistic school of Sweden
dating from 1880 . . . and reaching up to the time of the purchases." The list of
procured works contained the names of "5 and 50 [sic]" different authors, some
of whom were represented by a dozen volumes, and August Strindberg by more
than twenty-five. Several smaller purchases of recent Swedish publications

were made later on, most in the form of duplicates that were placed at the Central Library as well as at the South and East Side Branches.[17]

Nilsson went on to note that he had himself delivered half a dozen lectures in an effort to acquaint the Swedish American public with the new literary production of the home country. These lectures were subsequently published in the local press, both Swedish- and English-language, as well as in other papers in the United States and Sweden. Following a brief run-down of the types of Swedish authors represented by these purchases, Nilsson concluded by saying that financial reasons had prevented the MPL from keeping abreast of public demands for highly current Swedish literature. Yet, he said, "This deficiency appears . . . less grave when it is considered that the only two great Swedish authors, August Strindberg and Ola Hansson, have settled permanently [at that time] in Germany and only occasionally write in Swedish. There is no new talent of any real importance or greater promise that is not represented in the Minneapolis Public Library, except Selma Lagerloef."[18]

The Nilsson article is significant, then, not only for its information on the type of Swedish literature acquired by the Central Library and its branches during this formative period but also for its insights into Nilsson's efforts, as scholar-educator-library professional, to present Swedish literary trends to the larger public and to focus attention on what he considered to be the "literary canon" of the time.

Some years later, however, in April 1897, there appeared to be signs of unrest or disagreement within the Twin Cities' Swedish American community on the issue of Swedish-language materials in the MPL. In two successive articles published in a local Swedish-language newspaper, Swedes expressed their discontent over the "poor representation" of Swedish literature in area libraries. These commentaries reveal the following observations. First, the Swedish holdings of the Franklin Avenue Branch, "located in the most densely populated Swedish section of the city," were deemed too few, largely out of date, not representative of works by the younger generation of poets and authors, and nearly deficient of literary magazines and journals. Under these circumstances, the Swedish American youth of Minneapolis risked growing up with the totally false assumption that the Swedish language was conspicuously devoid of literature. Second, the Central Library had only one Swedish newspaper, and its personnel apparently could not distinguish between a Norwegian American paper and a Swedish literary magazine when requests for the latter were made by Swedish patrons. And finally, Minneapolis had approximately 10,000 more Swedes than Norwegians, and therefore this "injustice" was all the more abhorrent.[19]

Whether or not the above should essentially be regarded as overblown expressions of ethnic pride is perhaps best left unanswered here. It does, however, indicate that there was a "grass roots" concern for the type of Swedish literature held by area libraries of the MPL, and this concern apparently led to action. According to the second of these newspaper articles, a decision was made by the MPL to purchase a new supply of Swedish books with money available (a sum of $100) for the purpose. More funds were promised in the future, providing demands and interests made themselves both visible and strong. All interested individuals were encouraged to draw up book suggestion lists and forward them to Victor Nilsson, who was charged with the task of reviewing and submitting them for final approval by the Library Board.[20]

It is worth noting here that Swedes voiced general praise for the Library Board, which in their eyes had "always been willing to meet public demands." On the other hand, they were fairly critical of their own failure to take an initiative, make their demands heard, and see to it that they were represented by at least one board member. This, it was said, was the reason why so few Swedish literary works were to be found in Minneapolis libraries. If, as this article went on, the Norwegians could organize themselves and retain Sven Oftedal in his board position, from 1885 to 1894, why should it be so difficult for the Swedes? "True respect for our countrymen cannot be won until Americans see that we lay claim on offices which, although they do not pay well, can, if well filled, contribute to raising the intellectual level of our society."[21]

As mentioned earlier, the Franklin Avenue Branch (South Side Branch, B) became the first special library of the MPL in 1904, functioning as the main depository and distribution point for all Scandinavian books (about 6,000 at the time), magazines, and newspapers for the entire city. This meant, among other things, that the branch could continue to serve the needs of the Swedish and Scandinavian populations regardless of subsequent trends in the geographic mobility of immigrant patrons. Although the immediate Cedar-Riverside area acquired two sub-branches of its own, one at Seven Corners in 1905 and another at 24th and Franklin avenues in 1908, the Franklin Avenue Branch emerged as the "Scandinavian Mecca" on the city's south side. In 1912 it supplied Scandinavian books to ten different points within the MPL system according to a fixed exchange schedule. Despite its central location and vital functions, the branch would wait until July 1914 for a new building that specifically addressed its needs and functions. Formally opened in January 1915, the building's main floor plan accommodated two large reading rooms, one for the Scandinavian collection and the other for English-language materials. The new surroundings were to have an immediately positive effect on the circulation figures of the branch.[22]

Although the *Annual Reports* of the MPL from 1890–1913 provide tabular circulation statistics for both the central and branch libraries, the lack of specific breakdowns for foreign literature makes it fairly difficult to study the Franklin Avenue Branch in any detail during this period. Generally speaking, this branch consistently led all others in the circulation of "foreign literature" from 1890 to 1904 (the year of its designation as a Scandinavian collection center) and again from 1905 to 1915. On the other hand, a careful reading of the texts to these reports for the latter ten-year period can shed some light on conditions at this branch.

By 1908, the MPL leadership was painfully aware that the Franklin Avenue Branch had outgrown its rented quarters and that the lack of space for both books and readers had curbed its circulation figures in contrast to developments elsewhere in the system. In 1909 it was reported that all books for adults had been placed in the front section of the reference room except for the foreign books, mostly Scandinavian, which were still kept in the back section of the juvenile readers' room. In 1912, the largest circulation of any class of books in the MPL system, outside of juveniles, fiction and magazines, was that of foreign literature (a 63 percent gain), chiefly Swedish and Norwegian (Franklin Avenue and Seven Corners branches). Again, however, it was noted that the Franklin Avenue Branch had lost ground in terms of total circulation, primarily as a result of inadequate accommodations. A major contributing factor was the opening of the new Seven Corners Branch only three-quarters of a mile away; in 1912 its total circulation figures were more than double those recorded in 1911 at the old location. Nonetheless, in 1913 the Franklin Avenue Branch was reported to have led all other branches in the circulation of foreign literature, including 9,047 books in the Scandinavian languages alone.[23]

Language-specific circulation figures for foreign literature are recorded for the first time in the MPL annual reports of 1914 and 1915. Focusing on these, one can note the following developments. Of the books circulated in twenty different languages in 1914, the Swedish led in total figures with 11,987, followed closely by the Norwegian with 10,491. German-language holdings ranked third with 5,281. Among all system reporting libraries, including Central, the Franklin Avenue Branch headed the list of Swedish circulation with 6,375, followed by Seven Corners with 1,175, and, strikingly enough, the Camden (Park) Branch, on the North Side, with 1,068. In total circulation figures for foreign literature, the Franklin Avenue Branch ranked first (12,496) and well beyond its closest rival, the Sumner Branch (5,237, of which the majority was Yiddish literature).[24]

These trends are reinforced by the statistics in 1915, which show that Swedish literature had the highest total circulation (14,117) of all foreign-language literature, followed at some distance by the Norwegian with 10,858. The Franklin Avenue Branch alone circulated 7,431 of the Swedish total as well as 6,045 of the Norwegian, its closest rival being the Seven Corners Branch with a Swedish circulation of 1,386. As a depository source of Scandinavian books for the entire system, the Franklin Avenue Branch also loaned a total of 2,370 volumes to other branches and stations, an undertaking that was still in its infancy in 1915. In total circulation figures for foreign literature the Franklin Avenue Branch again led the list of reporting libraries with 13,817 volumes, its closest rival being the Central Library with 5,749. It is interesting to note that the Cedar-Riverside Branch managed to edge out the Camden Branch for a third-place ranking in total Swedish circulation (969 volumes to 946 volumes), despite its closing in November 1915.[25]

The above statistics doubtlessly reflect certain purchasing and accessioning trends in Scandinavian literature that make themselves visible around 1909. In that year, the MPL Order Department announced the purchase of books in six foreign languages, including Swedish, Norwegian, and Finnish. Although the Scandinavian collection was considered a good one at the time, it apparently

Immigrants and laborers reading books and newspapers at the Minneapolis Public Library Reading Room, Bridge Square (old City Hall), ca. 1910.

showed signs of wear and tear, and the Order Department encouraged the purchase of a fairly large addition "in another year" to "meet the demands of our very excellent Scandinavian patronage." No less than 563 foreign-language volume replacements, chiefly Scandinavian, out of a general replacement total of 1,946 volumes, were acquired by the system in 1910.[26]

Four years later, however, the MPL Order Department noted that Scandinavian book orders constituted "by far the larger number of any foreign purchase." Other smaller or larger purchases made in 1914 included books in Dutch, Italian, Syrian, French, Yiddish, Hebrew, Romanian, Polish, and Hungarian. The Branch Superintendent's report that same year characterized the Scandinavian collection at the Franklin Avenue Branch as a large and useful one and indicated that it was the ambition of the MPL to make it "one of the best, if not the best, Scandinavian library in the country." In 1915, the Franklin Avenue Branch report showed a total of 1,546 book accessions, of which over two-thirds were Scandinavian and children's literature. Most of the Scandinavian additions went to the Swedish collection in a stated effort to make it equally as strong as its Danish-Norwegian counterpart. The report added that "the larger Swedish circulation seems to warrant a greater supply of books in that section."[27]

This is an appropriate juncture to step away from the Minneapolis public library scene and look at the situation across the river in neighboring St. Paul. Related developments in the St. Paul Public Library for the period 1882–1916 are sparsely covered in its *Annual Reports*. In fact, little is said about purchases of foreign-language materials for the express use of immigrant patrons or the operations of branches or delivery stations in districts with distinct ethnic profiles. There is general mention of a Delivery Station B at the Bodin and Sundberg Drug Company (896 Payne Avenue), in existence between February 1905 and May 1916, and the establishment in 1915 of a branch station at the Swedish Methodist Church in Arlington Hills. Although the 1905–15 *Reports* present circulation figures for the various branches and stations, they do not specify the types or classes of books covered by these statistics. It is not until 1914 that overall circulation is broken down into broad classes, including "foreign literature." No attempt is made, however, to itemize this literature or record its circulation by specific branches. The same is largely true of accession statistics in the foreign literature category, which make their initial appearance in 1891 with a total of 109 unspecified volumes and cross the 9,000 volume level (again unspecified) in 1913. The first real mention of book purchases in specific language and literature categories appears in 1912, when "considerable additions" were made in French, Swedish, Norwegian, and Yiddish titles.[28]

An examination of available finding-lists and supplements for the St. Paul

Public Library in the years 1891, 1895, 1896, and 1899 reveals that only German and French-language titles are given substantive representation. It is difficult, however, to determine whether these purchases were intended solely for immigrant readers. Prior to 1895, the general category of Scandinavian language and literature is limited to three dictionaries and a scattering of English-language titles on the literary and cultural history of Scandinavia. Only three Scandinavian-language titles are listed among the "Books in Foreign Literature" section of the 1895 *Supplement*: two are editions of early medieval *edda* [saga] literature, and one is a classic history of Swedish book printing from 1483 to 1883.[29]

It is not until 1913, and the issuance of *Class List No. 7: Literature*, that a broader spectrum of Swedish literature and, by comparison, an even larger selection of Danish-Norwegian titles make their appearance in the holdings of the St. Paul Public Library. Surveying the Swedish listing, one is struck by a number of things: the total absence of the popular novel *genre*; the general attention to literature perspectives and compilations, including a developing set of *Sveriges national-litteratur, 1500–1900* (which began publication in 1908); and a major emphasis on the categories of poetry and drama, including English-language translations. Imprints range from 1866 to 1912, and the entire collection comprises eighty-six volumes. The pre-1880/1890 period in Swedish and Swedish-Finnish literature is represented by a maximum of ten authors in eighteen volumes, covering the categories of poetry, drama, and "miscellany." Late nineteenth- and early twentieth-century authors are essentially six in number, falling under the categories of poetry, drama, essays, and "miscellany." They include Heidenstam (two titles/volumes), Snoilsky (one title/volume), Strindberg (poetry: two titles/volumes; drama: eleven titles/volumes, including four translations; essays: two titles in five volumes), Leffler (one title/volume), Geijerstam (one title/volume), and Ellen Key (one title/volume). Swedish American contributions are limited to Johan A. Enander's editorial compilation of nineteenth-century Swedish poetry, *Ur svenska sången* (1901).[30]

By contrast and comparison, the MPL expanded on its initial (1899) Swedish finding list with the issuance of printed supplements (arranged by subject categories and classes) both in 1908 and 1913, as complemented by a *List of Additions*, beginning in 1917. While the popular novel *genre* of the mid-nineteenth century is well represented (authors such as Louise Stjernström, G. H. Mellin, C. F. Ridderstad, and Marie Sophie Schwartz), including favorites in "collected works" format, the 1908 supplement shows increasing attention to the later generation of Swedish literature (works by Bondeson, Geijerstam, Hallström, Heidenstam, Lagerlöf, Lundegård, Strindberg, and Söderberg). There is also an interesting sprinkling of Swedish American literary contributions by such

authors as Henning Berger, Vilhelm Berger, Johan Jolin, Gustaf Sjöström, and
Ninian Waernér. Some of these authors are also listed under the separate categories of poetry and drama, with Strindberg (d.1912) represented by no less than
twenty titles/volumes. The 1913 supplement edition and the 1917 listing reinforce these trends to some extent, although one can notice a new and comparatively strong selection of translated fiction representing American and general
European authors in post-1900 editions.[31]

An overview of the selection and purchasing methods followed by the MPL
regarding foreign-language literature is provided by the *Annual Report* of 1912,
and it deserves special mention here. The selection of such literature was apparently a difficult problem for the MPL Chief Librarian and the Order Department but had been resolved in a resourceful manner.

> When a collection of any foreign literature is first started, a person of that
> nationality in the city is sought who seems to be well informed, and he is
> asked to give titles of some of the best known standard books in his native
> language and supply us with catalogues. He interests his group of people and
> between them a very creditable list is usually furnished which the library
> corrects or supplements by reference to other library catalogues or by his-
> tories of the literature of that country. Translations of English titles into that
> language are used freely and find favor. . . . There is usually danger in getting
> the first list of books a little too heavy for the class of people who are to use
> them, so that a small number only is purchased at the beginning to test the
> reading tastes of the community.[32]

While the above comments do not necessarily apply to the Scandinavian
collection at the Franklin Avenue Branch, which was generally well established
by 1912, they do provide an appropriate frame of reference for remarks made
three years later by the then coordinator of all Scandinavian library work in
Minneapolis, Emma B. Nilsson. The younger sister of the former East Side
Branch librarian, Nilsson was a singer and actress of some standing in Swedish
American circles, having made an opera debut in Berlin in 1884. Joining the MPL
system as an assistant in 1893, she served at the Central Library and various
branches from 1893 to 1895 and again from 1897 to 1909. In September 1909, she
was chosen to succeed Halvor Askeland as Head Librarian of the Franklin Avenue Branch, a post she retained until her appointment in 1914 as coordinator
of all Scandinavian work in the city.[33]

In the judgment of her professional superiors, Nilsson was well qualified to
select books in the Swedish and Norwegian languages, and she had the assistance of educated Scandinavian men and women. It is reported that her selec-

tion expertise was sought out at times by libraries in other states, and both faculty and students from the University of Minnesota and Augsburg Seminary came directly to the Franklin Avenue Branch for reference and research assistance. Use was made of folders in Swedish and Norwegian informing patrons about the nature and use of the library as well as procedures for obtaining borrowing privileges. Reading lists of various kinds, mostly related to the Scandinavian collection, were also printed and distributed on a weekly basis, both in the city and elsewhere in the state.[34]

As a member of the Minnesota Library Association, Emma Nilsson served on its Foreign Book List Committee, contributing to an awareness of trends in Scandinavian literature, while at the same time publicizing the work of the Franklin Avenue Branch to other libraries in Minnesota. Two of her published contributions happen to date from 1915 and therefore tie in handily with what has been sketched above.

In an article entitled "Scandinavian Literature," Nilsson summarized the development and work of the Minneapolis Scandinavian collection up to that time, commenting in detail on the range and quality of Scandinavian writing, especially the "realistic literature," as represented in the holdings of the MPL system. She noted that most of the Scandinavians in the United States, especially the Swedes and Danes, were of a conservative mind and education and fond of the more "old-fashioned" books, embracing the categories of historical fiction and "every-day romantic novels of home life." This conservative class of readers included individuals "who, because of one single outspoken phrase or situation, will utterly condemn a whole work really of a serious purpose or artistic form." At the same time, she said: "There is among the newcomers of every Scandinavian country a class steadily growing which is made up of quite advanced and liberal-minded people, mostly working men and women. Many of them are militant in the temperance, socialist or suffrage causes." These people, she added, "demand modern books to read, the literature that has the works of August Strindberg and Ellen Key as its starting point. Few, indeed, are the authors like Selma Lagerlöf whose books are with equal eagerness sought by readers of all classes and all ages."[35]

That the standing problem of fictional literature in American public libraries also concerned the librarian of foreign-language literature is spelled out in Emma Nilsson's delegated contribution to the Minnesota Library Association's annual meeting of September 1915, entitled "Report of the Committee on Foreign Book Lists." Nilsson reminded the association that the purpose of including foreign books in public libraries was not to educate people in the languages of these countries, but rather "chiefly to preserve the elements of culture in the foreign born of our people, elements which would otherwise be lost, for lack of an English education." At the same time, she noted, foreign booklists were an acutely felt need of any librarian, and their preparation mainly involved problems of a *linguistic* nature:

> In making such lists one cannot always put the literary value of a book in its first place. The principal thing to ascertain in each instance is the cleanliness and wholesomeness of the mental food.
>
> A big author's name does not always guarantee the fitness of his products. Discretion is necessary for the guidance of readers.
>
> Still, it must be remembered that the foremost fiction writers of Scandinavia distinctly are leaders of thought and cultural development. Therefore we could not eliminate the realistic masterpieces of these writers from library booklists.
>
> For average libraries and small groups of readers fiction is primarily needed; only larger library centers require the full equipment of classed books and works of reference.
>
> Where resources permit the buying of classified books, it will be found that the Scandinavians are not lacking in appreciation of this kind of reading. Especially is this true of the men.[36]

The above excerpts from Emma Nilsson's work with the Scandinavian section of the MPL and the Minnesota Library Association's Committee on Foreign Book Lists are striking in a number of respects. Here, as with her brother Victor Nilsson, we have a good example of a foreign-born, public library professional from the years around the turn of century who straddles both the American and immigrant communities and, in so doing, addresses the responsibilities connected with general public education and immigrant community advocacy. Emma's comments on the social backgrounds and literary-cultural tastes of Swedish immigrant readers shed additional light on studies that have been made of the "reading/take-home menus" of Scandinavian immigrants who were members of private reading societies or who frequented and borrowed from private, ethnocentric libraries.[37]

At the same time it seems clear, perhaps more so than with Victor Nilsson, that Emma is not only concerned with the interpretation and cultural preservation of a "literary canon" but also with the ongoing evaluation of this canon for both the American and immigrant public. The attention she draws to "the cleanliness and wholesomeness of the mental food," including the works of then contemporary Swedish authors such as Strindberg, places her in the mainstream of a century-long debate, both civic and professional, on the role and nature of fictional literature, regardless of national origin or language medium, on the shelves of the American public library.

* * * *

NOTES

1. See, for example, the published remarks of a Connecticut public library administrator, David Bryant, "Multiculturalism: The New Racism," in the column "Backtalk," *Library Journal* (hereafter *LJ*) (Feb. 1, 1994): 54. One example of the ALA's continuing efforts on behalf of a multicultural focus for American public libraries is its published and electronic (on-line) reference compilation, *Multicultural and Ethnic Materials: A Selected Bibliography of Bibliographies* (LARC Fact Sheet, No. 23) (Chicago: The Association, 1996–), reportedly updated and revised on an annual basis.

2. Immediate background is provided by my unpublished academic paper, "Americanization, Foreign-language Books, Immigrants, and Public Libraries: A Conceptual and Bibliographic Essay on American Public Library Opinion, as Reflected in the Library Literature of the Period 1894–1920" (Univ. of Minn. Graduate School of Library Science, Minneapolis, May 1977), 8, and cited literature (separate articles or announcements in *LJ*, Jan.–Oct. 1894); also cited in my article, "In Private and Public: The Dialogue of Libraries, Immigrants and Society," in *Scandinavian Immigrants and Education in North America*, Philip J. Anderson, Dag Blanck, and Peter Kivisto, eds. (Chicago: Swedish-American Historical Society, 1995), 203n19.

3. See, in particular, my unpublished, academic research contribution, "Books and Reading in a Swedish-American Community: A Case Study of the Lending Library of the *Vega Litterära Förening* (Vega Literary Society), St. Paul, from 1881 to 1948, with Emphasis on Bookstock Characteristics, Patronage and Circulation Statistics, and Popular Reading Tastes" (Univ. of Minn. Graduate School of Library Science, Minneapolis, Apr. 1977), *passim*; see also Westerberg, "In Private and Public," 193–98.

4. Sidney H. Ditzion, *Arsenals of a Democratic Culture: A Social History of the American Public Library Movement in New England and the Middle States from 1850 to 1900* (Chicago: American Library Association, 1947). See also, on this topic, Sidney Louis Jackson, *Libraries and Librarianship in the West: A Brief History* (New York: McGraw Hill, 1974), and Michael Harris, "The Purpose of the American Public Library: A Revisionist Interpretation of History," *LJ* (Sept. 15, 1973): 2509–14; Ditzion, *Arsenals*, 75, and cited literature. See also the American library literature survey reported and commented on by Deanna B. Marcum and Elizabeth W. Stone, "Literacy: The Library Legacy," *American Libraries* (Mar. 1991): 202–5. For evidence that the American immigrant's relationship to and involvement with the American public library movement of the late nineteenth and early twentieth centuries had an even wider significance for the traditional and evolving role of the library in its societal setting, see Jesse H. Shera, *Introduction to Library Science: Basic Elements of Library Service* (Littleton, Colo.: Libraries Unlimited, Inc., 1976), 49f. Shera specifically cites the acculturation experience of the American immigrant vis à vis the host society and the public library movement as the "most notable" example of what he envisioned (at that time) as a new discipline of societal knowledge called "social epistemology" (p. 50).

5. The standard bibliography of the early professional literature on these issues is H. G. T. Cannon, *Bibliography of Library Economy: A Classified Index to the Professional Periodical*

268   KERMIT B. WESTERBERG

Literature in the English Language Relating to Library Economy... From 1876 to 1920 (Chicago: American Library Association, 1927). One example of the period's professional opinion is George Watson Cole's "Fiction in Libraries: A Plea for the Masses," originally published in *LJ* in 1894 and reprinted there June 15, 1996, S8. I have studied these and related issues for the period 1894–1920 in my unpublished research paper, "Americanization, Foreign-language Books, Immigrants, and Public Libraries." See also Westerberg, "In Private and Public," 197ff. An example of Swedish opinion and concern on the issue of *smutslitteraturen* ("filth literature") around the turn of the twentieth century is found in John Landquist, "Billighetslitteraturen och den litterära överproduktionen," *Tidskrift för det svenska folk-bildningsarbetet* 2 (1913): 252–58. See also Ulf Boëthius, "Nick Carter som ungsocialist. Det socialdemokratiska ungdomsförbundets kamp mot 'smutslitteraturen'," in *Litteraturens vägar. Litteratursociologiska studier tillägnade Lars Furuland* (Stockholm: Gidlund, 1988), 136–52.

6. Aksel G. S. Josephson, "Scandinavian Books in American Libraries," *LJ*, 19:1 (Jan. 1894): 4; "Swedish Books for American Libraries," *LJ*, 19:7 (July 1894): 224.

7. "A List of Swedish Books for American Libraries," *LJ*, 19:10 (Oct. 1894), 340f.

8. Ibid., 340.

9. "The Proposed Publication," *LJ*, 19:10 (Oct. 1894), 328.

10. Josephson, "Foreign Books in American Libraries," *LJ*, 19:11 (Nov. 1894), 364.

11. See my unpublished research papers, "Americanization, Foreign-language Books, Immigrants, and Public Libraries," *passim*, and "Books for the Immigrants. I. Swedish" (Univ. of Minn. Graduate School of Library Science, June 1976), *passim*; Gratia Alta Countryman, "Shall Public Libraries Buy Foreign Language Literature for the Benefit of the Foreign Population?" *LJ*, 24:6 (June 1898), 229ff., esp. 229. Brackets are mine.

12. Countryman, "Shall Public Libraries," 230f.

13. Westerberg, "Books for the Immigrants. I. Swedish," 8, and n29–30 (cited literature).

14. Ibid., 8f. n31 (cited literature), and n32 (cited literature and commentary). For historical and statistical surveys of Swedish and Scandinavian settlements in the Twin Cities, including shifts and changes over time, see Helge Nelson, *The Swedes and the Swedish Settlements in North America*, 2 vols. (Lund: CWK Gleerup, 1943), 1: 185–89 and fig. 62, 189; Byron Nordstrom, ed., *The Swedes in Minnesota* (Minneapolis: T. S. Denison, 1976); Byron Nordstrom, "Swedes in Minneapolis," *Sweden & America* (Autumn, 1996), 12–17; and, in particular, Calvin F. Schmid, *A Social Saga of Two Cities: An Ecological and Statistical Study of Social Trends in Minneapolis and St. Paul* (Minneapolis: The Minneapolis Council of Social Agencies, 1937).

15. Ibid., 9 and n33 (cited literature and commentary).

16. Victor Nilsson, "The Public Library: A Talk on its Swedish Collection," *Minneapolis Journal*, Dec. 28, 1894, as cited in Westerberg, "Books for the Immigrants. I. Swedish," 9f. and n34–35.

17. Ibid.

18. Ibid.

19. *Svenska Amerikanska Posten*, Apr. 20, 1897, p. 12, and Apr. 27, 1897, p. 12, as cited in Westerberg, "Books for the Immigrants. I. Swedish," 10f. and n36–37.

20. Westerberg, "Books for the Immigrants. I. Swedish," 11 and n37.

21. Ibid., and n38–39.

22. Ibid., 12 and n41.

23. Ibid., 13 and n42–45.

24. Ibid., 13f. and n46. It should be noted here that in 1905 the Camden area, on Minneapolis's north side, had a higher percentage of Swedish-born residents than any other part of the city, save the Cedar-Riverside district.

25. Ibid., 14, and n47–48.

26. Ibid., and n49–50.

27. Ibid., 14f. and n51.
28. Westerberg, "Books and Reading," 72f. and n73.
29. Ibid., 73 and n74.
30. Ibid., 73f. and n75.
31. Ibid., 71f. and n72.
32. Westerberg, "Books for the Immigrants. I. Swedish," 15 and n52.
33. Ibid., and n53.
34. Ibid., 15f. and n54.
35. Ibid., 16f. and n55–57; Minnesota Public Library Commission, *Library Notes and News*, IV (1913–15): 10 (June 1915), 183–86. Ms. Nilsson's article provides an overview of Scandinavian authors whose fiction could be "safely recommended" to public libraries and their readers along with comments on the period's literary publishing trends (by countries/genres) as well as observations on literacy standards, socio-cultural conditions, and library developments in the Scandinavian countries.
36. Westerberg, "Books for the Immigrants. I. Swedish," 17 and n59–60; Minnesota Public Library Commission, *Library Notes and News*, IV (1913–15): 12 (Dec. 1915), 224f. It is essential to point out that, in this context, and vis à vis the referenced sources in n35 above, that much of the realistic, sometimes decadent, socio-critical literature published by some late nineteenth- and early twentieth-century Scandinavian authors (including, most prominently, August Strindberg) became the focus of heated debate and censure in home countries and, by consequence, emerged as a matter of concern for both the consuming and reviewing audiences in North America. For striking evidence of this from Swedish and Swedish American commentators of the period, who grappled with the literary and cultural identity of the Swedish immigrant, see H. Arnold Barton, *A Folk Divided: Homeland Swedes and Swedish Americans, 1840–1940* (Carbondale: Southern Ill. Univ. Press, 1994), esp. 88, 122, 144, 207, and 290. Regarding the background of the so-called *Strindbergs-fejden* and the larger *osedlighetsdebatten* ("the immorality debate") in Swedish literary and cultural circles, see, for example, the chapter "Åttiotalet," in Gunnar Brandell, *Från 1870 till första världskriget*, vol. 1 of *Svensk litteratur, 1870–1970* (Stockholm: Aldus, 1974), 110–56. For insights into the possible relationship between the Nilsson siblings' contributions and what has been termed "inventional cultural tradition-making," see *The Invention of Tradition*, Eric Hobsbawm and Terence Ranger, eds. (Cambridge: Cambridge Univ. Press, 1986), esp. 1–14.
37. See Westerberg, "Books and Reading" and "In Private and Public"; also, see Steven J. Keillor, "Rural Norwegian-American Reading Societies in the Late Nineteenth Century," *Norwegian-American Studies* (Northfield, Minn.: Norwegian-American Historical Association, 1992), 139–63.

As Others Saw Them:
Swedes and American Religion in the Twin Cities

MARK A. GRANQUIST

The largest and most complex institutions within Swedish America were the congregations and ethnic denominations formed by the immigrants. It is surprising that Swedish Americans were willing to devote so much of their time and resources to the building of these institutions, but even more surprising was their facility in adapting their religious traditions to the radically peculiar world of American religion. In their quest to form religious institutions for their community, Swedish Americans borrowed heavily from the religious institutions of their American neighbors, but often the borrowing was accomplished with a uniquely, sometimes stubbornly, Swedish cast. This essay will survey the rich dimensions of Swedish American religion in the Twin Cities, especially the relationship between the immigrant religious leaders and their American counterparts, to see the interplay between the immigrant community and the world of American religion.[1]

Before exploring its connections with American religion, it is necessary to examine the scope of religious life within the Twin Cities Swedish American community. The diversity of congregations and denominations is striking—there were Swedish Lutherans, Mission Covenant, Free, Congregational, Baptist, Methodist, Episcopal, Seventh-Day Adventist, Salvation Army, Presbyterian, Pentecostal, Unitarian, Universalist, and Spiritualist congregations—and this is only surveying the self-consciously Swedish groups. Perhaps many other immigrants moved into the American denominations, making the transition directly into American religious life. Although by 1920 only about 20 percent of Swedish Americans were formally affiliated with one of the ethnic denominations, it is credible to suggest that their "sphere of influence" was larger than their membership, perhaps in the range of 40 to 50 percent of the whole immigrant community. Using 1920 as the high-water mark of Swedish America, we can see the strength and variety of these ethnic religious groups.[2]

The largest religious group among Swedes in the Twin Cities was the Augustana Lutheran churches, with eighteen congregations in the Minneapolis district of the Minnesota Synod and twelve congregations in the St. Paul district, comprising 13,000 members. The organization of city congregations was difficult and proceeded slowly; the first congregation, First Lutheran Church in St. Paul, was founded in 1854 but had no permanent pastor until 1871. The first congregation in Minneapolis, Augustana Lutheran Church, was organized as a Scandinavian congregation in 1866. Its initial course was rough; the Norwegian members left the congregation in 1868, and during the 1870s another pastor temporarily led the congregation out of the Augustana Synod. The formation of congregations proceeded slowly. Of the thirty Lutheran congregations in 1920, fifteen were founded after 1900, while only five were founded before 1880.[3]

Moreover, the work of gathering in urban Swedes lagged behind the growth of membership in rural areas. While up to 30 percent of Swedish Americans in rural Minnesota belonged to Augustana congregations, the rate of membership in the urban areas averaged about 15 percent. Given that up to one-third of Swedish Americans in Minnesota lived in these urban areas, these figures were quite distressing to Augustana leaders. In an attempt to address this problem after 1900, the Synod began to form English-language Augustana congregations, often as offshoots of established Swedish churches. Congregations founded in this way included Grace and Messiah in Minneapolis and Gloria Dei and Arlington Hills in St. Paul. But still this effort was an attempt to make up for years of missed opportunities, and many Swedes were lost to American congregations, including English-speaking Lutheran congregations of other synods.[4]

Another denomination active in the Twin Cities early on was the Swedish Baptists, whose presence in the area began in the 1850s and 1860s with small groups of immigrants who had adopted the Baptist denomination. The first congregation, the First Swedish Baptist Church of Minneapolis, was formed in 1871 and for a number of years enjoyed the strong leadership of Pastor Frank Peterson. Other congregations included Bethel Baptist, founded in 1884, and Elim Baptist, founded in 1888. In St. Paul, the largest and oldest Baptist congregation, also named First Swedish Baptist Church, was founded in 1873, followed by Central Baptist in 1893 and Bethany in 1898. The membership in these congregations in 1920 numbered approximately 2,600, which comprised about one-third of the Swedish Baptists membership for the entire state.[5]

The Baptist educational institutions, Bethel College and Theological Seminary, were another important Swedish presence in the Twin Cities. Founded in 1871, Bethel Seminary was moved a number of times, including a brief period in St. Paul (1884–85), until it was finally returned to St. Paul in 1914, where it was combined with an academy founded nine years before in Minneapolis.[6]

Swedish Methodism was a third early presence among the Swedish American community, with five congregations. One of the first Swedish congregations in the Twin Cities was the Scandinavian Methodist Episcopal Church of St. Paul, founded in 1854 as a joint congregation of Swedes, Danes, and Norwegians. Out of this congregation eventually came an all-Swedish congregation, the First Swedish Methodist, sometimes known as the Temperance Street Church. The Arlington Hills Swedish Methodist congregation was organized in St. Paul in 1889. Three ethnic congregations were formed in Minneapolis: First Swedish Methodist in 1873, Ebenezar Swedish Methodist in 1897, and Emmanuel Swedish Methodist in 1911. The membership of these five congregations totaled 1,020 in 1920.[7]

The movement that eventually brought forth the Mission Covenant and Evangelical Free churches began in the 1860s and involved a struggle over the implications of the Pietist and Lutheran heritage, a background that many Swedish immigrants shared. Some Swedish Americans, both inside and outside of the Augustana Synod, were struggling to achieve congregations of "awakened" Christians that would resemble the Pietist conventicles of Sweden. The conflict intensified during the 1870s over the ideas of Swedish theologian Paul Peter Waldenström, a debate that hardened divisions within the community. Soon independent congregations of Swedish American Pietists were being gathered together, a movement that led eventually to the formation of the Mission Covenant and Evangelical Free denominations.[8]

The beginnings of the Mission Covenant congregations in the Twin Cities come from this time of ferment. First Covenant Church of St. Paul (known in the early years as the St. Paul Tabernacle) was formed in 1874, as a split-off from First Lutheran. First Covenant Church in Minneapolis (known after 1886 as the Swedish Tabernacle) was founded the same year with a core of former Augustana Lutheran and other pietistic Swedes. Additional congregations, begun usually as offshoots of the Minneapolis congregation, were Salem (1888), Broadway (1890), Camden Place (1899), and Bethany and Elim (1904). In St. Paul, the Elim church (1914) also began as a Sunday school chapel of the mother church on the East Side. Total membership of these congregations in 1920 was 2,160.[9]

Some of the more radical congregational and antidenominational leaders formed congregations that would eventually become a part of the Evangelical Free Church, though this group was slow to organize. First Evangelical Free Church (originally Scandinavian Church of Christ) of Minneapolis was formed in 1884. A split-off of members from this congregation formed the Swedish

Mission Temple in 1894; this congregation was affiliated with the Swedish Con-gregationalists until 1926, when the Swedish Temple merged with the First Evangelical Free congregation. Another congregation, the Scandinavian Evan-gelical Free Church, was organized in 1908. In St. Paul a Free Church congre-gation was organized in 1883. This congregation split over the issue of the de-gree of organization allowable, but the two congregations reunited in 1906 to form the Swedish Evangelical Free Church.[10]

Mention of the Covenant and Free congregations brings up the issue of the Swedish Congregational churches. Among these groups the organizational sit-uation was rather fluid, with congregations and pastors often belonging to both the Covenant and Free denominations *and* the Congregational Association at the same time. The American Congregationalists made a strong and definite effort to extend their influence over the ethnic congregations, under the lead-ership of Marcus Whitman Montgomery, the Scandinavian superintendent of the Congregational American Home Missionary Society (AHMS). The AHMS supported at least thirty congregations in the Upper Midwest, and many Swedish pastors were trained at the Congregational Chicago Theological Sem-inary. The Congregationalists also maintained a Scandinavian presence at Car-leton College for a time, and some Swedish Congregational pastors were trained there. There was even a Swedish Congregational Ministerial Association orga-nized in Minneapolis in 1898, in which up to 200 pastors would eventually par-ticipate. By the 1920s, however, the previous fluidity of association was gone (along with interest on the part of the Congregationalists), and most of the pas-tors and congregations in the Swedish Congregational movement had moved permanently to the Mission Covenant Church, with a few associating with the Evangelical Free denomination.[11]

Another American denomination with a strong outreach to Scandinavians in Minnesota was the Episcopal Church. Episcopal work among Swedes in the Twin Cities dates back to a visit by Gustaf Unonius to St. Paul in 1851, but this initial effort did not bear much fruit. A more serious attempt began in the 1890s, when a number of Swedish Episcopal congregations were formed in the Twin Cities. St. Ansgarius was formed in Minneapolis in 1892, and Olaf Toffteen was called as priest of the congregation. From St. Ansgarius, Toffteen organized two additional Minneapolis congregations, St. Johannes (1893) and Messias (1895). In St. Paul, a dispute erupted within the First Lutheran congregation over the issue of Masonic membership, and a group left this Lutheran congregation to form St. Sigfrid's Episcopal congregation, also organized by Toffteen. Many Swedish Episcopalians were former Lutherans who resented the Augustana Synod's strict morality code and stance on membership in secret societies. But it also seemed clear that many nonaffiliated Swedish Americans employed the services of Swedish Episcopalian priests for occasional pastoral duties, such as baptisms, weddings, and funerals.[12]

The Presbyterians were a third American denomination that ventured into Swedish work. During the 1890s, the Synod of Minnesota began a mission in Minneapolis called Immanuel Presbyterian Church, with August Wadensten as pastor. Later there is mention of a second congregation in Minneapolis, First Swedish Presbyterian Church, but both of these congregations were very small and soon disappeared from sight after only about six years.[13]

During the 1870s, some Swedish Baptist congregations split over the message and incursion of Seventh-Day Adventism. Some Baptist pastors, such as J. G. Matteson and August Swedberg, became Adventists and began to spread the Adventist message in the Swedish American community. In Minneapolis, Adventist work was begun in 1884 by J. P. Rosequist, who gathered in a mixed Scandinavian Adventist congregation; this arrangement continued until 1919, when the congregation was divided into separate Swedish and Danish-Norwegian congregations. A similar Scandinavian congregation was begun in St. Paul in 1887.[14]

Another group having at least partial origins within the Swedish Baptist tradition was the Swedish Pentecostal churches. From 1905 to 1910, many Swedish Baptist congregations underwent a renewal known as the "New Movement," which exhibited many of the characteristics of the new Pentecostal movement. Swedish American Pentecostalism grew partially out of this movement, as well as through Pentecostal immigrants from Sweden. In 1922, three groups of Swedish Pentecostal pastors and congregations came together in St. Paul to found the Independent Assemblies of God (unincorporated). The largest Twin Cities congregation was the Bloomington Temple, founded before 1920, which would later be decimated by a schism involving a faith-healing evangelist, Charles Price. Another congregation, the Philadelphia church, was formed in Minneapolis around 1926. An informal group of Swedish Pentecostals met in St. Paul, beginning in 1917, under the leadership of Almeda and Charles Engquist, and this group grew into the Bethel Christian Fellowship, formally organized in 1930.[15]

A small religious group with a great impact on the immigrant community was the Swedish Salvation Army corps. This movement began in the 1880s among Swedish Americans in Brooklyn, New York, and soon spread to Swedish communities throughout the United States. A Swedish-language newspaper was launched in 1891, and the work was organized into separate Scandinavian divisions. The largest of the Twin Cities Scandinavian corps (akin to local congregations) was Minneapolis No. 4, organized on April 8, 1888; by 1901 it had eighty-seven officers. In 1891 there were four separate Scandinavian corps in

Minneapolis and two additional corps in St. Paul. These groupings were especially valuable in tracing missing persons within the immigrant community
and in providing charitable relief.[16]

Small but interesting were the congregations of Swedish Unitarians and
Universalists—both American denominations with at least a token representation in the Swedish American community in the Twin Cities. The First Swedish
Universalist Church was organized in 1886, with August Dellgren as its first pastor; it existed until at least 1901 and at one point had sixty members. Axel Lundberg and John Mattson organized a Swedish Unitarian congregation in 1890.
Lundberg was the congregation's first lecturer, until his resignation in 1894. The
congregation was unable to find a suitable replacement, and the congregation
closed in 1896.[17]

As is surely apparent by now, the diversity of the various Swedish congregations within the Twin Cities was immense. The largest part of the work belonged to the Augustana Synod, but both within Swedish ethnic denominations themselves and within their American counterparts there was a lively
religious interest in, and competition for, Swedes living in the Twin Cities. And
yet the majority of urban Swedish Americans were not formally a part of any
of these congregations. In 1920, on average only one in five Swedish Americans
belonged to one of these groups, and, if the Lutheran experience in the Twin
Cities was typical, the figure was probably lower for this urban area.

Where were the rest of the Swedish Americans? There are some hints, if
not answers. Some attended the ethnic churches but were not formally members. The American system of voluntary affiliation must have seemed unusual
to many immigrants, rooted in the automatic parish system of the Church of
Sweden. Many of these congregations had stiff membership regulations that
discouraged causal affiliation. Others were glad to escape the sphere of formal
religion altogether.

How many urban Swedish Americans joined American congregations and
denominations is difficult to assess, for the only evidence of this is anecdotal.
Some left because they found the morality and theology of the immigrant
churches oppressive; for example, David F. Swenson, Covenant leader and professor of philosophy at the University of Minnesota, was driven from the Swedish Tabernacle in Minneapolis by fundamentalist preacher Gustaf F. Johnson,
who labeled Swenson a "modernist." Others found that "American" congregations offered the immigrants more social prestige, or an easier chance to attain
their goal of becoming American. George Trabert, the "English" Lutheran
home missionary in Minnesota, recounted what he saw as a typical example of
a Swedish couple:

Neither he nor his wife are very proficient in English, but they have a daughter and want to form more prominent social connections than the leading Swedish congregation to which they belong affords. On the plea that their daughter does not understand Swedish . . . they land in the leading Presbyterian church.

Many younger Swedish Americans either could not understand Swedish or were impatient with the slow language transition within the ethnic congregations. Given the mobility and proximity afforded by the religious diversity of the urban Twin Cities, no doubt these scenarios were common.[18]

On the other hand, Swedish pride could often resent heavy-handed and paternalistic home mission work by American denominations. Two Minneapolis Scandinavians remarked in 1901:

Many attempts have been made by the different American denominations to do mission work among the Scandinavians in the state. More money has been expended, and more brain-work wasted for this purpose in Minnesota, especially in the Twin Cities, than in any other state in the Union.

After suggesting the large sums of money expended, they concluded:

But the fact that neither money, devotion, nor moral scruples have been spared, yet the results has not been very great. . . . Many Northmen, both church members and outsiders, also feel it as a humiliation that they should be treated as fit subjects for missionary work the same as are the savages of Africa.[19]

Some Swedish Americans, not formally affiliated with any congregation, utilized them for occasional religious services. This seemed especially common with the Lutheran and Episcopal congregations. In 1929 it was estimated that, since its founding in 1893, there had been 903 baptisms and 510 confirmations at St. Ansgarius Episcopal in Minneapolis, although its total membership never reached anywhere near those levels. Episcopalians claimed that many of these joined local American parishes, but this is difficult to substantiate.[20]

Swedish Americans seemed quite open to the religions of their new country, and their interest was reciprocated by the American denominations. Swedes were much more likely than their Scandinavian neighbors to adopt American religious forms and denominational life, and the Americans saw in the Swedish community fertile ground for the growth of their own denominational groups. Since in the Twin Cities, more than anywhere else in the United States, Swedes and Americans met on equal religious terms, this area was a center for contacts between the two communities. The contacts did not always go smoothly, and the hopeful visions of some did not always come to fruition, but their views of each other provide an interesting insight into Swedish American religious life in the Twin Cities.

There was a genuinely reciprocal interest between the Swedish and American denominations, even if such interests were not always identical. Almost all of these Swedish American religious groups had a corresponding American denomination with which they were affiliated in some way or which provided aid or assistance. Sometimes these identifications were organic; the Swedish Episcopalian parishes, for example, formed no national organization but existed within normal diocesan line. Most Swedish American denominations existed as separate units within the larger denominational framework, in the case of the Methodists, Adventists, Salvationists, and others, as special "Swedish" units within their parent denominations. Others, like the Lutherans and Baptists, had their own independent organization but affiliated with an American group, the General Council Lutherans and Northern Baptists respectively. For some Covenant and Free churches, there was a strong identification with the Congregationalists on the local level until the close of World War I, where pastors and congregations often had dual allegiances.[21]

These connections were important for more than material support, although that was crucial in the early days. Ties to American denominations gave the ethnic groups models for organization and an entry into the world of American religious life. American denominations saw these new immigrants as desirable, especially as a way to possibly extend their own denominational reach. Ironically, as the Swedish denominations become stronger and more "Americanized," they began to pull away from their American counterparts. This movement can be seen most vividly in the decade from 1910 to 1920, and among the Lutheran, Baptist, Covenant, and Free churches, and to a lesser extent among the Methodists. The Twin Cities were often an area of focus, where American and Swedish denominational leaders could meet and converse.[22]

One early American proponent for work among the Swedish immigrants was Marcus Whitman Montgomery, a Congregational leader who came to Minneapolis in 1881 and headed Scandinavian efforts for the American Home Missionary Society. Montgomery was an enthusiastic supporter of Swedish Congregational work and developed close ties to Covenant and Free Church congregations in the Upper Midwest. His enthusiasm is explained in a book written in 1884, after a trip to Scandinavia: "*The Scandinavians are, all things considered, among the best foreigners who come to American shores.* . . . They who love liberty *and* religion will make the best citizens for this republic. Just such are the Scandinavians." After a long passage where Montgomery contrasted Scandinavians with other "foreign elements" ("peddlers," "organ grinders," "beggars," "socialists," "nihilists," "communists," etc.), he concluded: "I am clearly of the opinion that *they* [the Scandinavians] *are more nearly like Americans than are any other foreign peoples.*" To Montgomery, these Protestant northerners were much more desirable than the southern and eastern European Catholic immigrants who were making up an increasingly large part of emigration to America. He believed that it would not take much to transform the nominally Lutheran Swedish immigrants into good American Congregationalists, but this was to overlook many of the differences between the two groups.[23]

Some leaders within the Swedish Congregational movement echoed these sentiments. A. P. Nelson, a Swedish Congregational pastor published a history of this movement in Minneapolis in 1906, in which he claimed:

> The day will surely come when these three branches of Swedish-American free mission work [Covenant, Free, and Congregational] will be united. . . . It is self-evident that three such similar groups will . . . quite naturally affiliate with the Congregationalist—that denomination which in every respect is so much like themselves.[24]

Mrs. Larson's Swedish class, Swedish Tabernacle, ca. 1900.
In the "Swede School," Swedish church groups offered first- and second-generation immigrants a means to preserve the culture of their homeland.

But other Covenant and Free Church leaders, whose congregations were often the focus of Congregational assistance and interest, although grateful for financial assistance from Montgomery and the AHMS, were sometimes defensive and wary of Congregational motives. They saw a distinct social and theological difference between their movement and the Americans' and resisted any form of closer affiliation with them. Eventually, by the 1920s, the Swedish Congregationalists had moved almost entirely into the Covenant church.

A situation similar to this can be seen in the relations between the Swedish Baptists and the Northern Baptists. The Americans in the Northern Baptist Convention sought to establish connections with quite a few immigrant groups, the Swedish Baptists being one of the largest. Like Montgomery, Baptist leaders mixed religious and racial reasons for special attention paid to the Swedes. Henry Morehouse, the secretary of the Baptist Home Mission Society, delivered an address at the fiftieth anniversary of the Swedish Baptists, praising their growth and faithfulness. Morehouse attributed the strength of the Swedish Baptists in part to their racial qualities, suggesting that northern European groups made a better and easier transition to becoming American Baptists than did groups from southern Europe. Some Swedish Baptists agreed, among them Frank Peterson, the long-time pastor at First Swedish Baptist Church, who would later become a district secretary for the Home Mission Society. In an article on Scandinavians in America for a Baptist publication in 1886, Peterson suggested that Scandinavian immigrants made the best Baptists and Americans; they were Protestants, religious, not socialists or communists, and very few of them were "peddlers, organ grinders, or beggars."[25]

But relations between the two groups did not always go smoothly, and, especially after 1910, Swedish Baptists became concerned about theological trends within the Northern Baptist Convention, especially the rise of liberal and modernist theology. The Swedish Baptists refused to participate in the ill-fated "New World Movement" drive of the Northern Baptists and began to pull back from participation in cooperative ventures.[26]

Episcopal interest in Swedish immigrants had one of its major centers in Minnesota, especially during the tenure of Henry Whipple as Bishop of Minnesota. Whipple had known Gustav Unonius when they both were priests in Chicago, and Whipple had cared for Unonius's St. Ansgarius congregation after Unonius returned to Sweden in 1857. In an address to an Episcopal convention in 1868, Whipple stated:

> The position of the members of the Church of Sweden in our state has long been of deep interest to me. With a valid ministry, a reformed faith, and a

liturgical service, they ought to be in communion with us. For lack of their own Episcopate as a bond of union between them, they are becoming divided.

Whipple, too, saw the Swedish immigrants as social and religiously desirable and sought ways to bring them into the Episcopal fold. In 1897 he reflected, "Often and often I have tried to devise plans whereby these children of a sister church might become fellow heirs with us." Such plans included directing Swedish immigrants to local Episcopal congregations, and later a scheme to bring the Augustana Synod into the Episcopal Church as its own synod with its own bishop. These plans were strenuously opposed by the Augustana Synod.[27]

In 1892 Whipple's dreams began to be realized, when he brought the Swedish American priest Olaf Toffteen to Minneapolis. Toffteen himself echoed much of Whipple's language about the unifying force of the Episcopal Church. In an 1897 article, Toffteen suggested that "The Protestant Episcopal Church's teaching and object are in complete harmony with those of the Church of Sweden and most faithfully represent Swedish Christianity." The Episcopal Church, he added, "offers Swedes a real church . . . with all their praiseworthy Christian activities other denominations can never offer a real church; they are poor works of man doomed to perish." But like the Swedish Congregationalists, Toffteen managed to overlook the real theological and social differences between the two groups. The Swedish Episcopal movement never would become a unifying force resistant to the divisive effects of denominational splintering.[28]

The Swedish Lutherans had a long relationship with one branch of American Lutheranism, the General Council of the Evangelical Lutheran Church of North America, a confederation of regional American Lutheran synods. The Augustana Synod was not a regional synod but a national one and was not always comfortable in the General Council. One main area of friction concerned the issue of "English" home mission work. Most member synods of the General Council were English speaking, but there was no English work going on in the Upper Midwest, a territory closely guarded by the Augustana Synod. As American Lutherans moved into the Upper Midwest, there were no English-language congregations for them to join. In 1883, the General Council sent George Trabert to Minnesota as an English home missionary, and he established congregations in the Twin Cities and Red Wing. In deference to the Augustana Synod, Trabert and his congregations joined the Augustana Synod, but it was an odd connection, for they were not, for the most part, Swedish and had a hard time settling into the Augustana Synod.[29]

Despite Trabert's concessions to Augustana, many Swedes saw his efforts as an attempt to lure younger Swedish Americans into English-speaking congre-

gations and away from the Synod. There were also issues of language preservation and national pride involved, questions that Trabert saw as harmful to the
Lutheran cause as a whole. In 1894 he complained to a sympathetic Augustana
leader, "There is, in my humble opinion, one thing that may eventually do great
harm to the Augustana Synod, and that is a sort of selfish Swedish pride on the
part of some of the younger pastors. . . . here it is Svensk! Svensk! Svensk!" Trabert experienced opposition from foreign-language Lutheran groups: "As soon,
however, as an English Lutheran mission is established, there is not only vigorous protesting, but every effort is put forth to prevent the people from going
to English services. Some pastors would sooner see the children of their people go to the Sunday schools of the sects than to an English Lutheran mission
Sunday School." Trabert and his congregations found their situation within the
Augustana Synod to be a handicap, and in 1891 they left the Augustana Synod
to form the English Lutheran Synod of the Northwest, which was received into
the General Synod.[30]

The Augustana reaction was to pull back from cooperative efforts with the
General Council, and, when in 1918 the General Council merged with other
American Lutheran groups, the Augustana Synod was the only synod not to
participate. But the formation of the English Synod of the Northwest was also
an incentive to Augustana's own English-language work. In 1894, Minnesota
Augustana leader Eric Norelius suggested to a convention of the Minnesota
Conference that the question facing them was this: "Shall we permit English
Lutheran Synods to take over the English work among us, or shall we do this
ourselves, and retain the generation now growing up in our conference and
Synod?" Even so, English-language work remained stalled for another decade,
until the foundation of English-language congregations in the Twin Cities, be-
ginning after 1900.[31]

One interesting evaluation of the Swedish immigrants came from none other
than the Roman Catholic bishop of St. Paul, John Ireland. In 1889, a Roman official sent a message to Cardinal Gibbons in Baltimore, wondering if there were
Swedes in America who might be converted to Roman Catholicism and sent
back to Sweden as missionary priests. Gibbons forwarded the message to Ireland, assuming that he might have some contacts with the Swedish American
community. Ireland wrote back at length with his views on Swedish Americans: "They are intelligent, industrious, aggressive . . . learn English rapidly . . .
they were addicted to drunkenness, but . . . are now the most temperate element of the population, next to the Irish American. I have not seldom spoken
in their temperance gatherings." In addition, Ireland saw the Swedes as ideal
candidates for the Roman Catholic Church, since they accepted "nearly all our
dogmas, claiming the same sacramental system, and freed in America from so-

cial pressure and local conditions. . . . I have always believed that the Church rightly presented to them would gain among them many adherents." Ireland mentioned that he had tried for fifteen years to find priests to work among the Scandinavians, without much success. Here again we find another religious group who viewed the Swedes as ideal candidates for their own denomination, again by elevating the character of the immigrants and minimizing the points of doctrinal disagreement between themselves.[32]

Swedish ethnic denominations and congregations found the Twin Cities to be a vital and sometimes fruitful area for their efforts, and the range of denominational offerings for the immigrants was large. Given the size of the Swedish American community in the Twin Cities, it was imperative that any group wishing to claim Swedish Americans had an important presence in this area. In the Twin Cities too, the leaders of many American denominations looked to the Swedish immigrants in fear or in hope—in fear of being overwhelmed by the rush of immigrants, and in hope of gathering the more desirable Swedish immigrants under their own denominational wing. Some American efforts were successful, at least for a time, but often such efforts were possible only when American denominational leaders, or their Swedish immigrant allies, overlooked the very real religious and social differences between themselves and the new immigrant community. The larger ethnic denominations were more successful at gathering in their fellow immigrants and in differentiating themselves from their American denominational counterparts. Yet they, too, were only partially successful, for much of the Swedish American community remained unaffiliated with their organizations. However, many of the lasting elements of the Swedish American community in the Twin Cities—churches, educational and social institutions, and others—grew out of the efforts of these ethnic denominations.

Perhaps the most striking success of Swedish American religion in the Twin Cities was its ability to adapt and to adopt American forms of religiosity without being totally absorbed into American religion. Religious Swedes avidly raided the American religion culture, but managed to create a strong and particular religious world that combined elements of both Sweden and America but that belonged wholly to neither world.

* * * *

NOTES

1. In addition to the denominational histories of the Swedish American groups, see George M. Stephenson, *The Religious Aspects of Swedish Immigration* (Minneapolis: Univ.

of Minn. Press, 1932); Mark Granquist, "The Swedish Ethnic Denominations in the United States: Their Development and Relationships, 1880–1920" (unpublished Ph.D. diss., Univ. of Chicago, 1992); Frederick Hale, *Trans-Atlantic Conservative Protestantism in the Evangelical Free and Mission Covenant Traditions* (New York: Arno Press, 1979); and Mark Granquist, "Smaller Religious Groups in the Swedish-American Community," *Swedish-American Historical Quarterly* 44 (1993): 217–30.

2. Granquist, "Swedish Ethnic Denominations," 45, table 10. Regarding Swedish influence, see Conrad Bergendoff, "Augustana in America and Sweden," *Swedish Pioneer Historical Quarterly* 24 (1973): 238. One very optimistic report from the turn of the century suggested that the total might reach two-thirds, but such figures are doubtful. O. N. Nelson and J. J. Skordalsvold, "Historical Review of the Scandinavian Churches in Minnesota," in O. N. Nelson, ed., *History of the Scandinavians and Successful Scandinavians in the United States*, 2 vols. (Minneapolis: O. N. Olson and Co., 1901), 1:336.

3. For the history of the Minnesota Conference of the Augustana Synod and the Swedish Lutheran congregations in the Twin Cities, see Emeroy Johnson, *A Church is Planted: The Story of the Lutheran Minnesota Conference, 1851–1876* (Minneapolis: Lutheran Minnesota Conference, 1948), and *God Gave the Growth: the Story of the Lutheran Minnesota Conference, 1878–1958* (Minneapolis: T. S. Denison and Company, 1958); *Referat öfver förhandlingarna vid Luth. Minnesota-Konferensens af Augustana Synoden Sextio-Andra Årsmöte Först Svenska Evangelisk-Lutherska Kyrkan, St. Paul, Minnesota, den 9–15 mars 1920.*

4. Emeroy Johnson, *God Gave the Growth*, 197–200.

5. On the Minnesota Swedish Baptists, see Adolf Olson, *A Centenary History: As Related to the Baptist General Conference of America* (Chicago: Baptist Conference Press, 1952), esp. 174–255; *The Minnesota Baptist Annual, 1920*, Report of the Swedish Conference.

6. Norris A. Magnuson, *Missionskolan: The History of an Immigrant Theological School, Bethel Theological Seminary, 1871–1981* (St. Paul: Bethel Theological Seminary, 1982).

7. On Swedish Methodism in Minnesota, see J. Olson Anders, "A First Step Towards the Organization of Swedish Methodism in Minnesota," *Swedish-American Historical Bulletin* 1 (1928): 76–93; Carl H. Linden, Guds Lilla Skara: *The Story of Swedish Methodism in Minnesota* (Minneapolis: Commission on Archives and History, Minnesota Conference, United Methodist Church, 1983); and Arvid Lakeberg, "A History of Swedish Methodism in America" (unpublished Ph.D. diss., Drew Univ., 1937), esp. 245–88; *Minutes of the Annual Conferences of the Methodist Episcopal Church: Fall Conferences, 1920* (New York: Methodist Book Concern, 1920), 770.

8. On these developments, see Hale, *Trans-Atlantic Conservative Protestantism*; and Karl Olsson, *By One Spirit* (Chicago: Covenant Press, 1962). Although the histories of these two denominations were closely linked, and at times they even discussed a possible merger, there are distinctive differences between the two that have kept them apart.

9. On the Covenant congregations in Minnesota, see Philip J. Anderson, *A Precious Heritage: A Century of Mission in the Northwest, 1884–1984* (Minneapolis: Northwest Conference of the Evangelical Covenant Church, 1984); *Svenksa Evangeliska Missions-Förbundet i Amerika, årsberättelse* (Chicago: 1920).

10. On the Free Church congregations, see H. Wilbert Norton et al., *The Diamond Jubilee Story of the Evangelical Free Church of America* (Minneapolis: Free Church Publications, 1959), and Arnold T. Olson, *The Search for Identity* (Minneapolis: Free Church Press, 1980). On the history of the Twin Cities Free Church congregations, see *Golden Jubilee: Reminiscences of Our Work Under God, Swedish Evangelical Free Church of the U.S.A., 1884–1934* (n.p., 1934), 125–44.

11. On the Swedish Congregationalists, see Olsson, *By One Spirit*, 334–56, and Anderson, *A Precious Heritage*, 68–72; Leal Headley and Merrill E. Jarchow, *Carleton: The First Century* (Northfield, Minn.: Carleton College, 1966), 23; Anderson, *A Precious Heritage*, 70.

12. On the Swedish Episcopalians, see Thomas Burgess, *Swedish Folk Within Our Church: The Rise, Normal Decline and Glorious Results of Half a Century's Work* (New York:

National Council, Department of Missions, 1929), 16-page pamphlet. On the Minnesota parishes, see George Clinton Tanner, *Fifty Years of Church Work in the Diocese of Minnesota, 1857–1907* (St. Paul: n.p., 1907), and E. L. Sheppard, *The Second Fifty Years: The Diocese of Minnesota and the Diocese of Duluth from 1907 to 1957* (Minneapolis: The Diocese of Minnesota, 1972), 50.

13. On Presbyterian work among the Swedes, see Maurice Dwight Edwards, *History of the Synod of Minnesota, Presbyterian Church U.S.A.* (Minneapolis: Synod of Minnesota, Presbyterian Church U.S.A., 1927), 226f.; *Minutes of the General Assembly of the Presbyterian Church in the United States of America, Proceedings of the 113th General Assembly*, n.s. vol. 1, no. 1 (Philadelphia: Office of the General Assembly, 1901). Nelson and Skordalsvold, "Historical Review," suggests that the modest results were purchased with quite an outlay of funds: "A Scandinavian Presbyterian church cost the American Presbyterians about $1000 a year for a half dozen years, or nearly $100 annually for each communicant" (337).

14. On Swedish American Seventh-Day Adventism, see Ingemar Lindén, *Biblicism, apokolyptic, utopi. Adventismens historiska utveckling i USA samt dess svenska utveckling till och med 1939* (Uppsala: Studia Historico-Ecclesiastica Upsaliensis, 1971); and Louis Martin Halswick, *Mission Fields at Home* (Brookfield, Ill.: Pacific Press Publishing Association, n.d.), 43–45.

15. On the Swedish American Pentecostals, see Henry Jauhiainen, "History of the FCA" (tape-recorded lecture), Fellowship of Christian Assemblies, Edmonton, Alberta, Canada, Apr. 1990; Arthur Carl Piepkorn, "Holiness and Pentecostal Groups," in *Profiles in Belief* (San Francisco: Harper and Row, 1979), 3: 152ff.; and Warren L. Heckman, "History of the Fellowship of Christian Assemblies" (unpublished M. A. thesis, Olivet Nazarene Univ., 1994), 61ff. The FCA is the body that continued most of the Independent Assemblies of God (unincorporated); Adolf Olson, *A Centenary History*, 588–91.

16. On the Scandinavian Salvation Army, see William A. Johnson, *O Boundless Salvation: The Story of the Scandinavian Salvation Army in the United States* (New York: Salvation Army Literary Department, 1988); Alfred Söderström, *Minneapolis minnen. Kulturhistorisk axplockning* (Minneapolis: Svenska folkets tidnings förlag, 1901), 9, 242.

17. Söderström, *Minneapolis minnen*, 236f.

18. Anderson, *A Precious Heritage*, 74; George Henry Trabert, *English Lutheranism in the Northwest* (Philadelphia: General Council Publication House, 1914), 68f. Trabert relates a number of similar anecdotes.

19. O. N. Nelson and J. J. Skordalsvold, "Historical Review," 336ff.

20. Burgess, *Swedish Folk*, 7.

21. Granquist, "Swedish Ethnic Denominations," 163–65.

22. On this dynamic, see Frederick Hale, "Nordic Immigration: The New Puritans," *Swedish Pioneer Historical Quarterly* 28 (1977): 27–44, and Norris Magnuson, "Along Kingdom Highways—American Baptists and Swedish Baptist in a Common Mission: An Introductory Essay," *American Baptist Quarterly* 6 (1987): 125–48. On tensions within Methodism, see Carol Norén, "A Study of Wesley's Doctrine of Christian Perfection in the Theology and Method of Nineteenth-Century Methodist Preachers in Northern Illinois, with Particular Emphasis on the Writings of Nels O. Westergreen" (unpublished Ph.D. diss., Princeton Theological Seminary, 1986).

23. M. W. Montgomery, *A Wind from the Holy Spirit in Sweden and Norway* (New York: American Home Missionary Society, 1885), 6, 7.

24. A. P. Nelson, *Svenska Missionsvännernas i Amerika Historia* (Minneapolis: Utgifven på författarens eget förlag, 1906), quoted in Olsson, *By One Spirit*, 339f.

25. See Lawrence B. Davis, *Immigrants, Baptists, and the Protestant Mind in America* (Urbana: Univ. of Ill. Press, 1973), esp. 106, 108f.; and Virgil Olson, "An Interpretation of the Historical Relationships Between the American Baptist Convention and the Baptist General Conference," *American Baptist Quarterly* 6 (1987): 156–71.

26. Adolf Olson, *A Centenary History*, 591–93.

27. Henry Benjamin Whipple, *Lights and Shadows of a Long Episcopate: Being Reminiscences and Recollections* (New York: MacMillan Co., 1899), 434, 435. On relations between the Augustana Synod and the Episcopalians, see Hugo Söderström, *Confession and Cooperation: The Policy of the Augustana Synod in Confessional Matters and the Synod's Relations with Other Churches up to the Beginnings of the Twentieth Century* (Lund: CWK Gleerup Bokförlag, 1973).

28. Olaf Toffteen, "De två syster-kyrkorna," *Kyrkotidningen* (Worcester, Mass., June 2, 1897), quoted in Oscar Olson, *The Augustana Lutheran Church in America 1860–1910: The Formative Period* (Davenport, Iowa: Arcade Office and Letter Service, 1956), 37.

29. See Söderström, *Confession and Cooperation*, esp. 138–58.

30. G. H. Trabert to P. Sjöblom, Nov. 5, 1894, quoted in Emeroy Johnson, *God Gave the Growth*, 218; Trabert, *English Lutheranism*, 69f.

31. Eric Norelius, *Referat* (Minnesota Conference, 1894), quoted in G. Everett Arden, *Augustana Heritage: History of the Augustana Lutheran Church* (Rock Island, Ill.: Augustana Press, 1963), 241f.

32. John Ireland to James Gibbons, Dec. 5, 1889, quoted in Marvin R. O'Connell, *John Ireland and the American Catholic Church* (St. Paul: MHS Press, 1988), 266.

Ethnicity and Religion in the Twin Cities:
Community Identity through Gospel,
Music, and Education

SCOTT E. ERICKSON

In his autobiography, Carl V. Bowman wrote that Erik August Skogsbergh often described Minneapolis as a "glorious city," where great possibilities existed for Christian ministry and for the building of Swedish American institutions. Bowman, who served as president of the Mission Covenant Church from 1927 to 1933, remembered that Skogsbergh described the Twin Cities as the "center of the universe." For a large number of Swedish immigrants during the latter part of the nineteenth century, the Twin Cities had become a new home and a lively center of activity. Earlier Swedish American rural settlements had been supplemented by these urban enclaves. Common religion, politics, culture, language, and traditions allowed Swedish Americans to express ethnicity in their immigrant community and through institutional form.[1]

Many of these ethnic settlements consisted of people connected by shared religious experiences. The present focus is on those immigrants associated with the Swedish renewal movement among Mission Friends. Many of them participated in efforts to revitalize the state-established Church of Sweden, while at the same time they did not join religious bodies more directly inspired by Anglo-American influences—for example, the Baptists and Methodists. In 1856 they were involved in the establishment of *Evangeliska Fosterlands Stiftelsen* (the Evangelical National Foundation), a national organization that coordinated neo-evangelical activities in Sweden and was an official, yet voluntary, association within the bounds of the state church. The leaders of the foundation, among them Hans Jakob Lundborg and Carl Olof Rosenius, perceived this organization as their ideal of a church within a church. Although they generally supported the state church's Lutheran devotion and theology, members of the foundation were skeptical of any church policy that employed birthright membership as a means whereby God's grace was mediated. Instead, they considered religious conversion as the "one thing needful" for salvation. In the 1870s, some Mission Friends began more strongly to question church tradition, doctrine, and confession, as well as state-established religion. Paul Peter Waldenström challenged the Church of Sweden's atonement doctrine in 1872–73 and argued for a nonconfessional stance. In 1878, Carl Johan Nyvall and Erik J. Ekman proposed the founding of an association more independent than the Evangelical National Foundation, and the Mission Covenant Church of Sweden was born.[2]

In America, many Swedish immigrants were associated with the Augustana Synod. Founded in 1860 and generally consisting of Swedish (and, until 1870, Norwegian) Lutherans, the synod adhered strongly to the Augsburg Confession and developed rather clear guidelines on membership and doctrine. Mission Friends, most of whom arrived in America after the Civil War, wished to express their religion in a manner different from those who founded the Augustana Synod. Events in Sweden had recharted the religious map in the homeland and among Swedish immigrants. Waldenström's ecclesiastical challenges in the 1870s initiated questions about theological freedom, and many Mission Friends in America supported Waldenström's views while confessional Augustana leaders and ministers generally did not. Active missionary work among Swedish Americans was also undertaken by non-Lutheran groups, for example, the Baptists and Methodists.[3]

Thus, as migration from Sweden increased to high levels in the 1880s, many Swedish immigrants who arrived in the Twin Cities were concerned about religion and the communal expression of their Christian faith. Mission Friends often sought out conventicles, or small group-meetings, held in homes throughout Minneapolis and St. Paul. They were inspired by Rosenius to gather for Bible study and prayer. They were not dramatically anti-Augustana, as their devotional life was generally Lutheran, but were caught up in the currents of theological freedom and remained unsure about the necessity of formal church membership. In 1874, a group of Minneapolis Mission Friends gathered to organize a non-Augustana body, "The Swedish Evangelical Lutheran Mission Church," which would later become the Swedish Tabernacle, and is presently First Covenant Church.[4]

The establishment of immigrant communities and Swedish American churches is related to the central problem that confronted all immigrant groups, that is, identity. Ethnic institutions, including churches, were the result of the desire of immigrants to preserve Swedish heritage while somehow relating to the adopted country. One cannot blame them for seeking mutual contact in homes, stores, secular associations, historical societies, churches, and schools. After all, prevailing rhetoric and societal pressure suggested that immigrants could indeed be uprooted from their homeland and should be integrated rapidly into American culture, that is, melted into the diverse American pot. Working against these pressures, immigrants were active in communities where there was a lively interaction of people and innovation of ethnic traditions. Even if a majority of them did not write eloquently about ethnicity, many were involved in the process of defining a common ethnic identity. Religion played a key role in ethnic identity and in helping Swedish Americans in the Twin Cities develop a shared immigrant vocabulary.[5]

This shared ethnicity, or communal expression of religion and Swedish American ethnicity, was often shaped by immigrant leaders, who mediated between their Swedish compatriots and those outside Swedish American enclaves. John Higham has written that ethnic leaders worked with the "consolidation and maintenance of [America's] ethnic groups," and served a "mediating function, weaving a web of ethnic mutuality on the one hand and encouraging their people to reach beyond it on the other." In the same line of thinking, Victor Greene has called ethnic leaders "mediating brokers" between immigrant communities and American society. Like conduits, these leaders conveyed information and influenced their people to define ethnic and religious identity through a shaping of community life, rather than allowing their identity to disintegrate into the chaos of melting pots and unavailing assimilation.[6]

From the mid-1880s until after the turn of the century, three immigrants from Värmland, Sweden, were key leaders among Mission Friends in the Twin Cities. Erik August Skogsbergh (1850–1939), Andrew L. Skoog (1856–1934), and David Nyvall (1863–1946) were community developers in the Twin Cities. They did not negotiate, but rather mediated, their own ethnic identity and that of their community. They taught the Mission Friends how to express their religion and ethnicity through gospel, music, and education. This essay addresses the relationship between these leaders and focuses on the means through which they contributed to immigrant identity: Skogsbergh through preaching, Skoog through music, and Nyvall through education. The importance of religion in understanding ethnicity in the Twin Cities is evident through the efforts of these leaders to define the nature of Swedish American community life.[7]

Each of these immigrant leaders from Värmland found their way to Skogsbergh's "center of the universe" within the first year of their arrival in the United States. Skoog, the future song leader, was the first to arrive. His father preceded the family over the ocean, and in 1869 Andrew emigrated to St. Paul with his mother and siblings. His education was very basic and sporadic, for his assistance was required in the family's tailoring business. He also studied music, but this, too, was intermittent. Skoog had time for only twelve lessons on a small reed organ; his other tasks did not allow for much formal training.[8]

In 1876 Skogsbergh arrived in the United States. He had accepted a call to serve as preacher at the North Side Mission Church on Franklin Street in Chicago, a position that required him to immigrate from Sweden, which he did following many weeks of indecision. He first collaborated with J. M. Sanngren, pioneer preacher and president of the Mission Synod, an association of non-Augustana congregations that was organized in 1873. The ailing Sanngren sought Skogsbergh's assistance with his ministry among Swedes in the Chicago area. Before long, Skogsbergh was known as a stunning preacher and great evangelist, and the church building on Franklin Street was deemed too small for the crowds he attracted. He therefore asked the American revival preacher Dwight L. Moody if his large auditorium could be used for a Swedish service on Sunday afternoons. This request was granted, and Skogsbergh began preaching to large crowds in the 10,000-seat church. Promptly nicknamed "the Swedish Moody," Skogsbergh was leading a Swedish-language revival that rivaled the success of Moody's services in English.[9]

Skogsbergh's revival was increasingly dissimilar to the Rosenian form, which was identified by small conventicle meetings in candlelit homes and chapels. In contrast, Skogsbergh was a lively, busy evangelist who attracted great attention in his new country, as evidenced by the large worship spaces he required. The small mission chapel in Chicago had insufficient space, and he preferred a large American auditorium. Having moved across the city to establish a new work in 1877, he soon convinced his own congregation to construct a tabernacle for Swedish immigrants on the south side of Chicago. Skogsbergh noted that his revival "success" in Chicago would not have been possible in Sweden. He reflected later that he appreciated the spontaneity found in American cities, including the positive aspects that allowed for a wealth of possibilities and the negative aspects that forced him to confront a complex and foreign society. Skogsbergh was seldom dismayed because, he wrote, "everything is successful in America."[10]

But the popular evangelist could not long avoid the "center of the universe." Less than a year following his arrival in Chicago, he sought to take a vacation from his preaching duties. This opportunity for rest turned into a "Macedonian call" to preach in the fall of 1877. He gave up his vacation plans because he "felt a special urging toward Minneapolis" and believed that "a revival was imminent." Indeed, it would have been uncharacteristic for "the Swedish Moody" to give up the opportunity to lead a religious revival. While in the Twin Cities, he noticed two difficulties that confronted Mission Friends. First, their communities were served by preachers who were too few in number, forcing them to travel great distances among a growing number of congregations. The number of activities and the needs on the field outweighed the trained workers. Financial resources and organizational structures did not exist. Skogsbergh worried that many Mission Friends were not connected to a common church life and a wider immigrant community.[11]

Second, Skogsbergh was deeply concerned about the spiritual status of the increasing number of Swedish immigrants in the Twin Cities. He had already set dozens of revival fires ablaze in Chicago, and he sought to do the same during his crusade in the Northwest. He gained much inspiration from Moody in desiring to help as many as possible experience a religious conversion. It did not matter how they were brought to Christ as long as they got there as quickly as possible. Writing about these spiritually hungry Swedish Americans, Karl A. Olsson noted that "people wanted God." And Skogsbergh was prepared to convey this gospel message in a blazing manner. He described the climax of his revival services as "a battlefield after a bloody engagement." Continuing, he noted: "Wherever one looked, people lay in the pews or hung like dishrags over the backs. Everywhere could be heard the weeping and sobbing of people who were asking earnestly what they could do to be saved. Believers from the various churches had learned to participate in the work for the salvation of souls."[12]

One young man who heard Skogsbergh's message and responded like so many others was Andrew Skoog, who had been living in the Twin Cities for eight years. Skoog's mother, out of concern for her son's spiritual state, entreated Skogsbergh to employ her son as an organist for his worship services. She claimed that if Andrew were not used for Christ's work, he would serve the secular world through a career in the theater. Skogsbergh obliged, and Andrew soon

Reverend Erik August   *Andrew L. Skoog, hymnwriter,*
Skogsbergh, 1897   *composer, and publisher*

experienced a religious conversion. The meeting of Skogsbergh and Skoog initiated a lifelong partnership. Together, they would shape religious and ethnic community life among Mission Friends; Skogsbergh concentrated on the gospel and Skoog on the music.[13]

Gospel and music, as ways to express Swedish American religion and ethnicity, were part of the Mission Friend community in Chicago, a city to which Skogsbergh convinced Skoog to relocate in 1879, despite the fact that the song leader moved without any assurance of full-time work or salary. In the next several years, their cooperation produced a variety of results: a large Swedish tabernacle was built on the south side of Chicago; revival meetings were undertaken in other parts of the Midwest; song groups were organized; music programs were developed; a school for Swedish Americans was founded; a Swedish songbook was published (*Evangelii Basun*, 1883); and the Mission Covenant denomination was founded in 1885, the organizational meeting of which was held at the tabernacle.[14]

But Skogsbergh was not one to tarry in one place if he sensed that God was leading him to start a revival somewhere else. He believed that he best served God by establishing his evangelical revival center in Minneapolis, becoming pastor of the small congregation that had been organized in 1874 and to which he was called early in 1884. After eighteen months, Skoog, the increasingly well-known song leader, joined "the Swedish Moody" in the Twin Cities. By the time Skoog arrived in the summer of 1885, Skogsbergh had already initiated many activities, including a building program. After all, the preacher was inspired by an America where many things were big and busy, including revival programs and churches. He planned to erect the largest Swedish American tabernacle in existence by convincing the immigrants in Minneapolis to take the necessary financial risks. He already had "revealed" this vision during his 1877 revival, at a time when, as he later noted, "the news fell like a bomb on the people." In 1884, now appointed pastor and spiritual shepherd, Skogsbergh proved his skill at raising funds within one month of his arrival, and plans were drawn under his close scrutiny. The ground floor was completed in 1886, and the Swedish Tabernacle was dedicated in the fall of 1887. The construction of this place of worship was not an attempt to impress people with a grand and "stately temple." Rather, Skogsbergh wanted his congregation to have a "practical" American auditorium in which many could gather. Function, not style, was paramount.[15]

The preacher did not concentrate his efforts exclusively on the construction of a large tabernacle. During his pastorate of this significant church for almost twenty-five years, Skogsbergh traveled extensively on preaching and revival missions, seeking to establish and care for new churches while giving encouragement to his colleagues in ministry. His entrepreneurial bent, coupled with tireless journeys to every corner of the district, led him to envisage many activities that joined congregations and pastors into a common mission program. Under Skogsbergh's leadership, the Northwestern Missionary Association had been formally established as early as 1884, four months earlier than the organization of the Covenant Church. With some humor, Skogsbergh claimed to be the "Bishop of Minneapolis," partly because of the several new Covenant churches in the city that grew out of his Swedish Tabernacle.

While many were uncertain (or even jealous) of his intentions and successes, and even though Skogsbergh often did act independently, his ambitions paved the way for many district and national organizations among Covenanters. He was not to be out-maneuvered by either people or conflicting events. He believed that all gatherings of immigrant people were opportunities to build Swedish American religious culture—a work he believed would grow because of a vigorous revival attitude. Ethnicity and religion, as developed by first-generation immigrants, was an inheritance to pass on to the second and third generations. This inheritance was not expressed in buildings, but rather through a living culture in which conversion was the "one thing needful" and living a Christian life the goal. Skogsbergh was clear in his conviction that immigrants were living a "pioneer life" and that what they built would bear fruit in future generations.[16]

As an immigrant community leader, Skogsbergh also sought to express a shared religious vocabulary. He believed that the proclamation of the gospel was the best way to pass on a Swedish American religious inheritance. Further, the building of immigrant institutions was the best way to pass on a Swedish American ethnic inheritance. Erik Dahlhielm, the preacher's biographer, stated that Skogsbergh did this with the flurry of a "hurricane." If he were too inactive, would that not look like religious idleness? Dahlhielm provided an even more revealing interpretation when he noted one of the reasons why the preacher could carry on hurricane-like activities: "Skogsbergh supplied the ideas, the energy, the inspiration. Skoog did the work—most of the work, at any rate."[17]

Indeed, much of the time, Skogsbergh was the one to initiate and Skoog the one to implement. With great precision and attention to detail, Skoog organized his colleague's vision, ideas, and creations into workable routines. In the Twin Cities, as in Chicago, he was intimately involved with Sunday school, an American-inspired Christian education program. He also did most of the editorial work for *Söndagskol-Vännen* (The Sunday School Friend), a children's paper founded by Skogsbergh in 1886. Because of the careful administration provided by Skoog and others, the Sunday school programs in the district and denomination received timely attention and development.[18]

In 1884, Skogsbergh began publishing a Swedish American religious newspaper, *Svenska Kristna Härolden* (The Swedish Christian Herald), which was renamed *Minneapolis Veckoblad* (The Minneapolis Weekly) in the fall of 1887. Skoog published a wide variety of religious materials, and this newspaper was a major communication link for many Swedish Americans. While it certainly had competitors, the weekly's long life (from 1884 to 1934) is a witness to the significant role its journalists played in the dissemination of information, devotional materials, and matters of interest to the immigrant community.

Skoog's publishing efforts converged with his desire to develop the musical life of Swedish Americans at the Tabernacle and in the wider Mission Covenant Church. A volume of hymns was published in 1889 (*Evangelii Basun II*) and was followed a year later by a songbook for Sunday schools (*Lilla Basun*). In 1891 a book of choral music was added to the increasing number of Skoog's copyrights. That same year, the Skoog Publishing Company began operations in Minneapolis, and several books, hymnals, and choral music pieces rolled off the printing press. Skoog's music journal, *Gittit*, offered advice to church musicians and new material for their choirs and congregations. This plethora of activity and productivity evidences a great versatility, one of Skoog's traits that most impressed Theodore W. Anderson, president of Minnehaha Academy in Minneapolis and future president of the Mission Covenant Church, and many others. During his years in the Twin Cities, Skoog proved himself to be an accomplished editor, translator, publisher, composer, teacher, fundraiser, and choral leader. His music helped immigrants express their Christian faith through song, and this would bear fruit in future generations. As a community leader, Skoog developed a religious musical culture that allowed many Swedish Americans to participate in worship and relate to their Christian faith. Religion, as expressed through music, bound immigrants together within their ethnic community.[19]

Skoog's ethnicity and religion were public, not private, issues. His published music was used in his own tabernacle choirs and through congregational singing at services led by Skogsbergh. Like Ira Sankey, though not as famous, Skoog wanted to encourage lively and robust congregational singing as a complement to the preaching of his colleague. Like J. S. Bach, though not as prolific, Skoog translated, transcribed, and composed music for the church. Like F. Melius Christensen (who as a young Norwegian-immigrant music student often attended the Swedish Tabernacle just to hear Skoog's choirs), though probably not as precise, Skoog led choirs. This was a task for which he lacked training, according to his own critique. He reflected later: "I actually knew nothing about choral conducting, but I reasoned thus: First and foremost, singers need a little knowledge about sight-reading, and in any event, I was so far advanced in music

that I could keep myself ahead of them." Regardless of his own feelings of in-
adequacy, reports of excellent singing in the filled-to-capacity Tabernacle reveal his manner of leading choirs and congregations in song. And the statistics
are impressive. One of his children's choirs had 500 members. During a festival
in 1901, Skoog led a combined choir of 300 singers. A reunion choir in 1908 had
a list of 400 names. He also gave instruction in singing and lectured his choral
singers on how to become skilled in "hitting the tone," as he called it. One so-
prano in Chicago hit the tones quite well, and she became Skoog's wife. Many
in his choirs, however, were not so accomplished in "tone-hitting," but Skoog
was undaunted. In Christian worship, "spiritual tonality" was more important
than absolute or perfect pitch.[20]

When David Nyvall arrived in Minneapolis in the fall of 1886, Skoog gained
a colleague to assist in the implementation of Skogsbergh's hurricane of ideas.
Nyvall had voyaged to America to visit his father, Carl Johan Nyvall, the respected Swedish preacher who was then traveling in the United States. Two
months after his arrival, the twenty-three-year-old Nyvall preached the opening sermon at the Mission Covenant Church's annual meeting in Rockford,

Skoog's children's choir, Swedish Tabernacle, Minneapolis, ca. 1895

Illinois. Following the service, Skogsbergh offered Nyvall a teaching position at his immigrant school in Minneapolis. Nyvall accepted and gave his first lectures at "Skogsbergh's School." Thus, as the preacher was dreaming up new methods with which to impact the Northwest district with the gospel, and while Skoog spent a good deal of time publishing music, Nyvall concentrated his efforts on shaping Swedish American education. People needed a school and an educator to lead it, and Nyvall seemed the appropriate person to develop an academic strategy.

Classes at "Skogsbergh's School" were first held in the pastor's home. When Nyvall arrived in the Twin Cities, his classroom was a store and eventually a room in the basement of the Tabernacle. Skogsbergh had not been intrinsically interested in the training of preachers, although pastors could supplement their education at this school. He mainly sought, however, to provide general coursework for immigrants and their children. Nyvall designed the course schedule to include English language and grammar, American history, United States geography, music, business, religion, Swedish language, and Swedish history. This was a "practical Christian school," with a beneficial curriculum for Swedish Americans who longed for knowledge about the language and history of their inherited Swedish culture, as well as the language, history, and culture of their adopted country. Non-English speakers learned English so they could function outside the Swedish American community. Non-Swedish speakers learned Swedish in order to understand Skogsbergh's sermons in church. Nyvall also offered courses in religion as part of his vision to teach Mission Friends about their religious heritage, eventually hoping to offer training for ministers associated with the Mission Covenant Church.[21]

Nyvall's school in Minneapolis was certainly not similar to Uppsala University, where he had engaged in higher studies. Rather, he was required to study many subjects in preparation for lectures that dealt with a wide range of topics. He stated later that he taught "everything" he "could persuade anybody to learn." C. V. Bowman, a student of Nyvall's, wrote in his autobiography about the difficulties the teacher faced while disseminating knowledge to immigrants with little or no educational background. Nyvall attempted to "awaken thought" and "sharpen insight" in the frigid winter temperatures of his classroom. Despite this cold environment and some frozen (or inactive) brain cells, Nyvall's classroom was warm with ideas and humming with activity. Bowman continued:

> It was . . . cold in Professor Nyvall's classes when King Boreas made his great incursion through Minneapolis. . . . The respected man, with unruly hair, thin beard, and nose red from the cold, taught in a fur coat with his cap in one coat pocket and his mittens in the other, and we students sat there stiff

and blue so that not even our thoughts wanted to move. Under such conditions how can one give an account of everything D. A. Sundén has to say
about Swedish grammar? Of course the professor had it all at his five frozen
fingertips and thought that we should have been able to get it into our brains.
How we clambered and tripped over the language roots! How we fumbled
and stumbled through the exercises with sentences and verbs! At times the
answers were so stupid that even Job would have lost his patience; no wonder then if Professor Nyvall lost his! And sometimes they were so foolish
that the whole class exploded with laughter and the teacher could not resist
joining.[22]

The Swedish American community was supported through the learning
that went on in Nyvall's classroom. His work with education indicated his and
the community's attention to the intellectual development of Swedish American young people. Nyvall critically considered the role of general and religious
education in his ethnic community. He wrote about the combination of Swedish
and American themes in a curriculum that would prepare immigrants for making contributions to American society. He reminded his compatriots that cultural assimilation and melting pots were not the goals of an emerging ethnic
identity. Rather, building on the work of Skogsbergh, Skoog, and Nyvall, the
immigrant community would sharpen its understanding of both its ethnic heritage and its migration experience through immigrant community life and culture, religion and education, song, and literature.[23]

The educational convictions of Nyvall, Skogsbergh, and Skoog went beyond the Minneapolis geography, as "Skogsbergh's School" was offered to the
Mission Covenant Church as the site for the denomination's academy and seminary. This offer made it possible for the denomination to train its ministers and
offer general education to its lay people starting in 1891. But from the beginning
the Minneapolis location was considered temporary, and Nyvall realized that
the school needed its own space for its increasing number of students. While
Skogsbergh hastened to secure a building in the Minneapolis area, a favorable
proposal of land, a building, and an endowment was offered by a group of
Swedish Americans in Chicago. The denomination accepted this offer, and the
school—eventually named North Park University—moved south in 1894. This
relocation from the "center of the universe" was not accepted favorably by Skogsbergh, who retaliated by organizing a new school, Northwestern College and
Bible Institute.[24]

Even as Nyvall moved south, Swedish Americans in the Twin Cities contin-
ued to discuss their educational needs. In 1905 a group of leading Minneapolis
Covenant people met under the leadership of Daniel Magnus, a graduate of
Carleton College, to initiate discussions on the establishment of a Christian

high school. The Minnehaha Academy Association was organized, and Skoog, along with many others, worked tirelessly to raise money for a building and to increase interest in the founding of the school. Minnehaha Academy opened its doors on September 15, 1913.[25]

As Swedish migration to America reached its highest levels in the two decades prior to the turn of the twentieth century, three Swedes from Värmland were building and developing immigrant community life in the Twin Cities. Numerous activities informed the traditions Skogsbergh, Skoog, and Nyvall helped shape among Swedish Americans in the Twin Cities: the thousands of people who attended morning and evening services at the Tabernacle; the tons of newspapers and musical scores that were published; the large choirs and their weekly rehearsals; the hundreds of children who studied Swedish and English in school; the countless youth who listened to lectures about Swedish history and American history; and the numerous ministerial meetings and conferences.

For many of these Swedish Americans, in seeking to define their identity in the New World and perhaps realizing that they were unsure exactly how to do so, their community in the Twin Cities must have seemed like a "center of the universe." And for them it was. It was their ethnic home. The Mission Friends knew they were no longer living in their home country of Sweden. At the same time they were pilgrims who wished to express their religion and who generally valued America, but they were unwilling to accept being forced into the chaos of a melting pot, thereby losing their religious and ethnic identity. After all, they were reminded, as Scandinavian Americans, of their cultural inheritance from a time when there were "giants in the earth" (Ole Edvart Rølvaag). These were a thoughtful people who appreciated Esaias Tegnér's poem *Svea*, with its patriotic descriptions of Sweden, and who also responded by joining the army in large numbers when the United States entered World War I. They sang the Swedish revival hymns with the same vigor as when they joined Skoog in the singing of Swedish translations of Bliss and Sankey songs. They attended Skogsbergh's church, but also attended the revival meetings led by Moody. Although Swedish was their daily language during much of the first generation, many of the immigrants learned English and sought to educate their children in English and Swedish by sending them to Nyvall's lectures and Skoog's "Swede School" for children. Their newspapers reported American news as well as information from the homeland. Thus, life was a daily dialectic—both Sweden and America defined them. When they asked themselves if they were Swedes or Americans, they probably looked to their developing ethnic and religious culture—to gospel, music, and education—as the means by which they were preserving Sweden and embracing America at the same time. They looked to

Skogsbergh, Skoog, and Nyvall for leadership and found that within this di-
alectical immigrant identity they shared a common ethnicity and religious
vocabulary.

In order to illustrate this immigrant identity process, it is important to note
another Skogsbergh innovation, that is, his retreat center on the north shore of
the West Arm, a bay on Lake Minnetonka. Although this plot was originally intended as a summer home for his family, it became a well-used community resort for immigrants. As a summer conference center for Swedish Americans,
Skogsbergh's Point offered programs very similar to John H. Vincent's summer
workshops, which developed into programming offered by the Chautauqua
Institution in western New York. Skogsbergh's ideal was also similar to that of
Moody's work at his conference grounds in Northfield, Massachusetts. On Lake
Minnetonka, people had the opportunity to engage in religious worship services, biblical lectureships, recreation, theological discussions, and singing services. They were inspired by the gospel through preaching, moved by their
musical heritage through singing, and challenged by intellectual discussions
while walking in Skogsbergh's orchards.[26]

Skogsbergh's Point was a microcosm of the larger immigrant community. It
was a place where people experienced and lived the ethnic dialectic, where
they shared a common religious heritage and ethnicity. The community language contained a vocabulary influenced by gospel, music, and education. This
shared religion and ethnicity informed immigrant identity and defined their
community; it was also an inheritance that would be passed on to future generations. Changes of the religious revival in Sweden and disconcerting pressures of the migration experience in America did not jettison ethnic structures
into chaos. Rather, for the Mission Friends in the Twin Cities, ethnic identity
was shaped in the context of a religious community that was defined, in part,
through the leadership of Skogsbergh, Skoog, and Nyvall.

* * * *

NOTES

1. Carl V. Bowman, *Son of the People: The Autobiography of C. V. Bowman* (Chicago:
Covenant Publications, [1989]), 187.

2. Karl A. Olsson, *By One Spirit* (Chicago: Covenant Press, 1962), 81–87; Axel Andersson, *Svenska Missionsförbundet. Dess uppkomst och femtioårliga verksamhet, Inre missionen*
(Stockholm, 1928), 27–31.

3. Hugo Söderström, *Confession and Cooperation: The Policy of the Augustana Synod in
Confessional Matters and the Synod's Relations with other Churches up to the Beginning of the*

Twentieth Century (Lund, 1973), 56–69. Cf. Olsson, *By One Spirit*, 181–96; Carl V. Bowman, *The Mission Covenant of America* (Chicago: Covenant Book Concern, 1925), 19–32.

4. Philip J. Anderson, *A Precious Heritage: A Century of Mission in the Northwest, 1884–1984* (Minneapolis: The Northwest Conference, 1984), 25.

5. For example, note the terminology of J. Hector St. John de Crèvecoeur, *Letters from an American Farmer* [1782] (New York, 1957), 39; Israel Zangwill, *The Melting Pot* (New York, 1909). For representative sources in which scholars suggest an older immigration historiography (preoccupied with the notion that Swedes quickly assimilated into or adjusted to American society), see Adolph B. Benson, "The Assimilation of Swedes in America," *Swedish Pioneer Historical Quarterly* 7 (1956): 139; Oscar A. Benson, "Problems in the Accommodation of the Swede to American Culture," *University of Pittsburgh Bulletin* 30 (1933): 47. Cf. Gene Lund, "The Americanization of the Augustana Lutheran Church" (unpublished Ph.D. diss., Princeton Univ., 1954); Carl M. Rosenquist, "The Swedes of Texas" [1930], in *A Report on World Population Migrations: As Related to the United States of America* (Washington, D.C., 1956). Martin E. Marty has written that "ethnicity is the skeleton of religion in America because it provides 'the supporting framework,' 'the bare outlines or main features,' of American religion" ("Ethnicity: The Skeleton of Religion in America," *Church History* 41 [1972]: 9).

6. John Higham, "Leadership," in *Harvard Encyclopedia of American Ethnic Groups*, ed. Stephan Thernstrom (Cambridge: Harvard Univ. Press, 1980), 642, 646. Cf. John Higham, *Send These to Me: Immigrants in Urban America* (Baltimore: Johns Hopkins Univ. Press, 1975); *Ethnic Leadership in America*, ed. John Higham (Baltimore: John Hopkins Univ. Press, 1978); Victor Greene, "'Becoming American': The Role of Ethnic Leaders—Swedes, Poles, Italians, Jews," in *The Ethnic Frontier: Essays in the History of Group Survival in Chicago and the Midwest*, eds. Melvin G. Holli and Peter d'A. Jones (Grand Rapids, Mich.: Eerdmans, 1977), 144–75.

7. For a biography of Skogsbergh, see Erik Dahlhielm, *A Burning Heart: A Biography of Erik August Skogsbergh* (Chicago: Covenant Book Concern, 1951). For the life of Skoog, see E. Gustav Johnson, *A. L. Skoog: Covenant Hymn-Writer and Composer* (Chicago: Covenant Book Concern, 1937); Oscar E. Olson, "A. L. Skoog: Pioneer Musician of the Evangelical Mission Covenant of America" (unpublished M.M. thesis, Northwestern Univ., 1941); Skoog Papers 4:7, Covenant Archives and Historical Library, North Park Univ., Chicago; Hjalmar Sundquist, "A. L. Skoog," *Covenant Weekly*, Dec. 4, 1934, 5. For treatments of David Nyvall, see Philip J. Anderson, "David Nyvall and Swedish-American Education," in *Swedish-American Life in Chicago: Cultural and Urban Aspects of an Immigrant People, 1850–1930*, eds. Philip J. Anderson and Dag Blanck (Urbana and Chicago: Univ. of Ill. Press, 1992), 327–42; Leland H. Carlson, "David Nyvall—An Appreciation," *Our Covenant* 17 (1942): 33–43; Steven Elde, "The Hearth and the Chimney: Covenant Attitudes Toward Education," *The Covenant Quarterly* 49 (1991): 3–43; Scott E. Erickson, *David Nyvall and the Shape of an Immigrant Church: Ethnic, Denominational, and Educational Priorities among Swedes in America* (Uppsala: Acta Universitatis Upsaliensis, 1996); Scott E. Erickson, "Ethnic and Religious Education in Swedish America: David Nyvall and the Nature of Academic Culture for Immigrants," *Swedish-American Historical Quarterly* 47 (1996): 197–217; Zenos E. Hawkinson, "The Pietist Schoolman," in *Amicus Dei: Essays on Faith and Friendship*, ed. Philip J. Anderson (Chicago: Covenant Publications, 1988), 96–108.

8. Johnson, *Skoog*, 6.

9. For discussions on Skogsbergh as "the Swedish Moody," see Anderson, *Precious Heritage*, 37; Herbert E. Palmquist, *The Wit and Wisdom of Our Fathers: Sketches from the Life of an Immigrant Church* (Chicago: Covenant Press, 1967), 87.

10. Dahlhielm, *Burning Heart*, 56–85; Erik August Skogsbergh, *Minnen och upplevelser under min mer än femtioåriga predikoverksamhet* (Minneapolis, 1923), 180.

11. Erik August Skogsbergh, *Ett tjugofemårsminne* (Minneapolis, 1899), 26. Manuscript trans. by Karl A. Olsson, E. A. Skogsbergh Papers 1:17, Covenant Archives and Historical Library. Anderson, *Precious Heritage*, 27f.

12. Skogsbergh, *Minnen*, 149–60. Cf. Skogsbergh, *Ett tjugofemårsminne*, 26–29; Olsson, *By One Spirit*, 463. For a narrative about Skogsbergh's first preaching tour of the Twin Cities, see Dahlhielm, *Burning Heart*, 63–73; Skogsbergh, *Ett tjugofemårsminne*, 27. Cf. Skogsbergh's description of revival meetings as "battlefields" in *Minnen*, 98.

13. Skogsbergh, "Minnen," 160f. Cf. Dahlhielm, *Burning Heart*, 65f. Skoog called Skogsbergh his "spiritual father" and credited the preacher with allowing his work to bear so much fruit. Andrew L. Skoog, "Minnen från min körverksamhet," 17, Covenant Archives and Historical Library.

14. Skoog, "Minnen," 4–10.

15. Skogsbergh, *Ett tjugofemårsminne*, 31; Skogsbergh, *Minnen*, 195–203, 208f.

16. Anderson, *Precious Heritage*, 36–43. As a matter of fact, there were very few occasions when Skogsbergh was out-maneuvered by other church leaders or members of his church. The eventual move of the Covenant school to Chicago in 1894 was one occasion when Skogsbergh's view did not rule the day. For insight into aspects of Skogsbergh's personality, see Skogsbergh, *Ett tjugofemårsminne*, 9; Anderson, *Precious Heritage*, 37; Skogsbergh, *Minnen*, 167f.

17. In his *Memoirs*, Skogsbergh often mentions his revival work. He calls it fishing and hunting for souls, or sowing and harvesting the conversion crop. Skogsbergh, *Minnen*, 274f. Cf. Skogsbergh, *Ett tjugofemårsminne*, 20–26; Dahlhielm, *Burning Heart*, 80, 145.

18. Dahlhielm, *Burning Heart*, 112.

19. Although many of Skoog's texts were available in Swedish, it is interesting to note that his work went generally unnoticed in Sweden, even in Svenska Missionsförbundet (Mission Covenant Church of Sweden) circles. Concerning the American Covenant, twelve Skoog hymns were published in the hymnal used until 1973. In the American Covenant hymnal published in 1996, four Skoog hymns and four of his translations are available. The Swedish hymnal presently used in most Mission Covenant churches, *Psalmer och Sånger*, contains only one Skoog hymn, "Snart randas en dag" (We Wait for a Great and Glorious Day); Skoog, "Minnen," 11–15. Cf. Anderson, *Precious Heritage*, 39; Palmquist, *Wit and Wisdom*, 193.

20. Skoog, "Minnen," 9. Although Skoog lamented his lack of musical training, Skogsbergh wrote that the song leader was "born a composer" (Skogsbergh, *Minnen*, 180). Skoog, "Minnen," 3, 14–16; lecture by A. L. Skoog, MS., Skoog Papers 3:21, Covenant Archives and Historical Library.

21. Erik August Skogsbergh, "Minneapolis kristliga skola för unga män," *Svenska Kristna Härolden*, Apr. 15, 1885, 278; Erik August Skogsbergh, "Svenska kristna skolan i Minneapolis," *Svenska Kristna Härolden*, Apr. 7, 1886, 4. Cf. Untitled and undated manuscripts, Skogsbergh's School Papers, Covenant Archives and Historical Library.

22. Bowan, *Son of the People*, 165–66.

23. For Nyvall's representative statements on ethnicity and education, see David Nyvall, "Förbundet och kongregationalisterna," *Missions-Vännen*, Dec. 4, 1889, 1; David Nyvall to Erik J. Ekman, Mar. 19, 1896, Nyvall Collection 24:1:36–37, Covenant Archives and Historical Library; Nyvall, "Att amerikaniseras," Mar. 1896, Nyvall Collection 24:1, Covenant Archives and Historical Library; Nyvall, *Söken Guds rike! Sex undomstal* (Stockholm, 1898); Nyvall, "Among Swedish-American Colleges," *North Park College Journal* (Oct. 1899): 2.

24. Erickson, *David Nyvall*, 250–57. Skogsbergh wrote in his *Memoirs* that the move of the Covenant's school from the Twin Cities to Chicago was an "enormous mistake" and was a decision resulting primarily from "church politics" (Skogsbergh, *Minnen*, 205).

25. For Minnehaha Academy, see Anderson, *Precious Heritage*, 77–82.

26. Winthrop S. Hudson and John Corrigan, *Religion in America: An Historical Account of the Development of American Religious Life*, 5th ed. (New York: Macmillan, 1992), 231. For descriptions of Skogsbergh's Point, see Anderson, *Precious Heritage*, 40f.; Dahlhielm, *Burning Heart*, 117–27; Palmquist, *Wit and Wisdom*, 93.

David F. Swenson, Evolution,
and Public Education in Minnesota

PHILIP J. ANDERSON

In February 1927, Prince Wilhelm, younger son of Gustaf V of Sweden, visited Minneapolis to present an illustrated lecture at the Kenwood Armory, sponsored by the Hennepin County Sportsmen's Club. The flamboyant adventurer, according to a Twin Cities newspaper, was to talk about his "narrow escapes from death in the hunt for big game in central Africa." As an added attraction, "the prince will also throw on the screen a graphic picture of the Batwa pigmies." When asked about the anti-evolution bill that the Minnesota legislature would be voting upon within a few days, the prince commented that it was "very bad" and that "professors in Sweden teach what they believe to be true. Legislation against science is impossible in Sweden." "Educators," he said, "are the best judges of what they teach."[1]

The prince could not have been aware that he had stepped into the most heated and virulent controversy of religion and politics in Minnesota history. Between 1922 and 1927, the crusade against the teaching of evolutionary theory in all tax-supported institutions had been led by militant religious fundamentalists in Minnesota, notably one of the few northern states to entertain such legislation. Consequently, it was an intense battle that received considerable national attention.[2]

This essay addresses the controversy by assessing the participation of David F. Swenson, professor of philosophy at the University of Minnesota from 1901 until his premature death in 1940. His efforts, along with those of faculty colleagues and President Lotus Delta Coffman, accompanied by a massive dose of student pressure, assured the bill's overwhelming defeat. Swenson's public defense stands out, however, in the ways in which it combined academic freedom, logic, the nature of science, and, above all, the passionate character of religious experience. This requires seeing Swenson's role in the larger context of his life and work, where he has been best known as the pioneer English-language scholar and translator of the work of the nineteenth-century Danish philosopher and theologian, Søren Kierkegaard.

The Swedish American David Ferdinand Swenson was born in Kristinehamn, Sweden, on October 29, 1876, and emigrated at the age of six with his parents, Gustaf and Augusta, to the Cedar-Riverside neighborhood of Minneapolis. In a Fourth-of-July speech to the John Ericsson League for Patriotic Service at Minnehaha Park in 1918, in the midst of wartime xenophobia, Swenson spoke of his shoemaker father and deeply religious, literary mother:

> [They] were steerage immigrants, in common with so many others impelled and buoyed by the hope of bettering their condition. So far as they were personally concerned, this hope was scarcely fulfilled. They found conditions of life in the new world not easier and perhaps even somewhat harder than in the old. . . . But what life had denied to the parents, it granted in generous measure to the children. America afforded them, in spite of initial hardship and poverty, an education beyond the elementary, and she gave them the possibility of modest careers as students and teachers.[3]

As for so many immigrant children, education—nurtured in the home and at school—was the vehicle of opportunity for Swenson. He repeatedly voiced his gratitude for the Minneapolis public schools and later served on its Board of Education. A graduate of the University of Minnesota in 1898, having first pursued engineering, Swenson combined his love of mathematics with philosophy, modeled by the young philosopher Frederick Woodbridge, who subsequently went to Columbia. Swenson joined the philosophy department as an instructor in 1901 and never left. He was revered by students and colleagues alike and was among the handful of faculty who helped shaped the character of the University of Minnesota in the twentieth century.[4]

Prior to 1914, Swenson's involvement in the Swedish American community occurred most directly within the Swedish Evangelical Mission Covenant Church of America; he was active at every level of the denomination's life. Raised in the large Swedish Tabernacle (now First Covenant Church) on Seventh Street and Chicago Avenue, Swenson experienced both the intense pietistic and mission-minded faith of the people and the overt entrepreneurial ministry of its evangelist-pastor, Erik August Skogsbergh—known as the "Swedish Moody." As he matured, Swenson became especially involved in the educational work of the congregation, working alongside Andrew L. Skoog. He served for several years as a deacon, and as secretary of the congregation from 1909 until his departure in 1914, principally because of his disgust with the strident agendas of the new fundamentalist pastor, Gustaf F. Johnson, who considered him a dangerous modernist.

The final extant minutes recorded by Swenson at the congregation's annual meeting on January 1, 1912, included a resolution that he drafted to the Minneapolis Board of Education, a petition that it "not embark on the doubtful enterprise of turning the schoolhouses which belong to all the people into public dance halls . . . and not to use the educational machinery supported by all the people for the purpose of encouraging the modern social dance, thus nullifying the parental discipline of a large proportion of our citizenship." While this may seem ironic in light of the very progressive and controversial positions taken in later years, it demonstrates Swenson's commitment to and leadership in the moral values of his religious community.[5]

Swenson was intimately connected to Covenant leaders and work in the regional Northwestern Missionary Association. He was one of the founders of Minnehaha Academy and was the speaker at its groundbreaking ceremony in June 1912 at a dairy farm at Lake Street and West River Road, purchased in 1908. He also served for many years on the board of Minneapolis Veckoblad Publishing Company and wrote often for its Swedish weekly, *Veckobladet*, as well as other Swedish American periodicals.[6]

On the national level, Swenson jointly authored a catechism and helped create the first graded curricula for Sunday schools. In a lengthy pamphlet published and distributed at his own expense, he ably defended his friend David Nyvall, who as founding president of North Park College in Chicago had been pressured into voluntary exile in 1905 over his unpopular yet correct stand in the Alaska gold crisis, which involved the entire Covenant Church in turmoil and was surely one of the more dramatic episodes in Swedish American his-

David F. Swenson,
faculty portrait

tory, a matter ultimately settled by the Supreme Court of the United States. In all these activities, Swenson's interest in religion and education is evident.[7]

Swenson's broader concerns in Scandinavian American affairs are demonstrated, for example, by his detailed fourteen-page paper, written in 1912 at the request of President George Edgar Vincent and the Board of Regents, proposing a

Center for Scandinavian Studies at the University of Minnesota. The plan would expand the Scandinavian department in a new building to include "the gradual establishment of collections, museums and libraries, a staff of investigators and teachers, exchange professorships and lectureships in conjunction with the Scandinavian Universities." He thought that Minnesota, of all the states, by the sheer size of its Scandinavian population, was most positioned to assert an "institutional individuality" that would make the university distinctive. This was not "a mere arbitrary whim," he claimed. "A powerful one-sidedness is preferable to a weak and superficial all-sidedness." Swenson believed that the pre-migration cultural heritage of immigrants, which was being "transplanted" in their new lives and communities, was crucial and enriching to national self-understanding. "America," he wrote, "can better afford to receive [them] empty-handed than empty-headed."[8]

Moreover, Swenson's patriotic address in 1918, defending Swedish American loyalty to the war effort, had received considerable attention. Before its oral delivery, it had been published in the Minneapolis *Journal*; his own Swedish translation was then printed in *Minnesota Stats Tidning* by the Scandinavian Bureau of the Committee on Public Information. Letters of appreciation poured in, among them ones from President Burton, Guy Stanton Ford (then with the Committee on Public Information in Washington), Swedish American Governor J. A. A. Burnquist, and Swedish-born former Governor John Lind, who wrote that he had read the essay with "mingled feelings of appreciation and pride." Swenson had also served on a committee that examined forty to fifty German textbooks for objectionable propaganda, subject, he insisted, to fair criteria.[9]

There are several aspects of Swenson's public life in Minneapolis and statewide that made him already a known and respected figure when the evolutionary debate erupted. None was perhaps more visible than his involvement with the Minneapolis school board. Elected by the City Council to fill a vacancy in 1911, Swenson was re-appointed under the same circumstance in 1917, but the law then required an open election. In the months before November 1918, the election was hotly contested by his opponent, J. D. Lyon. Swedish American friends like Aaron Carlson, owner of a large millwork company in Northeast Minneapolis, promoted Swenson as a "character of proven loyalty and unselfish patriotism."

The major point of contention was nativist Americanism, occasioned by Swenson's argument (which Woodrow Wilson had endorsed) that school buildings could be used for neighborhood political meetings, including those of so-cialist locals. As late as 1938, Swenson defended the right of a Communist club to meet at the university, and he had backed several teachers threatened because they were alleged socialists or members of the International Workers of the World (IWW). Lyon accused Swenson of being in the "twilight zone" of socialism for defending an old schoolmate, O. J. Arness, who was a "Wobblie." The Minne-apolis *Journal* reported that at a meeting on June 9 Swenson "spoke with heat" when his loyalty was questioned implicitly by Lyon because he was foreign born:

> I love this country and I love our language. I love our American people. My wife [Lillian Marvin] is a D. A. R. [Daughters of the American Revolution], but she does not love America any more than I do. I love republicans, I love democrats, and I love the thousands of good, honest, loyal socialists. Some claim we cannot be 100 per cent American and not hate socialists. That is not the spirit of America.

This was courageous rhetoric when compared with Theodore Roosevelt's ugly speeches about hyphenated Americans, an irony for many of the Swedish Amer-icans who had been politically devoted to him for two decades.[10]

Swenson was even more indignant when the *Journal* challenged him "to step out of the twilight zone into the clear light." In a lengthy editorial, where he described himself as a "reasonably modest and retiring man, a student and teacher of philosophy," Swenson responded with astonishment:

> Of all the newspapers of Minneapolis *The Journal* has from my boyhood been my paper. As a youngster of 8 or 10 I sold it on the streets, buying my stock from the rear of 'Oscar's' wagon at Cedar av and Third st; and many a time do I remember how my childish heart quaked with fear lest I should be unable to dispose of my five or ten copies before night fall. For five years while attending high school and college I earned my way by daily carrier de-liveries of *The Journal*. My first education in American politics was obtained by reading the editorial page of *The Journal*, to which I used to turn as a boy of 10 before anything else was read.

A socialist? "Beg pardon, Mr. Editor, but I am not entirely unknown to the cit-izens of Minneapolis. I have lived here 34 years, while [Lyon] . . . has lived here five years." Swenson outlined his record of public service and explained his philosophical critique of socialism, saying that "by instinct, training and per-sonal temperament I am a conservative." For him, this was a matter of princi-ple and fairness. He repeated what he would say on many occasions when his integrity was called into question: "Socrates took pride in the fact that he al-ways said the same things about the same things. In this respect I humbly fol-low in his footsteps."[11]

A week before the election, the venerated Maria L. Sanford supported Swenson in the Minneapolis *Journal*. She scoffed at the notion that he was a socialist and noted with maternal affection: "I have known Professor David F. Swenson ever since he was a pupil in my classes at the University." She praised Swenson's honesty, scholarship, and moral courage, urging women's suffrage and the welfare of children: "Because I love our schools and seek their highest interest, I appeal to the women of Minneapolis to vote for Professor Swenson." Swenson had already received endorsements from the Woman's Club of Minneapolis, the Women's Welfare League, and the Alice Paul Branch of the National Woman's Party. He also qualified the endorsement he received from the Nonpartisan League, which he had defended on more than one occasion. Swenson won a decisive victory with 64 percent of the vote. Among his contributions as a board member, Swenson authored a comprehensive study, *The Finances of the Minneapolis Schools*, in December 1919, analyzing the deficit, as well as the budget and faculty salaries for 1920.[12]

Between August 1922 and December 1923, Swenson had an interesting exchange of letters with the author Upton Sinclair, answering questions and reading drafts of Sinclair's exposé on American education and academic freedom, later published as *The Goose-Step* (1923) and *The Goslings* (1924). Sinclair wrote in his autobiography that he "meant to muckrake the colleges, showing where they had got their money and how they were spending it," by probing the stories of disaffected teachers and professors. In the case of the University of Minnesota, Sinclair had pursued the political problems of professors A. J. McGuire (a dairy specialist in the Department of Animal Husbandry), John H. Gray (head of the Department of Economics and an expert on public utilities), and A. J. Todd (head of the Department of Sociology).[13]

These are some of Swenson's longest and most brilliant letters, and he was exasperated by the swashbuckling journalism relative to "The University of the Ore Trust" (Sinclair's name for Minnesota), as well as the Minneapolis schools. Swenson attempted to straighten the facts, promote fair judgment, care for context, and encourage judicious language—in short, to force Sinclair to think more deeply, more ethically, and to do his homework. He called much of the work "nonsense" and "inferior," with "too much second-hand stuff, and too much easy guesswork to make an impression." He defended the actions of presidents Northrup and Vincent, while couching his critique of the Board of Regents in careful, constructive words: "The management of our University is undoubtedly in conservative hands," he wrote. "Especially are they likely to confuse the demands of patriotism and loyalty to country with the interest they have in the preservation of the status quo, and the established balance of power, politically and economically." When Sinclair appeared unruffled after more than a year of this, Swenson finally told him with some humor, "You write like a journalist . . . facts, near facts, and total error." Saying he had no more time, Swenson added: "I conclude that you are a real brick, that is to say, a real man." Nevertheless, when Sinclair's books appeared, he honored Swenson's request not to be named, and his treatment of issues in Minnesota was modified.[14]

These letters demonstrate Swenson's care for the ambiguities that attend the truth of persons and events, his rigorous and thoroughly logical thought, and the high principles of academic freedom that Sinclair, in his more idealistic, left-wing passion, would in the end harm. Swenson had been vocal for many years on issues of academic freedom, was one of the architects of the university's tenure policy, and had recently authored a statement entitled *"Academic Freedom" at the University of Minnesota* (1920). His efforts to elevate journalistic standards remained a lifelong passion. On December 9, 1926, a report in the *Minnesota Daily* praised Swenson's critique of the loss of personality and ethics, particularly in rural journalism. He received a letter of appreciation from Minnesota's ancient and ageless first president, William Watts Folwell, who noted wryly: "For 45+/− years I have been giving such counsel to students. I hope you will have more influence than I seem to have had."[15]

The controversy over the teaching of evolution in Minnesota occurred between 1922 and 1927. Ferenc M. Szasz unraveled the complex sequence of events in his award-winning essay in the pages of *Minnesota History* in 1969. That general framework will be followed here in order to see in greater detail Swenson's own involvement, which has yet to receive any attention.[16]

Unquestionably, the principal protagonist in the story was William Bell Riley, at the time the nation's leading militant fundamentalist, who was pastor of First Baptist Church in Minneapolis from 1897 until his retirement in 1941, with his influence extending to his death in 1947. Riley was a tireless organizer who built his congregation from 585 to 3,350 members and established the Northwestern Bible and Missionary Training School in 1902, to which a seminary and college were added near the end of his life. On his deathbed, Riley succeeded in enlisting as his successor the young Billy Graham, who departed in 1951 to give full attention to his evangelistic crusades. On the national level, in 1919 Riley had organized the World's Christian Fundamentalist Association, of which he became president, the springboard for much of the agitation concerning evolution.[17]

In the autumn of 1922, Riley and his Bible institute invited William Jennings Bryan to deliver two lectures in the Twin Cities. Three times a populist Democratic presidential candidate, secretary of state under Wilson, and soon to be center stage in the Scopes trial in Dayton, Tennessee, Bryan characterized evolution as "a menace to civilization." He addressed 2,600 people at the State Theater in Minneapolis and more than 9,000 at the Hippodrome on the state fair grounds, a crowd that included curious university students.[18]

This crystallized the ferment that had been growing for more than a decade, and within a few days Riley gathered some Minneapolis ministers at his church to draft a resolution against the teaching of "anti-Christian theories." This led to the formation of the Minnesota Anti-Evolution League, soon to be a national organization with divided, and frequently contentious, leadership. Riley explained that its purpose was "to force the teachings of the evolutionary hypothesis from the public schools, and to lend all possible aid to the evangelical denominations in ridding their schools of the same pseudo-science." These words would be repeated like a mantra throughout the controversy: professors at the university taught "science, falsely so-called." The League demanded that President Coffman personally investigate and purge as necessary the assigned texts of 800 faculty members. He skillfully diffused the issue, but knew well the meaning of the gathering storm.[19]

At a public rally in October 1922, Riley singled out professors like Charles P. Sigerfoos, animal biologist in the Department of Zoology. David Swenson wrote to Riley asking that he verify the accuracy of quotations reported in the *Minneapolis Star* and the *Minnesota Daily* for October 30 concerning his colleague's alleged "vitiating teachings." "Too many of the young men and women of the state," Riley had charged, "have already been poisoned by the same."

Riley failed to reply, but Swenson had launched his own campaign for personal accountability, accuracy, and integrity.[20]

"Shall Moses or Darwin Rule Minnesota Schools" was the title of an article in the *Literary Digest* for January 1923, based on a poll of Protestant ministers around the state. One hundred-fifteen clergy were against the teaching

Cartoon illustrating the evolution debate, from the Minnesota Daily, *March 8, 1927*

of evolution; seventy-seven were supportive. By far the largest number opposed (sixty-two) were Lutherans, and Riley optimistically believed that it was this body of Germans and Scandinavians that would assure victory. While correct about the conservatism, he underestimated the lack of concrete support for his efforts, as Lutherans reasoned out of their theory of the two kingdoms—the distinct spheres of the secular and the sacred. G. M. Bruce, professor of ethics and sociology at Luther Seminary in St. Paul, spoke for them when he said that there were other weapons than "the sword of the state." The following month, Riley led a spirited rally at the Swedish Tabernacle in Minneapolis, an event recorded word-for-word by two Minneapolis court stenographers.[21]

Throughout 1925 and 1926, Riley debated evolution around the country with scientists who were willing to engage in a one-hour debate, followed by a rising vote, on the question: "Resolved, That Evolution Is an Established Fact and Should Be Taught in the Tax-Supported Schools of America." As he usually "preached to the choir," it is little wonder that Riley rarely lost. These debates also took place in Minnesota (he defeated the hapless field secretary of the Science League of America, Edward Adams Cantrell, for the seventh time at the Kenwood Armory), yet because of ways that the University of Minnesota restricted his presence on campus, Riley turned up the heat. He rented, at his own expense, the Kenwood Armory March 7, 1926, and to a capacity audience flailed the university for its one-sided prejudice. The meeting ended with jubilant cries from the audience that they would support the Anti-Evolution League in its campaign "that neither a dozen regents nor a hundred deceiving and faithless professors shall be the owners or controllers of the University of Minnesota."[22]

Matters came to a head during the first two months of 1927. With the assistance of the Wichita fundamentalist Gerald B. Winrod, Riley prepared the legislation against the teaching of evolution in all tax-supported schools in Minnesota, though it was not introduced in the state senate until the end of February; it was voted upon two weeks later. This drew Swenson openly into the fray, and he became the most articulate critic of the legislation in the pages of several publications and in intense public and private debate with Riley about the nature of science and religion.

Swenson made his case at some length in the February issue of the *Journal of the Minnesota Educational Association*. While he was concerned about the freedom of academic inquiry, especially when trained scientists tended strongly to agree, and wanted to insure the highest quality of education for students, the proposed legislation was above all "foolish" and "inimical to the interests of religion even more than the interests of science." In his correspondence with George T. Rygh, on this issue a particularly arrogant Norwegian Lutheran pastor who misquoted sources freely, Swenson accused him of being "a wilful [sic] slanderer and liar." He told Rygh that his own opinion about "your small theological faction" was justified, "as one who has for many years taught the Bible in an orthodox Christian church, as one who has for many years been an acceptable lay preacher." This affair was no less than "public slander upon a whole class of University scholars," which should make any participating minister ashamed of his calling.[23]

It was with Riley, however, that Swenson honed his arguments about religion as that which stood the most to lose. Even though the bill should pass, surely it would be repealed, he believed, for no free society could tolerate such disregard for law. But consequences for youth and for churches would be catastrophic to the interests of true faith. In an exchange of private correspondence, open letters to the Minnesota Daily, and a closed doors debate at the Leamington Hotel to the Town and Gown Club of the University of Minnesota, the two men went at it—admittedly laymen at science but experts from widely different perspectives in religion. While vitriolic at times, there was mutual respect, though Swenson believed that Riley frequently crossed the boundaries of civility in public. More importantly, he suffered from a "disorganized" and "confused mind," careless in thought, shifty and evasive, and "abysmally ignorant" if he believed that a popular audience could decide in one hour the truth or falsehood of the evolutionary hypothesis.[24]

Swenson wrote "as one whose most profound interest in life has from childhood until now been the cause of religion," claiming "the fruit of long reflection and religious experience." The truth of evolutionary theory was not his ultimate concern. He told the readers of the Daily:

> [Riley] heard me exalt the ministry of religious truth . . . infinitely above the ministry of scientific truth; he heard me criticize his own theory of biblical inspiration as essentially heterodox, because it unduly magnified the importance of science, and sought to put mere scientific accuracy on the same plane with a divine message to the consciences of men. It is I who am seeking to maintain the respect properly due the ministry.

Science, Swenson argued, is by nature neutral and demands disinterested research. Religion, on the other hand, requires the passionate interest and inwardness of the individual. Science is accessible only to the competently trained and is bound by objective reason. Religious experience is open to all in the firsthand subjectivity that finds truth beyond the merely objective and empirically demonstrable. Swenson believed that the real tragedy of the controversy was that it led people to embrace popular secondhand convictions about both science and religion. Fundamentalists, therefore, were not only uncivil and incapable of meaningful discourse, they misplaced passion. Religion was being used to serve, according to Swenson's categories, non-religious ends. Though Swenson never invoked the name of Kierkegaard in debate, the categories are generally his, shaped by Swenson's thought and experience to fit the moment.[25]

Swenson authored the resolution from the Faculty of the College of Science, Literature, and the Arts to the Senate and House Committees on Education. When the legislative hearing occurred on March 8, he made an eloquent speech, along with President Coffman, who addressed the legislature in a truly memorable appeal to the spirit of the university's founders. The bill died on March 9 by a vote of 55 to 7. At the end of the month, the Minneapolis *Journal* printed an article entitled "Philosophy Head Holds Religious Faith Main Need." And as part of a series of four public lectures on "Evolution and Civilization" in February 1932 at Northrup Auditorium, Swenson presented his comprehensive views in a lecture entitled "Evolution and Life Values." Though the debate was beyond fundamentalist resuscitation in Minnesota, of course it has not disappeared and has been revived in numerous school boards across the country following the new creation science of the past three decades.[26]

Swenson died on February 11, 1940, in Lake Wales, Florida, following a massive stroke, having suffered for a quarter-century from an advancing and debilitating deafness, as well as occasional bouts of depression. The greatest legacy of this remarkable philosopher and man of faith, however, resided among colleagues and a generation of students. As a Swedish American, he was a notable example of an immigrant whose heart was not divided. Passionately and securely a citizen of Minnesota and the United States, he said in 1918: "I have never seen fit to apologize for my Swedish ancestry nor sought to avoid any of its natural implications. . . . I have always believed that much of this inheritance may and of right ought to be used to enrich American life." In the case of David Swenson, it most certainly did.[27]

* * * *

NOTES

1. Undated, unidentified newspaper clipping in B Sw 42, Box 1, File 8, David F. Swenson Papers, Univ. of Minn. Archives, Minneapolis. At the end of January, Prince Wilhelm had joined his brother, Crown Prince Gustav Adolf, in a visit to the University of Minnesota, which included an event at Memorial Stadium attended by 35,000 people. Speakers included the crown prince, Lotus D. Coffman (president of the university), Frank B. Kellogg (secretary of state), and the Norwegian American governor, Theodore Christianson. A. A. Stomberg, professor of Scandinavian language and literature, reported that this event had received favorable coverage in Swedish newspapers.

2. Thirty-seven anti-evolution bills were introduced to twenty state legislatures between 1921 and 1929. Five were passed in varying degrees: Oklahoma, Florida, Tennessee, Mississippi, and Arkansas. See Ronald L. Numbers, ed., *Creation-Evolution Debates* (New York: Garland Publications, 1995); Willard B. Gatewood, Jr., *Preachers, Pedagogues & Politicians: The Evolution Controversy in North Carolina, 1920–1927* (Chapel Hill: Univ. of N.C. Press, 1966); Kenneth K. Bailey, "The Enactment of Tennessee's Anti-Evolution Law," *Journal of Southern History* 16 (1950): 472–90; Elbert L. Watson, "Oklahoma and the Anti-Evolution Movement of the 1920's," *Chronicles of Oklahoma* 42 (1964–65): 396–407; R. Haliburton, Jr., "The Nation's First Anti-Darwin Law: Passage and Repeal [Oklahoma]," *Southwestern Social Science Quarterly* 41 (1960): 123–35; R. Haliburton, Jr., "The Adoption of the Arkansas Anti-Evolution Law," *Arkansas Historical Quarterly* 23 (1964): 271–83; Virginia Gray, "Anti-Evolution Sentiment and Behavior: The Case of Arkansas," *Journal of American History* 57 (1970): 352–66; R. Haliburton, Jr., "Kentucky's Anti-Evolution Controversy," *Register of the Kentucky Historical Society* 46 (1968): 97–107; and Willard B. Gatewood, Jr., ed., *Controversy in the Twenties: Fundamentalism, Modernism, and Evolution* (Nashville: Vanderbilt Univ. Press, 1969).

3. David F. Swenson, *The Spirit of America in the War* (Minneapolis: Minneapolis Veckoblad Publishing Co., 1918), 3f. This pamphlet printed the above-titled address by Woodrow Wilson and included Swenson's "Independence Day Address." Later in life, Swenson collected several of his mother's poems and published them in a small edition (a copy is in Wilson Library, Univ. of Minn.). Swenson's sister was a French professor at Knox College, Galesburg, Illinois.

4. Little has been written biographically about Swenson. For the most comprehensive and insightful essay, see Paul L. Holmer, "Something About Swenson," *Swedish Pioneer Historical Quarterly* 7 (1956), 123–35. Following Swenson's death in 1940, the philosophy department published a series of tributes by colleagues, "Eight Informal Talks on the Nature of Morality" by Swenson, and a bibliography of his published writings. See *David F. Swenson: Scholar, Teacher, Friend* (Minneapolis: Univ. of Minn., 1940). For Swenson's most extended autobiographical account, specifically of his study of Kierkegaard, see his editorial introduction to Eduard Geismar, *Lectures on the Religious Thought of Søren Kierkegaard* (Minneapolis: Augsburg Publishing House, 1937), xi–xlix.

5. Swedish Tabernacle, Minneapolis, Minute Book, Jan. 19, 1903, to Jan. 1, 1912, p. 294, microfilm copy, Covenant Archives and Historical Library, North Park Univ., Chicago, Illinois. The fact that the extant minutes do not resume until Jan. 1, 1915, may well indicate a lost minute book. It may also reflect the congregational turmoil of finding a successor to Skogsbergh, who after twenty-five years had left for Seattle in 1909. C. G. Ellström, pastor from 1909 to 1913, though much loved, had problems because of his personal financial mismanagement and active Christian socialism. Vilified in the Covenant Church, this no doubt had an effect on Swenson's commitment to defending the rights of those with different political convictions.

6. For a discussion of this, see Philip J. Anderson, *A Precious Heritage: A Century of Mission in the Northwest 1884–1984* (Minneapolis: Northwest Conference of the Evangelical Covenant Church, 1984), 78ff.

7. Swenson's meticulous sifting of the unfolding complex legal matters and the messy ecclesial politics accurately corresponds with the definitive study of this tragic scandal. The pamphlet, dated June 3, 1907 (as well as an English translation), is in the Covenant Archives. See Leland H. Carlson, *An Alaskan Gold Mine: The Story of Number Nine Above* (Evanston: Northwestern Univ. Press, 1951); and Scott E. Erickson, *David Nyvall and the Shape of an Immigrant Church: Ethnic, Denominational, and Educational Priorities among Swedes in America* (Uppsala: Acta Universitatis Upsaliensis, 1996), 173–203.

8. Untitled paper, 14 p., Swenson Papers, Box 1, File 13. This ambitious program, which proposed the construction of a building to house all the activities, never materialized.

9. "Marvelous Unity of Spirit Seen in U.S. War Preparations: Diverse Elements Swing Into Line to Down World Peril, Declares Swenson," *Journal*, May 19, 1918; *Minnesota Stats Tidning*, June 17, 1918; M. L. Burton to David Swenson, Aug. 21, 1918; Guy Stanton Ford to David Swenson, Aug. 14, 1918; J. A. A. Burnquist to David Swenson, Aug. 1, 1918; and John Lind to David Swenson, May 21 [1918], Swenson Papers, Box 1, File 1.

10. "Loyalty Issue Is Dominant, Assert School Candidates," *Journal*, June 9, 1918, Swenson Papers, Box 1, File 3.

11. *Journal*, June 11, 1918.

12. "Maria Sanford Vouches for Swenson, and Appeals for His Election to School Board," *Journal*, Oct. 29, 1918. This was also printed as an "Open Letter" broadside for mass distribution (Swenson Papers, Box 1, File 3). The letters of endorsement are in Box 1, File 3, of the Swenson Papers. See esp. David Swenson to O. E. Nordstrom, May 27, 1918. Nordstrom was secretary of the Nonpartisan League. Swenson makes clear his position in this letter: he has an open and fair mind, but is critical of elements of the party platform and some candidates who had received endorsement.

13. *The Autobiography of Upton Sinclair* (New York: Harcourt, Brace, and World, 1962), 224–27.

14. Swenson Papers, Box 1, File 5. There are nine letters in this exchange between Aug. 21, 1922, and Dec. 26, 1923. Swenson believed that the Regents had always been honest and fair with regard to himself:

> There is another side to the picture. Take my own case. I have been in the newspapers with a vengeance. I served on the Minneapolis Board of Education during the war; voted to open the school auditoriums for political meetings, the Socialists taking most frequent advantage of the opportunity thus afforded them; I took an active part in the campaign here a few years ago to defeat a proposed street car franchise which I thought was unfair, and have been generally credited with influencing the result of that campaign decisively; I have publicly defended the Non-Partisan League against what I believed to be unjust criticism, and I have said my say about the newspapers in and out of my classes. Yet I have never been molested by any official of the University in these activities and my academic career has been as smooth sailing as it deserved to be [Swenson to Sinclair, Oct. 25, 1922, p. 5].

15. William Watts Folwell to David Swenson, Dec. 11, 1926, Swenson Papers, Box 1, File 17.

16. Ferenc M. Szasz, "William B. Riley and the Fight Against Teaching of Evolution in Minnesota," *Minnesota History* 41 (1969): 201–16.

17. The definitive biography of Riley is William Vance Trollinger, Jr., *God's Empire: William Bell Riley and Midwestern Fundamentalism* (Madison: Univ. of Wisc. Press, 1990). Cf. also C. Allyn Russell, *Voices of American Fundamentalism: Seven Biographical Studies* (Philadelphia: Westminster Press, 1976), 79–106; and Trollinger, ed., *The Anti-Evolutionary Pamphlets of William Bell Riley* (New York: Garland Publications, 1995). Much continues to be written about the history of American fundamentalism. For differing interpretations of the origins of the phenomenon, see Ernest R. Sandeen, *The Roots of Fundamentalism: British and American Millenarianism, 1800–1930* (Chicago: Univ. of Chicago Press, 1970); and George M. Marsden, *Fundamentalism and American Culture: The Shaping of Twentieth-Century Evangelicalism, 1870–1925* (New York: Oxford Univ. Press, 1980). For a larger contextual discussion, see Martin E. Marty, *The Irony of It All, 1893–1919* (Chicago: Univ. of Chicago Press, 1986); and Marty, *The Noise of Conflict, 1919–1941* (Chicago: Univ. of Chicago Press, 1991). See also Joel Carpenter, *Revive Us Again: The Reawakening of American Fundamentalism* (New York: Oxford Univ. Press, 1997).

18. For Bryan, see Lawrence W. Levine, *Defender of the Faith: William Jennings Bryan, 1915–1925* (New York: Oxford Univ. Press, 1965); Bryan, *Orthodox Christianity versus Mod-*

ernism (New York: Fleming H. Revell, 1923); and Russell, *Voices of American Fundamentalism*, 162–89. Bryan's role in the larger evolution debate is found in Ronald L. Numbers's definitive study, *The Creationists: The Evolution of Scientific Creationism* (New York: Alfred A. Knopf, 1992).

19. Quoted by Szasz, "Riley and Evolution," 205.

20. David Swenson to W. B. Riley, Nov. 4, 1922, Swenson Papers, Box 1, File 6. In Jan. 1927, Swenson had a brief but interesting exchange of correspondence with Sigerfoos relative to the credentials of the fundamentalist's leading scientific expert, Rev. Harry Rimmer of Los Angeles, who was holding rallies around the country. Sigerfoos had written to Rimmer asking him to support his claim that he was an anthropologist. Affronted, Rimmer told him to check with the American Association for the Advancement of Science. Sigerfoos learned that Rimmer (along with Riley) had in 1925 begun subscribing to the Association's journal, whose secretary told him that he hoped "the Reverend gets badly disappointed in his antiknowledge campaign." Sigerfoos also told Swenson that the Presbyterians had credentialed Rimmer only as an Evangelist, and that he had no right to put D.D. after his name or be called "Doctor." Furthermore, his claims to expertise in medicine could only be supported by a quarter of pre-medicine as an undergraduate (Swenson Papers, Box 1, File 6).

21. "Shall Moses or Darwin Rule Minnesota Schools," *Literary Digest*, vol. 76, no. 31 (Jan. 13, 1923). As Coffman sought support in opposing the legislation, only the presidents of Hamline, Carleton, St. Olaf, and St. Cloud pledged their help, though there was overwhelming faculty support in all the liberal arts colleges (Szasz, "Riley and Evolution," 212); "Mass Meeting at Swedish Tabernacle, March 18, 1923," Swenson Papers, Box 1, File 9.

22. Szasz, "Riley and Evolution," 209.

23. David F. Swenson, "The Proposal to Limit Science Teaching by Law," *Journal of the Minnesota Educational Association*, Feb. 1927; David Swenson to George T. Rygh, Feb. 14, 1927, Swenson Papers, Box 1, File 6.

24. Open letter to Riley, *Minnesota Daily*, Mar. 11, 1927. Swenson called these popular debates "hocus-pocus, a charlatan's trick . . . to fool the public" (*Minnesota Daily*, Feb. 4, 1923). Paul L. Holmer stated that sometime in 1946–47 he had invited Riley to speak on his relationship to David Swenson to a gathering at the Minneapolis YMCA. Holmer recalled that Professor George M. Stephenson was in attendance (interview with the author, Oct. 23, 1996).

25. "A Reply to Dr. Riley's Open Letter," *Minnesota Daily*, Mar. 12, 1927.

26. Swenson Papers, Box 1, File 7; David F. Swenson, "Evolution and Life Values," *Minnesota Alumni Weekly*, Aug. 1932. This was also published posthumously in Lillian M. Swenson, ed., *Kierkegaardian Philosophy in the Faith of a Scholar* (Philadelphia: Westminster Press, 1949), 49–82. For a survey of recent creationism campaigns, see Ronald L. Numbers, *Darwinism Comes to America* (Cambridge: Harvard Univ. Press, 1998); Edward J. Larson, *Trial and Error: The American Controversy over Creation and Evolution* (New York: Oxford Univ. Press, 1985); Larson, *Summer for the Gods: The Scopes Trial and America's Continuing Debate over Science and Religion* (Cambridge: Harvard Univ. Press, 1998); Paul K. Conkin, *When All the Gods Trembled: Darwinism, Scopes, and American Intellectuals* (London: Rowman & Littlefield, 1998); Langdon Gilkey, *Creationism on Trial: Evolution and God at Little Rock* (Charlottesville: Univ. Press of Va., 1998); and Kary Doyle Smout, *The Creation/Evolution Controversy: A Battle for Cultural Power* (New York: Praeger, 1998).

27. For letters from former students, see Swenson Papers, Box 1, File 17. As one student wrote, "I always said I learned more religion in your course than I had in church. As you said at the time, you 'unlearned' us things that did us no good" (Kathleen Carling to David Swenson, Dec. 8, 1939). After Swenson's death, his wife received letters from former students J. Oliver Buswell, Jr., fundamentalist Presbyterian and president of Wheaton College, who remembered "with great appreciation his kindliness in talking with me that night

on the train going down to Kansas City for the 1913–14 Student Volunteer Convention" (Apr. 17, 1940); and from Howard Hong of St. Olaf College, the editor and translator of the definitive Princeton edition of Kierkegaard's writings, who wrote that Swenson's "point of view" and "life conviction" was the reason he remained at the Univ. of Minn. for graduate studies (Mar. 3, 1940). In the Swenson Papers are graded student essays from courses in logic and in the philosophy of Plato; Swenson had required students to attend Riley's four lectures at the university in Nov. 1926 and write critical analyses (Box 1, File 10); "Independence Day Address," 4.

Swedish Americans and the
1918 Gubernatorial Campaign in Minnesota

DAG BLANCK

When Minnesotans went to the polls in 1918 to choose a governor, the preceding months had been characterized by a bitter political campaign. "Violence and physical danger were common during the campaign," notes Bruce Larson, an expert on Minnesota politics, who also has characterized the campaign as "one of the most acrimonious contests in Minnesota political history." Scholars have attributed the bitterness of the campaign to the role of World War I and the question of loyalty. Larson has observed that the campaign was conducted in an atmosphere of "war-time hysteria," and Carol Jensen has commented that "the explosive loyalty question" could be used to drown out other issues.[1]

The campaign was also of importance from a Swedish American perspective. In the primary election within the Republican Party (which is the focus of this essay), Governor J. A. A. Burnquist, the incumbent, was challenged by former congressman Charles Lindbergh. Lindbergh had represented the Sixth Minnesota Congressional District in the House of Representatives from 1907 to 1917, and Burnquist had served as governor since 1914. Both of these candidates were Swedish Americans; Lindbergh was Swedish-born and had emigrated as a child, whereas Burnquist was a son of Swedish immigrants, born in Iowa.

Not only did two Swedish American candidates oppose each other, Swedish Americans also played an important role as voters. At the time of this election, Minnesota had the largest Swedish American population of any state in the Union, which in 1910 included some 240,000 persons. This represented 11.5 percent of the state's entire population, making the Swedish Americans the second largest ethnic group in the state. Although Swedes had been emigrating to Minnesota since the 1850s, it took about a half-century for the Swedes to make a mark on Minnesota politics, and the first Swedish American governor, John Lind, was elected in 1899. Going back to the beginnings of Swedish mass immigration to the U. S. in the 1850s, a strong Swedish American loyalty to the Republican Party had developed, political preferences that persisted through the following decades. By the turn of the century, however, Swedish American loyalty to the G. O. P. was weakening. One reason for this was a Republican tendency to assume the Swedish American vote as a given, and consequently to think little about the nomination of Swedish American candidates. The election of Democrat John Lind as Minnesota governor is an example of Swedish American frustration with the Republicans and a willingness to let the ethnic factor be decisive in changing political allegiance. The election of 1912 also showed how Swedish American political opinion was becoming more diversified, as there was strong support among the Swedes for Theodore Roosevelt and his Progressive Party, as well as for the Democrats in that year. As this essay illustrates, there was also considerable political support for Populism and third party politics among Swedish Americans in Minnesota during the 1910s.[2]

What might be said about the Minnesota Republican gubernatorial primary election in 1918 from a Swedish American perspective? This investigation discusses Swedish American opinions concerning the candidates, as well as the way the Swedish American community voted. The sources for the analysis include the two leading Swedish-language newspapers in Minnesota in 1918, *Svenska Amerikanska Posten* and *Minnesota Stats Tidning*, both published in Minneapolis, as well as census data and official election return statistics. By using this election campaign as a unit of analysis, it is also possible to address the larger issue of political and ideological loyalties among Swedish Americans in Minnesota. The ethnic and religious factors in American politics have been discussed in recent decades, and the ethno-cultural interpretation of Midwestern politics by scholars such as Richard Jensen, Paul Kleppner, and more recently Jon Gjerde, have underscored how ethnic and religious differences tended to be important determinants of party loyalty. Earlier studies by Sten Carlsson and Bruce Larson of the Swedes in Minnesota's political history have also emphasized the role of ethnicity in determining Swedish American voting patterns in Minnesota. Jørn Brøndal has also recently argued for a distinct Scandinavian political behavior in Wisconsin during the decades around the turn of the century. Alternative interpretations, such as those by labor historians, which emphasize the role of class for political preferences have also been advanced. This essay does not seek to reconcile these two positions. Following Gjerde's sophisticated analyses of ethnicity in the Midwest, it does maintain, however, that Swedish Americans in Minnesota maintained complementary identities, in which ethnicity and social class could and did coexist.[3]

Before turning to the discussion of Swedish American opinion, it is necessary to comment on the issues at stake in the most bitter election campaign in Minnesota history. Two interrelated factors explain the campaign's bitterness: loyalty and war. Because the political campaign occurred during World War I, the "loyalty" of the Swedish ethnic group to the United States became dominant in the discussion. The reason for the focus on loyalty was that at the time of the election challenger Charles Lindbergh strongly identified with the opposition to American participation in World War I. Consequently, much of the campaign revolved around Lindbergh's positions on the war. Lindbergh argued that the war was not about making the world safe for democracy, as President Woodrow Wilson would have it, but rather that it was a way for "special interest groups," such as speculators and industrialists, to make money. In a congressional debate during his last year in Congress in 1916, Lindbergh had, for example, stated that "lords of special privilege" with "their selfish glees [were] counting billions of profit from the rage of war."[4]

Lindbergh's position on the war was in many ways a result of his overall political views. Lindbergh had served as a Republican in the U. S. House of Representatives from 1906 until 1918, representing what was known as the progressive or insurgent wing of the party. This movement can be linked to the general Populist movement from the late nineteenth century, which was especially strong in the Midwest. It was largely rooted in opposition to what was seen as the East Coast economic, industrial, and political establishment, among other things advocating control and regulation of the railroads and cheap money. There was strong support in rural and agrarian sectors of the Midwest for this kind of political program, and during his years in Congress Lindbergh had been one of the most loyal progressive Republicans, consistently voting against the regular Republican party-line on a number of key issues. One of the main vehicles for the agrarian Populist movement in the upper Midwest was the Nonpartisan League (NPL), an organization with its roots in the agrarian areas of the Upper Midwest. The League had its origin in the Dakotas but had made significant inroads in Minnesota by 1917. Its platform called for an economic program of public ownership, government regulation of transportation conglomerates, and state assistance to labor. Bruce Larson has commented that the League's appeal to both farmers and laborers was "a powerful one" and "that without question it had the potential for national influence." Lindbergh had become

Charles A. Lindbergh, Sr.

involved with the League in 1917, and, at its annual conference in St. Paul in
March of the following year, the NPL officially endorsed Lindbergh as its gubernatorial candidate.[5]

Lindbergh's views on the war were best explained in a book entitled *Why
is Your Country at War and What Happens to You After the War and Related Subjects.* It was published in June 1917, following the American entry into World
War I, and was, in Larson's words, "a summation" of Lindbergh's political and
economic views. Lindbergh made two main points in this book. First, in a typical midwestern Populist manner, he attacked big business and the East Coast
capitalists. The leading American capitalists had, in Lindbergh's opinion, not
performed any great services to America. They had instead been destructive—
he called them "the cancers in American business" or "destroyers of America"—
and must be brought under control. In order to break the power of the privileged
classes, the system "that makes them and their like to exist" must be changed.
Lindbergh's proposal for reforms included placing the large conglomerates that
controlled transportation, communication, and finances in America under government control and regulation. By doing so, he argued, the foundations would
be laid for a fair and equitable policy that would provide "equal opportunity to
all and special privileges to none."[6]

Second, he argued that the reasons for the ongoing war were fundamentally
economic. It was, Lindbergh claimed, "a war of economics" and a "war for
profit." The large economic interest groups had "counterfeited patriotism for
commercial ends and counterfeited the flag for the same purpose—all in all an
attempt to perpetuate the selfish plans of that group." American farmers in the
Midwest thus had no stake in this war of the economic elite and profiteers. Speculators and wealth grabbers were taking advantage of the war under a cloak of
patriotism to further their own interests. The way to win the war, according to
Lindbergh, came through economic and political reforms. The only "true victory" would be an "economic victory" for the "masses of the world," Lindbergh
concluded. Lindbergh's link between domestic politics and his view on the war
was also clearly expressed at the convention of the Nonpartisan League in 1918,
when he accepted its support for the governorship. In Lindbergh's thinking, the
war was a result of economic factors, mostly domestic. Therefore, Lindbergh
argued that it was of little avail "to win a war for democracy abroad, if in the
prosecution of that war all the traditional rights and privileges of the people of
this nation have been surrendered and abrogated. . . . The battles for industrial
democracy are still to be fought at home."[7]

How were the progressive insurgent Republican challenger Lindbergh and the regular Republican and incumbent Governor Burnquist discussed in the two major Swedish-language weekly newspapers in Minnesota, *Svenska Amerikanska Posten* and *Minnesota Stats Tidning?* They were the two largest Swedish-language papers in Minnesota, and one scholar has characterized them as the most prominent of the many Swedish-language publications in the state. *Minnesota Stats Tidning* was owned by a group of ministers in the Swedish Lutheran denomination, the Augustana Synod, and its profile has been characterized as "conservative" and "Lutheran," closely allied to the Republican Party. In 1915, it reported a circulation of 12,500. *Svenska Amerikanska Posten*, on the other hand, was a much more modern paper, owned by the successful editor and publisher Swan Turnblad, and represented "the liberal secular leanings among Swedes in Minnesota." *Posten* claimed a circulation of 56,000 in 1915.[8]

Turnblad's *Svenska Amerikanska Posten* came out strongly in support of Governor Burnquist. In addition, the paper covered the campaign quite extensively. The paper began commenting on the candidates and the issues involved in March, in connection with the NPL endorsement of Lindbergh. Beginning with the April 10 issue, *Posten* has articles and commentary about the election until the polling date in June. The main reason *Posten* gave for its support of Burnquist was his undisputed loyalty to Wilson's war policies. Burnquist was often compared to Lindbergh, whose questionable loyalty *Posten* did not fail to underscore. On April 10, 1918, *Posten* ran a story that in very positive terms commented on a Burnquist rally, at which the governor gave, in *Posten*'s words, "one of his forceful and patriotic speeches," which was received with "thunderous applause." In this speech (which *Posten* presented in such a positive light), Governor Burnquist asserted that those persons who did not completely support the United States in its current struggle to preserve its "free institutions" ought to lose their citizenship. And if they were immigrants, then they should be deported from the United States.[9]

Throughout the month of May, *Posten* ran many editorials on the primary election, all strongly supporting Burnquist for reasons of loyalty. "The first question for each candidate," the paper wrote on May 22, "must be: Does he correctly understand what we fight for, and can we expect him fully to support the government in this war?" *Posten* was also very severe in its criticism of the

J. A. A. Burnquist, ca. 1917

Nonpartisan League and its support of Lindbergh. The paper argued that the
League was an authoritarian organization run by "bosses," and accused it of
having close contacts with "lawless I. W. W. members and with red socialists."[10]

In order to enlist further support for Burnquist, *Posten* also employed the argument that the governor enjoyed strong support outside of the Swedish American community. A lengthy editorial on April 17 quoted positive editorial comments from four English-language Minnesota papers, and *Posten's* final editorial
before the election was a Swedish translation of an editorial from the *Minneapolis Tribune*, a newspaper which, among other things, was openly hostile
to the Nonpartisan League. A parallel was drawn in the editorial to the days of
the Civil War, when Minnesota Governor Alexander Ramsey was one of the
earliest supporters of President Lincoln. It concluded with an appeal to Minnesotans not to elect Lindbergh, "an open opponent of the war" and a person
supported by pro-German organizations: "The good name and reputation of
the state of Minnesota is at risk! Do not forget our state's record from the
1860s!"[11]

A quite different picture emerges from the pages of *Minnesota Stats Tidning*. Most importantly, it devoted far less attention to the election than did
Posten. One early reference to the campaign came in February, when the *Stats
Tidning* raised the question of whether the Nonpartisan League was a patriotic
organization. The paper noted that the League had been accused of disloyalty
and pro-German sympathies, but a closer examination of its program showed
that it included "many acceptable views." The League's problems were not so
much its ideas, the paper argued, but that of an "incompetent" leadership,
which often misrepresented the League's program.

After this cautiously positive assessment of the League, the *Stats Tidning*
made no references at all to the election until less than a month before the
June 17 polling date. At that time, an ad for Governor Burnquist appeared. The
only articles about the election to appear in the *Stats Tidning* came two weeks
prior to the election. A news story appeared about the Lindbergh campaign, in
which the candidate was quoted as saying that although he had opposed American entry in the war, he now "loyally supported the declaration of war and the
American war effort." In that same issue, the paper's only editorial comment
on the subject was given. The *Stats Tidning* argued that the main issue at hand
was to bring the war to a happy conclusion for both the United States and the
rest of the world. Furthermore, the *Stats Tidning* argued, "we cannot afford to
experiment" and, "without examining the qualifications of the other candidates," the candidate who had demonstrated the greatest degree of loyalty was
Governor Burnquist, which is why the paper endorsed him.[12]

Although the *Stats Tidning* came out in favor of Burnquist, it seems to be a rather lukewarm endorsement, especially as the paper chose not to examine the "other candidate." Moreover, the very limited coverage of a very intensive campaign also suggests that the paper wanted to minimize and perhaps even avoid the issue. It is reasonable to assume that the *Stats Tidning* harbored much more positive views of Lindbergh but felt unable to voice them during the vicious campaign against Lindbergh. In 1916, before the U.S. had entered the war and when Lindbergh unsuccessfully ran for Minnesota senator, the *Stats Tidning* showed less restraint in its opinions. It expressed sympathies for Lindbergh as "a friend of the people," one who was "free of any connection with the financial hierarchies." It also agreed with many of his ideas, including his analysis of World War I. The paper argued strongly against any kind of American involvement in the war, suggesting that those advocating American participation represented the capitalists and industrialists of Wall Street. "The capitalists have made an enormous profit from the fabrication and export of weapons and ammunition, and seek to increase these possibilities," although these motives were, the paper argued in May 1916, "hidden behind many hyper-patriotic phrases." The following month, the *Stats Tidning* maintained that it was not unpatriotic to suggest that America must address its own domestic problems before getting involved abroad. To criticize a war like this, and to argue that American domestic problems should be addressed prior to involvement abroad, was not to be unpatriotic.[13]

Even though both the major Swedish American newspapers in Minnesota thus endorsed the incumbent governor, it seems likely that *Minnesota Stats Tidning* did so under the influence of the bitter campaign against Lindbergh, whereas *Svenska Amerikanska Posten* supported Burnquist much more wholeheartedly. The question then becomes what impact did these discussions have on the Swedish American electorate? For whom did Swedish Americans in Minnesota vote in the 1918 Republican gubernatorial primary? Was it Lindbergh the insurgent or Burnquist the party regular? Did the Swedish American voting pattern differ from the Minnesota population in general, which gave Burnquist a victory, with 54 percent to Lindbergh's 41 percent of the vote?

One way of answering this question is by analyzing the election returns based on an ethnic analysis of the state counties. The counties have been grouped according to their ethnic composition, and those counties in which a particular ethnic group is predominant have been noted. Those counties in which no single group can be said to dominate have been classified as mixed. This analy-

sis cannot be expected to give absolute correlations between political preferences and ethnicity. Other factors have surely also played an important role.
Still, analyses of previous Minnesota elections by Sten Carlsson and Bruce Larson have yielded significant and consistent results, making the method's appli-
cation in this case meaningful. Table 1 shows the ten counties with the highest
concentration of Swedish Americans in Minnesota in the censuses of 1910 and
1920, which constitute the starting point for the statistical analysis of Swedish
American preferences in the Republican 1918 primary election.[14]

Next, a comparison of the returns for Lindbergh and Burnquist in these
counties with the state as a whole will be made in order to assess the level of
support for each candidate in these core areas of Swedish Minnesota. The results are shown in Table 2.

As Table 2 shows, there seems to have been strong support for Lindbergh in
the Swedish American core areas of Minnesota. In all of the ten Swedish counties, his support was stronger than in the state as a whole, ranging from 3 to 33
percent. On average, Lindbergh's result was 14 percentage points higher in the
Swedish counties than it was statewide. In seven of the counties he even defeated Burnquist. Likewise, Burnquist performed poorly in the Swedish counties. He only did better in one county—Pine—than in Minnesota as a whole. In
all other counties he polled fewer votes than in the state—by 11 percentage
points on average.

Moreover, an analysis of the return figures shows that Lindbergh did much

Table 1
The ten Minnesota counties with the highest share of Swedish-born
and American-born of Swedish parentage in 1910, and Swedish-born
in 1920, in percent of total population.

	1910	1920
1. Isanti	67	24
2. Chisago	60	22
3. Kittson	41	25
4. Kanabec	46	14
5. Lake	27	14
6. Mille Lacs	30	11
7. Meeker	31	10
8. Kandiyohi	28	9
9. Douglas	25	9
10. Pine	23	8
Minnesota	11.6	4.6

Sources: *United States Census* (1910 and 1920)

Table 2
Election results in percent for Lindbergh and Burnquist in ten Swedish Minnesota counties, and their differences in percentage points from the state average.

	Lindbergh		Burnquist	
	% of votes	Difference	% of votes	Difference
1. Isanti	74	+33	25	−29
2. Chisago	49	+ 8	49	− 5
3. Kittson	57	+16	41	−13
4. Kanabec	51	+10	48	− 6
5. Lake	55	+14	43	−11
6. Mille Lacs	52	+11	46	− 8
7. Meeker	48	+ 7	50	− 4
8. Kandiyohi	58	+17	40	−14
9. Douglas	68	+17	31	−23
10. Pine	44	+ 3	56	+ 2
Minnesota	41		54	

Source: *Legislative Manual for the State of Minnesota* (St. Paul, 1919), pp. 250f.

better in counties in which one ethnic group was predominant. Among Lindbergh's best fifteen counties, only two have been classified as mixed—i.e., no single ethnic group dominated. Among the remaining thirteen counties, five were dominated by Norwegians, four by Germans, three by Swedes, and one with a Scandinavian dominance. Burnquist's fifteen best counties show a different profile: ten were of mixed composition, while only five showed a particular ethnic dominance (four Scandinavian and one Norwegian). It seems as if there is a relationship between areas with a strong concentration of ethnic populations and electoral success for Charles Lindbergh.[15]

This observation is born out by an analysis of the election based on nativity. The Minnesota counties have been grouped in three categories: those where the native born dominated; those where the foreign born were predominant; and those which were characterized by native born of foreign parentage (foreign stock). Only those counties in which the share of the category in question exceeds 10 percent of its Minnesota average have been included (thirty-eight of the state's eighty-eight counties). The candidate's relative strength in these counties has then been analyzed. The results can be seen in Table 3.

Lindbergh, therefore, had his electoral strength among the ethnic communities in Minnesota—both in those counties dominated by immigrants and in those characterized by native-born citizens with immigrant parents (first- and second-generation immigrants). Burnquist, on the other hand, was strongest among the native-born Minnesotans. His average among the native born was 11 percentage points higher than in the state as a whole.

A final point regarding the urban/rural dimension of the election must also be made. The analysis of Swedish American voting patterns has largely been based on returns from rural areas in Minnesota, where the counties in which Swedish Americans clearly dominated could be found. But what of the thousands of Swedish Americans in the Twin Cities? For whom did they vote? That question is not easily answered, as many different immigrant and ethnic communities were found in the urban milieu of the Twin Cities, making it difficult to isolate the electoral behavior of one particular ethnic group. The election returns from Hennepin and Ramsey counties showed a clear victory for Governor Burnquist. His results in Hennepin County were far better than in the state as a whole, polling over 60 percent of the votes and receiving twice as many votes as his opponent. The returns from Ramsey County were more on the level of the state in general. It is possible then to conclude that Charles Lindbergh had strong support in rural areas of the state and also among the Swedish Americans there, whereas urban Minnesota clearly favored Governor Burnquist. The fact that *Svenska Amerikanska Posten,* which supported Burnquist so strongly, was published in Minneapolis and had a general political and social orientation, suggests that the support for Lindbergh in the Twin City Swedish American community may have been weaker than in rural areas.[16]

Having examined the way in which two of the leading Swedish-language newspapers in Minnesota covered the campaign, as well as the way in which heavily Swedish American counties in the state cast their votes, what about the

Table 3
The average results for Lindbergh and Burnquist in three groups of Minnesota counties and their differences in percentage points from the state average.

Group of counties	Lindbergh		Burnquist	
	% of votes	Difference	% of votes	Difference
Native born	33	− 8	65	+11
Foreign stock	56	+15	42	−12
Foreign born	46	+ 5	49	− 5
Minnesota	41		54	

Sources: *United States Census* (1920); *Legislative Manual for the State of Minnesota* (St. Paul, 1919), pp. 250f.

standing of these candidates in the Swedish American community? First, it should be noted that, although both of the newspapers came out in support of the incumbent Governor Burnquist, it seems very likely that *Minnesota Stats Tidning* did so because of the exceptional role the loyalty issue played during the campaign. Its coverage of the election was minimal and its endorsement of Burnquist was mild at best. An examination of the paper's position in the election of 1916, when the absence of the war seems to have allowed the *Stats Tidning* greater opportunities to voice its ideas, also shows much greater sympathies to issues associated with Charles Lindbergh, the Nonpartisan League, and the Populist movement in general. It seems as if Lindbergh and his ideas reverberated strongly within the Swedish American community and, despite the heated campaign against him, Swedish American opinion did not rally unanimously for Governor Burnquist.

Such an interpretation is also borne out by an analysis of the election returns. Although Governor Burnquist carried 54 percent of the vote statewide, his support in the typical Swedish American counties was much weaker and voters there tended to give the challenger Lindbergh support to a much larger degree than he received in Minnesota as a whole. As noted above, Lindbergh also defeated Burnquist outright in many of these areas. Further analysis of the election returns also demonstrates that Lindbergh not only showed greater popularity among Swedish Americans, he also did much better in areas dominated by immigrants and their children in general than in the state as a whole. Consequently, it may also be said that Lindbergh became the candidate of Minnesota immigrants and their children, whereas Burnquist had a much greater appeal among native-born Minnesotans, whose foreign background was at least two generations away.

Finally, it remains to assess Lindbergh's relative popularity among Minnesota Swedish Americans, even during such a harsh campaign as that of 1918. The ethnic factor is often an important explanatory variable in American political history, and, as both Sten Carlsson and Bruce Larson have shown, Swedish ethnicity has historically played an important role in Minnesota politics. But in the Lindbergh-Burnquist election of 1918, both candidates were Swedish Americans, and, although Lindbergh certainly emphasized his Swedishness less than Burnquist, it does not seem fruitful to interpret the outcome of the election in purely ethnic terms.

Instead, the gubernatorial election could be seen as an illustration of the spectrum of political and social ideas within the Minnesota Swedish American community. The relatively strong Swedish American support for Lindbergh in 1918 should be seen as an important indication of the promotion of "protest politics," as Bruce Larson described it, among Swedish Americans in Minnesota.

In the 1920s and 1930s, this would translate into Swedish American support for the Farmer-Labor Party in Minnesota, including such well-known names as Senator Magnus Johnson and Governor Floyd B. Olson.[17]

Lindbergh's Swedish American support was rooted in rural Minnesota. The counties in which he received Swedish American endorsement were all agricultural in nature, such as areas north and east of the Twin Cities, including Isanti, Chisago, Mille Lacs, Pine, and Kanabec counties, as well as an area to the west, including Kandiyohi and Meeker counties. These were areas where the program of the Nonpartisan League and Lindbergh resonated among Swedish American farmers. These were also places where Swedish American religion had its strongest hold over the population. Being so firmly rooted in rural Swedish American communities, it is not surprising, therefore, that the Augustana Synod-owned *Minnesota Stats Tidning* had sympathized with Lindbergh's cause in 1916 and had expressed cautious support for the Nonpartisan League and only reluctant support for Burnquist in 1918.

Svenska Amerikanska Posten, on the other hand, represented the urban community and, by 1918, a slowly growing Swedish American middle-class. Here, agrarian radicalism à la Charles Lindbergh found little support, and, in a campaign when loyalty to the newly adopted country was an issue, it was natural for this faction within the Swedish American community to throw its support to the candidate identified with loyalty. For this segment of the community it also gradually became important to distance itself from radical politics, especially in the form of socialism. *Svenska Amerikanska Posten's* attempt to link both the Nonpartisan League and Lindbergh to socialism can be seen as a part of this process.

In conclusion, then, the 1918 Republican gubernatorial primary election campaign illustrates the relatively broad spectrum of opinion within the Swedish American community, also pointing to the differences between urban and rural Swedish America. It was the agrarian areas in Minnesota that provided the foundation for an agrarian Populism of Lindbergh's kind, whereas the growing Swedish American middle-class was found in the cities, especially the Twin Cities, where organs like Swan Turnblad's *Svenska Amerikanska Posten* formulated its political and social ideas.

* * * *

NOTES

1. Bruce Larson, "Swedes in Minnesota Politics," in Byron Nordstrom, ed., *The Swedes in Minnesota* (Minneapolis: Denison, 1976), 93; Bruce Larson, *Lindbergh of Minnesota:*

A *Political Biography* (New York: Harcourt Brace Jovanovitch, 1973), 234; Bruce Larson, "Swedish Americans and Farmer-Labor Politics in Minnesota," in Nils Hasselmo, ed., *Perspectives on Swedish Immigration* (Chicago: Swedish Pioneer Historical Society, 1978), 208; Carol Jensen, "Loyalty as a Political Weapon: The 1918 Campaign in Minnesota," *Minnesota History* 44 (1972): 43.

2. The largest ethnic community in Minnesota in 1910 was the Germans (305,000 persons or 14.7 percent of the population). The Norwegians were in third place, with 231,000 individuals, making up 11.1 percent of all Minnesotans. For these figures, see U.S. Bureau of the Census, *Thirteenth Census of the United States, 1910* (Washington, D.C.: U.S. Government Printing Office, 1913), 2: 996; Sten Carlsson, "Swedes in Politics," in Hans Norman and Harald Runblom, eds., *From Sweden to America: A History of the Migration* (Uppsala & Minneapolis: University of Minnesota Press, 1976); Ulf Beijbom, *Mot löftets land. Den svenska utvandringen* (Stockholm, 1996), 196; Fritiof Ander, *T. N. Hasselquist: The Career and Influence of a Swedish-American Clergyman, Journalist and Educator* (Rock Island, Ill., 1931), 231. Cf. Larson, "Swedes in Minnesota Politics," 90. The sense of political frustration was probably more pronounced outside of Minnesota. It should be recognized that in Minnesota Swedes had been elected to local offices during the nineteenth century, and beginning in the 1890s Minnesota Swedish Americans ran for positions in both houses of Congress. Still, as Harald Runblom has pointed out, Swedish Americans were less successful than the Norwegians in Minnesota politics, which may explain a continued lack of political influence among Minnesota Swedes (Harald Runblom and Hans Norman, eds., *Transatlantic Connections: Nordic Migration to the New World after 1800* [Oslo: Norwegian University Press, 1988], 222ff.).

3. Richard Jensen, *The Winning of the Midwest: Social and Political Conflict, 1888–1896* (Chicago: University of Chicago Press, 1971); Paul Kleppner, *The Cross of Culture: A Social Analysis of Midwestern Politics* (New York: Free Press, 1970); Jon Gjerde, *Minds of the West: Ethnocultural Evolution in the Rural Middle West, 1830–1917* (Chapel Hill: University of North Carolina Press, 1997); Sten Carlsson, *Skandinaviska politiker i Minnesota 1882–1900. En studie av den etniska faktorns roll i politiska val i en immigrantstat* (Uppsala, 1971); "Scandinavian Politicians in Minnesota Around the Turn of the Century," in Harald Naess and Sigmund Skard, eds., *Americana-Norvegica, vol. III, Studies in Scandinavian-American Interrelations Dedicated to Einar Haugen* (Oslo, 1971); Larson, "Swedish Americans and Farmer-Labor Politics"; Jørn Brøndal, "National Identity and Midwestern Politics: Scandinavian-American Involvement in the Progressive Movement of Wisconsin, c 1890–1914" (unpublished Ph.D. diss., Univ. of Copenhagen, 1999). Cf. Richard Oestreicher, "Working-Class Political Behavior and Theories of American Political Behavior," *Journal of American History* 74 (1988), for a discussion and analysis of these approaches.

4. Quoted in Sture Lindmark, *Swedish America 1914–1932: Studies in Ethnicity with Emphasis on Illinois and Minnesota* (Uppsala, 1971), 95.

5. See Robert L. Morlan, *Political Prairie Fire: The Nonpartisan League 1915–1922* (Minneapolis: University of Minnesota Press, 1955), and Millard L. Gieske, *Minnesota Farmer-Laborism: The Third Party Alternative* (Minneapolis: University of Minnesota Press, 1979), 3–31 for a background to the Nonpartisan League and Minnesota Populism. Richard Lucas, *Charles August Lindbergh Sr.: A Case Study of Congressional Insurgency 1906–1912* (Uppsala, 1974), is a study of Lindbergh's political stance as a Congressman; Larson, *Lindbergh of Minnesota*, 219ff., 223.

6. Pamphlet published in Washington, D.C., 1917; Larson, *Lindbergh of Minnesota*, 211; *Why Is Your Country at War?*, 19f., 214f.

7. *Why Is Your Country at War?*, 73ff., 118f., 214. Cf. Morlan, *Political Prairie Fire*, 189f.

8. Janet Nyberg, "Swedish Language Newspapers in Minnesota," in Hasselmo, ed., *Perspectives on Swedish Immigration*, 250. For circulation statistics, see Lindmark, *Swedish America 1914–1932*, 331. See also Ulf Jonas Björk's chapter on *Posten* in this volume.

9. *Svenska Amerikanska Posten*, Mar. 27, Apr. 10, 1918.

10. Ibid., May 22, 1918; Feb. 27, Mar. 20, 1918.

11. Ibid., Apr. 17, 1918; Larson, *Lindbergh of Minnesota*, 228.

12. *Minnesota Stats Tidning*, May 22, 1918. See also May 29, 1918.

13. Ibid., Apr. 19, May 3, June 14, 1916.

14. Carlsson, *Skandinaviska politiker i Minnesota*; Carlsson, "Scandinavian Politicians in Minnesota Around the Turn of the Century"; Larson, "Swedish Americans and Farmer-Labor Politics."

15. Lindbergh: *German:* Carver, Brown, Sibley and Stearns; *Norwegian:* Pennington, Roseau, Clearwater, Chippewa, Yellow Medicine; *Swedish:* Isanti, Douglas, Kandiyohi; *Scandinavian:* Marshall; *Mixed:* Mahnomen, Red Lake. Burnquist: *Scandinavian:* Freeborn, Goodhue, Hennepin, Sherburne; *Norwegian:* Fillmore; *Mixed:* Fairbault, Rock, Anoka, Rice, Dodge, Mower, Houston, Martin, Murray, Lyon.

16. *Legislative Manual for the State of Minnesota, 1919* (St. Paul, 1919), 250f.

17. Gieske, *Minnesota Farmer-Laborism*, chapters 4–7.

Gubernatorial Politics
and Swedish Americans in Minnesota:
The 1970 Election and Beyond

BRUCE L. LARSON

In 1973, in a lead cover story, *Time* magazine praised Minnesota as "A State That Works" with "almost unnaturally clean" politics and success due to "its ethnic traditions," noting that: "In many respects, the Scandinavians, long the largest single group in the state, have shaped Minnesota's character. They, together with the large Anglo-Saxon and German strain, account for a deep grain of sobriety and hard work, a near-worship for education and a high civic tradition in Minnesota life." The 1970 Minnesota governor's race between Democratic-Farmer-Laborite (DFLer) Wendell R. Anderson (a lawyer and state senator from St. Paul, and the grandson of Swedish immigrants) and Republican Douglas M. Head (a lawyer and Minnesota's attorney general from Minneapolis, of English ancestry) set the stage for such national attention. This race also provides an opportunity to examine a Minnesota campaign and its long-term impact.[1]

The 1970 election represented a pivotal shift in political party history to virtual one-party control of state government by the DFL party. In general, Minnesota during its recent past from World War II to the present has been a competitive two-party state. The only exceptions have been the Republican resurgence from the governorship of Harold Stassen beginning in 1939 through C. Elmer Anderson in 1955, and then during the 1970s when the DFL gained control. As political scientist William Hathaway has observed: "Wendell Anderson's victory in the gubernatorial contest of 1970 marked the beginning of [this second] era." Thus the following themes will be discussed: (1) background to the 1970 race; (2) the 1970 campaign; (3) the Anderson administration, 1971–76; (4) the Twin Cities and Swedish heritage factors; and a summary and survey of 1976 and beyond will be offered.[2]

To understand the 1970 gubernatorial race, brief comment on Minnesota po-
litical history, particularly in the 1950s and 1960s, is necessary. During this period there was healthy competition between Minnesota's unique Democratic-
Farmer-Labor party (DFL)—the result of a 1944 merger between the Farmer-
Labor Party and the Democratic Party—and the Republican Party. By the 1960s,
such Minnesota DFL politicians as Hubert H. Humphrey, Eugene J. McCarthy,
Orville L. Freeman, and Walter F. Mondale had gained national prominence.
The DFL party was also torn, however, by two major internal struggles. First was
the 1966 governor's race in which Lieutenant Governor A. M. (Sandy) Keith
won the DFL endorsement over Governor Karl F. Rolvaag at an embattled state
convention. This was followed by a bitter primary challenge in which Rolvaag,
the son of Norwegian American author Ole Rølvaag and running on the slogan
"Let the People Decide," won by a two to one margin. Second was the 1968 presidential race in which U.S. Senator McCarthy and Vice President Humphrey
became embroiled in the bitter debate on America's role in Vietnam while
seeking the Democratic nomination. For Republicans in Minnesota, the decade
began with a gubernatorial victory by liberal leaning Elmer L. Andersen, a St.
Paul business executive of Norwegian and Swedish roots, who defeated DFL
Governor Orville Freeman, also of Swedish and Norwegian heritage, in his attempt for an unprecedented fourth term. In 1962, in the closest race for governor
in Minnesota history and the first four-year term, Rolvaag won over Andersen
by 91 votes after a recount.[3]

The 1966 DFL split provided an opportunity for Republicans, and Harold
Le Vander, a South St. Paul lawyer, the son of Swedish immigrants and a well-
known Lutheran lay leader, emerged as the endorsed candidate for governor.
Against a sharply divided DFL, Le Vander, with good rural support, conservative
backing, and probable DFL crossover votes, was easily elected in November. As
governor, Le Vander surprised many Republicans by supporting the creation of
a state Human Rights Commission, a new Metropolitan Council, a state Pollu-
tion Control Agency, and increased funding for postsecondary education—all
of which put him in the camp of progressive Republicanism. By 1969, however,
the state legislature had overridden Le Vander's vetoes of a state sales tax, and
his comments that "some small towns must die" in regard to regional government met with strong criticism from rural Minnesota. Yet he seemed likely to
be re-elected in 1970, and his decision early in the year to step down shocked
many Minnesotans. In his January 26, 1970, announcement, Le Vander, who had
never held public office before the governorship, explained that he believed in
the citizen politician, that he "never considered [himself] a career politician,"
and that holding public office was "an honorable but temporary privilege."
Other factors in his decision included his dislike for the political side of the job

and extensive demands on his time. As a case in point, Le Vander did not participate as an active leader in the Republican Party. Bernhard Le Vander, the governor's brother and a longtime Republican operative, also noted that (although not known at the time) another "underlying cause" to step aside was an earlier painful hip injury that made travel and movement difficult.[4]

The unexpectedly open 1970 gubernatorial race opened the door for potential candidates in both parties. On the GOP side, immediate response evolved into a contest between state Attorney General Head, a former state legislator and Yale law graduate with moderate political leanings, and James B. Goetz, the lieutenant governor and radio station owner from Winona, with a conservative and partly rural base. Head, who had already entered the U.S. Senate race against Republican Representative Clark MacGregor to run against Hubert Humphrey, emerged as the front-runner. Goetz claimed 42 percent of the delegates going into the state GOP convention in June, and it took several ballots before Head claimed victory. According to Head, there was bitterness within the party following the nomination struggle; for example, Head was strong among Hennepin County Republicans while Goetz carried Ramsey County delegates. To strengthen the ticket and consolidate this division, Head asked Goetz to be his running mate for lieutenant governor at the time, but Goetz declined. In fact, he remained politically inactive until early October when he then campaigned for Head. Ben Boo, the popular mayor of Duluth, after a heated contest with conservative state Senator Harold Kreiger of Rochester, won endorsement for lieutenant governor at the convention, while MacGregor received the nod for U.S. Senate.[5]

On the DFL side, there were five principal candidates for governor. They included two state Senators, Wendell Anderson and Nicholas Coleman of St. Paul, a University of Minnesota law professor, David Graven, a Minneapolis hotel owner, Robert Short, and Hennepin County Attorney George Scott. In the spring and early summer of 1970 they competed for DFL votes from the state convention to be held in Duluth in late June. With former Vice President Humphrey, who had narrowly lost the presidency to Richard Nixon in 1968, heading the DFL ticket as a candidate for the U.S. Senate, the election looked promising for the DFL. The main gubernatorial competition at the convention was between Anderson and Coleman. On the sixth ballot, after a meeting by candidates with Humphrey and party leaders, Coleman and Graven withdrew and Coleman made a motion for a "unanimous" endorsement for Anderson. Rumors on the convention floor were that a "deal had been struck" and urged delegates to get on with the Humphrey nomination. Spirited competition also developed for the lieutenant governor position between state Senator Rudy Perpich, a Hibbing dentist and the son of a Croatian immigrant mining family,

Jon Wefald, a Gustavus Adolphus College history professor who had run for
Congress in 1968, and Thomas Byrne, a former mayor of St. Paul. Byrne withdrew after the first ballot, and Perpich received enough votes to win endorsement on the second ballot. Perpich's political experience, his appeal in St. Louis
County and northern Minnesota, and his ties to Nick Coleman were factors in
his successful bid. Wefald then received the DFL endorsement for state auditor.[6]

Although not the main issue in controlling DFL candidate choices at the
convention, antiwar supporters were vocal in the hall following the unpopular Cambodian invasion ordered by President Nixon in May. Most identified
with the antiwar cause was Earl Craig, an African American University of Minnesota faculty member and Humphrey's rival for the DFL endorsement for the
U.S. Senate. Humphrey won the Senate endorsement by roughly a 4 to 1 delegate vote over Craig.[7]

With candidates Anderson and Head in place, the election campaign began.
In the opinion of most political observers and the two major participants, it was
a "program-oriented" and "positive" campaign. Indeed, both candidates framed
specific position papers on a wide range of issues, including crime control, education, taxes, legislative reform, commercial interest rates, the Metropolitan
Council, and the environment. Anderson proposed a major shift in school funding, calling for a reduction in property taxes offset by an increase in sales taxes
and income taxes. Head predicted that the plan would result in inordinately
high tax increases, and in contrast he promised to "hold the line" on all major
taxes. When Anderson sharply criticized the Le Vander administration for a
"feeble hold" on state government, Governor Le Vander quickly countered that
Doug Head had "superior qualifications" and more leadership experience than
Anderson. As the campaign progressed, Head seemed to have the support of
most state daily newspapers, including both Duluth papers (perhaps partly due
to Ben Boo on the Republican ticket). Anderson had strong support from labor
and the AFL-CIO, stressing his personal working class family history (his grand-
father was a streetcar motorman and his father was a meatpacker) and carry-

ing ads in the *Union Advocate*. Anderson also had
some rural farm support, particularly from the
Farmers Union. But rural southern Minnesota likely
remained good Republican country.[8]

Another factor in the campaign was the effec-
tive use of television and the media by Wendy
Anderson. Arthur Naftalin, the former mayor of
Minneapolis, later said that Anderson won the TV

Wendell Anderson, ca. 1971

competition with "the set of his jaw," his blue eyes, his "sincere and direct" approach to the camera, and his general vigorous appearance, which projected well in ads and during a series of TV debates with Head. Even the opposition press admitted that Anderson had a "better image," was a "charmer," and, as the "DFL's screen star," looked good, but pointed out that in "terms of ability" Head had the edge and that Minnesotans should elect him. While both Anderson (at age 37) and Head (at age 40) were young and articulate, Head, who earlier had conquered a bout with polio, projected less well on camera. Both Head and Anderson by common consent did not mention this issue, but journalist Gerry Nelson noted at the time that "It is the difference in their physical make-up—probably not a legitimate issue but one which could influence voters." To some voters, Nelson further commented, Anderson seemed almost too "youthful," and he began wearing dark conservative suits.[9]

The issue of Scandinavian and Swedish name identity was also present in the campaign. Indeed, Douglas Head stated that he considered it a "substantial issue" in the campaign, while observer Bernhard Le Vander declared that Anderson was a "good political name" in Minnesota. At the same time, some newspapers pointed out the confusion in 1970 when three Andersons were running on the statewide ticket: Wendell Anderson for governor; and, for a seat on the Public Service Commission, Ronald Anderson, an incumbent; and former Governor C. Elmer Anderson. Moreover, according to the Hibbing *Daily Tribune*, some Republican leaders were worried that the campaign effort to elect DFLer Anderson for governor and Republican Boo for lieutenant governor (in 1970 candidates need not be elected on the same party) might lead some "uninformed voters" into thinking that they were voting for popular former Republican Governor Elmer L. Andersen. Swedish or not, polls from August to October showed a tight race, with predictions in the 5 percent spread range for either Head or Anderson, and by late October they were predicting a race "too close to call." A *Minneapolis Tribune* poll in late October 1970 showed Head with 48.5 percent and Anderson with 48 percent. On the Sunday before the election, a rumor circulated that Hubert Humphrey had suffered a heart attack, but the former vice president quickly dispelled the issue while winding down his Senate campaign.[10]

The results on November 3 were not as close as the polls, with DFL candidate Anderson elected governor over Head with 53.4 percent of the vote and carrying fifty-one of Minnesota's eighty-seven counties. Rudy Perpich was

Douglas Head

elected lieutenant governor, although Ben Boo did slightly better than Head in
the state totals. Other aspects of the 1970 results include Anderson's strong support from the Twin Cities vote and the Scandinavian and Swedish vote. In both
Minneapolis, with 58.7 percent of the vote, and St. Paul, with 63.3 percent of the
vote, Anderson outperformed statewide results. He also had crucial DFL backing in Duluth, with 65.3 percent of the vote, and in St. Louis County, with 72
percent of the vote. In a sample of Minnesota's thirty-one most Scandinavian
counties, Anderson carried twenty-seven. Based on the 1940 census, the geographical and ethnic distribution of these "most Scandinavian counties" is as
follows: a majority of Swedes in northern and central counties, a majority of
Norwegians in northern and western counties, a majority of Finns in northern
and eastern counties, and a majority of Danes in southern counties. Within this
sample Anderson carried thirteen of the fourteen most Swedish counties, nine
of the eleven most Norwegian counties, three of the four most Finnish counties, and both of the most Danish counties. Anderson lost Clay, Douglas, Otter
Tail, and Wadena counties. Thus, most Scandinavians supported Anderson, including most of the politically active and farm-oriented Norwegians in the Red
River Valley. DFLer Warren Spannaus won the attorney general race in 1970, but
Republicans claimed the other three major state offices, including victors Arlen
Erdahl as secretary of state, Rolland Hatfield as state auditor, and longtime incumbent Val Bjornson as state treasurer. Hubert Humphrey easily won his bid
to return to the U. S. Senate, garnering 57.8 percent of the vote and carrying
sixty-eight of Minnesota's eighty-seven counties. One surprise in the 1970 election was the defeat of powerful legislator Gordon Rosenmeier of Little Falls, a
thirty-year veteran of the state Senate, to Winston Borden of Brainerd, in part
the result of the abortion issue.[11]

On what basis then did Minnesota voters choose Anderson over Head in
the 1970 governor's race? A well-organized and issue-oriented campaign by the
Anderson camp was the first major factor. It had started well before 1970, and,
according to active participants, the main "architects of the Anderson campaign" were attorney David Lebedoff, Anderson campaign manager and close
friend, and Tom Kelm, longtime Second District DFL operative. Doug Head said
simply that Anderson "ran a good campaign." Second, Anderson ran a successful and effective television media campaign. Print journalism after the 1960s
was "not as credible" in campaigns according to political scientist Bob Barrett.
Indeed, it could be argued that the 1970 Anderson/Head race and the impact
of TV debates in Minnesota played a role similar to the national TV debates in
the John Kennedy/Richard Nixon 1960 presidential race. Third, Hubert Humphrey provided great strength by heading the Democratic ticket. Humphrey
carried Minnesota easily and helped the state ticket; the others rode the "coattails of Paul Bunyan," said the *Duluth Herald*. Jon Wefald, candidate for state

auditor in 1970, emphasized the same point, noting that "I personally campaigned with Humphrey throughout the state in the summer and fall of 1970.
I have never seen any political leader work harder or more effectively than
HHH. He is, without a doubt, the greatest grassroots campaigner I have ever
worked with." Yet, the Republican *Mankato Free Press* argued that the "Victory
was Anderson's" and that he ran a good campaign and would have won even
without HHH; not so with Perpich and Spannaus. Anderson's ties to Humphrey were strong; he had been Minnesota campaign manager for Humphrey's
1968 presidential bid.[12]

A fourth reason was the strong showing of Anderson in the Twin Cities and
St. Louis County. In the analysis of political scientists, Republican voters up to
1974 made up roughly half of Minnesota outstate voters: "Heavy DFL margins in
the major cities usually are enough to carry the state for statewide DFL candidates even if Republicans win narrow margins outstate." Fifth, Anderson had
the ability to bring together elements within the DFL; namely, the diverse farmer,
labor, and intellectual wings of the party. He was identified as a "liberal of the
blue-collar variety," and his political style was to work toward compromise both
within the party and his administration. His models and heroes were Humphrey
and Harry Truman. His election brought a "quiet upheaval" in state government,
stated one opinion in 1970. Sixth, Anderson benefited from the bitterness generated by the competition in the primary between Head and Goetz. This internal schism likely hurt Head and the Republican ticket. Would a Head/Goetz
ticket have overcome any of Anderson's strengths? And finally, the results in
the Scandinavian sample counties underscore the role of Scandinavian and
Swedish name identity; this was also noted by several participants and observers. They include Head, Le Vander, Anderson, Val Bjornson, and Elmer L.
Andersen, as well as Martin Olav Sabo and Joan Anderson Growe, both of
whom purposely added the Scandinavian names "Olav" and "Anderson" in earlier political campaigns.[13]

Next, let us turn our attention to the Anderson administration between 1971
and 1976 and the politics beyond that time, as well as the ongoing impact of
Swedish and Scandinavian factors. The role of the Twin Cities is also crucial.
Immediately following the election, Anderson and his family appeared in photo
opportunities and press coverage with Hubert Humphrey, and it was an attractive new first family for Minnesota. With his wife Mary, an articulate former Bemidji homecoming queen and the daughter of conservative state legislator John McKee, and three very young children (Amy, Beth, and Brett; ages
three, two, and five months), it was a happy moment.[14]

As governor, Anderson introduced his ambitious plan of tax equalization
and school finance reform. After three special sessions, the program, dubbed
the "Minnesota Miracle," passed, largely because of bipartisan support. In 1974,

Anderson faced a re-election campaign against a less well-known Republican candidate, state Senator John W. Johnson. Despite Republican attacks of "Spendy Wendy" and charges that the governor could only be found for a debate on the golf course, Anderson stood on his record. It was a landslide for Anderson/Perpich in the aftermath of Watergate, as the DFL swept all state constitutional offices. Anderson won the 1974 election with 62.8 percent of the vote and carried all eighty-seven counties, including all of the Scandinavian/Swedish sample counties. Moreover, Anderson/Perpich again ran better in the Twin Cities than statewide, winning 71.7 percent of the vote in Minneapolis and 74.6 percent of the vote in St. Paul. Expectedly, Anderson/Perpich also did well in northeastern Minnesota, taking 68.9 percent of the vote in the Eighth Congressional District, including Duluth and St. Louis County.[15]

During Anderson's second term, with a DFL-controlled legislature, other reforms such as the unionization of public employees and environmental laws were passed, but there was also some criticism of his handling of the Reserve Mining tailings case and his apparent national political aspirations. In any case, the Anderson administration remained on firm political ground, including high approval in the polls, and the governor's success drew praise from politicians and the press. "The best friend public education ever had," stated former DFL Minnesota House Speaker and current Congressman Martin Sabo. Longtime former Republican legislator and State University Board chairman Rodney Searle agreed, asserting that Anderson was the "best prepared to handle education issues" of the seven governors with whom he had served. Anderson's commissioner of agriculture, Jon Wefald, rated him an "excellent" governor with many successful programs. The *Minneapolis Star* at the time termed him a "forceful leader," while the cover story in *Time* (1973) found him "almost too good to be true." Homer E. Williamson, a Minnesota political scholar, studied the governors who had served since World War II and ranked them according to such gubernatorial powers as legal/constitutional, institutional, political, and personal style. Anderson placed among the top four, along with popular three-term governors Republican Luther Youngdahl and DFLer Orville Freeman and two-term (1983–91) DFLer Rudy Perpich.[16]

During the Anderson years there were at least three occasions on which the governor's Swedish heritage drew public notice: (1) visits to the state by Charles Lindbergh in 1973; (2) the Anderson family visit to Sweden in the summer of 1975 to receive awards; and (3) King Carl XVI Gustaf's visit to Minnesota in the spring of 1976. Like many other Scandinavian American governors, Anderson was proud of his ethnic heritage (all four grandparents were Swedish and came from Västergötland, Värmland, and Hälsingland provinces), and he willingly engaged in contacts with the Swedish king and the president of Finland during his terms in office. In 1973, at a function at the governor's mansion, the state

honored Lindbergh with a plaque noting his achievements in promoting conservation, while in the fall Lindbergh gave the main address at the opening of
the Minnesota Historical Society's Lindbergh Interpretive Center at Little
Falls, at which time this writer also delivered comments on Lindbergh's Swedish
origins and his congressman father, Charles A. Lindergh, Sr. Unknown at the
time, Governor Anderson had asked Lindbergh to speak at the National Governor's Conference, which Anderson chaired. Although Lindergh was considering the offer, his death in 1974 of cancer precluded such an appearance. After
Lindbergh's death, Anderson released a thoughtful statement on Lindbergh
and the "rare privilege" it had been to meet him.[17]

On the second occasion, the Anderson family traveled to Sweden in the summer of 1975 where the governor was honored during "Minnesota Day" celebrations at the Emigrant Institute in Växjö and recognized as "Swedish American
of the Year" in Stockholm. There he presented the Swedish king with a Native
American peace pipe and commemorative plaque, joshing that he could trace
his Swedish roots farther back than the king, to the 1600s. The events were well
covered in the Swedish press. The third occasion was the visit of King Carl XVI
Gustaf to Minnesota in April 1976. There were several events in Minneapolis
and St. Peter celebrating Swedish heritage in Minnesota, including a meeting
with the governor, the awarding of fifteen gold and silver medals by the king
(among the recipients, for example, were Bernhard Le Vander, for his work as
Bicentennial chair, and businessman Curtis Carlson), the commissioning of a
medal for the king by Paul Granlund of Gustavus Adolphus College, and the
publication of a book, *The Swedes in Minnesota*, by the Swedish Bicentennial
Committee. It was a warm reception indeed for the king in Minnesota.[18]

Minnesota politics beyond 1976 began when Jimmy Carter picked Walter
Mondale as his running mate ("Grits and Fritz"), and, in a fateful decision,
Anderson resigned the governorship to be appointed to Mondale's U.S. Senate
seat. Rudy Perpich was thus elevated to governor, the first governor of the
Roman Catholic faith and of eastern European roots. In the 1978 election, both
Anderson and Perpich fell victim to the "Minnesota Massacre," as Republican
Al Quie, a former congressman with Norwegian roots, won the state house,
and both U.S. Senate seats were captured by the Republicans. Rudy Boschwitz
defeated Anderson, and Dave Durenberger won over Bob Short after a bitter
DFL primary fight between Short and Donald Fraser (both Boschwitz and
Durenberger had German ethnic origins, Boschwitz was a German immigrant
of the Jewish faith). Anderson, who had never lost an election, won only St.
Louis County. Anderson later admitted that he "wanted to be a Senator" and
was politically ambitious, reflecting that "I thought it made sense. . . . It didn't,
and I accept that;" it was an "honest mistake." He had also been considering the
option of a third four-year term as governor, which had never been attempted

and might have been difficult to achieve. The stunning DFL turnabout in 1978 was the result, in part, of the loss of Hubert Humphrey, who had died of cancer in 1978, as party leader, the Fraser/Short struggle, the Anderson appointment issue, and attractive Republican candidates. Wendell Anderson continued his interest in education and public service, completing two six-year terms as a member of the Board of Regents of the University of Minnesota and serving as Honorary Consul for Sweden in Minneapolis.[19]

Gubernatorial politics in Minnesota in the 1982 election became more fragmented, with one-issue supporters, involving abortion and the Christian fundamentalist right, affecting both parties. Moreover, party loyalties had eroded. Both party-endorsed candidates, Warren Spannaus of the DFL and Lieutenant Governor Lou Wangberg on the Republican side, were defeated in the primaries. Perpich, teamed with Marlene Johnson (the first woman to run for lieutenant governor), made an amazing comeback and defeated liberal Republican Wheelock Whitney in the general election. As governor, maverick Perpich enjoyed support from both conservatives and liberals on a range of issues, whether it was pro-business for conservatives or education for liberals. In 1986, Perpich easily won reelection over conservative Republican Cal Ludeman of Tracy. Thereafter, in the unexpected developments of the 1990 election, with the discovery of a sex scandal involving Republican-endorsed conservative Jon Grunseth, Arne Carlson, the son of Swedish immigrants, emerged as the surprise Republican candidate for governor and defeated incumbent Perpich in a close race. Carlson was also a maverick, in this case in Republican circles, and, like Perpich, he fashioned support from liberals on social issues while appealing to conservatives with a tight fiscal agenda and reduced state spending. In 1994, Carlson easily won reelection over DFLer John Marty.[20]

What, then, can be said about the Twin Cities and Swedish/Scandinavian factors in the 1970 election and beyond? Clearly the Twin Cities vote aided Anderson and the DFL in 1970, and indeed the Twin Cities electorate has been a mainstay for the DFL, along with the Iron Range and Duluth, in Minnesota's recent political past. There have been exceptions, when internal party schisms or non-traditional candidates became more important than typical liberal or DFL leanings, such as the support to Republicans Harold Le Vander in 1966 and Al Quie in 1978, who carried normally DFL Hennepin and Ramsey counties. Is Swedish or Scandinavian ethnicity still a factor? It would seem by 1970 and beyond that ethnicity would be clearly less significant in shaping voters' views than political, economic, and social issues in America. Yet, as Sten Carlsson has observed about Minnesota politics, Scandinavian dominance has been "overrepresented" when compared to its population strength. For example, while there is a large German population, this group has tended to be less active politically, due in part to the split between German Roman Catholics and German Protestants, mainly Lutherans, and the stigma of being German American during the two world wars. Carlsson also pointed out that, in the United States, state governorships have had a proportionately "greater attraction for Swedish Americans than Congress." Note that twenty-one of the last twenty-six Minnesota governors have been of Scandinavian descent.[21]

It would seem, moreover, that Swedes and Scandinavians often tend to combine progressive political views with a conservative personal lifestyle. Scandinavian and Swedish name identity still seems to persist, at least in the races for governor of Minnesota, as expressed by those involved in the 1970 contest and other politicians of the modern period. In the judgment of Wendy Anderson, Minnesotans vote primarily on perception and trust in the candidate and second on the candidate's position on issues. Only then, he noted, might other matters such as ethnic identity play a role in the minds of voters. Another Andersen, former Governor Elmer L., suggested that the success of Minnesota Scandinavians in politics was due to a "good image" and was most important "statewide." Yet another Anderson, journalist Dave, put it simply: "Having a Scandinavian name is Way Ahead of Whatever is in Second Place." Or, in the words of former Governor Elmer L., partly in jest, "Whenever Minnesotans elect a Scandinavian, they never make a mistake."[22]

Addendum

Since the 1996 celebrations of the 150th anniversary of the Swedes in America, one further Minnesota gubernatorial election has occurred—in 1998, and it was a shocker! In a stunning political upset in the general election, Reform Party candidate Jesse (the Body) Ventura, a former pro-wrestler, Brooklyn Park mayor, and radio talk show host, won with a plurality of 37 percent of the vote, the lowest in Minnesota history. In a three-way race, he defeated career politicians Norman Coleman, mayor of St. Paul and former DFLer who had switched parties in 1996, and Hubert (Skip) Humphrey III, longtime Minnesota attorney general and the son of Hubert Humphrey, who received 34 percent and 28 percent of the vote, respectively. Of Minnesota's eighty-seven counties, Ventura carried thirty-eight, Coleman thirty-two, and Humphrey seventeen. It should be noted that over 60 percent of Minnesotans did not vote for Ventura, with Coleman and Humphrey carrying northern Minnesota and much of outstate southern and western Minnesota. Ventura carried the Twin Cities and suburbs and a wide band of counties extending into north central, west central, and southern Minnesota. Among the sample Scandinavian counties, Humphrey carried fourteen, Ventura ten, and Coleman seven.[23]

The general election had been preceded by a hard-fought DFL primary, involving three powerful names in Minnesota political history, which also had

342

BRUCE L. LARSON

partly Scandinavian roots (mainly Norwegian) in each case. They included DFL-endorsed Hennepin County attorney Mike Freeman, the son of former Governor and U.S. Secretary of Agriculture Orville Freeman; Ted Mondale, the son of former Vice President Walter F. Mondale; and Humphrey, the son of former Vice President Hubert Humphrey.[24]

Ventura's victory tended to draw on the independent tradition of Minnesota voters. However, it did not fit earlier third party successes and agrarian protest in Minnesota, which normally occurred during times of major economic difficulties, such as the Populist success in the 1890s and the Farmer-Labor Party success in the 1930s. The Ventura (his real name is James Janos—of Slovakian ethnic descent) phenomenon seemed to reflect, in early analysis: first, a vote against politics as usual, and a need for both major parties to move toward the

Table 1
Minnesota Governors, 1961–1999

Date	Governor of Minnesota	Ethnic Ancestry	Political Party
1961–1963	Elmer L. Andersen	Norwegian & Swedish	Republican
1963–1967	Karl F. Rolvaag	Norwegian	DFL
1967–1971	Harold Le Vander	Swedish	Republican
1971–1976	Wendell R. Anderson	Swedish	DFL
1976–1979	Rudy Perpich	Croatian	DFL
1979–1983	Albert Quie	Norwegian	Ind. Rep.
1983–1991	Rudy Perpich	Croatian	DFL
1991–1999	Arne Carlson	Swedish	Ind. Rep.
1999–	Jesse Ventura (James Janos)	Slovakian	Reform

Table 2
Percentage of Vote for Minnesota Governors, 1960–1998

Arne Carlson (Ind. Rep.)	1994	63.3%
Wendell R. Anderson (DFL)	1974	62.8%
Rudy Perpich (DFL)	1982	58.6%
Rudy Perpich (DFL)	1986	55.8%
Wendell Anderson (DFL)	1970	54.3%
Harold Le Vander (Rep.)	1966	52.6%
Albert Quie (Ind. Rep.)	1978	52.3%
Elmer L. Andersen (Rep.)	1960	50.6%
Arne Carlson (Ind. Rep.)	1990	50.1%
Karl F. Rolvaag (DFL)	1962	49.7%
Jesse Ventura (Reform)	1998	37.0%

Sources: *Minnesota Legislative Manual, 1961–1962* to *1995–1996; Congressional Quarterly, Guide to U.S. Elections,* 1998.

The Republican Party of Minnesota used the label "Independent Republican" in the elections from 1978 through 1996.

center; second, high name-recognition for a former pro-wrestler and radio talk show host who was comfortable with TV and media appearances; third, the mobilization of nonvoters and young voters by Ventura; fourth, an underestimation by his opponents and lack of thorough challenge by them or the media on issues; fifth, an appeal to blue-collar workers as "one of us"and to some hard-pressed farmers; and finally, a broad theme of less government and fewer taxes, although details were vague.[25]

Thus Jesse Ventura represents the first non-Scandinavian to be elected Minnesota governor since Rudy Perpich. While the 1998 gubernatorial election seems contradictory to the themes of Scandinavian identity presented earlier in this essay, it does not change the overall trend of electing Scandinavian American

Table 3
Twin Cities and Statewide Vote for Governor, 1970 and 1974

1970 General Election

Location	DFL Vote	Percentage	Republican Vote	Percentage
Minneapolis	86,969	58.7%	61,249	41.3%
St. Paul	67,057	63.3%	38,849	36.7%
Minnesota Total	737,921	54.3%	621,780	45.7%

1974 General Election

Location	DFL Vote	Percentage	Republican Vote	Percentage
Minneapolis	83,299	71.7%	32,841	28.3%
St. Paul	60,630	74.6%	20,679	25.4%
Minnesota Total	786,787	62.8%	367,722	29.4%

Table 4
Scandinavian/Swedish Counties and Minnesota Elections for Governor, 1962–1982 and 1998

	87 Total MN Counties & Vote	31 Scand. Co. & Vote	14 Swedish Co. & Vote
1962	48 Rep. (55.2%)	19 DFL (61.3%)	8 DFL (57.1%)
1966	63 Rep. (72.4%)	16 Rep. (51.6%)	9 Rep. (64.3%)
1970	51 DFL (58.6%)	27 DFL (87.1%)	13 DFL (92.9%)
1974	87 DFL (100%)	31 DFL (100%)	14 DFL (100%)
1978	65 Ind. Rep. (74.7%)	20 Ind. Rep. (64.5%)	8 Ind. Rep. (57.1%)
1982	77 DFL (88.5%)	31 DFL (100%)	14 DFL (100%)
1998	38 Reform (43.7%)	14 DFL (45.2%)	9 Reform (64.3%)

Sources: *Minnesota Legislative Manual, 1961–1962* to *1983–1984*; U.S. Bureau of the Census, *Census of the United States, 1940*, Population; Minnesota Secretary of State, 1998 election returns on website.

*Statistical computations are by the author.

1970 Governor's Race: General Election

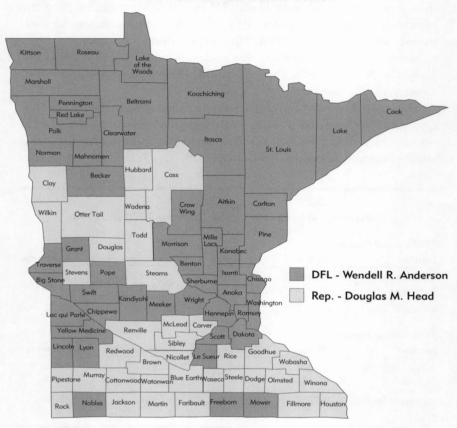

- ■ DFL - Wendell R. Anderson
- □ Rep. - Douglas M. Head

Source: *Minnesota Legislative Manual, 1971–1972*

Minnesota State University, Mankato, Department of Geography

I am grateful to David Sulze, graduate assistant in History, and Professor Cynthia Miller, Geography, for their assistance with these maps.

1970 U.S. Senate Race: General Election

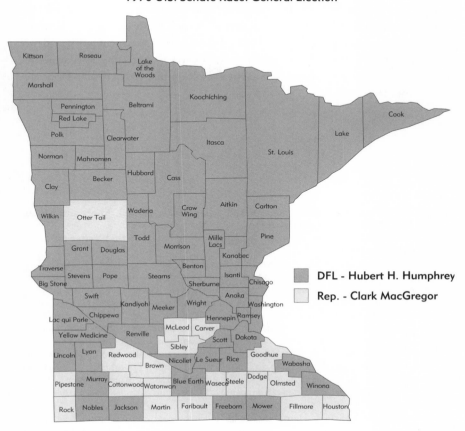

Kittson | Roseau | Lake of the Woods
Marshall
Pennington | Beltrami | Koochiching | Cook
Red Lake
Polk | Clearwater | Lake
Norman | Mahnomen | Itasca | St. Louis
Clay | Becker | Hubbard | Cass
Wilkin | Otter Tail | Wadena | Crow Wing | Aitkin | Carlton
Grant | Douglas | Todd | Morrison | Mille Lacs | Pine
Traverse | Stevens | Pope | Stearns | Benton | Kanabec
Big Stone | Swift | Sherburne | Isanti | Chisago
Lac qui Parle | Chippewa | Kandiyohi | Meeker | Wright | Anoka | Washington
Yellow Medicine | Renville | McLeod | Carver | Hennepin | Ramsey
Lincoln | Lyon | Redwood | Sibley | Scott | Dakota
Pipestone | Murray | Cottonwood | Brown | Nicollet | Le Sueur | Rice | Goodhue | Wabasha
Rock | Nobles | Jackson | Watonwan | Blue Earth | Waseca | Steele | Dodge | Olmsted | Winona
Martin | Faribault | Freeborn | Mower | Fillmore | Houston

DFL - Hubert H. Humphrey

Rep. - Clark MacGregor

Source: *Minnesota Legislative Manual, 1971–1972*

Minnesota State University, Mankato, Department of Geography

governors in the twentieth century, as clearly demonstrated. Although Ventura's
wife Terry has partial Scandinavian roots as a native of rural southern Minnesota,
that was not a factor in the unusual 1998 election. Clearly an outsider, Ventura
and his governorship present a real test for divided government at work, with no
real Reform Party colleagues for the new governor and a state legislature divided between a DFL-controlled Senate and a Republican-controlled House of
Representatives.

* * * *

NOTES

1. "The Good Life in Minnesota: Gov. Wendell Anderson" (cover), "Minnesota: A State
That Works" (story), *Time*, Aug. 13, 1973, p. 24, 31–35; 24, 34 (quotes).

2. William L. Hathaway, *Minnesota Politics and Parties Today* (St. Paul: Carter and Lacey
Publications, 1978), 35, 44.

3. See Theodore C. Blegen, *Minnesota: A History of the State*, rev. ed. (Minneapolis: Univ.
of Minn. Press, 1975); Robert Sobel and John Raimo, eds. *Biographical Directory of the Governors of the United States*, vol. 2 (Westport, Conn.: Meckler Books, 1978); John E. Haynes,
"Reformers, Radicals, and Conservatives," in Clifford E. Clark., ed., *Minnesota in a Century
of Change: The State and Its People Since 1900* (St. Paul: MHS Press, 1989), 387–89; David
Lebedoff, *The 21st Ballot: A Political Party Struggle in Minnesota* (Minneapolis: Univ. of
Minn. Press, 1969); G. Theodore Mitau, *Politics in Minnesota*, rev. ed. (Minneapolis: Univ.
of Minn. Press, 1970), 27–38; Ronald F. Stinnett and Charles H. Backstrom, *Recount* [1962
gubernatorial election] (Washington, D.C.: National Document Publishers, Inc., 1964); and
Laura K. Auerbach, *Worthy to Be Remembered: A Political History of the Minnesota Democratic-Farmer-Labor Party, 1944–1984* (Minneapolis: Democratic-Farmer-Labor Party of Minnesota, 1984).

4. "Biographical Sketch: Harold Le Vander: Former Governor of Minnesota" and other
items sent to the author by Iantha Le Vander (wife of Governor Le Vander); Iantha Le Vander to Bruce L. Larson, Sept. 26, 1991; Mitau, *Politics in Minnesota*, 38, 42; Bruce L. Larson,
"Scandinavian and Scandinavian-American Governors of Minnesota and Education," in
Scandinavian Immigrants and Education in North America, Philip J. Anderson, Dag Blanck,
and Peter Kivisto, eds. (Chicago: Swedish-American Historical Society, 1995), 177ff.; "Harold
Le Vander," thirty-minute videorecording in Minnesota Governors series, written and produced by Arthur Naftalin (Minneapolis: Hubert H. Humphrey Institute, Univ. of Minn.,
1981); *St. Paul Pioneer Press*, Jan. 27, 1970; *Minneapolis Star and Tribune*, June 20, 1986; interview with Douglas M. Head, Oct. 15, 1996; interview with Robert A. Barrett (a political
scientist at Minnesota State Univ., Mankato, and an active Republican in Nicollet and Blue
Earth counties), Oct. 14, 1996; interview with Bernhard Le Vander (brother and political
adviser to Governor Harold Le Vander, Republican party operative starting with the Stassen
governorship, and former Republican party state chair), Oct. 14, 1996; Mitau, *Politics in
Minnesota*, 72. Governor Le Vander later had a hip replacement.

5. *St. Paul Pioneer Press*, Jan. 27, 1970; *Minneapolis Star*, June 8, 1970; *Duluth News-
Tribune*, Jan. 1970; Douglas M. Head interview; *Duluth Herald*, Oct. 2, 1970.

6. *Duluth News-Tribune*, June 28, 1970; *St. Paul Pioneer Press*, June 28, 1970; June 29,
1970; *Union Advocate* (St. Paul), June 29, 1970; interview with W. Scott Shrewsbury (a po-

litical scientist at Minn. State Univ., Mankato, a DFL activist in Blue Earth County, and a delegate to the 1970 DFL state convention), Sept. 25, 1996; interview with Jon Wefald, Oct. 11, 1996; Jon Wefald letter and commentary to Bruce L. Larson, Jan. 27, 1998. Wefald is the grandson of former Minnesota Farmer-Labor Congressman Knud Wefald of Hawley (1923–27). On Humphrey, see also Carl Solberg, *Hubert Humphrey: A Biography* (New York: W. W. Norton and Company, 1984); and Bruce L. Larson, "Scandinavian-Americans and the American Liberal Political Heritage," *Scandinavian Review* (Winter, 1998–99), 4–15.

7. *Duluth News-Tribune,* June 28, 1970; W. Scott Shrewsbury interview; Jon Wefald interview.

8. Douglas M. Head interview; interview with Wendell R. Anderson, Apr. 17, 1992. Advertisements, position papers, news releases and newspaper clippings on the 1970 campaign may be found in the Wendell R. Anderson Papers and the Harold Le Vander Papers, both at the MHS, St. Paul, and in the "Wendell Anderson" file at the Duluth Public Library; 1970 campaign items such as bumper stickers, buttons, and posters may be found in the MHS Museum collections. Data here is from *Mankato Free Press,* Oct. 27, 1970, Oct. 28, 1970; *Minneapolis Star,* Oct. 30, 1970; *Duluth News-Tribune,* Oct. 22, 1970; *Duluth Herald,* Oct. 22, 1970; *Union Advocate,* Oct. 1970.

9. "Wendell Anderson," videorecording, Minnesota Governors series; *Duluth News-Tribune,* Oct. 22, 1970; *Mankato Free Press,* Nov. 4, 1970; Douglas M. Head interview; *Fairmont Sentinel,* Oct. 10, 1970 (Nelson quote).

10. Douglas M. Head interview; Bernhard Le Vander interview; *Hibbing Daily Tribune,* Oct. 31, 1970; *Minneapolis Star,* Aug. 19, 1970; *Union Advocate,* Oct. 28, 1970; *Minneapolis Tribune,* Nov. 1, 1970; *Rochester Post-Bulletin,* Nov. 2, 1970; *Worthington Daily Globe,* Oct. 31, 1970, Nov. 2, 1970.

11. *Minnesota Legislative Manual, 1971–1972;* see also Bruce M. White, comp. et. al., *Minnesota Votes: Election Returns by County for Presidents, Senators, Congressmen, and Governors, 1857–1977* (St. Paul: MHS Press, 1977), 58f., 214ff.; *Brainerd Daily Dispatch,* Nov. 4, 1970. The sample of Minnesota's thirty-one most Scandinavian counties (Swedish–14, Norwegian–11, Finnish–4, Danish–2, Icelandic–0) is based on the 1940 U.S. Census. These figures do not include non-Scandinavian ethnic groups that may be larger in some of the same counties. These comparisons and statistical computations from the census and on selected voting patterns are by the author. See also the maps on the 1970 governor's race, the 1970 U.S. Senate race, and the breakdown of Scandinavian/Swedish sample counties at the end of this essay.

12. Jon Wefald interview (quote); W. Scott Shrewsbury interview; examples of campaign literature, position papers, and correspondence in the Wendell Anderson Papers, MHS; Douglas M. Head interview; Robert A. Barrett interview; *Time,* Aug. 13, 1973, p. 35; *Duluth Herald,* Nov. 4, 1970; Jon Wefald to Bruce Larson; *Mankato Free Press,* Nov. 4, 1970; W. Scott Shrewsbury interview.

13. *Minnesota Legislative Manual, 1971–72;* Robert A. Barrett interview; Hathaway, *Minnesota Politics and Parties Today,* 50; *Worthington Daily Globe,* Nov. 4, 1970; campaign literature in the Wendell Anderson Papers, MHS; *Duluth News-Tribune,* Nov. 5, 1970; Douglas M. Head interview; Robert A. Barrett interview (Republican Barrett was a Jim Goetz-for-governor delegate supporter in 1970); *Minnesota Legislative Manual, 1971–72;* see also maps at the end of this paper. Douglas M. Head interview; Bernhard Le Vander interview; Wendell R. Anderson interview, 1992; interview with Val Bjornson, Aug. 23, 1984; interview with Elmer L. Andersen, Sept. 9, 1991; interview with Martin Olav Sabo, Aug. 15, 1984; Joan Anderson Growe commentary to Bruce L. Larson, Aug. 8, 1984.

14. *Duluth Herald,* Nov. 4, 1970; *St. Paul Pioneer Press,* Nov. 5, 1970; *Minnesota Legislative Manual,* 1965–66, p. 48.

15. *Time,* Aug. 13, 1973, p. 35; Joyce E. Krupey and Alan Hopeman, "Minnesota School Finance Reform, 1973–1982," *Journal of Education Finance* (Spring, 1983): 490–501; Larson,

"Scandinavian and Scandinavian-American Governors of Minnesota and Education," 179–81; *Minnesota Legislative Manual, 1975–76;* White, *Minnesota Votes,* 216ff.; statistical computations by the author. See also charts on 1974 governor's race at the end of this essay.

16. Martin Olav Sabo interview; interview with Rodney Searle, Apr. 18, 1992; Rod Searle, *Minnesota Standoff: The Politics of Deadlock* (Waseca, Minn.: Alton Press, 1990), xiv–xiv; Jon Wefald interview; *Minneapolis Star,* Oct. 25, 1974; *Time,* Aug. 13, 1973, p. 34; Homer E. Williamson, "The Minnesota Governor: Potential for Power," in Carolyn M. Shrewsbury and Homer E. Williamson, eds., *Perspectives on Minnesota Government and Politics,* 3rd ed. (Edina, Minn.: Burgess International Group, Inc., 1984), 190ff., 198f.

17. The author was present with Lindbergh at both events in 1973. The Little Falls event was a dual ceremony, celebrating the new Lindbergh Interpretive Center opening and the publication of the author's study on his father, *Lindbergh of Minnesota: A Political Biography* (New York: Harcourt Brace Jovanovich, 1973). Having known Lindbergh both professionally and personally for nine years in 1974, I was surprised to learn that he had been seriously considering Governor Anderson's offer to speak at the National Governor's Conference. Although he was very articlulate and in control when he felt the issue outweighed his penchant for privacy, Lindbergh was cautious, often distrustful of the press, and reluctant about public exposure. Indeed, the Little Falls event was a concession on his part. See "Items" [Wendell R. Anderson], *Swedish Pioneer Historical Quarterly* 27 (1976): 72; *Little Falls Daily Transcript,* Oct. 1, 1973; Charles A. Lindbergh, "Some Remarks at the Dedication of Lindbergh State Park Interpretive Center," *Minnesota History* 43 (1973): 276; *Duluth News-Tribune,* June 5, 1974; Wendell R. Anderson interview, 1992; *Minneapolis Star,* Aug. 27, 1974.

18. *St. Paul Pioneer Press,* Aug. 8, 1975, Aug. 11, 1975; *St. Paul Dispatch,* Aug. 8, 1975; *Duluth News-Tribune,* Aug. 11, 1975. Ulf Beijbom, director of the Emigrant Institute in Växjö, Sweden, and a participant in the 1975 ceremony at Växjö, provided the author with Swedish documentation on the visit by Governor Anderson and his family, including: "Minnesotadagen 1975" (Minnesota Day 1975) program, Aug. 10, 1975; and newspaper stories carried in *Kronobergaren,* July 25, Aug. 9, 1975; *Växjöbladet,* Aug. 6, Aug. 12, 1975; *Svenska Dagbladet,* Aug. 10, 1975; and *Smålandsposten,* Aug. 7, Aug. 11, 1975. Information and specific items on the Wendell Anderson genealogy and its connection with the Swedish provinces were also provided by Lennart Setterdal of the Emigrant Institute. Conversations with Lennart Setterdal at Växjö, Sweden, Aug. 1993; Lennart Setterdal letter and Anderson records to Bruce L. Larson, Sept. 3, 1993; *Minneapolis Tribune,* Apr. 1976, May 15, 1976; *St. Peter Herald,* Apr. 8, 1976, Apr. 15, 1976; and a series of articles in the *Gustavian Weekly,* Mar. 12, Apr. 2, Apr. 23, May 14, 1976.

19. *Minnesota Legislative Manual, 1979–80; Duluth Herald,* July 15, 1976; *Duluth News-Tribune,* Sept. 19, 1976, Feb. 10, 1977; "Wendell R. Anderson," videorecording, Minnesota Governors series; Wendell R. Anderson interview, 1992. On Mondale, see also Steven M. Gillon, *The Democrats' Dilemma: Walter F. Mondale and the Liberal Legacy* (New York: Columbia Univ. Press, 1992), and Larson, "Scandinavian-Americans and the American Liberal Political Heritage."

20. *Minnesota Legislative Manual, 1983–84; Minnesota Legislative Manual, 1995–96;* Haynes, "Reformers, Radicals, and Conservatives," 389; Bruce L. Larson, "If Your Name Is Anderson, You're Probably Governor: Minnesota's Swedish Governors," *Sweden and America* (Summer 1998), 4–11.

21. *Minnesota Legislative Manual, 1967–68; Minnesota Legislative Manual, 1979–80;* Sten Carlsson, *Swedes in North America, 1638–1988: Technical, Cultural, and Political Achievements* (Stockholm: Streiffert and Co., 1988), 110, 116.

22. Interview with Wendell R. Anderson, Aug. 23, 1984; Elmer L. Andersen interview; Dave Anderson, "If Your Name is Anderson(sen) You're Probably Governor—Or You Should

Run," *Twin Cities: Scandinavia Today Minnesota* (1982–83), 133–36; "The Governors Anderson (e)," *Minneapolis–St. Paul* (Sept. 1996), 54.

23. Minnesota Secretary of State, "Vote for Governor and Lieutenant Governor by County, November 3, 1998, State General Election," *Minnesota Legislative Manual, 1999– 2000*, p. 370–73. *Minneapolis Star and Tribune*, Nov. 5, 1998; *St. Paul Pioneer Press*, Nov. 5, 1998; "Body Slam!: Minnesota's Governor-elect Jesse 'The Body' Ventura," *Time*, Nov. 16, 1998, p. 54–57.

24. Minnesota Secretary of State, "Vote for Nomination for Governor and Lieutenant Governor by County, September 15, 1998, State Primary Election," *Minnesota Legislative Manual, 1999–2000* p. 342–45. *Minneapolis Star and Tribune*, Sept. 16, 1998.

25. *Minneapolis Star and Tribune*, Nov. 4, Nov. 5, Nov. 8, 1998; *St. Paul Pioneer Press*, Nov. 4, Nov. 5, Nov. 8, 1998; *The Free Press* (Mankato), Nov. 7, 1998; "Body Slam," *Time*, Nov. 16, 1998, 54–57; *New York Times*, Nov. 8, 1998.

Notes on Contributors

PHILIP J. ANDERSON is professor of church history at North Park Theological Seminary in Chicago, Illinois, and is president of the Swedish-American Historical Society. He is a specialist in British and American religious history, and among his publications are *Swedish-American Life in Chicago: Cultural and Urban Aspects of an Immigrant People, 1850–1930* and *Scandinavian Immigrants and Education in North America.*

H. ARNOLD BARTON is professor of history emeritus at Southern Illinois University in Carbondale, Illinois. He served as editor of the *Swedish-American Historical Quarterly* from 1974 to 1990. He has published widely on Swedish, Scandinavian, and Swedish American history, including *Letters from the Promised Land: Swedes in America 1840–1914* and *A Folk Divided: Homeland Swedes and Swedish Americans, 1840–1940.*

WILLIAM C. BEYER is vice president of administration for Sufficient Systems, Inc., a Minneapolis software development firm, and a member of the graduate faculty in American studies at the University of Minnesota, where he also served as an administrator. His research interests include the African American author, Langston Hughes.

ULF JONAS BJÖRK is associate professor in the School of Journalism at Indiana University at Indianapolis. The topic of his doctoral dissertation was the Swedish American press, and he has since written several articles about Swedish American newspapers and editors.

DAG BLANCK is university lecturer in the Centre for Multiethnic Research at Uppsala University, Sweden, and director of the Swenson Swedish Immigration Research Center at Augustana College in Rock Island, Illinois. Among his publications are *Becoming Swedish-American: The Construction of an Ethnic Identity in the Augustana Synod, 1860–1917* and *Migration och mångfold. Essäer om kulturkontakt och minoritetsfrågor tillägnade Harald Runblom.*

MICHAEL BROOK is former special collections librarian at the University of Nottingham Library, England, and also served as reference librarian at the Minnesota Historical Society. He recently edited *On the Left in America: Memoirs of the Scandinavian-American Labor Movement* by Henry Bengston.

SCOTT E. ERICKSON is director of religious studies, chaplain, and a member of the faculty of humanities at St. Paul's School in Concord, New Hampshire, and an affiliated scholar at Harvard Divinity School. He edited the work *American Religious Influences in Sweden*.

MARK A. GRANQUIST is assistant professor of religion at Gustavus Adolphus College in St. Peter, Minnesota. The subject of his doctoral dissertation was Swedish American denominations, and he has written several articles on Scandinavian American religious groups.

ANITA OLSON GUSTAFSON is assistant professor of history at Presbyterian College in Clinton, South Carolina. She has published several essays addressing the Swedish immigrant community in Chicago, which was the focus of her doctoral dissertation.

LAWRENCE G. HAMMERSTROM is a retired employee of the United States Postal Data Center in Minneapolis and is a volunteer at the American Swedish Institute. He has a special interest in Swan J. Turnblad, and his research forms the core of the public tour narrative presented to visitors at the Institute.

ANNE-CHARLOTTE HARVEY is professor of theatre and teaching associate in women's studies and the Master of Arts of Liberal Arts and Sciences program at San Diego State University. She is active as a translator and dramaturg of Scandinavian drama, especially Ibsen and Strindberg, and during the 1970s she helped organize the Snoose Boulevard Festival in Minneapolis.

NILS HASSELMO is president of the Association of American Universities in Washington, D.C., and is president emeritus and professor of Scandinavian languages and literature at the University of Minnesota. Among his publications are *Swedish America: An Introduction* and *Perspectives on Swedish Immigration*.

PATRICIA HASSELMO (1930–2000) was senior advisor to the president of the Association of American Universities in Washington, D.C.

DAVID A. LANEGRAN is John S. Holl professor of geography and dean of social sciences at Macalester College in St. Paul, Minnesota. Several of his publications have addressed neighborhood communities and change in the Twin Cities, most recently *Grand Avenue: Renaissance of an Urban Street*.

BRUCE L. LARSON is professor of history at Minnesota State University, Mankato. He is a consultant to the Minnesota Historical Society and the Lindbergh Foundation, and his research interests include Minnesota history and Scandinavian American politics. He is the author of the political biography *Lindbergh of Minnesota*.

JOY K. LINTELMAN is associate professor of history at Concordia College in Moorhead, Minnesota. Her publications have focused especially on Swedish immigrant women, and currently she is researching relationships between Swedish immigrants and Native Americans, as well as the subject of Swedish immigrant children.

LARS LJUNGMARK was associate professor of history at Göteborg University in Göteborg, Sweden, until his retirement. He has written widely on the subject of immigration studies, including *For Sale—Minnesota: Organized Promotion of Scandinavian Immigration, 1866–1873* and *Swedish Exodus*.

DAVID MARKLE is a Minneapolis-based writer and acoustical designer specializing in high-quality loudspeakers. He has reviewed classical music performance and recordings and has devoted time to issues of government and the arts.

BYRON J. NORDSTROM is professor of history and Scandinavian studies at Gustavus Adolphus College in St. Peter, Minnesota, and since 1997 has been editor of the *Swedish-American Historical Quarterly*. He edited *The Swedes in Minnesota* and has recently published *Scandinavia since 1500*.

LARS OLSSON is professor of history at Växjö University in Växjö, Sweden. His research has focused on Swedish labor history, gender and ethnic relations in agrarian capitalism, and refugee and labor policy during World War II, including *On the Threshold of the People's Home of Sweden: A Labor Perspective of Baltic Refugees and Relieved Polish Concentration Camp Prisoners in Sweden at the End of World War II*.

NILS WILLIAM OLSSON is founding editor and publisher emeritus of the *Swedish American Genealogist*. He has published *Swedish Passenger Arrivals in the United States 1820–1850* and most recently *Swedish Voters in Chicago 1888*.

MARY TOWLEY SWANSON is professor of art history at the University of St. Thomas in St. Paul, Minnesota. She has curated several exhibitions, including

"Pictures for a New Home" (St. Paul) and "Konsten och fäderneslandet, om svensk-amerikansk konst/Elusive Images of Home" (Stockholm).

RUDOLPH J. VECOLI is professor of history and director of the Immigration History Research Center at the University of Minnesota. He has written extensively about immigration and ethnicity in American history, particularly about the experience of Italian immigrants, including his recent article "We Study the Present to Understand the Past," which appeared in the *Journal of American Ethnic History*.

KERMIT B. WESTERBERG is manager of cataloging projects and ongoing microform collection development for Primary Source Microfilm in Woodbridge, Connecticut, an imprint of Gale Group. He has served as archivist-librarian at the Swenson Swedish Immigration Research Center at Augustana College in Rock Island, Illinois, and on the library staffs of Uppsala University and Yale Divinity School.

Index

Picture Credits